MW01285204

DAILY LIFE IN

THE AGE OF SAIL

The Greenwood Press "Daily Life Through History" Series

The Ancient Egyptians
Bob Brier and Hoyt Hobbs

The Ancient Greeks
Robert Garland

Ancient Mesopotamia
Karen Rhea Nemet-Nejat

The Ancient Romans
David Matz

The Aztecs: People of the
Sun and Earth
David Carrasco with Scott Sessions

Chaucer's England
Jeffrey L. Singman and Will McLean

Civil War America
*Dorothy Denneen Volo and
James M. Volo*

Colonial New England
Claudia Durst Johnson

Early Modern Japan
Louis G. Perez

18th-Century England
Kirstin Olsen

Elizabethan England
Jeffrey L. Singman

The Holocaust
*Eve Nussbaum Soumerai and
Carol D. Schulz*

The Inca Empire
Michael A. Malpass

Maya Civilization
Robert J. Sharer

Medieval Europe
Jeffrey L. Singman

The Nineteenth Century
American Frontier
Mary Ellen Jones

Renaissance Italy
Elizabeth S. Cohen and Thomas V. Cohen

The United States, 1920–1939:
Decades of Promise and Pain
David E. Kyvig

The United States, 1940–1959:
Shifting Worlds
Eugenia Kaledin

The United States, 1960–1990:
Decades of Discord
Myron A. Marty

Victorian England
Sally Mitchell

DAILY LIFE IN

THE AGE OF SAIL

DOROTHY DENNEEN VOLO
AND JAMES M. VOLO

The Greenwood Press "Daily Life Through History" Series

GREENWOOD PRESS
Westport, Connecticut • London

Library of Congress Cataloging-in-Publication Data

Volo, Dorothy Denneen, 1949–
    Daily life in the age of sail / Dorothy Denneen Volo and James M. Volo.
        p.   cm. — (The Greenwood Press "Daily life through history" series,
    ISSN 1080–4749)
    Includes bibliographical references and index.
    ISBN 0–313–31026–2 (alk. paper)
    1. Seafaring life—History.   2. Navigation—History.   3. Sailing ships—History.   I.
Volo, James M., 1947– II. Title.   III. Series.
VK149.V65   2002
910.4'5—dc21   2001016186

British Library Cataloguing in Publication Data is available.

Copyright © 2002 by Dorothy Denneen Volo and James M. Volo

All rights reserved. No portion of this book may be
reproduced, by any process or technique, without the
express written consent of the publisher.

Library of Congress Catalog Card Number: 2001016186
ISBN: 0–313–31026–2
ISSN: 1080–4749

First published in 2002

Greenwood Press, 88 Post Road West, Westport, CT 06881
An imprint of Greenwood Publishing Group, Inc.
www.greenwood.com

Printed in the United States of America

The paper used in this book complies with the
Permanent Paper Standard issued by the National
Information Standards Organization (Z39.48–1984).

10 9 8 7 6 5 4 3 2 1

Cover art: The age of sail permeated all aspects of life. Even common household items
often bore references to the sea. This period delft-style tile depicts an artist's rather fanci-
ful interpretation of a lateen rigged coasting vessel. Note the lee boards.

Contents

Introduction

The first and most obvious light in which the sea presents itself . . .
is that of a great highway.

        —Alfred Thayer Mahan[1]

From ancient times to the nineteenth century, people came into contact
with no more complicated piece of machinery than a sailing vessel. The
wood from hundreds of trees was required to complete even small ships
in the eighteenth century. More than three miles of rope, some as small
as an inch wide and some the thickness of a man's leg, was needed to
support the rigging, set the sails, and control the vessel. The separate
labor-saving machines incorporated into the fiber of a ship were almost
numberless.

 Although appearing immense when viewed from the quay side, even
the largest sailing vessel shrank to a mere splinter when floating in the
vastness of the ocean. In merchant vessels, the crew were usually
crowded into the forecastle or found space on the open well-deck on
which to curl up in a blanket. In warships, they had the dubious luxury
of berthing in the between decks encumbered only by the guns. A French
naval officer, when first going to sea, wrote in his journal, "Now we saw
nothing but sky and water and realized the omnipotence of God, into
which we commended ourselves."[2]

 For many of the most skillful seamen, sailing masters, and captains,
open-ocean navigation remained a profound mystery. Many seamen

who regularly sailed from port to port in the Mediterranean Sea or along the coasts of Africa and Europe utilized a good deal of "dead reckoning," judgment born of long experience, and luck in setting courses from place to place once they left familiar local waters and landmarks.

The Portuguese first established a school for navigators in the fifteenth century, and Spain set up a similar institution a century later. Italian navigators dominated the discovery of the New World but faded thereafter as prominent figures in the development of transoceanic trade. The French were quick to produce up-to-date nautical treatises, instruments, and sea charts, and the Dutch were among the first to make transoceanic shipping a business. Strangely, the English, who would exit the era as the dominant ocean-trading nation, were particularly backward in accepting the new nautical sciences. As late as 1570, there were no schools for navigators in England comparable with those on the Continent. Not until the Armada fight in 1588 did the English take navigation seriously.[3]

Notwithstanding the habit of maritime historians to ascribe certain technological or exploratory events to individual nation-states, it was the accumulated experiences of the sailors of many nations, through their encounters with helpful or contrary winds, adverse tides and helpful currents, dangerous obstacles and reassuring landmarks, that dictated the most commonly used sea routes. The sea lanes established between the sixteenth and eighteenth centuries connected natural resources, suppliers, seaports, cities, and markets over remarkably wide expanses of ocean.

The economics of the age of sail was truly global. Englishmen drank French wine; Frenchmen used spices from the Dutch East Indies; Dutchmen cooked in Spanish olive oil; and Spaniards ate salted cod from New England. Sugar moved from the New World to the Old, Asian silks were sold in the markets of Italy, and African slaves were torn from their homes to labor in the American wilderness. For the European nations taking part in the economic expansion of the sixteenth through nineteenth centuries (1588–1815), sea power was the fundamental principle that could determine whether empires would rise or fall. Overwhelming sea power, and the quest to maintain or regain it, proved a decisive factor in the history of all of Europe during the period.[4]

In this regard, naval and maritime historians have bowed to the most influential of their number, Admiral Alfred Thayer Mahan, USN. As president of the Naval War College in 1886, Mahan prepared and gave a series of lectures that were the basis for the book *The Influence of Sea Power upon History*. Rewritten and carefully revised before its publication in 1890, this book has continued to exert a widespread influence of its own. It remains Mahan's best-known and most-quoted work. It has furnished authoritative guidance for a period in history filled with transitions and new departures in international affairs—a kind of gospel, furnishing facts for every discussion of naval procedures and supplying a sound basis for all thought on maritime policy for more than a century. According to one of his biographers, "His writings will retain a value little affected by the lapse of time."[5]

In modern times, no period has generated such a huge catalog of historical fiction as that of the age of sail. Pirates and buried riches came to life in Robert Louis Stevenson's *Treasure Island* and Rafael Sabatini's *Captain Blood*. Herman Melville's *Moby Dick* and *Billy Budd* brought the daily life of seamen to the public. Stories of naval fleets in action on the high seas have captivated readers for many decades. Among the most popular authors of seafaring yarns are Patrick O'Brian (20 volumes), Alexander Kent (23 volumes), Dudley Pope (18 volumes), and Richard Woodman (13 volumes).

However, C. S. Forester remains the dean of maritime novelists. Cecil Scott Forester's first naval adventure, *Beat to Quarters*, was published in 1937. Herein Forester introduced Horatio Hornblower, a fictional character so beloved by readers that many believed him to be an authentic person. For the next three decades, Forester filled out the life of Hornblower in eleven volumes from his days as a midshipman to his admiralty, possibly mirroring the real life of Admiral Sir Edward Pellew. Millions have thrilled to the exploits of the indomitable Hornblower, and Forester has become the standard by which all authors of naval fiction are now measured. No other author has proved so well equipped to dramatize the sea battles and mesmerize the armchair admirals of the reading public. The durability of his work more than thirty years after his death attests to Forester's continuing and particular popularity.

In researching the age of sail, the authors of this history have tried to separate the facts from the fiction and the politics from the policies. They have incorporated the words of mariners from the period wherever possible. However, most ordinary seamen put few of their thoughts on paper. Charles Nordhoff and Richard Henry Dana, Jr., are notable exceptions. As educated men, officers tended to write about contemporary events in journals and letters and to produce memoirs in their retirement as did Captain Samuel Samuels and admirals Thomas Hardy and Cuthbert Collingwood. Naval administrators and heads of state have also left a wealth of material. Admiralty Secretary Samuel Pepys, for instance, left more than 15,000 letters written at the end of the seventeenth century for historians to consider.

The hundreds of surviving documents, bills of lading, customs receipts, and logs of most merchant vessels are abysmally dull and were composed of largely repetitive details about stowing cargo, changing weather, shortening sails, and altering course. Those of warships are similarly boring. "A sea battle which, when written up in a historical novel, petrifies the reader with six pages of thrills, horrors, flaming heroism, and detestable cowardice, takes up about three lines in a ship's log," as shown in the following excerpt.[6]

Piped all hands to quarters and cleared for action. ¼ before 4 the enemy got under weigh [*sic*] to engage us. At 4 P.M. being within good gunshot commenced a brisk connonade on the starboard side which the enemy returned. 10 minutes past 4 P.M. she wore ship and struck her colors. Gave three cheers.[7]

NOTES

1. Allan Westcott, *Mahan on Naval Warfare: Selected from the Writings of Rear Admiral Alfred Thayer Mahan* (Boston: Little, Brown & Co., 1919), 16.

2. Nicholas Blake and Richard Lawrence, *The Illustrated Companion to Nelson's Navy* (Mechanicsburg, PA: Stackpole, 2000), 148.

3. G. J. Marcus, *The Formative Centuries: A Naval History of England* (Boston: Little, Brown & Co., 1961), 59.

4. Westcott, xiv.

5. Westcott, xiii–xiv, xix.

6. Bertram Lippincott, *Indians, Privateers, and High Society* (New York: J. B. Lippincott Co., 1961), 118.

7. Ibid.

Chronology

1547   First recorded English navigational chart.

1553   Edward VI dies. Mary Tudor (Bloody Mary), wife of Philip II
        of Spain, takes the throne. Protestants repressed in England.

1558   Elizabeth I becomes queen of England and re-establishes Prot-
        estantism.

        William Gilbert discovers terrestrial magnetism.

1567   A single English privateer fights off seven Portuguese ships in
        the Azores.

1569   Gerard Mercator produces a new type of chart known as a
        projection.

1570   The English develop the topmast.

1575   The "race built" galleon is perfected from the design of the
        Revenge.

1579   The Dutch declare independence from Spain under the Union
        of Utrecht.

1580   The absorption of Portugal by Spain.

        Sir Francis Drake completes a circumnavigation of the earth.

        The British Admiralty begins recording magnetic variances.

1581   William Boroughs writes a treatise on the use of the compass.

1586   Shipwright Matthew Baker drafts designs for galleon-built
        warships.

1587   Drake destroys a Spanish squadron in the harbor of Cadiz.

1588   The English defeat the Spanish Armada.

1595   The English under Sir Francis Drake attack Puerto Rico.

1598   The English under Sir George Clifford attack Puerto Rico.

1600   The English (Honourable) East India Company is formed.

1602   The Dutch East India Company is founded.

1603   James Stuart of Scotland becomes James I of England.

1607   The Honourable East India Company establishes it own ship-
        yards and fleet of ships.

        English colonists found Jamestown, Virginia.

1611   The Muscovy Company is chartered.

1612	A superior Portuguese fleet is defeated by two small English warships in India.
1614	The Dutch form the Noordsche Company to pursue whaling.
1615	A superior Portuguese fleet is again defeated by English warships in India.
	The English are given free leave to trade at any port in the Mogul empire.
1620	English colonists found Plymouth, Massachusetts.
1621	The Dutch West India Company is founded.
1623	The Dutch execute several factors (company employees) of the Honourable East India Company at Amboina in Java.
1624	The Dutch seize the Spanish capital of Brazil.
1625	The Dutch attack Puerto Rico.
1627	The French defeat an English fleet at La Rochelle.
1628	The Dutch capture two Spanish treasure galleons.
1640	English Civil Wars (1640–1649) begin.
	The Dutch force the Portuguese out of Malacca and Ceylon.
1643	Louis XIV becomes king of France.
1645	Americans begin whaling from Long Island.
1649	Charles II is executed, beginning the Republican Period (1649–1658) of English history under Oliver Cromwell.
1650	The Dutch control trade in the East Indies.
	Jan De Witt comes to power in Holland.
1652	Americans begin whaling from Martha's Vineyard.
	The first Anglo-Dutch War (1652–1654).
1653	First recorded use of "Line Ahead" tactics.
1655	The English take Jamaica.
1660	Charles II returns to the English throne.
	The first English Navigation Act is passed.
	The English return Dunkirk to France.

1661   Dutch traders leave Brazil.

        Jean-Baptiste Colbert becomes French finance minister.

1665   The Second Anglo-Dutch War (1665–1667).

        First use of the term *privateer* with regard to warships.

1666   The Great London Fire.

1667   The English fleet in London is burned by the Dutch.

        The Dutch win trading privileges in Sumatra.

1668   The Honourable East India Company begins operations in Bombay, India.

1669   Jean-Baptiste Colbert becomes French minister of marine.

1670   Americans begin whaling from Cape Cod.

        Samuel Pepys reorganizes the British Admiralty and creates the rank of midshipman.

1672   Jan De Witt is murdered, and William of Orange is established as the ruler of the Dutch.

1673   Henry Morgan (pirate) becomes the lieutenant general of Jamaica.

        Beginning of the Third Anglo-Dutch War (1672–1674).

1674   The original Dutch West India Company is dissolved.

1678   First recorded use of the term *cruiser* with regard to warships.

1688   The British Parliament deposes James II in favor of William and Mary.

        The Glorious Revolution and the War of the League of Augsburg (1688–1697). King William's War in America.

1690   Americans begin whaling from Nantucket.

        Captain Kidd (pirate) is active in New York.

1696   Howland Great Dock constructed at Depforth in London.

        The British crown takes steps to suppress piracy.

1698   Parliament opens the slave trade to private persons.

1701   Queen Anne ascends the throne of England.

1702	The War of Spanish Succession (1702–1713) begins.
	The British take Gibraltar.
1704	Battle of Malaga.
1708	The Prize Act openly encourages privateering in England.
1710	Long Wharf is built in Boston.
1714	The Peace of Utrecht ends the War of Spanish Succession.
	The Board of Trade offers a reward for the invention of a chronometer.
1715	Queen Anne dies, leaving the English throne to George I.
1728	The Navy Act provides a means for men to send pay to their families.
1729	First workhouse opened in Plymouth, England.
	John Harrison invents his No.1 marine timekeeper.
1731	First Articles of War established for the British Royal Navy.
1733	Dead men's shares established in the Royal Navy for widows.
	The Molasses Act is passed.
1739	British enter the War of Jenkins Ear (1739–1740) against Spain.
1740	Beginning of the War of Austrian Succession (1740–1748).
1744	The British declare war against France.
	Battle of Toulon.
1745	Americans take Fortress Louisburg.
	A particularly fast sailing French prize (*Amazon*) is taken. The hull type is used for the development of the British sloop-of-war.
1745–46	Scottish uprising ends with the Battle of Culloden.
1747	Battles of Finisterre.
1749	Navy Discipline Act established for the Royal Navy.
1754	Beginning of the French and Indian War in America (1754–1763).
1755	Americans begin whaling from New Bedford, Masschusetts.
	General Edward Braddock is defeated by the French.
	George Washington rises to prominence in America.

Tobias Meyer of Gottingen publishes tables of lunar movements.

1756   Beginning of the Seven Years War in Europe (1756–1763).

Americans defeat the French at Lake George, New York.

1757   British Admiral John Byng is executed.

1758   The Admiralty orders a survey of all uncharted waters.

Payment of wages is improved for naval ratings.

Admiral Edmund Boscawen, General Jeffrey Amherst, and General James Wolfe take Louisburg.

1759   John Harrison invents the modern chronometer.

Wolfe takes Quebec.

Admiral George B. Rodney attacks LeHavre.

Boscawen wins at Lagos Bay.

French fleet destroyed by Sir Edward Hawke at Quiberon Bay.

1760   George III begins ruling England.

1763   The Peace of Paris brings an end to French rule in Canada.

1764   The Navigation Acts crisis in America.

1768   James Cook's first voyage to the Pacific.

1772   The burning of the Royal Navy cutter *Gaspee*.

Cook's second voyage.

1773ʻ   The Boston Tea Party.

1774   France and Spain secretly support the American colonies.

1775   Battles of Lexington and Concord.

The siege of Boston.

American warships capture two British navy storeships and four troop transports.

The Continental Navy is established.

1776   The American Declaration of Independence.

First landing of the U.S. Marines.

Cook's third voyage.

1778   Numerary code developed for the Royal Navy.

        France enters the American war after Battle of Saratoga.

1779   Carronades developed at the Carron gun foundry.

        Spain becomes an American ally.

        Bonhomme Richard (John Paul Jones) fights the *Serapis* (Richard Pearson).

1780   Thirty-six Articles of War established for the Royal Navy.

1781   Improvements in naval gunnery adopted by the Royal Navy.

        Battle of the Chesapeake (Yorktown, Virginia).

        Holland becomes an American ally.

1782   Battle of the Saints in the West Indies, among the islands of the Caribbean.

1783   Peace of Paris ends the American War of Independence.

1785   American ships captured by Barbary pirates.

1786   The French Navy is reorganized.

1789   The French Revolution.

1793   The British enter the war against the French Republic (1793–1801).

        Battle of Toulon.

1794   Battle of the Glorious First of June.

        American navy re-established.

1795   The Admiralty establishes a Navy Hydrological Office.

        The Quota Act begins the worst period of impressment.

        Royal Navy dress regulations are formalized.

1797   The Spithead and Noire mutinies of the Royal Navy.

        Battles of Cape St. Vincent and Camperdown.

1798   British Admiral Horatio Nelson defeats the French at the Nile.

        American Department of the Navy established.

        The quasi-war with France (1798–1803).

1800   Sir Home Popham's *Telegraphic Signals or Marine Vocabulary* is adopted by the Royal Navy.

British perfect the copper-clad bottom.

1801   Nelson defeats the Danish fleet at Copenhagen.

America enters the Tripolitan War (1801–1805).

1802   The West India Company Dock is fortified.

Peace of Amiens (1802–1803).

Nathaniel Bowditch publishes *The New Practical Navigator*.

1803   Beginning of the Napoleonic Wars (1803–1815).

American frigate *Philadelphia* is taken in Tripoli.

1804   Napoleon becomes emperor of the French.

Lt. Stephen Decatur burns the *Philadelphia*.

1805   Nelson defeats the French at Trafalgar and is killed.

1806   British naval production reaches its peak.

American Congress passes the Non-Importation Act.

Number of lashes limited to twelve for all Royal Navy floggings.

1808   The Female Penitentiary for Penitent Prostitutes is opened in Plymouth.

British and Americans outlaw the slave trade.

Thomas Jefferson places an embargo on all foreign trade.

1809   The French port of Rochforte is attacked by the English.

1812   America enters the War of 1812 (1812–1815).

1815   Napoleonic Wars end with the Battle of Waterloo.

British seamen are enjoined from bringing wives to sea.

1816   Barbary Wars end.

1819   U.S. Congress authorizes the navy to suppress the slave trade.

U.S. Navy attempts to suppress piracy in the West Indies.

1832   British end race-based slavery in the empire.

The term *clipper* is first applied to an American packet.

1848	Gold is discovered in California.
1850	Matthew Maury charts worldwide winds and currents.
	Flogging outlawed in the U.S. Navy.
1851	Herman Melville publishes *Moby Dick*.
1854	The Crimean War.
1856	Declaration of Paris outlaws privateering.
1857	The Sepoys of the British Army in India revolt.
1861	The American Civil War (1861–1865).
1864	Flogging outlawed in the U.S. Army.
1865	The last of the Confederate cruisers, *Shenandoah*, returns to England.
1869	Americans cease whaling from Nantucket.
1871	American whaling fleet lost in the Arctic ice.
1872	Britain pays the United States more than $15 million as part of the *Alabama* claims, resulting from the Civil War.
1876	A second American whaling fleet is lost in the Arctic ice.
1880	The prime meridian (0 degrees) is determined to pass through the Royal Observatory at Greenwich, England.
1883	Robert Louis Stevenson publishes *Treasure Island*.
1890	Alfred Thayer Mahan publishes *The Influence of Sea Power Upon History*.
1937	C. S. Forester publishes *Beat to Quarters*.

1

Seaports

We're homeward bound across the sea,
We're homeward bound with sugar and tea.
We're homeward bound and the wind's blowing fair,
There'll be many true friends to greet us there.

—Nineteenth-century sea chanty

THE SEAPORT TOWN

The visitor to a thriving seaport town in the age of sail (1480–1880) was beset with a fusion of sights, smells, and sounds that could easily prove a sensory overload. For many, the intensity of this sensory experience rivaled the mythological beckoning of the Sirens in Homer's *Odyssey*, and "old salts" too frail with age or too crippled to return to sea were frequently drawn to the waterfront. The typical seaport town was set against a forest of spars, masts, and rigging whose leafless branches networked across the sky amid an almost incomprehensible web of ropes, cables, and lines. Warehouses lining the wharves opened their arms to the ships heavy with coveted cargoes. Blocks and tackles squeaked as they hoisted precious commodities to the second story lofts while wagons, carts, and wheelbarrows rumbled and clanged their iron rimmed wheels across the cobblestone streets. Each breeze bathed the waterfront with a diverse mixture of odors—the pleasant fragrances of spices, oils, and salt air offsetting the less inviting smells of tar, wet canvas, and rotting fish.

Notwithstanding the possibility of offensive odors, tavern owners and maritime outfitters located their shops close to the wharves so that they could entice mariners to spend their money with them before they reached the finer parts of town. These shopkeepers often employed runners, who were known to sailors as "landsharks." The runners watched for a signal that an incoming ship had been seen. They would then rush to meet the vessel, even racing out on a bumboat to reach the men before they set foot on shore. A contemporary observer noted:

> [T]he word was passed that the bumboats were alongside, and immediately a crowd besieged the narrow gangway anxious to examine their contents. . . . The boats themselves were the scenes of most dire confusion. The articles kept for sale were piled away in the bow and stern, the middle of the boat left as a gangway or passage for customers. There was a terrible din, every one speaking, or rather hallooing at the top of his voice. The boats were continually rolling from side to side, as those on board changed places, and not infrequently one would go gunwale under, and ship water, to the dismay of the owner, and the delight of mischievous sailors.[1]

In addition to selling wares, the landsharks hoped to get the men to sign up for another outbound voyage. If they were successful, they would be paid by the shipowners once the sailor boarded his next ship.

The Waterfront   In the Americas, particularly in New England where wood was plentiful, most wharves and docks were made of wood. In Europe where wood was valued at a premium, and in the Caribbean where the weather and temperature combined to shorten wood's useful life, log cribs filled with stone, brick, or accumulated rubble served as a building material. Long Wharf, built in Boston in 1710, stretched more than 2,000 feet out into the deep water of the harbor. Solid rows of warehouses, ropewalks, and sail lofts lined its center, and heavy cargo cranes adorned its edges.

The buildings that lined the waterfront were varied both in their construction and their purpose. Made of stone, brick, or wood, the buildings varied greatly from place to place. Many were done in gray and white stucco, others in simply gray wooden siding, pink marble, or red sandstone. Small single story sheds occupied positions next to clapboard houses and multi-leveled edifices.

Besides the essential workplaces, taverns, banks, marine insurers, and residences for the population, there were many shops stocking a variety of common consumer goods, such as carpeting, window glass, pewter ware, boots and shoes, firearms, wines, and spices. These were often unloaded directly from the vessels in port to the windows and shelves of the appropriate shops. Many shops dealt in fine fabrics, sewing notions, jewelry, and other items, and it was not unusual to see well-

A New England seaport town in winter. Note the shops and stores lining the wharf. James Volo Photo.

dressed women navigating the more distasteful districts along the wharves in order to view items directed specifically toward their interests. The better men's shops offered tailoring, wigs, tobacco products, and leather-bound books. Specialty shops dealt in silverware, cabinets, firearms, furniture, carriages, saddles, and harness, but these tended to be set back from the water. The majority of the waterfront shops served the needs of the mariners, offering ironwork, sails, hooks, lines, nails, coarse cloth for sailors' clothing, lead shot and gunpowder in kegs, axes, knives, swords, and even cannon and ball.

Each shop was identified with its own unique hanging wooden sign. The wigmaker might have the outline of a properly coiffured head, the apothecary a mortar and pestle, the gunsmith a pistol, the shoemaker a boot, and the chandler an anchor and chain. Coffee shops might sport a coffee pot and bookstores an open volume. Some signs represented the name of the establishment. The Ram's Head Tavern or the Golden Eagle might have pictures or carvings depicting them. Such signs were very important as many patrons could not read, and they supplied a simple remedy to strangers who needed to get around an unfamiliar town.

The most common sign found along the waterfront was probably the silhouette of a mug of ale or a bottle of rum. **Taverns** Sandwiched between buildings were the sailors' taverns, which dotted the entire harbor area. Sign boards bearing dolphins, anchors, capstans, and mermaids beckoned the sailor to groggeries with descriptive names such as the Jolly Tar, the Crow's Nest, the Spyglass, the Admiral's Cabin, the Flags of All Nations, or the Spouter Inn. The interiors of these haunts ranged from dives with long wooden benches beneath low-beamed ceilings hung with ships lanterns to plush, gilt halls festooned with velvet drapes.

Taverns and alehouses served a definite social purpose, providing both food and drink. Most did not provide rooms or overnight accommodations, however. These were left to the inns and ordinaries, a distinction in service well understood by seventeenth- and eighteenth-century patrons. Men, and even boys as young as twelve, were allowed to buy whatever alcoholic beverages they wanted. Popular drinks in cold weather were hot buttered rum and a concoction called flip. The common variety of flip was a mixture of rum, beer, and brown sugar into which a hot poker was plunged. The heat warmed the mixture without seriously diminishing its alcohol content. Warm weather drinks included many kinds of beer, ale, porter, cider, wine, and a long list of liquors. If ice was not readily available (and it usually was not) drinks could be chilled by placing the bottle on a rope or in the water bucket hanging in the cool water of a well. The temperature of the water in a well is rarely higher than 45 degrees even on the warmest day.[2]

Before the temperance movement gained popularity in the middle of the nineteenth century, taverns and alehouses were in many cases considered respectable men's clubs, and they served as public centers for political gatherings, assemblies of merchants or ships' officers, and fertile fields for the hiring of crews and workmen. These establishments provided wholesome entertainment in the form of card games, bowling, shuffleboard, music, and singing. Gambling was rampant and socially acceptable.

In 1860, *Harper's Magazine* described this waterfront scene induced by the arrival in port of a whaler long absent on a voyage:

A cart rumbles by, loaded with recently discharged whalemen . . . under the friendly guidance of a landshark, hastening to the sign of the "Mermaid," the "Whale," or the "Grampus," where, in drunkenness and debauchery, they may soonest get rid of their hard-earned wages, and in the shortest space of time arrive at that condition of poverty . . . that must induce them to ship out for another four years' cruise.[3]

Contrary to common perceptions, the woman and girls who served as "wenches" and waitresses in taverns and alehouses rarely provided illicit entertainment of a sexual nature. This business was reserved for the bordellos and alleyways of the town. Melville described such places as "that portion of the terraqueous globe providentially set apart for dance-houses, doxies, and tapsters, in short what sailors call a fiddler's green."[4] Nonetheless, street prostitutes could be brought into the tavern by patrons for as little as a dollar. The owners of these businesses, however, commonly frowned upon this practice as they could be fined by the authorities for running a disorderly establishment.

The fields along the water's edge were dotted with the simple sheds that served as offices, warehouses, and shel-   **Workplaces** ters to many of the mercantile establishments of any port town. The blacksmith's hammer chimed rhythmically as he beat out the bolts, plates, chains, tools, block sheaves, rudder irons, harpoons, and other nautical ironwork from his waterside shop.[5] Although the blacksmiths' sheds were usually placed some distance from the highly flammable hemp and flax that could cause a general fire along the waterfront, the smell of burning soft coal or charcoal still permeated the air when the wind blew from certain quarters. Apprentices tended the huge bellows feeding air to the fires that glowed like a mythical serpents' eyes amid the blackened recess of the ironworks, an image that was reinforced by the hiss of red hot metal being plunged into cold water to temper and strengthen it.

Shipwrights were more than mere carpenters or woodworkers. They expertly sorted through the collected stores of odd shaped wood stored in protective sheds to find the right piece to saw, carve, and shape into watertight and seaworthy vessels. Each was expert in a particular trade such as caulking, planking, joinery, and rigging. The shipyards, always near the water's edge, were the workplace of the shipwright and his men. The slipways were made of massive timbers smoothed on top and laid parallel to the shoreline about eight to ten feet apart. These "log beds" might reach thirty or forty feet inland from the high tide mark. Vessels were constructed on these and were launched from them. Great care was taken that the slipways were constructed at the correct angle and sloped down into the deepest part of the water. Permanent yards were built with stone-filled cribs at the waters edge to shield the slipways from the actions of water, wind, and tide.[6]

Low, narrow buildings several hundred feet long housed the ropewalks. Here long hemp fibers were cleaned and combed through rows of iron spikes. A man called a spinner would coil the fibers around his waist and walk backwards drawing the fiber taut while a boy at a wheel twisted the ends round into yarns. These were then rolled up, tarred, and rewound on bobbins where they would remain for a year while they seasoned. In time, they would be threaded through the holes of a large metal plate and pulled and twisted into strands. Combinations of the strands would then be parted out full length and twisted again into the desired size of rope or cable. As the yarns, strands, ropes and cables were twisted, they necessarily became considerably shorter. The total

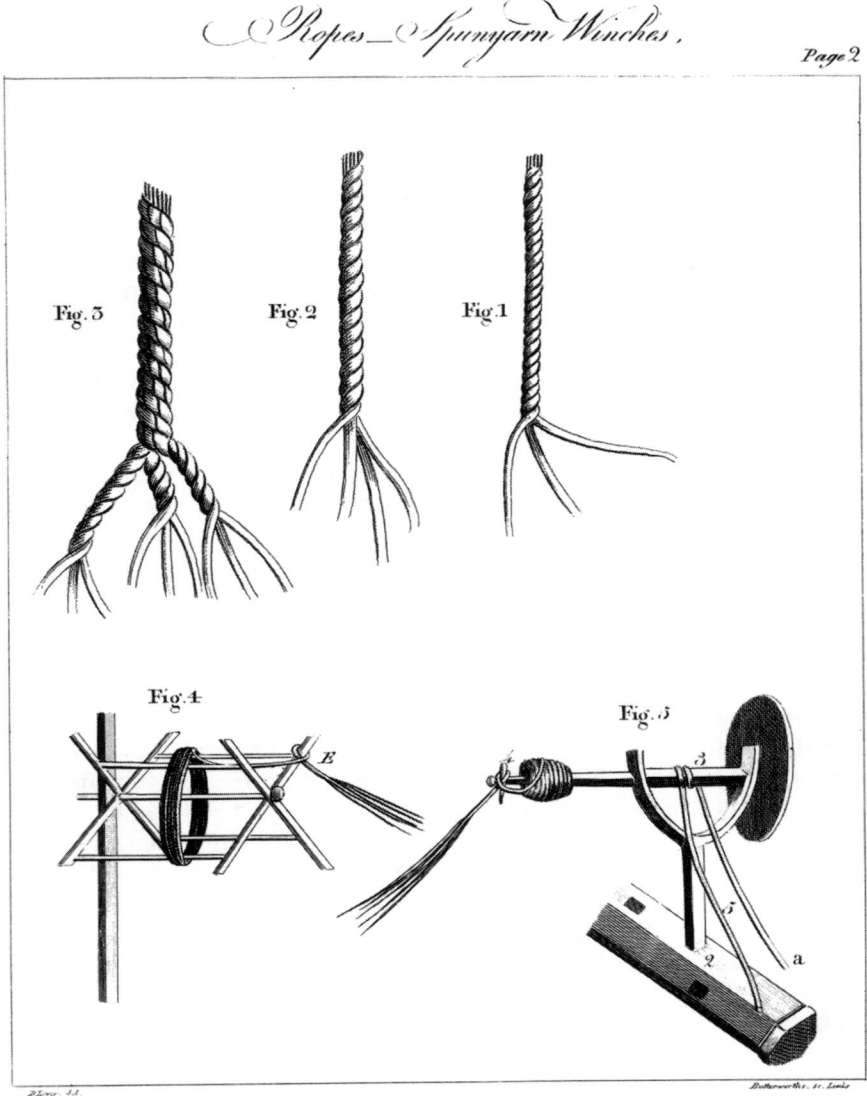

Simple rope making is illustrated in a plate from a nineteenth-century sailor's manual.

length of the ropewalk, therefore, dictated the maximum length of rope that could be turned so that these buildings were sometimes many hundreds of feet long.

The diameter of the rope found on almost all sailing vessels fell between two extremes. The thinnest ropes of under an inch in diameter were referred to as small stuff. A stout rope formed of several smaller ropes twisted together, known as cable, was usually the largest diameter product of a ropewalk. This could be several inches thick. The term *cable length* was often used by mariners to express a distance of about 200 yards (185 meters, 608 feet, or one-tenth of a nautical mile). This measure indicates to some extent the immense length of ropewalks in general.[7]

Sailmakers sat cross-legged in their sail lofts surrounded by canvas bags suspended from pegs to hold their simple tools. With only a leather palm and needle, countless yards of stiff canvas were fashioned into proper sails with the "belly" to draw well. Tucked in the raftered upper floors of warehouses or in large open buildings, with stoves suspended from above to optimize floor space, sailmakers sketched patterns on the floors whereupon they laid out the canvas, cut it, and sewed it to size before attaching the bolt rope around the outer edges.

The cooper's shop was littered with wood shavings and staves. Coopers spent much of their time making open containers such as buckets and pails, but they were expert in fashioning a whole series of containers loosely categorized as kegs, barrels, and hogsheads. Some of these were merely round, closed containers into which loose merchandise was packed in straw for protection and easy shipment. Others were waterproof, ensuring that the contents remained dry. Finally, the epitome of the cooper's art was the watertight container, or cask. This could hold liquids within and prevent contamination from without. The shape of the barrel was unique in its design from simple crates and boxes. Not only was a barrel stable on its flat ends, but it could be rolled efficiently for short distances on its curved sides without needing a separate wheeled truck or cart. Moreover, the round shape almost completely filled the available space when the barrels were stacked on their sides. These characteristics proved particularly useful in the cramped quarters found below and between the decks.

Blockmakers carved the large wooden pulleys needed to haul supplies and cargo aboard the ships. Woodcarvers made ornamental work, railings, and figureheads to adorn the the ships' bows. The ornamentation of sixteenth- and seventeenth-century vessels was often grandiose to the point of being garish and extravagant. The figureheads took the form of generals, statesmen, ladies, and Indians. Some even depicted the wives and daughters of captains and shipowners. Figureheads could be extremely elaborate with pieces that could be unscrewed. This feature enabled the figurehead to be removed and stored safely away once the ship was out to sea. When the vessel neared a port, it could be replaced. Sailors tended to be a superstitious lot, and they feared that a damaged figurehead foreshadowed hard times. Similar notions forbade figureheads from being painted black.

Homes
Seaports had their sheds, shanties, and shacks, but they also had their mansion rows, which were built by wealthy ship-owners and captains. The first big houses were generally built right beside the water where they faced the wharves and counting houses of their owners. Away from the immediate noise of the wharves, but close enough to oversee the activity, newer homes were often surrounded by lawns and gardens with flowers and fine trees.

One distinguishing characteristic of many of these homes was a flat, roof-top platform with ornamented rails. This structure afforded a grand view of the harbor and provided an early opportunity to see the masts of arriving ships as they broke the horizon. The concept may actually have been imported from the Caribbean islands as a means to take advantage of the sea breeze. Accessed by a ladder through a trap door in the roof, they also provided swift access for fighting chimney fires, and often, buckets of sand or water were kept handy at the ladder's base. When a husband's ship was expected, the wife of the ship's master could often be seen pacing the platform hoping to catch that first glimpse of her beloved's returning ship. The sight of the lonely woman pacing the lofty perch long after the ship had been expected earned them the designation of "widow's walks."

The physical and economic nature of the seaport was such that everybody knew everybody and their specific niche in the life of the community, but few formed very warm relationships outside their trade. The sailor who could not speak to the shipmaster aboard ship did not expect a warm collegiality when they met on the streets of town. A hierarchy developed wherein the deep-water captains, shipbuilders, bankers, underwriters, ministers, and other professionals became a sort of aristocracy.

The homes of the "first families" were graced with many fine appointments and details. Fences enclosed gardens of Chinese asters, roses, day lilies, peonies, and geraniums. Paths led the way through formal gardens. The tree-lined avenues were so lush and green that sailors remarked that walking along them was like a trip to the country. Inside, the spacious rooms were filled with delicate porcelains, carved soapstone, exquisite embroidered silks, and handsome teakwood furniture brought back from voyages to the Orient. Highly prized Cantonware graced the dining room tables. Recalling the awesome sight of her whaling captain uncle's parlor, Christine Pease wrote, "It smacked of travel, adventure, romance, the East. First, of course there were the Chinese Chippendale chairs, ribbon-backed, upholstered in rich Chinese brocade. Impressive draperies hanging from the tops of the high windows to the Brussels-carpeted floor. . . . Under one window, stood the Chinese sewing box full of little ivory gadgets to delight any needlewoman's heart.

... But it was the peacock tail table that lent luster to the parlor."[8] Returning sea captains also brought back exotic produce such as pineapples. It became a custom to place a pineapple on the front gate or door to alert visitors of the captain's return. From this practice, the pineapple came to be a symbol of hospitality, a tradition that survives today.

In sharp contrast to the more idyllic residences was the maze of alleys and by-ways meandering around the dockside or crisscrossing through the warehouse area. **The Backwater**

The backwater was often an area exposed to stagnant pools, pestilential insects, and noxious smells at low tide, but the term came to describe any place considered culturally or socially backward. The area was sometimes called a "Fiddler's Green." Clustered here were the poorer residences, shacks, and more disreputable taverns and shops.

Pawn shops littered the district. The three golden balls hanging outside the shop signaled that the owners were willing to take almost anything from South Sea shells to Eskimo harpoons. Visitors to such shops would find oddities from the four corners of the globe as well as items crafted by sailors in their quiet hours. "Back of the counter were all sorts of things, piled up and labeled. Hats, and caps, and coats, and guns, and swords, and canes, and chests, and planes, and books, and writing-desks, and every thing else. And in a glass case were lots of watches, and seals, chains, and rings, and breast pins, and all kinds of trinkets."[9]

Also in the backwater were tailors, or more correctly slops-merchants, who sold sailors a complete sea chest with kit to outfit them on their next voyage. "These thieves become security for the safe delivery on board of the new recruit, and then furnish him, in exchange for his three months' pay, with the articles of clothing enumerated in the navy regulations."[10] Having plied the unwary seaman with ale while the transaction took place, the notorious merchant would then present the bill for clothes and drink to the ships's master for payment from the sailor's wages. In some cases, a full share of the excess charged was given to the ship's master to ensure his ignorance. To further aggravate the injustice, once at sea, the sailor often found that he had little more than some ragged shirts and rocks in his sea chest—the contracted items having been discreetly removed before the chest was brought aboard. Such injuries were common enough to show up in song:

> The next I remembers I woke in the morn,
> On a three skys'l yarder bound south round Cape Horn
> Wid an ol' suit of oilskins an' two pair o' sox
> An' a bloomin' big 'ead, an' a sea-chest of rocks[11]

Even ratings on warships had to ensure that all was done fair and above board. "It is provided that the master-at-arms shall, on the rendering on board of the recruit, examine his clothing to see that the requisite number of pieces is there." Unfortunately, the quality of the clothing was not made a matter of regulation. The consequence of this was that the slop-seller, "while furnishing faithfully the number, made too in the fashion required, provides it of stuff which, it is safe to say, cannot be found anywhere else than the establishments of these thieving outfitters."[12]

Having shipped as a boy on a American warship for the first time, Charles Nordhoff discovered the poor quality of a kit purchased from a slops-merchant. "The white duck frocks and trousers were made of yellow bagging, which so course was its texture, would scarcely hold peas; and which was warranted not to last beyond the first washing. Instead of the 'neat' black silk neckerchief and shining pumps, articles of dress in the excellence of which a true man-of-war's man greatly delights, the recruits are furnished a rusty bamboo rag, and shoes made of varnished brown paper, which vanish before the damp salt air as mist in the bright sun."[13] The following day, the young man was called before the lieutenant and asked by the master-at-arms, a confederate of the slops-merchant, if he was satisfied with the kit he had been provided. "This worthy having previously instructed me that it was all right, or that if it was not, I would be sent ashore again, I very readily declared my entire satisfaction."[14]

Boarding houses made up a large portion of any Fiddler's Green. The most respectable ones were run by former seamen retired from the rigors of the life at sea. These offered the sailor what he needed most, a decent bed, fair victuals, and a few good drinks. There were plenty of boarding establishments of another sort. Prominently featured were a bar, a supply of women of loose morals, or some resident prostitutes. Rooms were furnished with straw mattresses on simple beds, a rough table, and a chair or two. The food was of questionable quality, and the liquor was often watered. Sailors who frequented these places sometimes fell victim to conniving characters called crimpers, whose job it was to find crews for ships needing men. Some of the more disreputable boarding houses overhung the water and contained trap doors so that crimps could easily slip a doped sailor to a waiting boat beneath.

Author Herman Melville summed up the hazards of the waterfront. He writes of "the variety of landsharks, land-rats, and other vermin which make the helpless mariner their prey. In the shape of landlords, clothiers, barkeepers, crimps and boarding house loungers, the land-sharks devour him limb by limb; while the land-rats and mice constantly nibble at his purse."[15]

SEAPORTS OF THE NEW WORLD

Of all the early European nations that colonized the New World, Spain was most favored in the natural excellence of so many of her ports. Havana, San Juan, Nombre de Dios (or Portobelo), Panama City, Callao (near Lima, Peru), and Veracruz all became important ports. Inside these ports ships could undergo repairs, resupply themselves with victuals and naval stores, and take on their cargo. They also offered crippled and storm-tossed vessels a safe haven. As each port came in time to be a target of enemy raiders, their defensive features proved as important as their economic geography.

Veracruz became the seat of the viceroy of New Spain. The small barren island of San Juan de Ulua, which faced Veracruz, rather than the city itself, provided the port facilities. Despite the fundamental military weakness of an exposed position in the Gulf of Mexico, the island of San Juan de Ulua provided water of sufficient depth to allow ships to sail virtually up to the shore. Although the island served as a shield against strong winds from the north, a large sea wall capable of securing more than twenty large vessels was built on its southern coast. Merchandise was carried to Veracruz by barges and lighters.

Nombre de Dios on the Caribbean side of the Isthmus of Panama was the primary treasure port for the Peruvian wealth that came overland from the Pacific, but the entire region surrounding the port was considered pestilential by the Spaniards. Panama City, on the Pacific side of the isthmus, proved drier and more hospitable. Cartagena de Indias, on the coast of Columbia, was one of the best natural ports in the New World. Like the Mediterranean port of Cartagena in Spain for which it was named, an island sheltered the mouth of a large bay in which ships could safely anchor. The climate of Cartagena de Indias proved to be one of the least harmful for Europeans living in the Caribbean.

The port of San Juan in Puerto Rico was one of the most easterly in the Caribbean. As such it guarded the entrance to the Caribbean and served as a last port for outbound shipping. It was also one of the best fortified ports developed by the Spanish. The system of fortresses that guarded the port was all but impregnable. Several attacks on Puerto Rico at the turn of the seventeenth century by both the Dutch and English failed to dislodge the persistent Spanish defenders.

Havana was the best port in all of Spanish America. The entrance to the bay was formed by a narrow mouth, which could be closed with a great chain and defended by shore batteries against attack. Across from the edifice of Moro Castle was the less imposing Punta Castle, and in the port itself were the Caban Fortifications and the Atares Castle. Moreover, throughout the eighteenth century, Havana ranked among the very best shipyards of the world easily outdistancing its American rivals. The Spanish warships built in Havana's four slipways "carried with them a reputation for strength and stamina" and were the envy of the Spanish shipyards in Europe.[16]

NORTH AMERICAN MERCANTILE PORTS

Early explorers of the New England coast came slowly to know what it looked like. The geography of the coastline had been dictated by the advance of at least two great ice sheets in the time before history. The first of these scoured the North American continent from a point in today's Wisconsin and deposited its leavings—a terminal moraine of sand, rocks, and boulders—at its line of furthest advance. This formed most of the Atlantic-facing body of Long Island. This ice sheet melted back more than 50,000 years ago. A more recent but not quite as extensive ice event made an additional deposit in a line of low hills that ran along the length of Long Island on the mainland side to Montauk Point, passed beyond Block Island, bisected Martha's Vineyard and Nantucket, and continued east into the ocean to form Georges Bank. The melt water from this event gouged out the river valleys of the Kennebec, the Merrimack, and the Connecticut and formed much of the Great Lakes. The water also raised the sea level, creating islands—such as those that dot the Boston harbor—from a series of partially drowned hills. The actions of surf and tides in the succeeding 15,000 years formed the smooth shores and Atlantic-facing barrier beaches of Long Island and created the profound hook of Cape Cod.

The shore line of New England south of Cape Cod is "the most changeable in North America." The combination of wind-driven waves and tidal variations keeps the seas in perpetual motion. Tidal variations alone range from as little as three feet to as much as thirty feet along the coast. In narrow passages, as at the eastern end of Long Island Sound, the tide races by the mainland at almost six knots. Yet much of the southern coastline is protected by the barriers of Long Island, Nantucket, and Martha's Vineyard. North of Cape Cod, the shore lies exposed and open to the ravages of the Atlantic from the northeast (hence the term *nor'easter* for a bad storm). A day or two of heavy weather can create inshore waters with a nasty chop and great swells in the ocean. Warm moist air from the south is cooled into impenetrable fog by the cold waters of the Labrador Current, lending the New England coast one of its most haunting characteristics. Until the fog burns off in the sun, the mariner moves cautiously, if at all, wary of the unseen rocks and shoals that dot the coast.[17]

The fishing fleets of several European nations set their nets and hooks in the waters off the New England shore. Some set up temporary quarters on the scattered islands to dry and salt their catch. Others wintered over. The English did not welcome these foreign fishermen, since they claimed the territory from Maine to Virginia for themselves. Not only did England covet the bounty of the sea, but also the timber, shingles, barrel staves, and pine pitch that the forests offered. Other commodities such as furs, potash, turpentine, and distilled rum were equally valued.

Until the 1760s, the town of Newport, Rhode Island, was the leading port in New England. Indeed, it was one of the leading ports in all of eighteenth-century North America. This apparent success was largely attributable to the "Triangular Trade." A number of Newport's most prominent merchants were involved in the slave trade with the islands of the West Indies. Molasses, imported from the islands, was distilled in New England into rum. The rum was a valuable commodity that could be used to trade for slaves on the west coast of Africa. The slaves were then traded to the sugar plantation owners in the islands thereby closing the triangle. At one point, Newport was rivaled only by Charleston, South Carolina, in the number of slavers that called the town a home port. The slave trade was outlawed by mutual agreement with Britain in 1808, and Newport came to rely on other New England towns for commodities to export.

Ultimately, Newport was surpassed in maritime activity by Providence, Rhode Island. The American cotton textile industry, founded at the end of the eighteenth century, centered in the region served by the port of Providence, ensuring the growth of the town. Located on the mainland at the head of a large bay, Providence had better communications with the surrounding country than the island of Newport. The town had a significant number of water-powered textile mills filled with machinery for spinning and weaving as well as banks and other mercantile enterprises. To the east, the ports of New Bedford, Barnstable, Plymouth, and Nantucket continued to flourish by following the traditional trades of whaling and fishing.

Boston and New York were rival ports. In the late eighteenth century, the shoreline of Long Island Sound was **Boston and** described as "a cask of good liquor, tapped at both ends, **Salem** at one of which Boston draws, and New York at the other."[18] Three times as many vessels began their passage from New York than from Boston Harbor. Yet the heart of maritime New England remained Boston. The city with its outlying towns north of the cape came to dominate the region's commerce. In 1807, Boston's total commercial shipping surpassed that of the next three New England ports combined. These were Portland, Salem, and Newburyport in order of tonnage. Nonetheless, the satellite ports of Boston (Portsmouth in New Hampshire; Gloucester and Marblehead in Massachussetts), as well as the "down east" ports of Maine, and the Long Island Sound ports of New

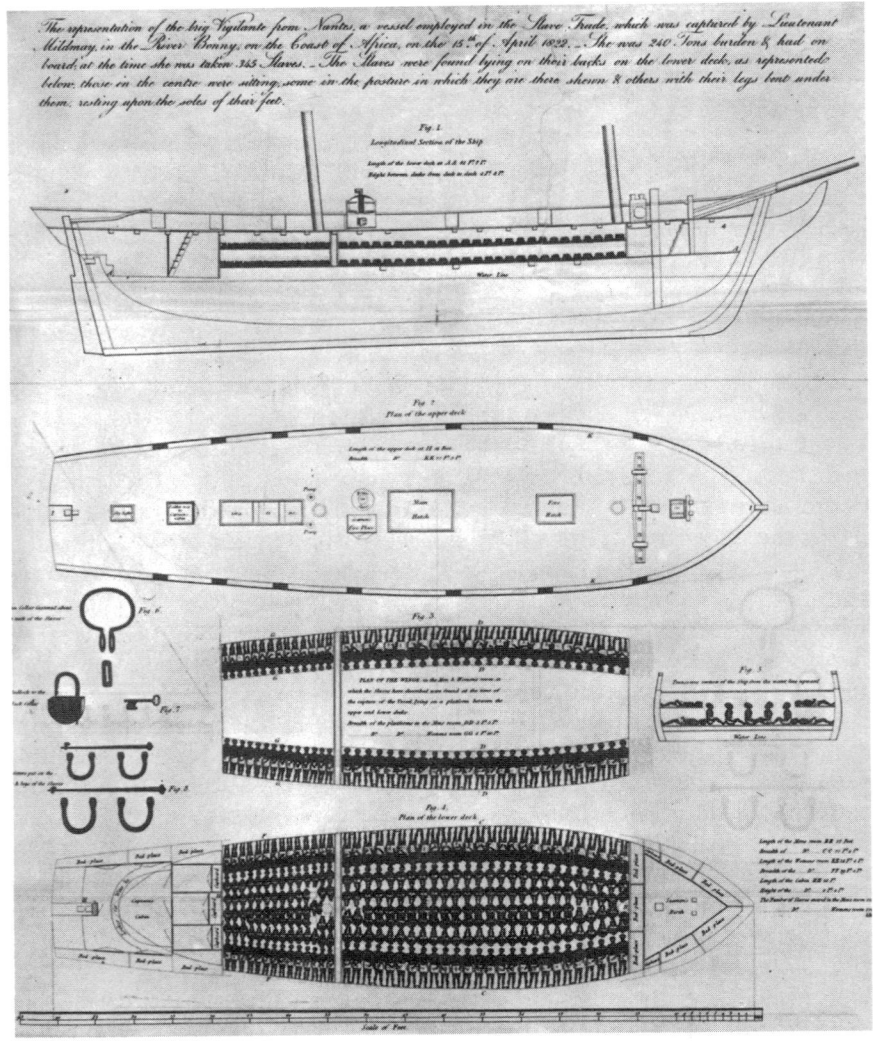

The plan of a French slave ship captured in 1822. At the time of the capture, 345 African slaves were crammed below the decks.

London and New Haven, Connecticut, developed independent commercial importances by doing business not only with Europe but also with the West Indies and the maritime provinces of Canada.

Salem, Massachussetts, may be taken as an example in this regard. Bound by dense wilderness, eighteenth-century Salem looked to the sea for its life and prosperity. It was one of the busiest ports in all of America during the first half of the nineteenth century. In the 1820s and 1830s, it was outranked as to the dollar value of its commerce only by New York and Baltimore. Shipyards were established in Salem almost as soon as the town was settled. There were so many shipbuilders around the creek off Norman Street that the sound of the hammers and mallets gave it the name Knocker's Hole. The first homes were built close to the water, facing the wharves and counting houses. During the American Revolution, Salem was home to 158 armed vessels serving as privateers. Richard Derby owned twenty-five of them and emerged from the war as one of New England's wealthiest men. One of his sons later established a navigation school for apprentice ship's officers and midshipmen, which produced many of Salem's famous shipmasters.

Trade with the Orient brought great wealth to Salem. Ships from the Indies were sometimes moored three deep at the wharves. The customs house recorded more than 1,000 ships entering the port with a trade valued at $7 million from 1800 to 1810. Warehouses were filled with silks and teas from China, pepper from Sumatra, coffee from Arabia, tallow from Madagascar, hemp from Luzon, cotton and fabric from Bombay, and palm oil from West Africa. Figs and raisins from the Mediterranean, wine and olives from Portugal, and ivory from Zanzibar also made their way into Salem's teeming storehouses.

Many of Salem's shipmasters were particularly partial to the porcelain trade despite the fragile nature of the cargo. Once wrapped and crated, it could be stored deep in the hold where dampness might spoil other commodities. The crates of porcelain provided both ballast and a flooring upon which other cargo could be stored. There was almost "an insatiable market for the radiant, translucent porcelain," and the possession of export china was "an enviable status symbol."[19]

Canton china was actually made at potteries many miles in the Chinese interior. The coastal town of Canton was not much more than a trading post, but it was widely visited by American merchant vessels. Cantonese middlemen, recognizing the demand, placed advertisements in American newspapers. The following example appeared in the *Providence Gazette* in May 1804:

Yam Shingua, Chinaware merchant at Canton, begs leave respectfully to inform American Merchants, Supercargoes, and Captains that he procures to be manufactured in the best manner, all sorts of Chinaware with Arms, Cyphers and other Decorations (if required) painted in a very superior style and on the most reasonable Terms. All orders carefully and promptly attended to. Canton (China) Jan. 8, 1804.[20]

With time and development, Salem's richest merchants and shipowners abandoned the crowded, treeless houses by the wharves for the ample front and back yards of the spacious area surrounding Washington Square. Three-story houses built of Flemish-laid brick, boasting four rooms to a floor, became the predominant architectural style. Front doors were arched and graced by fanlights and sidelights. Ionic columns added grace and dignity to the entrance ways. Inside, the Oriental influence was strong. Wives and daughters, dressed in elegant silk gowns and bedecked with gold bangles and lustrous pearls, served Hyson tea on custom designed sets of Canton chinaware. Homes became showplaces decorated with furniture made from teak, camphor wood, and sandal-wood. Oriental carpets adorned the floors while cabinets and sideboards flaunted porcelain punch bowls, tureens, and platters, which were used as much for decoration as for service.

New York   One year after Henry Hudson discovered the river that bears his name (1609), a Dutch trading vessel entered lower New York Bay. The vessel had come to trade with the Raritan nation, a native American tribe that inhabited the western shore across from the large hilly island occupied by the Manhattans. The ship had come to barter beads, knives, hatchets, and cloth for furs. Some of the crew had been with Hudson when he first sailed into the bay and traveled up the river looking for the Northwest Passage. Having reached Albany, Hudson became convinced that the great river would not lead through North America to the wealth of Japan and China, and he left. Yet New York (originally New Amsterdam) was one of the best natural ports in the world and the ocean terminus of a water route that led into the very heart of the continent.

Lower New York Bay contains more than 100 miles of shoreline with as little as six miles exposed to the ravages of the sea. The natural channel to the sea, called the Narrows, was up to 100 feet deep and three-quarters of a mile wide except at the sand bar (where there was almost 50 feet of water). The Upper Bay, containing more than 600 square miles of water, was practically landlocked. Besides the island of the Manhattans, which was separated from the mainland by a river (the Harlem River), there was a large island in the bay behind which flowed the Passaic, Hackensack, and Raritan rivers.

After the first trading vessels, others followed, particularly the Dutch. Adrian Block was the first to dare the passage of the East River into Long Island Sound, a passage so fraught with dangerous rip tides and currents that it was called the Hell's Gate. Block's maps were the first to show Manhattan and Long Island as separate entities. The harbor surrounding the island of Manhattan was situated in an estuary with a daily cycle of high and low tides. Block also discovered the Housatonic and Connecticut Rivers, the Norwalk Archipelago on Long Island Sound, the great Narragansett Bay of Rhode Island, and Block Island at the eastern entrance to the Long Island Sound from the Atlantic.

Strangely, it was not in the bay, but rather up the river at Fort Orange (Albany) that the Dutch planted their fur trading posts. In 1614, a group of Dutch shipowners had the remarkable foresight to form the New Netherlands Company (Dutch West India Company), a fur trading monopoly chartered by the States General. The small outpost of New Amsterdam was founded at the southern tip of Manhattan. The New Netherlands colony soon proved immensely rich in terms of the fur trade with the native population. The most valuable furs were those of beaver, taken in the winter when the coat was most heavy. There was an easy water route from the fur-rich interior of the continent—controlled by the immensely powerful Iroquois—down the river of the Mohawks to Albany, from Albany by way of the Hudson River to Manhattan, and from Manhattan to the sea.

The Dutch granted huge tracts of land along the Hudson River to friends of the company and expanded their trade up the Connecticut River and the other lesser streams that flowed into the Long Island Sound. They went further into the Narragansett country to trade for deerskins as well as beaver, and they expanded southward into the lands of the Delaware. Soon they found themselves in conflict with the trading companies of England to the north and of the Swedish to the south. Nonetheless, Fort Orange at Albany remained the greatest fur trading market in America throughout the seventeenth century. In less than fifty years, the Dutch were exporting beaver, deerskin, raccoon, marten, skunk, weasel, otter, and fox.[21]

The town of New Amsterdam grew slowly. By 1640, a fort (called Fort William for William of Orange) was built, and blockhouses for the garrison were erected at the tip of the island. A wall ten feet high separated these from the hinterland (Wall Street), and several churches and windmills were built. A fine house was built for the colonial governor, and a gallows was erected at the water's edge. The troops drilled on the common, and several cannon were placed in a well-located battery (Battery Park).

Notwithstanding the town's apparent readiness, in 1664 a squadron of five English ships entered the harbor and took possession of the town without a fight. Dutch New Amsterdam quickly changed to English New York (named for the Duke of York, later James II). The residents accepted the new name with little difficulty mainly because the English brought considerable trade to the town. Gradually, a significant trade developed that made New York competitive with Boston. The stimulus for this change came from the passage of the Flour Regulation Act in 1678. Large cargoes of flour shipped downriver from the Hudson Valley estates of wealthy Dutchmen were required by law to be "bolted" (a sifting process) in New York Town ostensibly to facilitate quality control. New York's flour was then sold to the sugar islands of the West Indies for molasses, to the colonies along the Atlantic seaboard for tobacco, and to the countries of Southern Europe for manufactured goods. Before the act, as few as eighteen vessels of any size used the port annually. Thereafter, almost 200 large vessels landed there annually.

By the eighteenth century, the New York waterfront was a maze of poorly lit alleys, canals, and docks surrounded by warehouses built largely of stone or brick. A few smaller vessels anchored in the river, and all of the larger vessels tied up at the wharves because of the current of the river and the daily cycle of tides. Sailors frequented taverns on Dock Street. The best food, immortalized in a sea chanty, was found in the taverns along Great Queen Street:

> If fresh meat be wanting to fill up our dish,
> We have carrots, and pumpkins, and turnips, and such,
> And if there is mind for a delicate dish,
> We haste to the clam banks and there we catch fish.[22]

It was reported that more than a dozen languages were spoken along the waterfront. Well-organized gangs of harbor pirates went along the docks and wharves stealing anything that was not tied down, chained up, or under guard. "Rope was taken by the coil, and sails cut from the gaskets, stripped from the ship's booms and yards." Brass and iron fittings, cleats, and anchors were pried loose, and blocks, stove pipes, and small boats were wisked away in the night. Watchmen were hired by shipowners in an attempt to suppress this thievery.

During the day, the garrison would parade on Broad Street (Broadway), and the sedan chairs of the wealthy began to appear. Negro servants and coachmen filled the streets. Gentlemen and ladies with brilliant clothing and incredibly high coiffures could be seen on Broad or Wall Streets in the afternoon. Those unwilling to spend time in the taverns might browse through the shops and bookstores. New York Town quickly took on many of the sophisticated characteristics of London. Nonetheless, at night anywhere along the waterfront sailors, workers, and civilians could be attacked by thieves armed with knives, swords, or firearms who suddenly appeared from the many alleys or popped out from the many barges tied along the dock side.

Nonetheless, New York continued to thrive with thousands of English and Germans entering the port destined for the lush Hudson and Mohawk valleys. Wheat and corn passed steadily down the river from the interior. A bustling scene was presented to any observer. A huge fleet of river craft was in service, among them hundreds of Hudson River sloops. This craft was broad of beam and heavily built. Some were rigged with fore and aft sails attached to 90-foot booms so that they could take advantage of the wind as they tacked back and forth up the river on the flood tide. Anchored during the ebb, these were often passed by the smaller, faster, and more "handy" vessels called "pinks." These had sharp ends both fore and aft and could make way even against the tide with a good wind blowing up the Hudson Valley. To these were added the boats, schooners, and masted barges that served as ferries from place to place across the harbor carrying vegetables from Fulton Street in Brooklyn or fish and oysters from the Jerseys.

By the beginning of the nineteenth century, the City of New York was thick with buildings and churches. Shipbuilding blossomed along the East River. The former Dutch trading post was quickly overtaking Boston as the largest port in the nation. In 1785, *The Empress of China* docked in New York with a fabulous cargo of tea and silk. A New York–built sloop, *Experiment*, thereafter made the first direct trip to China and came home with a highly profitable cargo of tea, silk, and ginseng. Such sailings firmly established New York in the China trade and led the merchants of Boston, Baltimore, and Salem to quickly enter the contest.

AMERICAN WHALING PORTS

One of the New England communities that turned to the business of whaling was Nantucket, an island off the coast of Massachusetts. Initially voyages were short. After the whales were caught, the blubber was cut up, packed in barrels, and brought back to the island to be rendered or "tried out." By 1730, voyages were becoming longer and the try-works were built right on the ships. It is doubtful that the residents of Nantucket missed the stink of blubber and boiling oil that hung heavy in the fog and strafed the island on the sea breeze. What remained was only the sweetish smell of oil stored in the casks carried ashore.

By 1775, the population of Nantucket had risen to 4,500 persons, and 150 vessels called it home. The American Revolution put a halt to whaling, but in the years after the War of 1812, Nantucket rose to its greatest days. By 1840, the wharves were filled with ships unloading or preparing for a voyage. At least one whaler entered or left the harbor every week. This generated numerous secondary businesses. Teamsters drove wagons to and from the wharf. Sail makers made and repaired sails in their sail lofts. Ropewalks were busy twisting rope of all sizes. Blacksmiths forged harpoons and lances. Coopers made the oil casks while carpenters fashioned other ship needs. Chandlers provided the ships with supplies. Stylish houses were built by wealthy whaling merchants and captains.

Nantucket was not the only American whaling port, nor was it the largest. New York had large commercial whaling ports at Sag Harbor, East Hampton, Southampton, and Amagansett. Whalers sailed regularly from Mystic, New London, and Stonington in Connecticut. Massachusetts hosted a number of ports that supported whalers including

A New Bedford whaler with its whaleboats hanging along its sides. The U.S. whaling fleet numbered many hundreds of similar vessels in the nineteenth century. Illustration from an early-twentieth-century text in the authors' collection.

Gloucester, Marblehead, Salem, Provincetown, Fairhaven, and Edgartown on the island of Martha's Vineyard.

But it was New Bedford, Massachusetts, which was to rise to be the whaling capital of the world. On Water and Union Streets were the outfitters who sold clothes for whalemen. Above the shops were fairly clean sailor's boarding houses. A church called the Seamen's Bethel was specifically dedicated to whalemen. Away from the smells and taverns were the mansions of the rich merchants with their gardens and lawns. In

1850, New Bedford was the richest city, per capita, in the world. The whale oil and bone entering the port was valued at $10 million annually. Such prosperity produced a community where expenditures for education and public buildings were among the highest in the country.

Former slave and abolitionist Frederick Douglass arrived in New Bedford in 1838 and was surprised to see that "the laboring classes lived in better houses, [and] that their houses were more elegantly furnished and were more abundantly supplied with conveniences and comforts than the houses of many who owned slaves on the Eastern Shore of Maryland." He also noted that this was true "not only of the white people in the city" but also of the free back population.[23] In fact, New Bedford had a larger population of blacks, 6.8 percent, than any other city in New England at the time.

EUROPEAN PORTS

European ports were quite different from those of eighteenth- and nineteenth-century America. Rather than a series of docks and piers extending directly from the seashore, the ports of Europe generally consisted of long narrow wharves clinging to the banks of rivers that led into the sea. The wharves, quays, and docks of a common seaport town were often built of a combination of stone and wood. In Europe the use of stone predominated. This was also true of the warehouses, shop buildings, and workplaces with many wooden structures having been replaced over the centuries after repeated waterfront fires.

The Great London Fire of 1666, for instance, had taken away most of the flammable materials in the city, as well as extensively damaging a large number of wooden waterfront structures, in a single catastrophe. Much of the damage was replaced in the next decade with the sweeping use of stone as a more fire resistant material. In London, much of the bank of the Thames River had stone steps or stairways leading down from stone-lined river banks to the water's edge. Water-gates, entrances cut into the ancient stone embankment wall built by the Romans, led to the small docks or "hithes" on the grassland.

During the reign of Elizabeth I (1558–1603) shipping from London was brisk. Small boats serviced the ships that lay at anchor in the river. However, by 1660, it had declined almost to the point of stagnation with English ships overshadowed by French, Dutch, German, and Scandinavian vessels. By the eighteenth century, prosperity had returned. Activity abounded as the trading ventures of the Virginia Company, Honourable East India Company, and Hudson Bay Company set out for the New World. The Muscovy Company went to Russia, the Turkey Company went to the Levant, and the Africa Company went to the Bight of Benin. As the pursuit of trade progressed, so did the waterfront, which became crowded with warehouses, chandleries, riggers, sail-lofts, and smithies. Taverns and coffee houses filled the alleys and narrow streets leading from the quay. Large merchant ships and privateersmen surrounded smaller ships like a cat with a large litter of kittens. Farther down the river were smaller vessels such as those used to transport prisoners to the penal colonies or packets used to carry mail to the colonies.

The first dock to be built in London was the Howland Great Dock. Constructed at Depforth in 1696, it was rebuilt as Greenland Dock in 1807. Along Wapping Wall stood the infamous Execution Dock where the bones of executed pirates and mutineers hung in chains as a stern warning. Some of these may have been river pirates who infested the waterfront stealing cargoes, stores, and rigging. By the nineteenth century, thieves proved to be such a menace that fortified docks were established along the London waterfront. Merchant companies built high walls that surrounded the warehouses, and the water gates were guarded day and night. The first fortified structure was the West India Company Dock, which opened in 1802.

Endless trains of barges and a forest of masts could be seen lining the quays of all the port cities of the Dutch Republic. Amsterdam was a port of antiquity. In the seventeenth century, it was the largest port in the world. Built on a series of ninety islands joined by approximately 200 bridges, many of its buildings were built on piers. Its warehouses, adorned with ornate gables, were known for their singular beauty. Amsterdam never developed the sleazy wharf culture of other seaport towns. It was almost inevitable that a city such as Amsterdam should develop as a center of this trade. A sea dike built on the north side of the city and dikes on either side of the Amstel River gave protection from flood waters and provided the first three streets. The broad dam built across the river gave the town its name. Besides Amsterdam, other Dutch ports such as Texel, Hague, Flushing, and Antwerp became great centers of trade.[24]

Hamburg was another active port even though the numerous independent "German" states that made up the region surrounding it were not noted for their maritime prowess until the nineteenth century. A few shore wharves existed along the Elbe River, but these were mainly used by the lighters to transport freight to and from the ships moored in the river. Dissected by a series of canals, the lower town was periodically beset with floods. The canals were lined with damp warehouses and workplaces. The lower-class dwellings were often situated on ground well below water level. During exceptionally high tides, residents needed to seek safety. Once the tide receded, the inhabitants would return to waterlogged neighborhoods and search the canals looking for anything of value to clean off and to sell.

The grand Spanish port of Seville was actually a series of ports stretching up the Guadalquivir River from Cadiz to Seville. The largest of the great merchant ships and war galleons could seldom sail more than half-way up the river. The majority of smaller ships were able to continue up river to Puerto de las Muelas. Notwithstanding its limited capacity to handle large vessels, Seville was able to supply "men to sail the ships, functionaries to dispatch them, victuals to feed the mariners, a good commercial distribution network, and the money to finance the expeditions." Seville's inland position also necessitated a laborious and time consuming journey downriver, but it also "provided protection against the assaults of all those who were tempted by the gleaming precious metals and other riches of the Indies."[25]

The port was flanked by the curtain wall of the old Almohad fortifications and by Triana, a suburb whose buildings ran right to the water's edge. Beyond the Arenal Gate were two small openings known as the "Doorways of Oil and Charcoal." The latter was the direct route to the royal palace. So many riches passed through this portal that it was designated the "Golden Doorway." One of the most notable buildings was the combination jail, warehouse, and custom's house, which extended over the protective wall to rest at the river's edge.

Between the city wall and the river was the Arenal or "sandy beach" where dozens of vessels nosed in side by side in an effort to save space. Like many other European ports of the period, Seville did not have wooden piers. The Arenal Gate connected to the cathedral through the Calle de la Mar or "Street of the Sea." Here was the hub of activity for mariners. It linked the port with the steps of the cathedral. Sailors hoping to join a crew waited here to be signed by ship's masters. Notaries positioned themselves in the archways surrounding the steps to make available their services in formalizing contracts for shipping, bookings, passages, or other maritime matters.

Around the waterfront warehouses were the residences of the stevedores, coopers, and other river workmen. Period documents describe a small cylindrical platform made of stone that served as a base for the only crane in the port. Seville had no shipyards for the repair or refurbishing of ships, or for the clearing of barnacles and seaweed from their bottoms. To complete such work, the ship's hull would be hauled out of the water and pulled over on one side by ropes and pulleys attached to the masts to permit work on the other (a process called "careening").

The French had a number of good and moderately good ports including Rochefort, Toulon, Lorient, Cherbourg, Nantes, Boulogne, and LeHavre, but only one port, Brest, was outstanding as a French naval base. The harbor at Brest was one of the best in all of Europe with an entrance two miles wide. As many as 500 ships could be moored in its roadstead, which was fourteen miles long and four miles wide. The port had a complete dockyard and shipbuilding facility. Unfortunately, Brest

was on a lee shore subject to a predominantly westerly wind. This necessitated a difficult outward passage against a headwind. Many departures were delayed until the wind shifted. Then scores of vessels would
make for sea.

Toulon had an inner harbor for about fifty ships with a dock, arsenal,
and victualing yard. However, the outer harbor and roadstead was capable of handling only three or four ships simultaneously. The town,
considered the most secure in Europe, was well fortified and impregnable from the sea. The prevailing north wind made the blockade of the
harbor very difficult at all seasons of the year.

Rochefort had a complete dockyard, an arsenal, a foundry, and a ropewalk, but it was ten miles inland from the sea on the Charente River,
which meandered through a marshland. The approach was protected by
the Ile d' Aix, but it suffered from silting and difficult winds. There were
two major roadsteads at the outer Aix and at the Basque roads. The port
city was thought to be well protected, but the unsuccessful British attack
of 1809 caused the French to reconsider the vulnerability of the harbor.

BRITISH NAVAL PORTS

The numerous seaport towns comprising the greater Portsmouth and
Plymouth areas were deluged with two destitute populations, each owing their status to British naval practice—seaman's families and prostitutes. The demands for crews to man British ships during the Georgian
era drove press gangs into coastal towns "pressing" men into naval service. During the height of the seamen shortage (1803–1815) press gangs
went so far as to intercept merchant ships returning to port and siphon
off their most experienced seamen to serve in the navy without ever
stepping on dry land. Some men simply disappeared until word was
sent from the processing ships to their distraught families. This cruel
system left many women and children in the most desperate of situations. Wives seldom knew when their husbands would return. Even if
they did, seamen had no right to shore leave and getting to the ship was
not easy for a family without the resources to pay for transportation.

It was important for a wife to be present when her husband was paid.
Seamen's wages seldom amounted to much, and they were quickly exhausted. The purser had to be paid for any tobacco used during the
voyage or for any clothing drawn from the slops chest. Additional
money was often due to the bumboats that met the ships as they came
into port, setting up stalls on board that offered fresh fruit, liquor, clothing, trinkets, and anything else a sailor might fancy. Even if a wife did
get some of her spouse's pay before he spent it, it was not likely to last
for very long unless there was a good deal of prize money to be distributed.

The number of impoverished seamen's families was an oppressive presence in most seaport towns. Supplementing the pittance they received from their husbands was not easy for most wives. Women of this period were generally prohibited from participating in many of the exclusively male trades that paid well. A shop or tavern required the investment of capital that was all too frequently unobtainable by a family whose income depended on a living made at sea. Domestic service offered the most possibilities for women but there were always few open positions. Those who resorted to begging could be arrested, jailed, and whipped for the offense before being sent back to their home parish.

Charitable organizations existed but their main strategy was to send these poor wretches back to their home parishes. While awaiting transport, they were sent to workhouses. The first workhouse was established in Portsmouth in 1729. The aged, blind, insane, and diseased were all housed together with the poor. The able-bodied inmates were put to work in the most menial of jobs such as plaiting straw for sailor's hats or picking apart old rope to make oakem, a hemp-like material mixed with tar and used to caulk ship's planking. The proceeds of these labors went to the workhouse so that when they left the inmates had neither a nest egg nor a new skill upon which to build.

Economic conditions in English seaports were so bad that some seamen's wives resorted to prostitution in order to avoid exposing their children to the dangers of the workhouses where infant mortality among children under one year of age ran as high as 70 percent. Once a family was transported home, their prospects were not much better unless they had relatives who could provide for them or assist them in finding work. As soon as word was received of a returning ship, wives scurried back to the ports starting the pitiful process once again.

Portsmouth and Plymouth were occupied by a large number of professional prostitutes. Prostitution, which was not illegal, was an institution in most large cities of England at this time. What made it so prolific in these ports was the presence of the Royal Navy. Although never policy, it was common practice for prostitutes to be brought out to the ships while in port. This was thought to lessen the incidence of desertion. Importing women to the ships was done in foreign ports as well especially in the West Indies.

Ships prostitutes were in the lowest echelon of their profession earning so little that they were often not even managed by a madam or pimp. In Plymouth, they rented rooms in the sailor's tavern district near the Quay. They were often forced to share accommodations with other prostitutes or with families of desperately limited means who would tolerate their profession.

Reform movements of the late eighteenth and nineteenth centuries spawned a number of institutions to assist the "wayward women." The

Female Penitentiary for Penitent Prostitutes was founded in Stonehouse outside of Plymouth in 1808. Built with private funds after the wretched conditions of the workhouse gained attention, the penitentiary, albeit clean, was austere and constrictive. Inmates were dressed in drab attire and their heads were shaved. They labored at domestic chores and those who did not run away generally entered the workforce in domestic service.

Charles Nordhoff, having traveled the world as a sailor for many decades, observed of seaports, "The sailor sees nothing of the world really worth seeing. Seaports, devoted entirely to the shipping interest, as the vast majority of such places are, contain but little that is of real interest to the traveler."[26] He concluded that in a lifetime of travel most sailors had "merely . . . informed themselves of the localities of the various grogshops; [and] they had possibly made the acquaintance of sundry other persons and places—not to be mentioned to ears polite."[27]

NOTES

1. Charles Nordhoff, *Sailor Life on Man-of-War and Merchant Vessel* (New York: Dodd, Mead & Co., 1884), 153–154.

2. Recent American tastes in beer and other beverages call for large quantities of ice, but European tastes, even today, call for wines and beers to be properly cooled only to the temperature of well water.

3. Quoted from *Harper's* in Richard Ellis, *Men and Whales* (New York: Alfred A. Knopf, 1991), 173.

4. Herman Melville, *Billy Budd* (New York: Literary Classics, 1983), 1361.

5. Blacksmith James Durfee of New Bedford made 58,517 harpoons during his lifetime.

6. Robert Carse, *Ports of Call* (New York: Charles Scribner's Sons, 1967), 46.

7. The reconstructed ropewalk at Mystic Seaport in southeastern Connecticut, an immensely long building, is still a small fraction of the length of period commercial ropemaking facilities.

8. Emma Mayhew Whiting and Henry Beetle Hough, *Whaling Wives* (Boston: Houghton Mifflin 1953), 95–96.

9. Herman Melville, *Redburn* (New York: Literary Classics, 1983), 26.

10. Nordhoff, 35.

11. Stan Hugill, *Sailortown* (New York: E. P. Dutton & Co., 1967), 78.

12. Nordhoff, 35.

13. Ibid., 36.

14. Ibid., 37.

15. Melville, *Redburn*, 152.

16. C. Douglas Inglis, "The Spanish Naval Shipyard at Havana in the Eighteenth Century," in *New Aspects of Naval History: Selected Papers from the Fifth Naval History Symposium*, ed. Frederick S. Harrod (Baltimore, MD: Nautical and Aviation Publishing, 1985), 56.

17. Robert G. Albion, *New England and the Sea* (Middletown, CT: Wesleyan University Press, 1972), 7.

18. Albion, 47.

19. Richard Heckman, ed., *Yankees under Sail* (Dublin, NH: Yankee, Inc., 1968), 98–105.

20. Ibid.

21. Carse, *Ports of Call*, 140–147.

22. Ibid., 154–155.

23. Russell Bourne, *The View from Front Street* (New York: W. W. Norton & Company, 1989), 154.

24. G. J. Marcus, *The Formative Centuries: A Naval History of England* (Boston: Little, Brown & Co., 1961), 197.

25. Pablo E. Pérez-Mallaína, *Spain's Men of the Sea: Daily Life on the Indies Fleets in the Sixteenth Century*, trans. Carla Rahn Phillips (Baltimore, MD: Johns Hopkins University Press, 1998), 3–5.

26. Nordhoff, 300.

27. Ibid., 300–303.

2

Sea Lanes

Notwithstanding all the familiar and unfamiliar dangers of the sea,
both travel and traffic by water have always been easier and cheaper
than by land.

—Alfred Thayer Mahan[1]

The sea initially presents itself as a great common highway over which
ships may pass in any direction, yet in the age of sail the majority of
travelers and traders determined to use certain paths across the sea to
the exclusion of others. These paths have come to be known as the sea
lanes. The reasons for the choice of one route over another in the age of
sail was controlled by several factors.

The principal factors affecting the choice of particular routes may include the relative positions of the port of departure and the destination,
any geographic features that served to enhance or detract from a particular course, and the combined effects of winds, currents, and tides. Economic demands created by the needs of trade such as the availability or
lack of certain products were particularly crucial, as was the strategic or
military value of maintaining or interdicting a particular sea lane. The
dangers posed by pirates and politicians were always a consideration
when choosing a route.

Many routes were dictated by formal political and economic agreements. Under such agreements some sea lanes were elaborately laid out.
Others were less well established and acted as detours around or away

from both political and physical obstacles. Ships that sailed to and fro upon the sea needed secure ports at the beginning and end of their voyages and convenient and dependable places along the way to obtain provisions and to execute repairs. The voyages were often long and dangerous.

Moreover, the periods of peace between maritime nations were often too short, and the seas were beset with enemies. The route had to allow a ship and cargo the protection of its country's navy throughout the voyage. Merchant seamen, seeking trade in new or unexplored regions, often gave up this security and protection for the promise of bountiful profits, but their courage also helped to establish new sea lanes.

Geographical Position

The geographic position of the great maritime nations of Europe dictated to a large extent many of the commonly frequented sea lanes. Circumstances have caused the Mediterranean Sea, for instance, to play a greater roll in the commercial and military history of the sea than any other body of water of equal size. Nation after nation has tried to control it. Italy, Spain, France, and the Barbary states of North Africa have all tried to maintain sole rights to travel its sea lanes. Yet the very existence of the posts of other nations along its coasts or among its islands has prevented such a circumstance from taking place. Thus Gibraltar, Malta, and Crete have each served in the capacity of maintaining some level of freedom of the sea. From ancient times, the relatively short and well-known sea lanes that crisscrossed the Mediterranean were dictated more by economic need and political influence than by physical or meteorological conditions met upon the sea.[2]

Although a formidable opponent, the French fleet was rarely in a condition to contest the English control of the Channel. Crossing the Channel, therefore, was politically safe. A trip to Bordeaux was simply an overseas, rather than a foreign voyage. It was also no great venture in navigation, but it did require a vessel capable of withstanding an ocean voyage, since the Channel weather could be very rough. Moreover, each voyage could easily be extended to Spain or Portugal. Accordingly, the Channel crossing became a regular route for outward-bound shipments of wool and home-bound cargoes of grain and wine loaded into broad-beamed merchant vessels propelled by square sails.

The same rivers that made much of Holland a swamp provided a convenient and inexpensive means of transporting goods through a great portion of western Europe. The earliest Dutch traders traveled far up these streams hauling their boats against the lazy current and floating back down carrying cargoes such as lumber, grain, and wine. By using the experience gained on the inland waterways, these traders expanded their enterprises into Denmark and across the North Sea to York and other English towns. Moreover, a series of natural disasters that struck the lowlands of Europe in the thirteenth century broke the dikes of Holland, admitting the sea deep into the heart of the country. This new inland sea (the Zuiderzee) never retreated and may have been the consequence of either the gradual subsidence of the land or a similar rise in the average sea level—possibly a little of both. Many thousands of people died when the dikes burst, but the calamity served, nonetheless, as a turning point in Dutch history. "With a large and protecting sea arm reaching deep within their borders, the Dutch turned to trade more vigorously than ever before."[3]

Portugal made the most meaningful advances in maritime technology and achievement during the critical early years of **Portugal** Europe's exploration of the world's sea lanes. The Portuguese were aided in these endeavors by their position on the Atlantic and their fine blue water port of Lisbon. Unlike many other European ports that required a difficult passage of vessels to and from the sea, Lisbon's geographical location and deep harbor allowed large vessels to make their way in and out with little aid or difficulty.[4] Before the end of the sixteenth century, the Portuguese had expanded their commercial empire by establishing trading relationships with the slavers along the African coast and constructing trading "factories" at Goa, Daman, and Diu in far away India. In this they were helped by the discovery of a pattern of winds that blew toward India between the east coast of Africa and Madagascar in the monsoon season and back toward the southern tip of Africa in the dry season.

Notwithstanding their early lead in maritime activity and exploration, Portuguese rulers became accustomed to having their discoveries made for free. Certainly privately funded voyages of exploration were rewarded by magnanimous grants of land, honors, and suitable titles, but royal funding for any enterprise requiring the risk of ships or money was almost unknown. Ultimately the Portuguese, like the Spanish, sought to acquire vast riches and to create a great national wealth not through "the healthy excitement of exploration and adventure, but [through] gold and silver." The absorption of Portugal by Spain in 1580 ended the period of Portuguese dominance and made Spain what it had not been before, an important naval power.[5]

Spain's position on the Iberian Peninsula was remarkably favorable with access to both the Atlantic and Mediterranean **Spain** coastlines. By 1720, the Spanish had four major ports with shipyard facilities on the Iberian peninsula: Guarnizo, El Ferrol, Cadiz (La Carraca), and Cartagena. With the ports of Cadiz and Cartegena straddling the entrance to the Mediterranean, Spain should have been able to control the trade coming from the Levant as well as that coming up the west African coast from the East Indies. The loss of Gibraltar to England, however, not only deprived Spain of the control of the mouth of the

This chart of the North Sea is typical of many of the early navigational aids used in the seventeenth century. Note the sounding numbers and the man with the cross-staff in the corner.

Mediterranean, but "also imposed an obstacle to the easy junction of the two divisions of her fleet," one in the Atlantic and the other in the Mediterranean.[6]

Nonetheless, as the age of exploration passed into the age of colonization, the great gateway to the New World proved to be the complex of Spanish ports stretching from Cadiz to Seville on Spain's southwest coast. It was at Cadiz that the New World fleets were gathered and dispatched, and it was through Cadiz (and ultimately Seville) that the treasures of the New World entered Europe. Yet sixteenth-century Spain, as a whole, had few ports with facilities for loading and unloading large vessels. Only Santander on the the Bay of Biscay and Malaga in the Mediterranean had cranes capable of loading heavy cargo.

Despite the fact that Seville did not have the port instillations to match its ultimate importance, this inland port, almost 100 kilometers up the Guadalquivir River from Cadiz, became the land base for the fleets that explored and exploited much of the western hemisphere. The passage of the Guadalquivir River was accomplished in slow stages over a period of several days. There was a very real risk of losing vessels among the many sandy shallows that posed an enormous danger for navigation in this river. Because of these shallows, only small vessels left Seville fully loaded with all their cargo and provisions. Larger vessels left practically empty with their provisions descending much of the length of the river on large barges. Once at the mouth of the Guadalquivir one serious obstacle remained: a sandbar that blocked the passage to the open sea. "[A] final departure could be delayed for many days until the conditions of wind, daylight, and tides were propitious" for clearing this obstacle. Once over the bar, all the ships were consigned to the care of harbor pilots experienced in finding the channel that led to Cadiz.[7]

Voyages to and from the New World were scheduled for either spring or summer in an attempt to avoid the Caribbean storm season. The first leg of the trip was a short hop to the Canary Islands where repairs could be effected and supplies topped off. The ships then faced the great leap across the Atlantic, a voyage of about a month with constantly favorable trade winds at their backs. The northeasterly trades blew with a steady 15 to 20 knots without changing direction by more than a compass point all year, and an equally unvarying current added 2 or 3 knots in the same direction. As a result, westward-bound vessels were given a speedy voyage. Arriving in the Antilles, some vessels made for Puerto Rico, Hispaniola, or Cuba; others, having left Spain later in the year, sailed further south for the mainland at Cartagena de Indias and Veracruz.

The return trip to Spain always began with a first leg to Havana, Cuba. The island of Cuba was located at the entrance to a circuit of winds and currents that led directly back to the Azores—a trip longer and more difficult than the outward voyage from Spain. Captains still had to claw

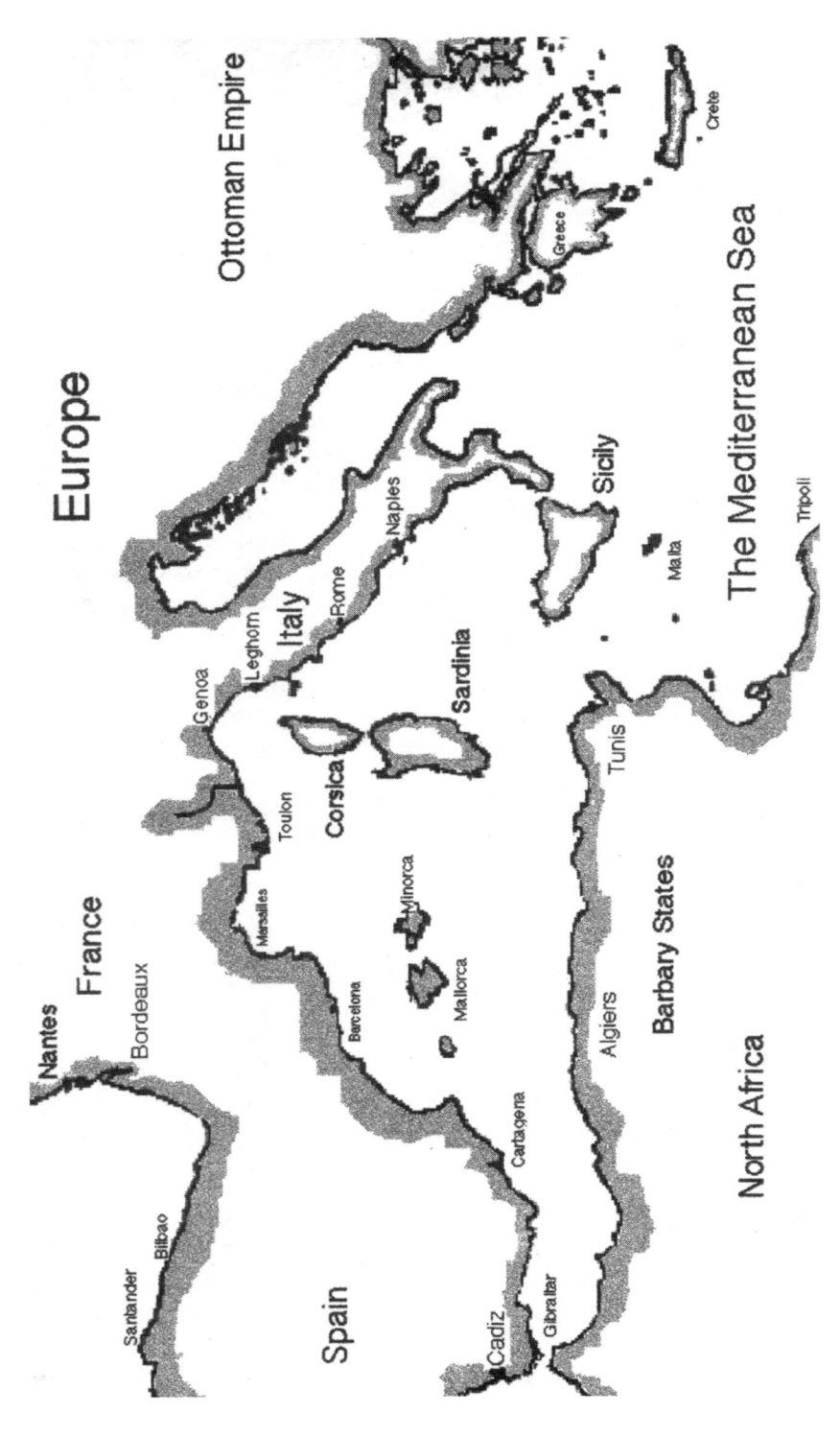

their way to the east against adverse winds, but the currents at least ran eastbound through the ninety-mile-wide strait between Florida and Cuba. Initially many vessels were lost to hurricanes, uncharted reefs, and sandbars, but with experience, navigators learned how to use the seasonal winds and currents to their best advantage.

Through most of the sixteenth century, Spanish fleets sailed back and forth across the Atlantic "largely unchallenged by European rivals." Only after the precipitous decline of the Spanish navy after the defeat of its Armada in 1588 did marauders begin to regularly attack the Spanish fleets.[8] "The fortunes of Portugal, united to Spain during the most critical period of her history, followed the same downward path." Maritime historian Alfred Thayer Mahan blamed the abandonment of commerce, manufacture, and trade by both Portugal and Spain, on "the mines of Brazil . . . [and] those of Mexico and Peru" respectively. "The English and the Dutch were no less desirous of gain," wrote Mahan, "[but] Spain and Portugal sought it by digging gold out of the ground." He noted that "all manufactures fell into insane contempt" leaving the Dutch and the English to provide both Spain and Portugal with clothing, merchandise, and all other commodities, "even to salted fish and grain."[9]

Spain's ultimate maritime impotence was not only a symptom of a general decay but an inevitable consequence of the Spanish attempt to rule an empire without shipping. The Spanish entered the eighteenth century with extensive holdings. On the European continent, they held the Spanish Netherlands (now Belgium), Milan, Naples, most of southern Italy, and other scattered provinces. In the Mediterranean they ruled Sicily, Sardinia, and the Balearic Islands—all perfectly located to control the sea lanes. In the western hemisphere, the Spanish ruled almost all of South America and half of the northern continent besides Puerto Rico and Cuba. They had scattered possessions in the Pacific and ruled the Philippines. During the next century, the list of Spain's possessions would shift with the vagaries of each ensuing war.[10]

The fact that the Spanish recognized the need for a navy to wage war and protect their possessions made their dependence on impressed merchant vessels instead of warships even more remarkable.[11] Military strength afloat, nonetheless, proved to be the natural and healthy outgrowth of a dedication to peaceful commerce and shipping. Thus the trading nations of northern Europe advanced their sea power at the expense of their southern neighbors by building foundations securely resting on sea-borne commerce.[12]

The Dutch Republic—alternately referred to as Holland, or the United Provinces—developed one of the earliest of the **Holland** great trading nations of Europe. Holland was particularly favored in this endeavor by its geographic location halfway between northern and southern Europe. A long line of dunes and dikes fringed the

coastal lands of Holland and Flanders, and the Zealand Islands protected
the mouths of the rivers Maas and Scheldt at their entrance to the North
Sea. Extensive lakes and marshlands secured the northern frontier almost
as effectively as the great rivers did in the south. Throughout its existence, Holland's history has been one of close association with the sea—
fighting it back by building and maintaining dikes and dams while the
sea periodically reclaimed some of the hard won land. Fighting the sea
ultimately proved impossible. With a population eight times greater than
their land could sustain, the Dutch turned to trade to supply their
needs.[13] It was economic need, therefore, that drove the Dutch to make
a living upon the sea, but it was their geographic location that helped
to make them successful "beyond their wildest hopes."[14]

The Dutch fished their own coast for centuries mainly for herring,
which they consumed fresh, but the need for an export product encouraged them to learn how to preserve the herring by salting it. The consequences of this discovery were immense. The Dutch found that they
could exchange an almost unlimited quantity of salted herring for other
products throughout Europe. The schools of herring were a gold mine
for the Dutch, but the best fishing grounds were off the coasts of Scotland
and England. Therefore, the Dutch concluded treaties with England for
the rights to fish in these waters—rights that they held until late in the
seventeenth century. The security of the fishing fleet was provided by
armed escorts built and fitted out for the purpose. It is no exaggeration
to say that the Great Fishery provided the experience and the means that
later enabled the Dutch Republic to become a maritime power of the first
magnitude. Here they learned the arts of seamanship, navigation, and
shipbuilding, and they used their skills to expand their trade into the
Baltic.

Dutch shipping quickly came to dominate northern Europe, and further expansion was equally successful. The growth of the Dutch carrying
trade kept pace with the generally increasing commerce of western Europe. Ultimately Dutch prosperity came to reside in moving luxuries
from all over Europe—cloth made from English wool; wine and olive
oil from France, Italy and Spain; and dried fruit and silks from Greece
and far away Persia and Turkey. As much as 75 percent of all goods
moving across Europe were carried in Dutch bottoms.

Moreover, their growing reliance on and comfort with the sea led the
Dutch to look beyond the horizon to the lands of spices in India, the
East Indies, and China.[15] By borrowing from the Portuguese the maps
and knowledge of the routes to the East Indies, Dutch shipping expanded into a great global trading empire. The powerful Dutch East
India Company, founded in 1602, built an empire largely by dispossess-
ing the Portuguese. By 1650, the company was the mistress of the Cape
of Good Hope and controlled trading posts in Ceylon and along the coast

of Malabar and Coromandel. Dutch colonies could be found in India, Malacca, Java, and in the Maluccas. More importantly, the Dutch post at Batavia controlled the sea lanes to Japan and China.

Moreover, the Dutch West India Company, founded in 1621 to regulate contraband trade already carried on in America and on the African coast, held portions of the coast of Guinea and Brazil as well as several colonies in North America—New Amsterdam being the most notable.[16] Although less profitable than its sister company, the Dutch West India Company was able to gain a valuable foothold in the sugar islands of the West Indies. In little more than a decade (1634–1648), the company occupied St. Eustatius, Curacao, Bonaire, Aruba, Saba, St. Martin, and several lesser islands. Although it was dispossessed of its Brazilian stations by treaty in 1661, it was able to maintain mainland establishments in Surinam and Essequibo (Dutch Guiana). In 1674, the original company was dissolved only to be reconstituted a number of times as less successful incarnations in the eighteenth and nineteenth centuries.

Mahan pointed out that England was so situated that it was "neither forced to defend itself by land nor induced to seek   **England** extension of its territory by way of the land." This gave England a natural advantage when compared with nations whose boundaries were "continental." Among the great maritime nations of the age of sail, the English were free to dedicate much of their wealth to the development of a navy and was also able to concentrate the force of their naval power around their own shores. England was further favored by the "strategic advantage of a central position and a good base for hostile operations against its probable enemies . . . facing Holland and the Baltic states on one hand and France and Spain on the other."[17]

Moreover, England lay astride the windward side of the Straits of Dover (the English Channel), one of the great thoroughfares of sea-borne trade. In the decades prior to the adoption of steam, a passage through the Channel by sailing vessels was still a serious endeavor, not to be taken lightly; yet much of the trade of Holland, Sweden, Russia, and Denmark had to pass through the Channel at the narrow strait between Dover and Calais. Here England could interpose her naval forces against any combination of enemies wishing to effect a junction of their fleets either to the north or to the south.[18]

For much of its history, the English held the port of Calais on the Continent. Thus astride the Straits of Dover, the English established ports that offered the shortest sea routes between Britain and the Continent. Among the best known of these English ports were the Cinque Ports (Hastings, Romney, Hythe, Sandwich, and Dover) lining the east coast of Britain facing the Continent. The naval dockyards at Woolrich, Deptford, and Chatham faced the Spanish Netherlands just as the naval base at Portsmouth faced France. Moreover, a number of small ports and good

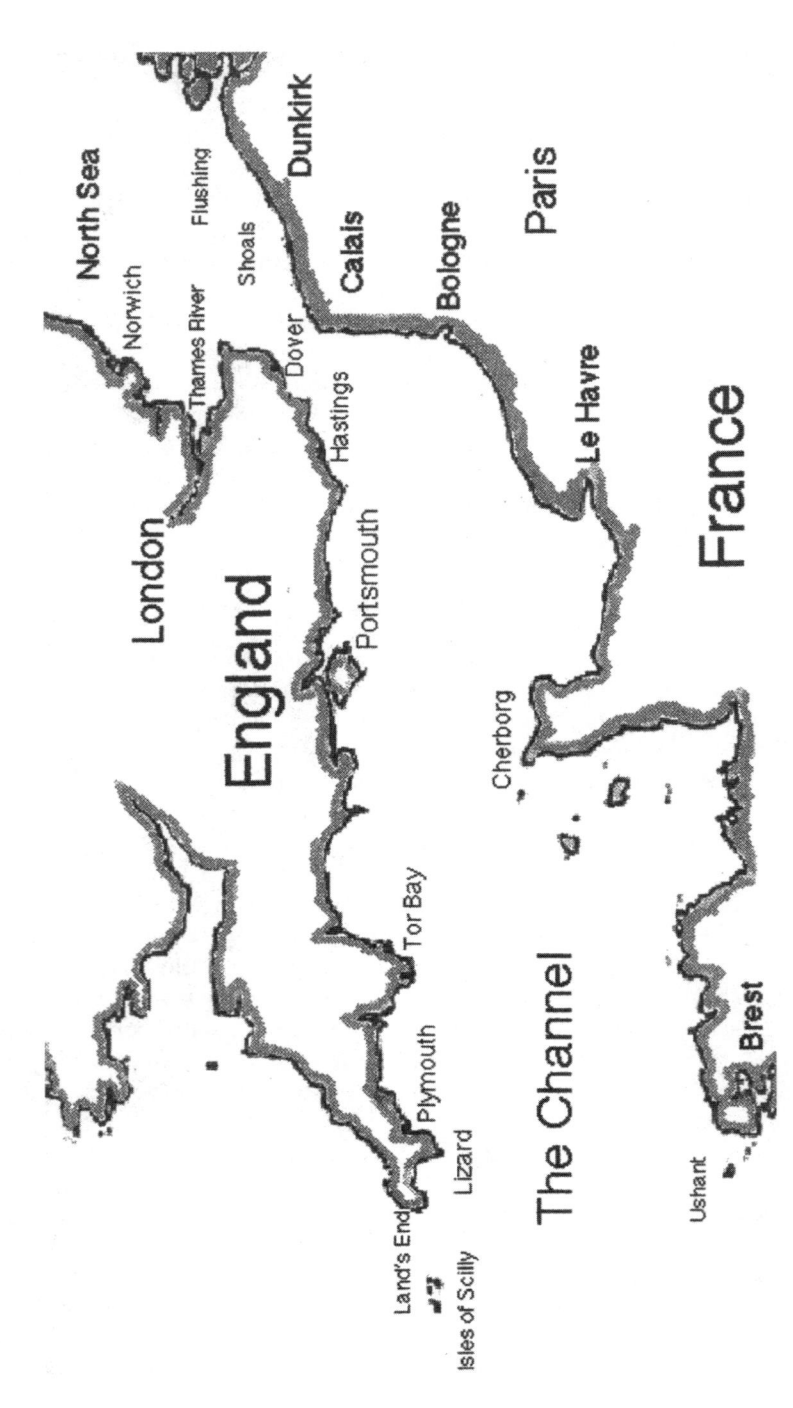

anchorages comprised the great Atlantic-facing Plymouth naval base and those in the north at Sheerness and Yarmouth.

Although other nations lined the Channel, the English had better ports and a safer coast to approach than most of their rivals. When English ships operated against the French ports at Brest, Dunkirk, or Le Havre, they based their fleets at Torbay, Plymouth, or Portsmouth (Spithead). In easterly or moderate westerly weather, English ships in the Channel could maintain their watch over the French with ease. When gale winds came from the west, the English ships made for their bases at home knowing that the adverse winds would prevent the French from getting out of port. When watching northern ports such as Antwerp, Hague, or Texel, the English used their ports at Sheerness or Yarmouth.

These geographical advantages were not without some negative consequences. The Irish Sea, for instance, resembled a large estuary separating the British Isles. It proved a great danger to the English time and again, giving their enemies access to the western reaches of Britain and interfering with English control of the generally hostile population of Ireland.[19] Moreover, French privateers were quite as close to interdicting many English trade routes as the English were to threatening the French Atlantic seaboard. The nearness of France to England "greatly facilitated her *guerre de course* directed at the latter. Having ports on the North Sea, on the Channel, and on the Atlantic, French cruisers started from points near the focus of English trade, both coming and going." The French port of Dunkirk was particularly effective in this regard.[20]

The English gave up some of the advantages inherent in defending only their island fortress by expanding their colonial holdings and trading posts into an immense global empire. Nonetheless, unlike the Spanish whose equally extensive colonies could not be protected from insult because of their declining maritime strength, the dimensions of the British empire peaked just as English seapower achieved the ability to secure them. Moreover, the English were particularly fortunate in the location of some of their foreign posts. Gibraltar, the classical example of a well-situated station, gave the English virtual control of the entrance to the Mediterranean from the Atlantic; Malta secured many of the Mediterranean's central crossroads; Aden secured the Persian Gulf and the land bridge at Suez; and Madras and Bombay controlled the Indian Ocean and the approaches to the East Indies. Although deprived of most of its Atlantic colonies by the War of American Independence, the English maintained excellent facilities in Nova Scotia at Halifax and in the West Indies.

Jamaica, in the Caribbean, located to the windward of the most important trading stations of her competitors, gave England a critical advantage in the Windward Islands, while Antiqua served as a base for the Leeward Islands. The British periodically occupied other islands such as Martinique and Curacao as well as a major fortification called Brimstone Hill on the sugar island of St. Kitts (St. Christopher's), which had an excellent anchorage. Oddly, for many years, the French occupied both ends of St. Kitts while the English held the center. The fort, located on top of an 800-foot monolith of volcanic stone jutting up from the island, overlooked the eleven-mile channel between St. Kitts and the Dutch island of St. Eustasius. The place was seemingly impregnable and, strengthened periodically throughout the eighteenth and nineteenth centuries, became known as the "Gibraltar of the West Indies."

The Honourable East India Company
In London, a board of directors oversaw the Honourable East India Company, which was described as "a government owned by businessmen." At its height, the company ruled virtually one-fifth of the world's population and had an army and navy of its own. It was almost as great a military force as it was a commercial one, and at one time or another, it was commanded by a number of heroic figures including Robert Clive, Warren Hastings, Lord Cornwallis (the British general of the American Revolution), and Arthur Wellesley (later the Duke of Wellington). In the 1820s, the Honourable East India Company maintained an army on foreign shores numbering well over a quarter of a million men—larger than any standing army in Europe at the time.[21]

The Honourable East India Company also maintained a dockyard at Bombay to serve one of the world's largest navies in the form of a giant mercantile fleet. Its naval service patrolled the Indian Ocean and the waters of the East Indies as well as the Persian Gulf. The East Indiamen of the eighteenth century were of about 500 tons with a crew of ninety. Recognized as a discrete category of vessel, they were built specifically for the India trade and, with time, some reached 1,000 tons. Large three-masted ships, East Indiamen were heavily armed for merchant vessels, carrying between 20 and 30 guns sometimes on two decks.

East Indiamen usually sailed in convoy with at least a dozen others of their kind and one or more Royal Navy frigates as escorts. The combined fire power of several East Indiamen was more visually impressive than real, however, as they were generally undermanned as fighting ships and were cluttered with passengers, baggage, and merchandise. Nonetheless, on at least one occasion a group of fifteen East Indiamen warded off the attack of four French warships by forming line ahead and running out their guns in an aggressive manner.[22]

The Honourable East India Company had a great influence on English shipping in general. Prior to the establishment of the company, English vessels had been built largely for the cross-channel and coasting trades or for fishing. The Portuguese, Spanish, Venetians, Genoese, and Dutch were the early builders of ocean-going vessels. In 1607, the Honourable East India Company began maintaining its own shipyards and building its own ships. About thirty ships were required each year, as after four or five voyages, they were considered to be "worn out." By 1621, the company was employing 500 shipyard workmen directly and had produced more than 10,000 tons of shipping. Two hundred years later, the company was valued at more than 21 million pounds. In the nineteenth century, the Honourable East India Company served as the administrative arm of British government for all of India.[23]

During much of the eighteenth century, English sea power was the superior of any two European nations. Fortified by worldwide territorial possessions and large colonial populations of loyal Englishmen in Australia, South Africa, India, and in North America, England found the support in terms of bases, supplies, and manpower that was needed to maintain a world trading empire. As the nineteenth century began, the English became the unchallenged global rulers of the seas, fearing no combination of the navies of Europe.

The French did not take to the sea with the eagerness of other European nations. Mahan suggests that a principal reason for **France** this attitude was "the physical conditions which have made France a pleasant land, with a delightful climate, producing within itself more than its people needed."[24] Yet with all of her natural advantages, French maritime power wasted away "because of the want of that lively intercourse between different parts of her own body . . . known as commerce." France, cut off from the world by the navies of England and Holland and girdled by enemies on the Continent, was the victim of an economic starvation from which only a dedication to effective control of the sea could have saved her. Such isolation "ate away the life of the nation, because it drew wholly upon itself and not upon the outside world, with which it could have kept contact by the sea." The subordination of sea power in this manner must be considered when analyzing French conduct on the world stage throughout the age of sail.[25]

Besides the disadvantage of being on a lee shore in the Atlantic, the French had no ports on the Channel for large warships east of Brest. However, the coastline between Dunkirk and Calais—to all outward appearances defenseless against attack—was in reality amply protected by lines of mostly submerged banks and shoals extending many miles out to sea.[26] France also had excellent harbors for trade in the Channel, in the Bay of Biscay on the Atlantic, and in the Mediterranean. Many of these were at the mouths of great rivers, which allowed trade goods and other merchandise to flow freely within the nation.

Brest was the best of the Channel ports (although it actually resides between the Channel and the Bay of Biscay). In the bay was the naval base of Rochefort. The city of Nantes stood at the limit of deep sea navigation on the River Loire, and Bordeaux was well inland along the shoal-filled Gironde, which was navigable to trading vessels only on the

high tide. Toulon and Marseilles were the only major ports that lined
the French Mediterranean coast, and only Toulon was a naval base. The
effectiveness of Toulon was largely negated by the English naval base of
Port Mahan on the island of Minorca.

The Fisheries   From Newfoundland to southern New England there was
a shallow area of the ocean called the banks. The south-
ernmost, opposite Massachusetts, were called the Georges
Banks. Those off the coast of Labrador and Newfoundland were called
the Grand Banks. These huge shoals on the edge of North America had
attracted fishermen for centuries because they were the waters from
which fishermen could catch cod. This singular cold water fish could be
found in no greater density than on the North American banks. The
countries of Europe and North America had been sending fishermen to
the banks since before the discovery of America. Vikings, Basques,
Frenchmen, Englishmen, and Americans had all fished the banks, and
the right to do so has been incorporated into many international treaties.[27]

The Atlantic cod is the largest species among five related fish: cod,
haddock, pollock, whiting, and hake. Cod has the whitest meat of the
five types. It has virtually no fat and is more than 18 percent protein.
Air dried, sun dried, smoked, or salted, the meat represented 80 percent
concentrated protein, and there was little waste in processing. In an age
before refrigeration, cod was the fish of choice for salting. It not only
lasted longer than other salted fish (such as the herring), but it tasted
better and presented a fine flaky texture, which could be restored
through soaking. To the Spanish, Italians, and Portuguese, fresh cod was
such a rarity that there was no word for it in those languages. But salt
cod was known as bacalao, baccala, and bacalhou, respectively, and for
many generations, it was a staple foodstuff of Mediterranean nations.[28]

From the seventeenth century, the common way to fish for cod was
to go to the banks in a ship and then drop off a number of dories, twenty-
foot deckless boats with two-man crews. The Portuguese were known
for working one-man boats. These could be propelled by a single sail
but were most often rowed. The fishing was usually done with a hand
line. Europeans crossed the ocean in large barks built with deck space
and large holds. New Englanders and Canadians went out in schooners
that could race back and forth to the shore with the catch.

The fishermen of Gloucester, Massachusetts, developed a unique type
of schooner that was fast and seaworthy. These schooners quickly became characteristic of the fishing fleets on the banks. They were also used
to make fast runs to the French islands of the West Indies where the
cod-molasses and cod-Madiera (wine) trades grew steadily until the
American Revolution. The salted cod was used to feed the plantation

slaves. Cod fishermen also used vessels called "smacks" with a wet-well to keep the fish fresh.[29]

Americans were the unchallenged masters of whaling throughout the world in the eighteenth and nineteenth cen- **Whaling** turies. Yet it is generally accepted that the first commercial enterprise in whaling history was accomplished by the Basques of France and Spain in the thirteenth century. The Basques took advantage of the abundance of Black Right whales in the Bay of Biscay. So numerous was this species and so close to the shore did it appear that hunters were able to put out from the open beaches in small boats to pursue them. This method was still being used as late as the sixteenth century.

Lookouts, established on high cliffs or other vantage points, would signal the appearance of the whales to the waiting hunters, who would launch their boats and follow the lookouts' signals to the pod (a group of whales). The whale would be struck with a harpoon attached by a line to drogues, huge pieces of wood two feet square. With the harpoon firmly embedded in its flesh, the animal was forced to expend its energy pulling the drogue through the water. The whalers followed, either under oar power or sail, until they could kill the exhausted animal with lances. They then towed the carcass back to the beach for processing (flensing). Heavier whaleboats, better harpoons with a metal head that secured it in the flesh, and more serviceable line led to the development of "fastening on" to the harpoon line and having the whale pull the boat.[30] The practice was dangerous, but it enabled the hunters to keep in closer touch with the whale and make an earlier kill.[31]

The advantage of a shore station was that while some of the men hunted others did the chopping and cutting of the flesh and operated the cookeries. However, as the whales, either through overkilling or other causes, became less plentiful near the shore, rowing out and towing back became impractical. The Basques adapted the caravel, a proven windship, for whaling away from the coast. If the voyage home was such that the blubber would arrive in reasonable condition, they flensed the whale along side the ship and stored the blubber in casks. If the distance was too great, they processed the blubber into oil at sea. The dual methods of processing whales both on land and at sea remained characteristic of the industry for centuries.

The invention of the method for processing whales at sea is generally attributed to a Basque captain, Francois Sopite, who erected a try-works on the deck of his ship. The try-works enabled blubber to be heated in a container placed over a fire on board. The oil was ladled out of the pot, and the remnants of fat were fed to the fire as fuel. The plume of black smoke from the fires could be seen from over the horizon. In later years, whaleships tied up to iceflows on which the flensing was done as both drifted through the whaling grounds on the currents. These processes, with minute refinements in the equipment, remained the predominant methods by which whalers brought home their catch into the twentieth century.[32]

The Basques were the only Europeans hunting whales on extended sea voyages until the sixteenth century. They were on the Grand Banks in the fourteenth century, as well as in the waters surrounding Iceland. They marketed the oil as a fuel for lighting; salted the flukes and meat as food; and crushed the bone and other residue to use as fertilizer. Although the early explorers of the Northeast and Northwest passages noted whales in Arctic waters, the first deployment of non-Basque European whaleships was not recorded before the end of the sixteenth century.

In 1611, the Muscovy Company, a chartered company searching for a passage to India through the North Sea, recruited six Basques to lead a whaling expedition of two ships. The unsuccessful enterprise was lead by Thomas Edge, but it was the earliest recorded English whaling venture. In the next year, two more vessels ventured forth and returned with 180 tons of oil. The company immediately asked for, and was granted, a monopoly on whaling by royal charter. When King James I granted a charter that included whaling rights to the Scottish East India Company, a dispute arose between the two companies that was finally settled by compromise.[33]

Nonetheless, a number of Dutch merchants, seeing the advantages of the trade, formed the Noordsche Company in 1614 as a competitor. They developed small-scale whaling into a large-scale industry by providing financial support and protection for their fleets of whaling ships. In 1614, a flotilla of fourteen whalers put to sea under the watchful protection of four men-of-war, each mounting 13 guns. In the same year, the Muscoy Company sent out thirteen ships and two armed pinnaces. The two fleets had an uncomfortable meeting in the North Sea whaling grounds, but good sense and a desire for profit prevailed. The two nations agreed on a permanent truce that divided the best regions for the hunt between them. The Dutch, with a bigger European market for their oil, ultimately dominated the industry in Europe and severely restricted English profits. The French appeared in the whaling grounds intermittently, but they were continually challenged by the Dutch claims of exclusive rights.

The Anglo-Americans were not to be so easily dismissed. Beginning by setting out from the shores of Southhampton, Long Island, English colonists in North America began a small whaling industry as early as 1645. Whales were being hunted in small boats by the people of Martha's Vineyard in 1652 and from the coast of Cape Cod in 1670.

The residents of Nantucket initially ignored commercial whaling, processing only those whales that came into shallow waters or grounded themselves on the shore as had the native Americans for centuries. In

1690, however, the Nantucket community, composed of hard working Quakers, made a concerted effort to develop a whaling industry. This has been described as "a successful enterprise unique in the annals of whaling."[34]

Once the whaling industry was established, it affected the lives of all the people on Nantucket. Young men were eager to serve on the whalers, and if unable or too old to go to sea, they turned their efforts to associated trades such as shipbuilding, sailmaking, or coopering. To make the voyages even more profitable, larger ships were constructed. The glow of success was brief, however, for sperm whales were becoming harder to find, and voyages were taking the whalers to the Arctic to hunt the right and humpback whales. Nantucket's harbor was blocked by a sand bar that prevented the larger ships with deeper drafts from entering. By 1869, the sand bar quickly proved an insurmountable obstacle.

By the end of the seventeenth century, a growing whaling industry had spread all along the New England coast. In 1755, the town of New Bedford began a whaling industry that was to make it the leading whaling community in North America. Its greatest days were from 1825 to 1860. Ships crowded the harbor. The wharves were lined with casks of whale oil covered with seaweed for protection from the hot weather. Whale-oil gaugers trod across the oil soaked ground to test the quality and quantity of the oil. On the cobblestone streets leading down to the waterfront, brick buildings were constructed to house the merchant offices and counting rooms. Banks, insurance underwriters, and law offices established themselves in the heart of the business district. Warehouses, oil refineries, and shops were built. Bakeries specializing in producing dry ship's bread sprung up. The traditional marine support crafts were in evidence as well, and all were kept very busy. New Bedford's greatest year was 1857 with 10,000 men making their living in the whaling industry.

As the New England industry expanded, Anglo-Americans found that they were producing oil and whale by-products beyond their own needs. But they found a ready market in England where the whaling industry had come to a standstill. Nonetheless, colonial whalers were encouraged by the British government, which passed major bounty acts in 1733 and 1749 for the building of whaleships of more than 200 tons. New England whalers began to range beyond the traditional whale fisheries, preferring the warmer and less risky waters of the South Seas inhabited by the sperm whale. "Up to the outbreak of the American War of Independence in 1775, the story of whaling in the colonies [was] one of expansion and seizure of opportunity." In 1774, the American whaling fleet numbered more than 360 vessels and employed almost 5,000 men. Although the industry was victimized by the war, the spirit of American whalemen

A wide variety of vessels were used every day by those who worked at sea. This scene of the Dutch coast in the middle of the nineteenth century is from an antique delft tile. (Author's collection)

survived into the nineteenth century to make them unrivaled around the world.[35]

However, the American Civil War (1861–1865) took its toll on the whaling industry. The Confederate cruisers *Alabama* and *Shenandoah* sank many whalers, and the federal government purchased forty whaling vessels, known as the Stone Fleet, to be sunk in southern coastal waters in 1861 to help blockade Confederate ports. Notwithstanding these losses, the remaining days of whaling were inevitably marked. In 1850, petroleum was discovered in Pennsylvania. As kerosene became available, whale oil was no longer needed for lamps. With a new era dawning, investments that formerly would have gone into the whaling industry were now put into industries having higher prospects of rapid growth and quick returns such as railroads, fabric mills, and oil wells.

NOTES

1. Allan Westcott, ed., *Mahan on Naval Warfare: Selected from the Writings of Rear Admiral Alfred Thayer Mahan* (Boston: Little, Brown & Co., 1919), 16.

2. The same argument can be made for the Caribbean with its many island posts or the East Indies.

3. George Masselman, *The Cradle of Colonialism* (New Haven, CT: Yale University Press, 1963), 10.

4. With Portugal under the rule of Spain from 1580, it was at Lisbon that Philip II gathered the Spanish Armada in 1588.

5. G. J. Marcus, *The Formative Centuries: A Naval History of England* (Boston: Little, Brown & Co., 1961), 86; Alfred Thayer Mahan, *The Influence of Sea Power upon History, 1660–1783* (1890; reprint, New York: Dover, 1987), 50–53.

6. Westcott, 26.

7. Pablo E. Pérez-Mallaína, *Spain's Men of the Sea: Daily Life on the Indies Fleets in the Sixteenth Century*, trans. Carla Rahn Phillips (Baltimore, MD: Johns Hopkins University Press, 1998), 8–9.

8. Pérez-Mallaína, vii.

9. Mahan, 50–53.

10. Ibid., 201–202.

11. William O. Stevens and Allan Westcott, *The History of Sea Power* (New York: Doubleday, Doran, 1943), 88.

12. Westcott, 21.

13. Ibid., 32.

14. Masselman, 7.

15. Ibid., 13.

16. Mahan, 97.

17. Westcott, 21–24.

18. Ibid., 23.

19. Ibid., 37.

20. Ibid., 24.

21. Brian Gardner, *The East India Company: A History* (New York: Dorset Press, 1971), 188.

22. Ibid., 96–97.

23. Ibid., 29, 203.

24. Mahan, 36.

25. Ibid., 198–199.

26. Marcus, 102–103.

27. Mark Kurlansky, *Cod: A Biography of the Fish that Changed the World* (New York: Penguin Books, 1997), 44.

28. Ibid., 37.

29. Ibid., 95.

30. An African-American blacksmith, Lewis Temple, invented a harpoon head, which, once inside the whale, turned at right angles to the shaft so that it would hold fast. This was known as the Temple Toggle Iron, and it was used by virtually every whaler.

31. Bill Spence, *Harpooned: The Story of Whaling* (New York: Crescent Books, 1980), 35. American whalers became so adept at this form of whaling that the phrase "Nantucket sleigh ride" was coined to describe it.

32. Ibid., 16.

33. Ibid., 27.

34. Ibid., 35–37.

35. Ibid., 44, 53.

3

Navigation

Now we saw nothing but sky and water and realized the omnipotence of God, into which we commended ourselves.
—A French naval officer, 1780

Most professional navigators utilized plain sailing methods. Although they learned the mathematics of their trade in the formal atmosphere of a class, a good deal of their practical training was accomplished at sea under the watchful eye of a master instructor. The original "plane" sailing considered a body of water as a flat geometric plane. Plain sailing (note the change in spelling) was a simplified method of determining a course by assuming that the earth was a flat surface crisscrossed with imaginary lines of longitude and latitude like a checker board.

Of course, even the crudest of sailors understood that the earth was not "flat." A flat earth was simply more convenient as an intellectual model than a curved one. The methods of plain sailing were remarkably accurate for short distances in the tropical and temperate zones of the earth, but they were much less precise as vessels approached the polar extremes of navigation. Here the lines of longitude took on a pronounced curve, and the absolute distances between the lines of longitude in terms of miles decreased radically.

NAVIGATORS AND PILOTS

English navigators rose to prominence in the Elizabethan era largely due to the development of advanced mathematics. The result of the labors of mathematicians such as Thomas Hariot, Edward Wright, and Robert Recorde changed navigation from an art acquired by experience to a mathematical science. Hariot served as a navigational advisor to Sir Walter Raleigh for his expeditions to Virginia. Wright lectured widely on the mathematics of navigation and the use of maps and charts, and Recorde's treatise, *The Whetstone of Witte*, was proclaimed "invaluable" to the development of scientific navigation. "It brought mathematics out of the scholar's closet into the merchant's counting-house and into the sea captain's cabin."[1]

In America, prior to the War of Independence, maritime activity reached its height in New England. The colonies produced a host of shipwrights, ropemakers, sailmakers, master ship designers, and other skilled marine artisans who built up an extensive maritime industry centered in Massachusetts, principally in Newburyport, Gloucester, Salem, and Boston. "The tough Yankee stock bred some of the very finest seamen and shrewdest merchants of their day," and New Englanders were considered "beyond comparison the most skillful, experienced, and enterprising whalers afloat." In the northern colonies, "successive generations of hardy, adventurous youngsters" studied, acquired skills and experience, and qualified to became masters and master's mates. Although practical skills were acquired only by experience at sea, formal navigation schools arose and prospered in almost every port of consequence on the New England coast.[2]

Nonetheless, well into the eighteenth century, it was rare to find a good navigator capable of moving with confidence across the open ocean. Precise navigation required the knowledge of several specific variables that could interact in various ways. Among these were position, speed, direction, and time. Simple instruments for measuring each of these were developed over the centuries, but few of them were accurate and dependable in all circumstances. Truly accomplished navigators were able to apply complicated methods of correction to the determinations of time, place, direction, and speed made with these instruments. Moreover, in so doing, they mastered many difficult concepts found in modern algebra, geometry, trigonometry, geography, astronomy, meteorology, vector analysis, and physics. In the absence of accurate maps and charts, precise instruments for determining speed and position, and accurate clocks capable of keeping time at sea, it is a wonder that seamen were able to navigate at all. In fact, one of every seven ships that left port before the modern era were never heard from again. That most ships arrived at their destination is a credit to the skill and imagination of seamen and navigators throughout history.

The first determination that a navigator needs to make most accurately is that of present position. Initially this seems to be **Position** quite a simple task, but it proved one of the most daunting difficulties to overcome. Position can be either absolute or relative. When standing on the corner of two cross streets most people know their absolute position in the city and can move around with relative ease by using a city street map. Not until the development of precision instruments for determining both the longitude and the latitude, the geographic crossroads of the earth, could seamen find out exactly where their ships were on the earth's oceans.

Relative position, a position compared to some fixed or known point, is useful if the direction and distance to some landmark or landfall is known even if the absolute position remains unknown. Mariners were able to determine their relative position at sea by using the four major directions of the magnetic compass compared with north, or the position of Polaris (the North Star). Sailing by celestial observation was the underlying principle by which all ocean navigation was done down to the nineteenth century.[3]

A series of well-known landmarks acted as absolute starting points and signposts along the way. Among these were the island groups in the Atlantic. Early explorers knew that if they sailed due east from the Canary Islands they ultimately reached the west coast of Africa. If they sailed due west, they came to the Bahamas in America. Sail due north from the Azores to reach Iceland and due south for the Cape Verde Islands. Follow the coastline of Africa to the Cape of Good Hope. Strike to the northeast from the cape and eventually a landfall can be made near the large island of Madagascar. Proceed through the channel formed by Madagascar and present-day Mozambique and reach the Arabian peninsula or India. This method of navigating the oceans came to be known as dead reckoning. The term derives from the habit of recording a "deduced" estimation of position as "de'd." in the logbook. Dead reckoning remained the most commonly used form of navigation into the twentieth century.

Navigation seems relatively easy when referring to a world map in an atlas or almanac. From any point on the **Displacement** map, a course (direction) and distance to any other point can be plotted. Nonetheless, when actually navigating a ship, the master needed to know not only where he was at the beginning of the trip (and where he was going), but also where he was at the end of each day's journey. This determination was not as easily reckoned as one would assume. Tides, currents, and the sailing qualities of the vessel were among several factors other than the direction of the wind that conspired to make the determination of the distance and the direction traveled by a vessel very difficult even for a single day.

One of the factors that made the determination of a seaman's present position difficult was the lack of a fixed reference point. A sailor moored in the harbor at Portsmouth, England, knew his absolute position. But once out of sight of land, he "saw nothing but sky and water and realized the omnipotence of God." Mariners might sail for days, weeks, or months without sighting land and needed to approximate position based on the estimated speed and direction of a vessel over long periods of time without the aid of accurate correction. These calculations were frustrated by changeable and erratic winds, unknown and complex currents, and the inconsistent performance of the vessel under a wide variety of weather conditions.[4]

An experienced sailor, who was familiar with his vessel and his route, might nonetheless make a quite accurate landfall. On an ocean voyage of several months, he might expect to sight a familiar landmark no more than ten miles from his intended destination—the approximate distance that can be seen from the masthead on a clear day. Such navigation was considered excellent and underlines the importance to sailors of prominent or unusual geographical features such as mountains, headlands, and cliffs. Manmade structures such as lighthouses and church steeples visible from the sea were also important. The destruction of steeples and conspicuous trees used as landmarks by mariners was prohibited under English law.

The speed of a vessel through the water was difficult to measure, but sailors developed several methods for approximating it. A simple expedient was to drop a piece of wood in the water from the bow of the vessel and watch it speed toward the stern. In reality, the wood remained almost motionless in the water while the vessel surged forward. The time for the wood to travel the length of the ship was a good indication of the ship's speed in the opposite direction. By the fifteenth century, mariners had attached a rope to a triangular board weighted with lead that was dropped from the stern of the moving vessel. Although triangular, this was still called a *log*. The rope was drawn from its storage reel by the resistance of the water on the log as the ship sped forward. Small knots were tied in the rope at definite intervals. A 30-second sand glass, much like the half-hour glass used to keep the watches, was used to determine the time. The number of knots pulled from the reel in the time that the sand took to fall was a reasonable estimate of the speed of the vessel. A vessel that pulled six knots from the reel was doing six nautical miles per hour.

The log was thrown out every half hour, and the number of knots was recorded. Since most sailors could not read or write, they recorded the speed by placing a peg in the hole corresponding to the speed on a traverse board. The traverse board had eight holes for speed each representing one of the eight half-hours that made up a watch (each watch being four hours long). The traverse board also had holes made up into concentric circles for recording the course according to the compass. The angle that the log-line made with the rear of the ship was also a good indication of how much the wind was pushing the ship off its course. This was called leeway—or motion of the ship away from the wind. Leeway could cause considerable error in measuring a ship's forward speed, and the amount of leeway was a unique sailing characteristic of each vessel that had to be taken into account by the navigator. A ship with little leeway was said to be weatherly.

At the end of a watch, the navigator could refer to the traverse board to make his calculations of the distance and course traveled. On a chart, he would plot the vessel's displacement from where it had sailed to where it now resided with a set of dividers. He would then calculate a new magnetic compass course or azimuth (from the Arabic *as-samut*, meaning "path") for the next watch—always hoping that the compass was true and that the speed had been measured correctly. At noon each day, and at midnight if the weather were clear, the navigator would attempt to "fix" his position by taking sightings of the sun or polar star respectively. These methods of calculation, the line and log, the 30-second glass, and the traverse board were in use during the Age of Discovery and remained in use into the late nineteenth and early twentieth centuries.

LATITUDE AND LONGITUDE

The position on the earth north or south of the equator is called latitude while the position around the globe east or west is called longitude. Both latitude and longitude are used today, and they seem to us an inseparable pair. With modern satellite global positioning systems, it is possible to locate the position of any point on the globe in terms of latitude and longitude to within a few meters.

Latitude is a more ancient practical tool for navigation than longitude. Although the precise measurement of latitude is only two centuries old, there is ample archeological evidence that for more than two thousand years, ancient mariners maintained their position north or south of the equator by using the shadow cast by a perpendicular rod, called a gnomon, held in the sun. A similar method was used by Eratosthenes to precisely measure the circumference of the earth in the second century B.C. A rod, set in the ground vertically, casts a shadow whose length varies with the time of day, forming a unique arc at different latitudes. The arc created by the end of the shadow could be scratched out over the period of a day. Scientists and thinkers quickly understood that this curve would be the same at any given latitude anywhere around the globe. The daily variations of the shadow hid a long-term consistency that varied only with the distance from the equator.

Mariners may have used a gnomon attached to a wooden disk set afloat in a bowl of water to maintain their latitude. There is evidence that Norse sailors used the sun in this manner as they sailed from east to west and back again. Odd shaped wooden devices, much like a toy top, have been unearthed from Norse graves and home sites in Europe. Each exhibits a telltale scratched or painted curve similar to that described. With such a device, mariners may have maintained their approximate distance above the bulge of the earth during the day by sailing in a direction that kept the length of shadow on the line scratched out on the disk beforehand. Of course, several cloudy days could put a vessel many miles off course, and some other method was needed to sail at night. Nonetheless, modern sailors have reproduced such instruments and have sailed east to west and back across vast distances maintaining their latitude with remarkable accuracy.

For convenience, the equator of the earth is designated as being at zero degrees latitude. Theoretically, the lines of latitude, measured in degrees, encircle the earth both to the north and the south of the equator, and each line is parallel to the next. For this reason, lines of latitude are called parallels, and the distance north or south of the equator is designated by a number of degree between 0 and 90 degrees north or south—90 degrees being at the poles. Latitude can be determined with simple instruments by taking the angle made by the sun with the horizon at noon and subtracting it from 90. On the equator at noon, this angle would measure 90 degrees, with the sun being directly overhead, hence the latitude is 0 degrees. At the north or south pole, this angle would measure 0 degrees with the sun sitting on the horizon, hence a position at the poles would be 90 degrees north or south latitude, respectively.

Once the latitude was found, the position along the parallel could then be determined by finding the line that crossed it, called longitude. Lines of longitude emanate from and converge at the poles. They are uniformly spaced about the globe like sections of an orange into 360 degrees. The longitude lines are called meridians. The prime meridian (0 degrees) was determined by common consent in 1880 to be that which passes through the Royal Observatory at Greenwich, England.[5] The 180-degree meridian is in the Pacific Ocean. All positions around the globe are, therefore, between 0 and 180 degrees either to the east or west of Greenwich. The spacing in terms of miles between meridians varies greatly with latitude. At the equator one degree of longitude represents a distance of approximately 67 statute miles. At the poles, there is no distance between meridians because all the meridians come together at a point. For this reason the distance between meridians proved impractical for determining position accurately.

THE NAVIGATOR'S TOOLS

Although the precise determination of longitude eluded mariners and inventors for centuries, a number of instruments were devised for measuring latitude, including the gnomon, the cross-staff, the backstaff, the quadrant, the astrolabe, and, ultimately, the sextant. Each of these allowed the mariner to determine the angle between the sun at noon and the horizon. Some could be used to find the "height" of the polar star in a similar manner. Each varied in its precision, and improvements among them were in the areas of scale and convenience. For instance, the cross-staff, a graduated rule with a sliding cross-piece, required that the navigator peer directly into the sun and hold the lower arm of the instrument on the horizon, an activity both hard on the eyes and difficult to perform on the rolling deck of a ship at sea. The backstaff, an improved version, cast a pinhole image of the sun onto the instrument allowing the mariner to turn his back on the sun and relieve his eyes of the glare. With the astrolabe, the navigator lined up the sun or the Pole Star through two holes made in plates attached to a graduated circle, which was free to rotate. The sextant mechanically brought the image of the sun and that of the horizon together in the navigator's view and provided shaded and darkened lenses to protect his eyes. Regardless of the instrument used to determine latitude, corrections for the time of year and the hemisphere were made by consulting a set of declination tables.

Finding longitude accurately presented the mariner with a great problem. Ultimately, it was determined that a knowledge of *when* you were, rather than *where* you were with respect to the prime meridian, was more useful than an absolute distance to the east or west. As early as the fifteenth century, the astronomer Regiomontanus had noted, "Since the world rotates by 360 degrees every 24 hours, in other words 15 degrees per hour, the number of degrees traveled can be calculated by multiplying fifteen by the difference between local time and the time of the place from where the ship set out."[6] While the distance between meridians change, the time on each meridian is the same as a vessel sails from the south to the north—even from pole to pole. This time can be determined from the apparent motion of the stars, from the motion of the moon and sun across the sky, or by consulting a precise and accurate clock set to Greenwich time. The difference in observed and Greenwich time can provide an accurate longitude with one hour equal to 15 degrees.

The German astronomer Tobias Meyer of Gottingen was the first to publish tables of lunar movements in 1755. These required some use of

Simple navigational instruments included (left to right): the backstaff, astrolabe, and cross-staff.

advanced mathematics but no special instruments. In less than a decade, the necessary mathematics was being taught in schools that prepared young boys for the naval and merchant services.[7]

Longitude has been precisely measured on land since the invention of the pendulum clock, but its determination at sea was difficult to accomplish. Changing temperature and humidity combined with the rolling of the vessel made otherwise accurate pendulum clocks all but useless. In 1530, the Flemish astronomer Gemma Frisius first pointed out the possibility of determining longitude at sea, but the initial attempts to do so were so fraught with apparently insurmountable mechanical difficulties that completion of the proposition seemed doomed. In the 1660s, the famed scientist Christian Huygens constructed several marine timekeepers controlled by pendulums and subjected them to actual sea trials. He and all other inventors were equally unsuccessful. Although built with exquisite care and accuracy on land, each clock proved dramatically unreliable at sea, gaining or losing many seconds each day with no uniform variation.

In 1714, the British government, through the Board of Trade, offered a reward of 20,000 pounds for the invention of any means of determining a ship's longitude within 30 nautical miles at the end of a six-week voyage. To accomplish this, a timepiece would have to be accurate to within 3 seconds per day, a precision that had not been attained on land at the time.

In 1729, John Harrison invented a timekeeping mecha- **The Harrison** nism that could fulfill this requirement. Nonetheless, al- **Chronometer** though his timepiece was precise, it was also complicated, delicate, ponderous, and costly. Over the next three de- cades, Harrison improved his mechanism four times, ultimately devising a sea-going timekeeper capable of meeting the testing condition set out in the government's challenge. Strangely, the No. 4 Timekeeper (or chro- nometer) bore little resemblance to Harrison's first successful but bulky attempt. By 1785, several marine timepieces were being produced, which in appearance and performance were hardly distinguishable from mod- ern marine chronometers.

The chronometer was essentially a well-made watch, suspended in a box by a set of two bearings connected to a ring at right angles. These are called gimbals, and they allowed the mechanism to remain horizontal whatever the inclination of the ship. It was therefore isolated from all but the most violent alterations in the position of the vessel. This was not a new idea. Gimballed compasses first appeared in the sixteenth century. The differences in the chronometer from those in an ordinary watch were mechanisms providing for a balanced helical spring and a spring-driven escapement. This mechanism required no oiling (an im- portant feature as differences in oil viscosity over a wide range of temperatures was a major factor leading to imprecision), and it tended to restart itself if it stopped. Moreover, a careful use of different metals in the construction allowed for the timepiece to self-compensate for ex- pansion and contraction due to the effects of heat and cold. Chronome- ters exhibiting these features proved to be capable of keeping time for six months with less than one second of error per day. In a month's voyage along the equator, this error would translate to a calculated po- sition within eight nautical miles.

The magnetic compass was a great boon to navigation. To a person familiar with only the basics of the magnetic **The Compass** compass, setting a course in a particular direction seems easy. Point the compass so that North lines up with the magnetic needle (which has itself lined up with the magnetic poles of the planet) and choose your direction from among the points of the compass. Sixteen of these were named including four principal points (north, east, south, and west), the major position between these (such as northeast), and the po- sitions between the lesser point (such as east north east). The angle be- tween the named points of the compass is 22½ degrees. This was then split into 11¼ degree "points" (as in "two points off the port beam"). This is approximately the angle made by the width of the palm of the hand held out at arm's length.

The early history of the ship's compass is obscure, but it is known that it was perfected over many centuries. William Gilbert, a physician to

Elizabeth I of England, is generally credited with the discovery of terrestrial magnetism. Because the earth is a giant magnet, a compass needle, which is also magnetized, will always lie in a north-south line with the earth. Unfortunately, the geographical poles of the earth are not in the same place as the magnetic poles. The North Magnetic Pole is much closer to the Arctic Circle than the North Geographic Pole (presently 1,200 miles closer). A compass pointed at magnetic north may, or may not, point to the geographic north. It all depends on where the compass is on the earth. If it is in the Great Plains of North America, it is more precise than if it is in London because in America the two types of pole happen to fall in the same line of longitude.

The difference between the observed compass reading of north and the actual location of the Geographic North Pole was discovered in the fifteenth century. It is called magnetic declination. Magnetic declination is not constant. It varies with the magnetic field of the earth, the position of the compass, and the position of the magnetic pole, which wanders with time. In 1580, magnetic north was 11 degrees east of the geographic pole. In 1820, it was 20 degrees west, and in 1970, it was 7 degrees west. Declinations have been recorded in London since 1580, and mariners could acquire tables of declinations from the Admiralty.[8]

Maps and Charts   Most charts used in the seventeenth century were produced by private companies. The first recorded English chart was drawn of the Thames River estuary in 1547. This is not surprising as navigational difficulties were more likely to be encountered near the land, in the approaches to and passage of sand bars, and in exiting ports and harbors than in crossing an ocean unencumbered by obstacles.

Besides writing a treatise on the use of the compass in 1581, William Boroughs was one of the earliest English hydrographers (map and chart makers for mariners). In the late sixteenth century, he produced a number of carefully drawn charts of northern European waters. On these the depth of water near the coasts was carefully noted. This data was collected by the use of a sounding-line and lead. The heavy lead weight at the end of this very long line was thrown into the water to measure the depth to the bottom. The line was marked in fathoms (about six feet). In the end of the lead was a hollow filled with sticky beef tallow. Some of the bottom material adhered to the tallow allowing the mariner to make a determination of its nature. Sailors used the sounding-line when making approaches to land or when passing over shallow or unknown waters.

In 1569, Gerard Mercator, a Flemish cosmographer and mathematician, produced a new type of chart known as a projection. Most of the charts produced after 1630 were based on Mercator's Projections in which the meridians and parallels were drawn at right angles. Since these were

A sampling of the many forms of navigational aids including parallel rulers, a small sextant, a gimballed compass, dividers, and a replica of an eighteenth-century chart. James Volo Photo.

curves on the actual globe, the lines on the charts were significantly misplaced at the polar extremes. Yet a bearing from the helm should have cut all the meridians or parallels at a constant angle if a single course was maintained following a Mercator chart.

A line of bearing taken through the stern and bow of a vessel at sea was called a rhumb line. A course that followed the rhumb line was not the shortest distance between two points on the surface of the globe. Rather, the shortest distance was a great circle—a circle whose center was the same as the center of the earth. Although the great circle route was the shortest distance, following it required constant changes in course. Sailing on the rhumb proved much more convenient as courses and bearings could be laid down on a chart using a ruler and a protractor. Though the distances on Mercator charts were distorted (Greenland is not nearly large as it appears), the compass bearing from place to place was correctly represented, and the distances could be measured with some precision as the amount of distortion was known. The advantages of the projections greatly outweighed the disadvantages.[9]

Besides regulating the Royal Navy, the British Admiralty set many of the standards adopted by navigators throughout the world. Among these were the standardization of the length of the log-line used in reckoning distances; the publication of research on the magnetic variation; and the production of more accurate charts and maps. An Admiralty order of 1758 required all sailing masters to make surveys and notes of any uncharted waters that they might visit. These were collected, evaluated, printed, and distributed by the agencies of the Admiralty. Developments like these improved navigation and greatly reduced the loss of shipping due to shipwreck. In 1795, the Navy Hydrological Office was set up to organize the Admiralty's charts and issue certified copies to ships.

In the middle of the nineteenth century, U.S. Navy oceanographer Matthew Maury charted a great deal of information on winds and currents worldwide. To obtain this data, Maury used the observations made by American skippers as they followed the migrating herds of whales from the Arctic to the South Seas. By consulting the logs of the whaling vessels, taking anecdotal evidence, and compiling the results, Maury produced the first truly comprehensive maps of ocean currents and prevailing winds. The U.S. Navy Hydrological Department shared the results with the American whaling industry, and the skippers of the clipper ships who set speed records around Cape Horn by using them.

CIRCUMNAVIGATORS

Ferdinand Magellan, a Portuguese navigator sailing for Spain, set sail with five ships in 1519 seeking a southwest passage to the Orient. In 1520, he entered the passage at the tip of South America that bears his name and came out in the Pacific. Magellan was killed by natives in 1521, but his crew completed the first circumnavigation of the globe. The account of the voyage was written by Antonio Pigafetta, an Italian member of the expedition sailing in *Victoria*, the only vessel to complete the trip.

Sir Francis Drake navigated around the globe as part of a scheme to raid the Spanish treasures of the Americas from 1577 to 1580. Drake weathered Cape Horn in *Pelican* (later renamed *The Golden Hind*) and fell upon the Spanish along the west coast of South America. He then traveled north up the American coast looking for a northwest passage back to Europe. Failing this, he sailed across the Pacific to the Mulaccas, loaded a cargo of spices, and sailed home via the Indian Ocean, the Cape of Good Hope, and Sierra Leone. Drake supplied his ship by stripping the Spanish vessels that he encountered of their provisions.

In 1768, James Cook explored the southern Pacific in *Endeavor*. He sailed to Tahiti and charted the coasts of New Zealand and eastern Australia with extraordinary accuracy. In 1772, he completed a survey of the southern hemisphere penetrating farther south than any other explorer. On his third voyage in 1776, he charted the Pacific coast of North America. He was killed in a skirmish with Pacific islanders in 1779. He is regarded as the father of modern hydrography.

NOTES

1. G. J. Marcus, *The Formative Centuries: A Naval History of England* (Boston: Little, Brown & Co., 1961), 63.

2. Ibid., 404–405.

3. Ibid., 63.

4. Ibid., 64–65.

5. Prior to this agreement, France used Paris as 0 degrees; Spain used Madrid; Holland used Amsterdam; and Portugal used Lisbon. The United States has always followed the English standard.

6. Brigitte Coppin, *The Compass: Steering Towards the New World* (New York: Penguin, 1995), 43.

7. N.A.M. Rodger, *The Wooden World: An Anatomy of the Georgian Navy* (New York: W. W. Norton, 1996), 52.

8. Coppin, 16–17.

9. Nicholas Blake and Richard Lawrence, *The Illustrated Companion to Nelson's Navy* (Mechanicsburg, PA: Stackpole, 2000), 148.

4

Hull Down on the Horizon

What ship is that?

—Commodore Edward Preble[1]

The waterfront of a seaport town, even a small one, was a virtual forest of masts, yards, ropes, and pulleys. A contemporary observer, trained in the nomenclature of the sea or educated by his immersion in the seaport environment, might be able to differentiate among the various types of vessels and rigs with little difficulty. Lacking such an environment, a modern observer might find the identification of the rigging of a single vessel a daunting task. There is considerable consternation among students of maritime and naval history with regard to the incorrect use of nautical terms in reference to sailing vessels. While a comprehensive education in this field is beyond the scope of this work, some consideration must be given to educating the reader in this area. Although the exceptions often outnumber the common elements, nautical terms are often quite discriminating.

NAUTICAL TERMS

Naval and merchant vessels were referred to largely with deference to their employment. Merchant vessels were categorized by their rigging (as in a ship, bark, or sloop), while naval vessels were largely referred to by the number of gundecks and the available armament on board (as in a 100-gun three-decker, a 74-gun third rate, or a 44-gun frigate). These designations can be found in parenthetical form in many reference works and primary source materials (as in *Emilia* [bark], *Victory* [100], or *Alfred* [20 × 9 pdrs.—i.e., 20 cannon firing nine-pound balls]). There is no universally accepted system for recording this information, but the meaning of each is usually clear from the context of the discussion.[2]

The accumulated variations in hull types, arrangements of masts, yards, sail types, and the rope riggings that controlled them determined the identification of the many types of sailing vessels.[3] The vocabulary introduced in this chapter is based on American and British terminology, which is different from that used in other countries and sometimes at variance within itself. Many sailing types defy general classification simply because of their limited use in a specific locality or trade. As Charles Nordhoff, a lifelong mariner writing in 1884, pointed out, the descriptions "will apply, with some slight variations, to all other [vessels], ships of the line, and frigates."[4]

The Hull
The foundation of the vessel, the watertight container that carried the crew and cargo, was the hull. The hull needed to provide a stable platform from which the sails could be set and the vessel controlled. The design was dictated by the use that was intended. The planning of a merchantman's hull provided primarily for buoyancy and cargo space; for a warship protection and the ability to mount and to sustain the stress of large guns; for a smuggler or privateer speed. In any case, the safety of the crew and passengers was of prime importance. Balance and stability were added by stowing stones, bricks, or coal in the lowest portions of the hull to counteract the pressure on the sails and rigging above the waterline.

From early times, hulls were made in clinker fashion with overlapping planks attached to a skeleton of flexible ribs. This style, known in the twentieth century as lapstrake, was favored in the design of the sharp-ended Viking vessels that plied the North Sea, the Mediterranean, and the Atlantic, possibly as far as North America. However, the very flexibility of the clinker-built vessel left it wanting in the strength needed to carry large cargoes or undergo a cannonade.

From the sixteenth century, ocean-going vessels were built with a new type of hull—carvel built—having planks that met flush at their edges and providing a smooth, solid surface above and in the water. The spaces between the planks were filled by driving in a fibrous caulking mixed with tar and coating the entirety with paint. In the last quarter of the eighteenth century, the bottom was commonly sheathed in copper to prevent the build-up of weeds and barnacles as well as the damage done by torpedo worms. Hulls of this period had a semicircular cross section with rather blunt bows and sterns. Ironically, in just a few decades, ship designers would return to the more pointed bows and "V" shaped cross

Plate CXLIX.

Fig. 2. Bilander

Fig. 3. Bomb-Vessel

Fig. 4. Brigantine

Fig. 5. Hoybeat

Fig. 6. Hoy

Fig. 7. Hulk

Fig. 8. Ketch

Fig. 9. Lighter

Fig. 10. Pink

Fig. 11. Boat

Fig. 12. Shallop

Fig. 13. Sloop

Fig. 14. Smack

Fig. 15. Yacht

Fig. 1. The Section of a First Rate Ship of War. Shewing its various Timbers and Apartments

Fore Mast

Main Mast

Mizzen Mast

A nineteenth-century diagram of the interior of a first rate ship of war. Note the different sail arrangements shown at the top.

sections of the early Viking ships in an attempt to design speed and weatherliness (having little leeway) into their vessels.

The carvel-built hull was supported by a framework of stout ribs attached to a heavy beam known as the keel. The wood most preferred for the keel was elm, since it best resisted rotting due to continuous immersion in sea water. If elm was not available, then oak would be used. In any case the ribs and skeleton of a vessel were usually formed from red oak. For many years, white oak from the Baltic was not considered to have sufficient strength, but the American variety of white oak was found to be a superior building material.[5] During the Napoleonic Wars, when the British needed huge numbers of vessels to maintain the blockade of Europe, pitch-pine or fir was used extensively. Fir-built vessels had a shorter life expectancy than those fashioned of oak, but they built faster.[6]

Wood for use in marine construction was chosen for its natural shape in the tree. Straight tree trunks suggested planking and decking; while naturally curved branches and junctions between the branches and the trunk suggested particular components of many designs. Sometimes trees were "trained" from saplings to grow into a particular shape. Foresters would stake and tie the branches of these to form specific parts of vessels that would not be built in their own lifetimes. When they had grown to sufficient size, these trees would be cut down and rough-hewn square. Called "ton timber," it was floated down rivers in huge rafts, the hard woods atop the pine, either to be used directly or exported to other shipyards.[7]

When the timbers for the construction of a vessel arrived at the shipyard, they were stored in open-air sheds for about a year. The "seasoning" of the green wood was an important step in shipbuilding. As wood dries, it tends to warp and twist into a shape dictated by its own natural tendencies. As each piece of timber dries, it applies forces of different magnitudes and in unique directions that are often at odds with the design of the vessel. It was important, therefore, to allow each timber to reach its own natural form before shaping it into a finished component. Timbers were sometimes "roughed out" and stacked in certain positions depending on their proposed use. Others were boiled or steamed to enable the shipwrights to bend them.

The timbers were fastened together by the use of mortise and tenon joints. Tenons were shaped to fit tightly into mortises, which were cut in the timbers. These joints were held fast by oak trunnels, or treenails, which varied from 1 to 2 inches in diameter and up to 3 feet in length. Holes were drilled through each joint with an auger, and the trunnels were driven through to act as large wooden pins. In a well-designed mortise and tenon joint, the trunnels carried very little stress acting only to hold the pieces in place. Similar systems of joinery had been used

The reproduction of the *Mayflower* in Plymouth, Massachusetts, brings an early-seventeenth-century vessel to life. James Volo Photo.

successfully in house and bridge construction for centuries. Nonetheless, as ocean-going vessels were constantly being rocked and twisted by the dynamic action of waves, even in calm or moderate seas, the trunnels quickly loosened or wore. In the worst cases, they rotted or actually fell out. Shipwrights who were experts at marine joinery received a different apprenticeship than simple house joiners and were highly esteemed for their specific skills.

With the keel laid and the ribs and skeleton in place, the vessel was left for another season before the planking was added (unless it was immediately needed). Besides the differences in their relative size, it was at this point that the construction of the generally smaller merchant vessels diverged from that of warships. Merchant vessels, more lightly ribbed than warships, usually had a single layer of planking. A warship—stoutly ribbed to withstand the pounding of an opponent's guns and the weight and stress of its own—had two layers of planking attached to the frame, one on the inside and one on the outside. This often gave the hull a thickness of over a foot. Planking took a long time, and the work was grueling. Treenails made of locust wood for use below the waterline, and of oak for use above, attached the planks. Only at the ends and butts were copper spikes and bolts used. Plankers were the highest paid men in the shipyard, and shipbuilders sometimes hired an entire planker's gang rather than individuals.[8]

The size of the hull was determined by its cargo capacity. The common containers for merchandise aboard ships were barrels and kegs. The generic name for these containers was casks. Wooden casks ranged in a wide variety of sizes, including small 2 to 3 gallon pipes, 40 to 50 gallon barrels, and giant containers called tuns. The capacity of the hold was measured by a formula that approximated the number of these large tun containers, or their equivalent (33 cubic feet each), that could be stowed therein. Small coasting vessels might have a capacity of 60 to 70 tons (note the change in spelling) while warships might range from 300 to 800 tons. Really large vessels were over 1,000 tons.[9]

Decks   The following descriptions of the structures in the hull of a ship are based on the average or common arrangement of decks found on a man-of-war. With the exception of guns, large merchant vessels were similarly arranged. Whereas warships used the deck space to hold fighting men and weapons, merchant vessels used almost all of their deck space for cargo. Although warships held hundreds of men, they were a good deal more comfortable than merchant vessels, where every empty square foot represented a loss of profit.

The decks of a ship may be regarded as so many floors. On the upper, or spar-deck, the space between the bows and the foremast was called the forecastle. The space between the foremast and the mainmast was the *waist*, and that from the mainmast to the stern was the quarter deck. Behind the mizzen mast was the poop deck, a raised deck beneath which was the captain's day cabin. All around the upper deck were bulwarks. Attached to these were square casings called hammock nettings in which the seamen and midshipmen deposited their hammocks.

Most men-of-war did not carry a full tier of guns on the spar deck, the waist (or well) being open to the sky with gangways on each side. The deck below the spar-deck was the main-deck. This and the one below, called the lower-gundeck or berth-deck, had full tiers of gunports and guns. Between and among these guns the men ate and slept. The upper gunports could be left open for ventilation. The lower-gunports were opened only in calm seas and for battle. Next below the lower-gundeck was the orlop-deck, the first without gun ports cut in the hull. The aftermost part of the orlop reached "quite into the bottom of the vessel" and had an enormous space for storing dry provisions. Below the orlop was the hold. Forward and aft in the hold were the powder magazines. The rest of the hold was used to store wet provisions (in barrels), chains and cables, and the shot-locker, which held the cannonballs. In the aftmost part of the hold was the spirits-room, holding the rum and liquor and guarded day and night by a sentry. Set between the beams that supported the tiers of the hold were the water tanks "fit nicely to the shape of the ship throughout" from which the water for daily consumption was pumped.[10]

WARSHIPS

The British developed the best-known system for classifying warships. A "rate" was a classification system for warships (first through sixth), which expressed the number of long guns (cannon) officially carried aboard. Because each gun required a given minimum of space, the number of guns generally reflected the size of the warship. All rated vessels in the Royal Navy, including frigates, were commanded by post-captains. These men had achieved the rank of captain and had been posted on the Admiralty list. All other British warships were unrated and were usually commanded by lieutenants. Most European navies adopted the system of rates or followed something similar to it.

Line-of-battle ships having more than 50 guns were either first, second, or third rates. First and second rates had three gun decks. Third rates had two. First rates carried in excess of 100 guns, second rates 90 to 98, and third rates 80, 74, or 64. The third rate "74" was the most common line-of-battle warship in eighteenth century European navies. These and larger warships were often called men-of-war. It was felt that ships of this size could sail efficiently and could fire a significant weight of metal (cannonballs) in the line of battle.

Fourth rates were 50-gun vessels with either one or two decks. In the late seventeenth and early eighteenth centuries, fourth rates would have been intimidating adversaries, but in the age of fighting sail they were simply under-gunned, too small, and weakly armed to serve in the line. They tended to be posted in northern waters (like the Baltic Sea), on colonial stations, or on convoy duty where they could expected to face ships of equal or inferior fire power. Many fourth rates were razed (cut down) as they grew older to create more weatherly one deckers.

The raised parts of the ship at the front and back respectively were called the forecastle and sterncastle (later quarterdeck). The center section was called the waist. Most large warship had a well-deck in the waist, open to the sky. This gave the vessel the up-down-up profile common in children's book illustrations. Extra spars were stored above the well-deck supporting the ship's boats. First through fourth rates exhibited this characteristic profile.

Most fifth and sixth rates were flush decked with no sterncastle or forecastle. These were usually ship-rigged and designated as frigates. Those with between 32 and 44 guns on their single gundeck were fifth rate, those with 20 to 28 guns were sixth rate. They were quick (up to thirteen knots) and weatherly. Frigates were the most glamorous and exciting ships in the navy, offering many opportunities for independent

The most exciting warships of the eighteenth century were the frigates. Young officers were particularly fond of serving in these fast and agile vessels that were sometimes called "the eyes of the fleet." Illustration from an early-twentieth-century text in the authors' collection.

action, single-ship engagements, and prize money from the capture of enemy merchantmen. Officers of every nation, who wished to advance themselves through acts of heroism and bravado, sought to command or to serve in frigates.

Notwithstanding the glamor, frigates were also used for dispatch services, convoy duty, the suppression of privateers and slavers, inshore service in shallow water, and reconnaissance—the eyes of the fleet. When attached to the battle fleet, they served to repeat the admiral's orders, to take possession of enemy vessels that had surrendered, and to tow crippled men-of-war to safety.

The ideal size and armament for a frigate was never established during the age of sail, and navies throughout Europe experimented with different combinations of numbers and sizes of guns. The French developed the corvette—a small quick frigate with 18 to 24 guns, which would be classified as a small sixth rate. But the Americans seemed to have hit upon a winning combination in the *Constitution*-class frigates made famous in the War of 1812. These flush two-deckers carried between 36 and 44 guns, were very seaworthy, and could outrun anything that they could not outfight.

The largest class of unrated vessels was the sloop-of-war. While a particular class of warship carrying less than twenty guns, any ship regardless of size that was commanded by an officer of less than post-captain rank **Unrated Naval Vessels** was referred to as a sloop. To add to the confusion, the sloop was a distinct merchant type having a single mast and a light hull, while the sloop-of-war was generally ship or brig rigged. The hull type of the British sloop-of-war was designed along the lines of a particularly fast sailing French prize (*Amazon*) taken in 1745.

Before the French Revolution, there were only 23 sloops-of-war on the Royal Navy lists. These had been built in the 1770s and 1780s to serve in the American War of Independence. At least three were on North American station as early as January 1775. Each vessel in this class carried between 14 and 16 light cannon (6 to 9 pounders). These guns were too few and of insufficient weight of metal to take on ships-of-the-line. The timbers of a warship could not be appreciably damaged by anything smaller than a 12 pounder, but 6 to 9 pounders were formidable armament against lightly built privateers and slavers.

When the Royal Navy was pressed for ships during the early days of the French Revolution, and later during the Napoleonic wars, sloops-of-war became essential to the war effort. While a 74 might take two to four years to build, sloops-of-war could be built of oak in as little as five to nine months—in pitch pine or fir in as little as two. In 1806, at the height of ship production, five were built in just three weeks. Moreover, their construction could be let out to private shipyards, leaving the Royal Navy dockyards free to work on larger vessels.

Only about three dozen sloops-of-war were built in the decade before the Peace of Amiens (1802–1803), but in the decade after more than 100 were launched. They soon became an essential and ubiquitous part of the Royal Navy. Sloops-of-war fought in the Baltic against the smaller warships of the Batavian Republic (formerly Holland) and Denmark—both allies of Napoleon. They supported the Duke of Wellington and the British army in the Spanish Peninsular Campaign, delivering supplies, attacking coastal forts and batteries, and getting into the harbors and estuaries to pry out the enemy. They patrolled colonial waters around the globe, and they attempted, with less success, to suppress both American trade and American privateers in the War of 1812.

Among the smaller unrated vessels were gun-boats and row galleys, both capable of independent movement with long sweeps (oars); gun-brigs, which could be sailed; bomb vessels commonly rigged as ketches, which carried mortars with high arching trajectories; and fireships, der-elicts converted to carry fire into the mass of moored enemy shipping in an anchorage. Many of the smaller unrated vessels were commanded by very junior officers (passed midshipmen or ensigns) who were expected to show good seamanship and tactical initiative.

Cutters and schooners were also an important part of the navy. The cutter was a single masted vessel with a light hull and a flush deck. The schooner was based on a two-masted American merchant design of the same name. Both types were usually captured, purchased, or hired by the Royal Navy and re-rigged to meet its particular purposes. They were commonly armed with 6 or 8 very light cannon (4 pounders) and swivel guns. Cutters were used in support of the fleet to deliver dispatches, as coastal cruisers, and as inshore scouting vessels. As vessels for the rev-enue service, they tried to enforce the navigation laws and to suppress smuggling by nosing into the shallow waters of inlets, coves, and iso-lated beaches. Schooners were used in much the same way, but their larger holds might also allow them to act as fleet tenders, carrying extra provisions and supplies for a larger vessel with which they traveled in consort. Both cutters and schooners were used in European waters, but they were conspicuously posted to American colonial waters and to the West Indies. Almost half of the Royal Navy vessels on North American station in 1775 were either cutters or schooners.[11]

BOATS

Many nautical experts arrogantly point out that not all the vessels that plied the seas were ships; but neither were they all boats. A ship was a large vessel with at least three masts and a particular arrangement of rigging and sails. A boat was a smaller craft often defined as of a size capable of being carried upon another vessel even if it never was so carried. One seamen's tale suggests that the proper relationship between boats and their ship was the same as that of fleas and their dog. When not on a dog, a flea is still a flea.

Boats could be either clinker built or caravel built. Although equipped with oars and a rudder, most boats had "V" bottoms or a small keel and could be adapted to a wide arrangement of sails usually set on a single mast. Others were flat-bottomed or round-bottomed and relied on oars or devices such as dagger boards and lee boards to permit sailing off the wind.[12]

Boats were often used to ferry passengers, members of the crew, and supplies back and forth from the shore or between other vessels. They were referred to by many names and came in a variety of sizes. A captain commonly had a gig reserved for his personal use. The gig was any small boat reserved for the use of the commanding officer of a vessel. Captains and masters often reached into their own purses to decorate their gig and smartly uniform its crew in keeping with their financial or social status. Large vessels also carried a compliment of other craft variously described as long-boats, jolly boats, and cutters.

The jolly boat was a small boat (16 feet) usually hoisted and carried at the stern of merchantmen. The term *cutter* also referred to a small boat (18 to 20 feet), and it should not be confused with the much larger sloop of the same name. The long-boat, later called a launch, was the largest boat (20 to 24 feet) on a merchantman usually carried between the fore and main masts. Warships carried their boats on the spars stored over the well-deck but towed them or cast them free when going into battle to prevent damage in the engagement. In this manner, they could be retrieved in victory or resorted to in defeat.

A whaling ship might carry a dozen or more whaleboats from which the actual hunt took place, and fishing vessels carried numerous dories. These were often hung from cranes at the sides of the vessel, or they were stored on deck. Lifeboats were a nineteenth-century innovation made popular by the increase in passenger traffic. Lifeboats were essentially long-boats reserved for a specific purpose. All the working boats on a ship were considered lifeboats in an emergency. In this regard, it was said that the ship belonged to the master, but the boats belonged to the crew.

Many boats were capable of an individual operation apart from a larger craft, and their seaworthiness was often remarkable. They were generally too small to efficiently carry cargo but were sometimes used to explore rivers and inlets, as dispatch vessels and ferries, or to send forces ashore in amphibious landings or "cutting out" expeditions. These included partially decked and open vessels capable of independent ocean travel such as launches and pinnaces.

A pinnace was a boat somewhere in size between the long-boat and the cutter. One of the three vessels to cross the Atlantic with the Jamestown colonists in 1607 was a pinnace, and the Pilgrims in the *Mayflower* brought an open pinnace with them to the New World in 1620. In this vessel, equipped with lee boards for sailing, they explored the coast of New England and mapped Cape Cod, and from it they set foot on Plymouth Rock. Launches were essentially long-boats. Captain William Bligh, in a remarkable feat of seamanship, traveled 3,000 miles in a 23-foot launch overloaded with nineteen men after the crew of *Bounty* mutinied. The 23-foot launch was a standard size in the Royal Navy.[13]

There were a wide variety of utility craft known as bumboats, lighters, and barges that were most often found plying the quiet waters of a harbor or anchorage. Bumboats were small harbor craft used for peddling

A reproduction of the pinnace brought to America by the Pilgrims. Note the leeboards stowed aboard. James Volo Photo.

items to the crews of ships in the harbor. Lighters and barges were generally large ungainly boats. In the sixteenth century, a barge was considered a highly ornamented ceremonial craft with two banks of oars (as in the Admiral's Barge), but the term was later more commonly applied to an ungainly craft used for hauling cargo to and from shore or along inlets and rivers.

Many small fishing craft were flat-bottomed boats. Their variety was limited only by the prejudices of each fishing village or locality. Their names and specific characteristics were legion, and no list would be exhaustive of the many variations. The smallest practical boat was the dinghy. This could be any of several types of small boats characterized by round, rather than flat or "V" shaped, bottoms. Dinghies were usually very light and nimble.

RIG BASICS

There were two basic types of sails: square and fore-and-aft. Square sails may be the older form having been used on Greek and Roman galleys and Viking raiders. They were generally set to make a perpendicular plane with the center line of the ship. These sails (actually trapezoidal in shape) were set and carried on a variety of wooden poles known as spars and were best suited to a following wind. Most of the sails on seventeenth- and eighteenth-century merchant ships and warships were square sails. Although efficient in propelling a large vessel, the square sail was labor intensive, requiring a large number of men to set or to furl.

Fore and aft sails generally required fewer hands. Cat-rigs, gaff-rigs, and lateen-rigs were all forms of fore and aft sails in which the plane of the sail generally ran with the long axis of the vessel, much like the sails of a modern day-sailer. The first fore and aft rigs of three- and four-sided sails were commonly found in Dutch vessels of the sixteenth century, but the less sophisticated lateen sails (a triangular fore and aft sail set on a long yard that crossed the mast at an oblique angle) had been common in the Mediterranean since the medieval times. Fore and aft sails sacrificed some efficiency in a following wind for the ability to sail better "into" or "slightly off" the wind.

The general name for all the timbers used aloft in setting up the rigging and sails was *spar*. It was a generic term used when **Spars** a timber's place or use on the vessel was unspecified. The term included more specific items such as masts, yards, booms, and gaffs. The immense size of even the smallest spars used on sailing vessels can be easily underestimated from their appearance on a vessel seen at a distance. Each spar was a huge piece of wood. The base, or butt, of the main mast, for instance, might have a diameter in inches equal to its overall length in yards. In the eighteenth century, large masts shipped from New England forests in America to English shipyards were 36 inches in diameter and 36 yards long.

The term *mast* was applied to those vertical timbers from which were swiveled horizontal timbers such as yards, booms, **Masts** or gaffs used to support the sails. From the fifteenth century, a ship was considered a three-masted vessel fitted with square sails on all of its masts. The three masts were named (from bow to stern) the fore, the main, and the mizzen. The main mast was a leftover from the great single masts that were centrally located in the hulls of the Viking raiders on the North Sea, Hanseatic cogs of the Baltic, and oar-powered galleys that plied the Mediterranean in medieval times. The fore mast was placed toward the bow of the ship where additional sails could be set to catch the force of the following wind. However, since the fore mast

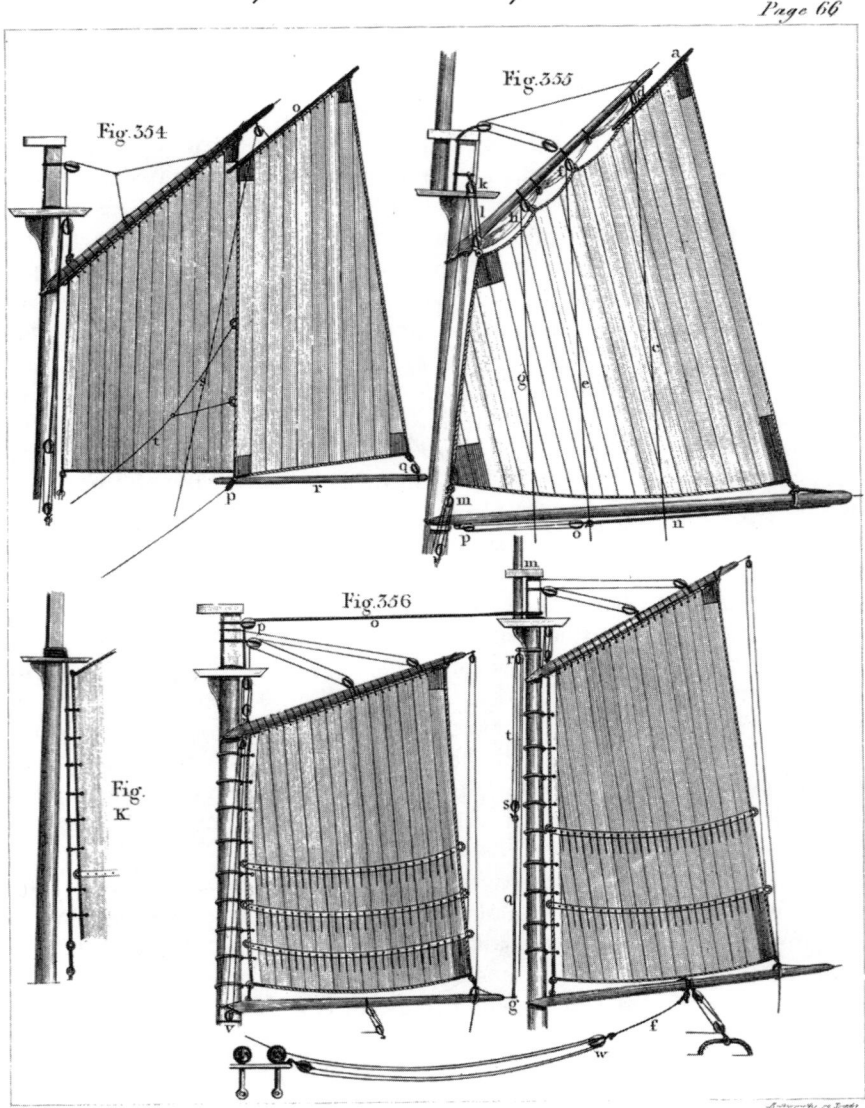

Types of fore and aft sails as illustrated in a nineteenth-century sailor's manual.

allowed the force of the wind to be applied in front of the center of gravity of the ship, it tended to drive the bow of the vessel off the wind when sailing at right angles to it. Therefore, the mizzen mast was added behind the center of gravity to balance the effect of the fore mast. The term *mizzen* derives from an Arabic word, *misan*, which means "balance."

Added to the vertical spars that served as masts was the bowsprit, a nearly horizontal timber protruding from the front of the vessel. The bowsprit was often 3 feet in diameter and 25 yards long on larger vessels. To this was often attached a jib boom, an extension that served as an attachment point for long triangular sails called jibs running forward on lines from the fore mast. In early vessels, a square spritsail was sometimes hung from a yard below the jib boom. In later vessels, a martingale stay was commonly located here, which helped to hold the jib boom down. An additional mast was sometimes set behind the mizzen. This was called the bonadventure.

The earliest square rigged vessels used masts and booms made from a single tree—ironically, so did many of the speedy coasting schooners and sloops of the late nineteenth and twentieth centuries. In the eighteenth century, however, square-rigged trading and naval vessels had grown so large vertically that the main mast—made in sections—might have four or five separate sections with as many sails set from them. The lowest sections of the masts (or lower mast) were the heaviest spars on the vessel, and they were set through the decks to rest firmly on the keelson at the bottom of the hull. Lower masts were sometimes bundled, or pieced together, from smaller diameter wood held together by giant metal bands. These "made masts" provided a solution to the scarcity of large diameter trees from the forests of the Baltic States or North America when supplies were interdicted in times of war.

The lower masts had little taper, but were flatten somewhat at their top to accommodate the attachment of additional vertical timbers. These additional sections eliminated the need for extremely long, single spars of uniform characteristics and high quality, and their smaller size facilitated the replacement of broken or rotting timbers. The first section set above the lower mast was called the topmast; the section above this— the topgallant mast; and so on—each section being named for the sails it supported.

At the junction of the lower mast and the topmast was a platform known as a top. Between the topsail mast and the **The Tops** topgallant mast were a set of cross trees. These structures helped to disperse the strain placed on the rigging and on naval vessels, they were used as fighting platforms for marines and sharpshooters. In the seventeenth century, as on the Pilgrim ship *Mayflower*, the tops were round, looking much like the fictional "crows nest" seen in cartoons. Later vessels had "D" shaped platforms with an opening known as a

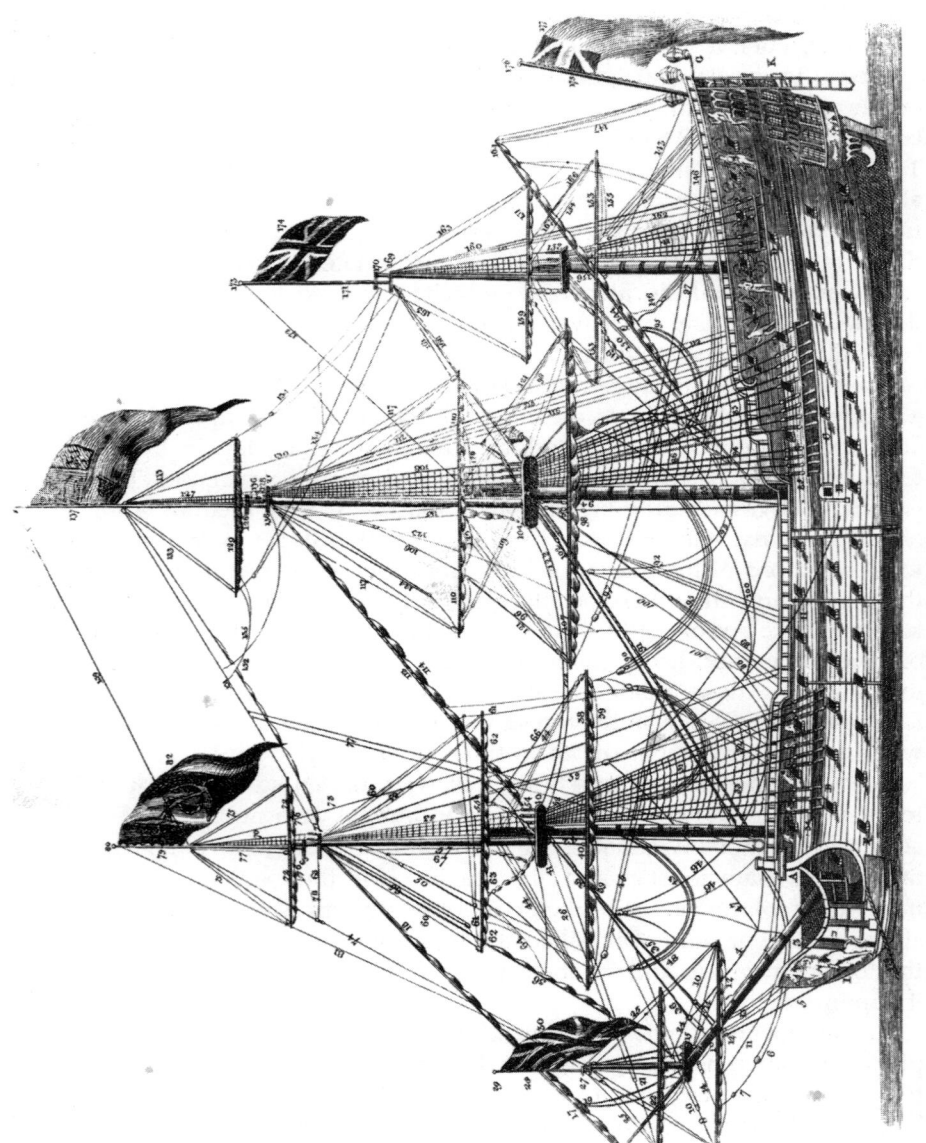

The rigging of a first rater from a nineteenth-century print.

"lubbers' hole" through which sailors could pass to attain the upper rigging. The term *lubber* was meant to be derisive, coming from landsman, or land lubber. A confident able-bodied seaman could climb around the top on the weather side futtock shrouds. This required that he hang almost upside-down from the rope rigging and ratlines as he passed under and around the platform. Even able-bodied seamen used the lubber's hole when doing hard work in the rigging or in foul weather.

Masts were usually raked. In other words, they leaned to some degree from being perpendicular with the deck and wa- **Raking** terline. Sixteenth-century vessels had a pronounced forward lean to the fore mast, while the main mast was upright, and the mizzen mast raked toward the stern. This gave to the vessel a silhouette shape somewhat like that of the hand held upward to the sky with the three longest fingers slightly spread apart. Most vessels of the seventeenth and eighteenth centuries retained this aspect but to a much smaller degree.

On nineteenth-century sailing vessels, all the masts were generally raked toward the stern. The rearward raking of the masts was instituted by designers in an effort to build superior speed into their vessels. Two-masted schooners might have an angle of 85 or even 80 degrees with the deck. Nonetheless, the masts were usually parallel to each other. On three-masted vessels, the masts usually raked to slightly greater angles as they passed from the bow to the stern. The foremast might have an angle with the deck of 88 degrees, the main mast 86 degrees, and the mizzen 83 degrees.

A vessel was considered seaworthy if it could sail "by and large." The term *by the wind* meant that the wind was blowing **Sails** from the front of the vessel. Sailing "large" meant that the wind was from behind the mast. "By and large" meant that the craft could do both and all things in her design were in balance between the extremes. A vessel could be rigged to carry only square sails, but this adversely effected its performance into the wind. No sail can propel a vessel directly into the wind, and square sails did not work as well as other types when sailing across or slightly into the wind. Fore and aft sails (triangular sails) worked fairly well at a small angle to the wind but were less efficient than square sails when it was blowing from behind because of their smaller area. By the eighteenth century, many smaller vessels carried "gaff" rigs. These were four-sided sails supported by the mast on one side, a large boom along the bottom, and a wooden support on top called a gaff. These could be set fore and aft for sailing into the wind and swung out to the side to take better advantage of a following wind than triangular sails.

A skillful combination of square and fore and aft sails became common in the fifteenth century. The main and fore masts were fitted with square sails, and the mizzen mast was fitted with a lateen rig to rectify any shortcomings. With this arrangement, small fifteenth-century merchant ships known as caravels, and naval vessels known as carracks, were able to negotiate the Mediterranean with crews of as few as twenty men. Both types of vessels proved capable of defying heavy ocean swells and were believed to be the only vessels capable of tacking into the winds that blew along the African coasts. Many pre-Columbian vessels carried lateen sails on both the mizzen and main masts when sailing the Atlantic coast of Africa or in the India Ocean. Although the type of rig used by Columbus in 1492 is not absolutely known, it has been suggested that he directed that square sails be set on all the masts for the outbound voyage to take advantage of the constantly following wind. A probably apocryphal story suggests that the lack of lateen rigging drove Columbus' crew to fear that they would be unable to sail back against the wind on the homeward voyage.

Sail Plan   Each section of the mast was named for the yard and sail that were suspended from it. The lower mast carried a lower yard fixed to the mast by trusses that allowed it to be swiveled from side to side. From the lower yard hung a large sail called a course. The topmast carried the topsail yards and the topsails. The topgallant mast similarly carried the topgallant yards and the topgallants. It was possible to name all the sails and yards arranged vertically by beginning at the deck: courses, topsails, topgallants, royals, and (infrequently) moon rakers. By adding the horizontal placement of the mast along the deck to the sail name, a particular piece of the rigging could be specified. The main topgallant sail would be found on the main mast (the center mast on a ship) hanging from a yard on the third section of the mast. Directly below the main topgallant sail would be the main topsail, and below this the main course. Directly in front of the main topgallant sail would be found the fore topgallant sail, while directly behind it would be the mizzen topgallant sail.[14]

VESSEL IDENTIFICATION

The identification of a vessel as a particular type was largely judged by the rigging aloft. A ship (or ship rigged craft) was a vessel with a fore, main, and mizzen mast, all of which were fitted with square sails. Sometimes a fore and aft sail was fitted directly behind the mizzen course to help sailing into the wind. A bark was a three-masted vessel with square sails on the fore and main masts, and fore and aft sails on the mizzen mast. A barkentine was also three-masted with square sails on the fore mast only and fore and aft sails on the main and mizzen masts. Each of these vessels could be of considerable hull size but would have afforded a unique silhouette to the observer. (Since there are today so few sailing vessels to observe, it is by their silhouettes that these different types are most easily learned by modern students.)

Smaller two-masted vessels included the brig (both masts fitted with square sails); the brigantine (fore mast square, main mast fore and aft, with a square main topsail), and the hermaphrodite brig (fore mast square, main mast fore and aft throughout). Vessels equipped with two or more masts rigged with fore and aft sails only were known as schooners, while single-masted vessels similarly rigged were called sloops. (These are not to be confused with a sloop-of-war, a single-decked naval vessel that was usually ship- or brig-rigged.)

The galleon class combined the lines of a large row galley with the strength of a ship, and the firepower of a fortress with the seaworthiness of an ocean-going privateer. The "race built" galleon was actually perfected by the English from the design of a single outstanding vessel—the *Revenge* of 450 tons built about 1575. The *Revenge* was thought to be the perfect galleon. New ships were modeled after it, and some older vessels were rebuilt along its lines. While most closely associated with the Spanish treasure fleets, the galleon was any large ornate ship from the sixteenth through eighteenth centuries that had a high poop deck and after structure, a high forecastle, and a pronounced bow. The galleon type, with minor modifications, dominated ocean traffic for almost 200 years.

English and American colonial records suggest that the bulk of waterborne transportation in the seventeenth and eighteenth centuries was carried by a variety of vessels indiscriminately classified as sloops, shallops, ships, brigs, barks, schooners, and topsail schooners, with little regard to a fixed maritime vocabulary. Naval historian G. J. Marcus, in a remarkable catalog of maritime terminology, noted the following:

The great Channel fairway was the principal trade focal of the world. Here, with a westerly wind, might be seen smart Falmouth *packets* standing in for the Lizard and St. Anthony's Head; heavily sparred *whalers* from the South Seas conspicuous by the "try-work" on their decks; fast fruit *schooners* hurrying home from the Mediterranean for the London Market; tall *East Indiamen*, with sterns sparkling with gilt and great cabin windows flashing in the sunlight, rolling majestically on past the English headlands, nine months out of Hoogli [India]: closer inshore, was a host of small coastal craft—*snows, brigs, brigantines, barquentines, hoys,* and *ketches*—skillfully working the tides, and the fleets of brown-sailed fishing *luggers*. Not a few of these merchantmen to be seen in the offing were foreigners—French *brigs* and Newfoundland *schooners*, Norwegian *cats*, Prussian *snows* and galliots, Dutch *bilanders, busses, hoys,* and *schoots*, and Danish *West Indiamen* . . . for in the days of sail ships hugged the English coast.[15]

These differences in terminology, however, were not taken lightly by the seafaring community at the time. For the modern student of maritime

Ship

Bark

Full-rigged Brig

Hermaphrodite Brig

Top-sail Schooner

Fore & aft Schooner

Sloop

Ocean-going vessels came in many types, distinguished by their sail plan.

and naval affairs, they can prove interesting and relatively simple to understand once learned. However, the entire design, operation, and safety of a vessel of the period depended on the use and understanding of specific unambiguous terms like these. Orders to set or furl the main topsail, for instance, sent sailors to those parts of the ship and rope rigging that were similarly named, such as in the main topsail braces or the main topsail clew lines.[16]

LEARNING THE ROPES

Large sailing vessels were equipped with an amazing quantity of rope divided into an almost bewildering web of shrouds, stays, lifts, sheets, braces, halyards, and lines. There may have been three miles of rope on even a small ship.[17] All rope rigging was divided into two general types: standing rigging and running rigging. Standing rigging supported the masts and yards. As such, its tension was rarely adjusted during a voyage. Since standing rigging did not need to be run through pulleys, it was often wrapped and heavily tarred to preserve it from exposure or wear and tear. Running rigging was passed through blocks and pulleys in order to adjust the position of the sails relative to the wind. It was constantly being handled and was used in its natural condition. Hemp fiber was the most common material used to make rope rigging throughout the period.

The main components of the standing rigging were the stays and shrouds, which supported the masts vertically. Each mast had its own set of stays and shrouds. The stays were strong cables running along the central line of the vessel that helped to hold the masts in place in that direction. Shrouds held each mast laterally and were attached to the sides of the vessel at the channels by the chains. These chains were often literally metal links but sometimes took the form of metal bars and brackets. The shrouds were crossed by smaller ropes called ratlines, which formed the distinctive ropelike ladder up which sailors scrambled to attain the tops.

Both stays and shrouds were tightened by pulling on the lanyards, which wound through wooden blocks descriptively called deadeyes. As rope rigging expanded and contracted with changing amounts of wetness, it was impossible and undesirable to set the stays and shrouds to piano wire tautness. The stress of the wind on the sails was ultimately carried by the masts, which bent a little under its force. The shrouds and stays only came into play when the masts had received stress enough to give them a decided bend. The total network of spars, including the masts and yards, was designed to distribute these bending strains, and the individual components were made large enough to do so without

The shrouds (side-to-side) and the stays (front to rear) support the foremast of the ship in this photo. Note the "crow's nest." James Volo Photo.

failing. This eased the strain on the masts and gave a springiness to the vessel that imparted life and speed to it.[18]

The yards of early vessels were tapered toward their ends or given an eight-sided shape. The ends of the yard were called yard arms. Later yards were tapered from their centers throughout their length. This gave them improved flexibility. Before 1800, sails were attached to the yards by lacing them through eyelets in their top edge and winding each lacing around the yard before going to the next eyelet. After 1800, jackstays were introduced. These were made by screwing eyebolts along the top of the yard and threading a rope (called a jackstay) through them from each end. The sails were then laced to the jackstay rope. The jackstay could be easily pulled out to release or replace the sail. Hanging about 3 feet below the yard and parallel to it was a rope supported by a series of metal stirrups placed at intervals. This was the footrope on which the

The "dead eye," a large wooden device used to
tighten the standing rigging. James Volo Photo.

sailors supported themselves when setting or furling sails. The footrope
was tied, or moused, to the stirrups to prevent the slack from giving way
beneath the feet of the first man out on the yard.[19]

Running rigging was composed of many ropes that were used to a
greater or lesser extent depending on the conditions of the weather and
the situation of the vessel. All yards other than the lower ones (which
were fixed in place) could be raised and lowered by means of ropes
known as halyards. The ends of the yards were supported by lifts, which
kept them from sagging under the weight of wet canvass. Prior to the
nineteenth century, the lifts were composed of an arrangement of blocks
and tackles that appeared complicated but were in their simplest form a
rope running from the ends of the yard to the mast and down to the
deck from which they could be activated.

Sheets, which held the lower corners of the sail on the yard immediately above them, were ropes leading through sheaves set in the lower
yard arm and along its bottom edge to blocks hanging under the middle

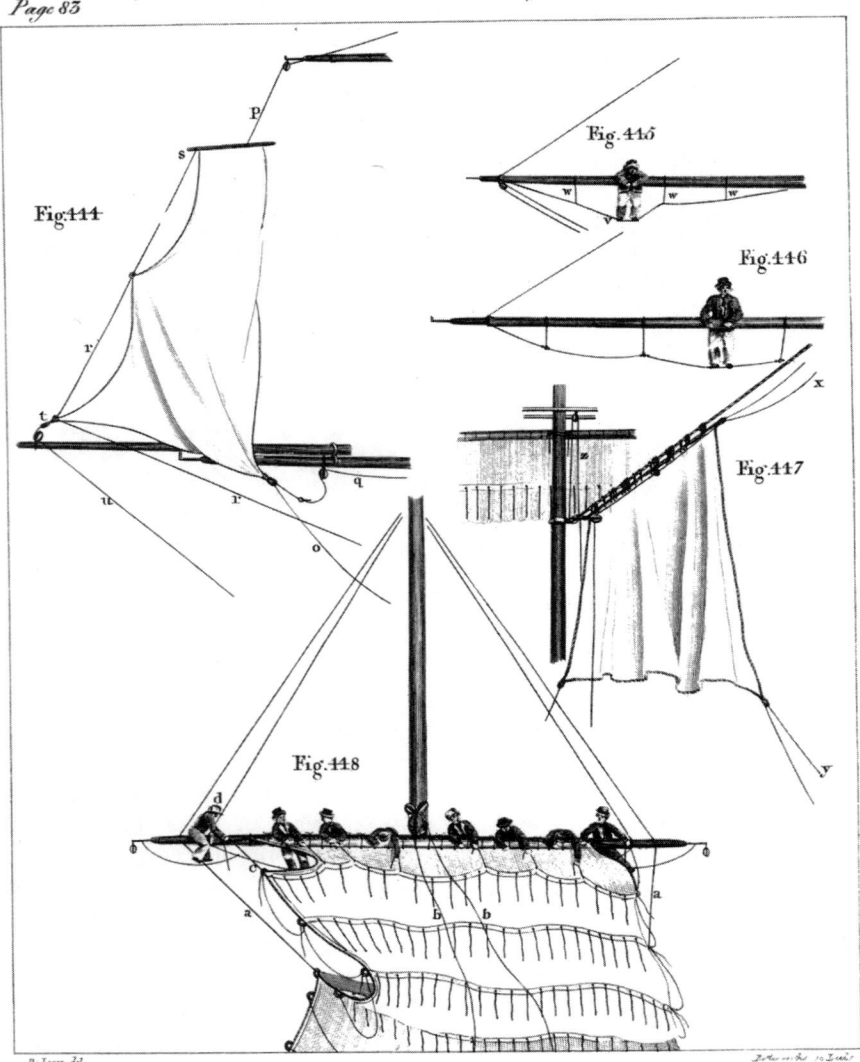

Taking in Studding Sails — Reefing Topsails &c.

Fig. 414
Fig. 415
Fig. 416
Fig. 417
Fig. 418

Reefing sails. Note the footrope on which the sailors maintained their balance.

of the yard and finally down along the mast toward the deck. The sheets allowed the sail to be securely fixed between the two yards—one above and one below. They took a great deal of strain and quickly wore thin. In later vessels, they were sometimes replaced by metal chains. The sheets for the courses—the lowest sails on the mast—had no yard below them and were attached from the lower corners of the sail to points in the hull of the vessel or along the railing.

Braces were attached to the yard arms at their ends. While the lifts were used to steady and adjust the yard, the braces were used so that the yard could be trimmed (rotated) to take the best advantage of the wind. The force exerted on the yard arms by the braces was multiplied by the use of a block and tackle. On merchant vessels the fixed blocks were located near the deck, while on warships, where the deck space was reserved for fighting, they were attached directly to the yard arms.

The final major piece of running rigging were the clew lines that led from each lower corner of the sail to blocks in the middle of the yard and thence down to the deck or top. The blocks were often the same ones as were used for the sheets. The purpose of the clew lines was to bring the sail up for furling. On warships, the blocks used to haul on the clew lines were once again secured aloft. Additional lines used for the same purpose were the leech lines and the buntlines drawing the sail in and up from the sides and bottom, respectively. The sail when furled was lashed firmly to its yard.[20]

MARINE DESIGN

The remarkable progress in ship design in the Elizabethan era was largely the work of the outstanding shipwright Matthew Baker. About 1586, Baker drafted designs for large warships with finer lines than those of earlier times. They were all galleon-built, with a long projecting beak, and a square stern. The sheer, or upward curve of the hull toward the bow and stern, was more pronounced than formerly.The sail plan was renovated to include topsails and a square spritsail under the bowsprit. Most importantly, the cut of all the sails was changed so that they were flatter. This made the ships faster, handier, and more weatherly. The high standard of English shipbuilding and design during this period can be attested by the fact that no English ship was lost through shipwreck during the whole of Elizabeth's reign. A contemporary observer noted in 1588, "The ships sit aground so strongly and are so staunch as if they are made of a whole tree."[21]

With the defeat of the Spanish Armada in 1588, the English assumed leadership in the field of marine design. The English had six naval dock-yards. By size the largest was Portsmouth, then Plymouth, with Chatham, Woolrich, Deptford, and Sheerness following. Each built and repaired hundreds of warships, yet in the eighteenth century, the British colonies along the northeastern Atlantic coast of North America provided almost half of the English shipbuilding capacity. After almost 200 years of shipbuilding, England was experiencing a scarcity of trees with the required firmness, weight, and compass (curvature) needed to build quality vessels.[22]

The existence of the vast North American forests, with their seeming superabundance of trees for masts and spars, played a vital role in the struggles for European supremacy between England and France in the eighteenth century. The white pine forests alone, which served to provide masts and planking, stretched in a broad belt from Nova Scotia to New Hampshire and back along the Connecticut and Hudson Rivers into the interior. By the latter days of wooden sailing ships, all the nations of the world were using masts from Maine.

The mantle of leadership in marine design, therefore, slowly passed to the Americans, particularly those along the New England coast. The development of a vast shipbuilding industry along the Maine coast was often attributed solely to the needs of the ports of Salem and New Bedford in Massachusetts. The vessels built in the American colonies were generally limited to between 400 and 600 tons burden, but some were as large as 1,000 tons. In 1742, at least forty vessels were built on the Maine coast.[23]

The War for American Independence ended the colonial period of shipbuilding. Thereafter, Americans built for themselves, becoming the premier shipbuilders and marine designers in the world of wooden sailing vessels. In the northern part of New England, particularly Maine and New Hampshire, there were more people engaged in shipbuilding than in agriculture, and in Massachusetts, it was estimated that there was one ship for every hundred inhabitants. In the decade after the adoption of the Constitution, American flag shipping increased by almost 400 percent, and by the American Civil War, it was nearly the equal to that of Britain. In 1861, the Americans and British each controlled one-third of the shipping of the world.[24]

The political revolution brought about by the struggle for independence also ushered in an era of revolution in marine design. American designers of the late eighteenth and early nineteenth centuries were quite successful in this regard. "[T]he resources of the country, the energies of the people, and their skill in the invention and application of machinery" have rarely combined to bring such large returns in material abundance. The Americans were also very quick to introduce labor-saving devices for managing the topsails, handling and lifting the anchor, and loading and unloading cargo. The Harbor Commissioners of Boston noted, "[T]he method of procedure in unloading at American wharves is greatly superior to that followed in the famous docks of London and Liverpool."[25]

The famous Baltimore clipper type, first built in the Chesapeake Bay area, came to be used wherever speed was paramount as in privateers, slavers, or smugglers. Their narrow beam, low freeboard, and V-shaped bottoms differed significantly from the rounder and wider British vessels.[26] In 1857, when the Sepoys of the British Army in India revolted, the British government hired a large number of American clipper ships to dispatch troops and supplies to their beleaguered forces. The "magnificent American-built clippers" almost completely dominated the India and China trade at the time.[27]

Still more celebrated were the American liners, which for a considerable period almost monopolized the carrying trade between Great Britain and the United States. A British observer noted,

This superiority consisted mainly in the fact that American ships could sail faster, and carry more cargo in proportion to their registered tonnage, than those of their competitors. But their improvements did not rest here. In considering the expenses of a merchantman, manual labor is one of the most important items: and herein [the Americans] by means of improved blocks and various mechanical applications, so materially reduced the number of hands, that twenty seamen in an American sailing-ship could do as much work, and probably with more ease to themselves, than thirty in a British vessel of similar size.[28]

It was a tradition of American shipbuilding that the keel, stempost, and sternpost of a ship were set down on the slipway, and the master builder shaped the hull by eye. For any craft other than a small boat, this would have been incredibly difficult. Not only is there no evidence that this was true, but surviving records indicate just the opposite. Master shipbuilders were highly skilled professionals, and they almost always worked from carefully drawn plans, many of which exist for naval vessels built under government contract. The fact that the plans for many merchant vessels no longer exist does not necessarily mean that there weren't any—the vessels also no longer exist.

The plans and elevation for the hull of each vessel under construction was commonly transferred to a half-hull model, many of which continue in existence as curiosities and collector's pieces. From this practice, it became common to refer to the practice of marine design as modeling, as in the following contemporary account: "Vessels of the United States at the time under consideration were better modeled, and, being better modeled and better handled, they sailed faster, and as a general rule

The use of half-hull models remained a part of shipbuilding into the nineteenth century, as can be seen in this illustration from a *Harper's Weekly* of 1877.

could make four voyages while the Englishman under similar circumstances and with similar vessels could make but three."[29]

NOTES

1. William Hutchinson Rowe, *The Maritime History of Maine: Three Centuries of Shipbuilding and Seafaring* (Freeport, ME: Bond Wheelwright, n.d.), 62.

2. The authors have attempted to be consistent in the forms that they use. However, primary sources such as journals, diaries, and traditional reference works—worthy of citation—may use slightly different methods to convey this information. The authors have decided to leave such material in the form found in the original works.

3. Rowe, 39.

4. Charles Nordhoff, *Sailor Life on Man-of-War and Merchant Vessels* (New York: Dodd, Mead & Co., 1884), 66.

5. American Live Oak from the Southern colonies was not considered as a marine raw material until used by the U.S. Navy. The U.S.S. *Constitution*, "Old Ironsides," had a keel of White Oak from New Jersey, timbers of Live Oak and Red Cedar from Georgia, and White Pines masts and spars from Maine. See Frances D. Robotti and James Vescovi, *The USS* Essex (Holbrook, MA: Adams Media Corporation, 1999), xvii.

6. In 1804, the Admiralty built and launched seven 32-gun fir-built frigates

in less than five months. In 1805, an additional five were built. See Nicholas Blake and Richard Lawrence, *The Illustrated Companion to Nelson's Navy* (Mechanicsburg, PA: Stackpole, 2000), 31–35.

7. Rowe, 58.

8. Ibid., 135–136.

9. Modern ship displacement does not use this system.

10. Nordhoff, 58–66.

11. Blake and Lawrence, 44–47.

12. John G. Rogers, *Origin of Sea Terms* (Mystic, CT: Mystic Seaport Museum, 1985), 19.

13. Richard Hough, *Captain Bligh and Mr. Christian: The Men and the Mutiny* (New York, E. P. Dutton, 1973), 67–68.

14. Try drawing a simple diagram of a three-masted ship with four sails on each mast.

15. G. J. Marcus, *The Formative Centuries: A Naval History of England* (Boston: Little, Brown & Co., 1961), 407. Italics added by the authors.

16. It is not the purpose of this work to give the reader a complete knowledge of the hundreds of terms and their derivations that can be found on this topic. However, a diligent person can expect to gain a layman's knowledge about the most characteristic sailing vessels after carefully reading these sections and referring to the accompanying illustrations.

17. Tom McGregor, *The Making of C. S. Forester's Horatio Hornblower* (New York: Harper-Collins Publishers, 1999), 60.

18. Charles G. Davis, *American Sailing Ships: Their Plans and History* (New York: Dover, 1984), 44.

19. Blake and Lawrence, 67.

20. George F. Campbell, *The Neophyte Shipmodeller's Jackstay* (Bogota, NJ: Model Shipways, 1969), 40–49.

21. Marcus, 84.

22. Marjorie Hubbell Gibson, *H.M.S. Somerset, 1746–1778: The Life and Times of an Eighteenth-Century British Man-O-War and Her Impact on North America* (Cotuit, MA: Abbey Gate House, 1992), 2.

23. Shipbuilding in the colonial American South is often ignored; however, some of the best designs for eighteenth-century vessels developed in the Chesapeake Bay area of Maryland and Virginia.

24. David Wells, *Our Merchant Marine: How It Rose, Increased, Became Great, Declined and Decayed* (New York: G. P. Putnam's Sons, 1890), 4, 8–9.

25. Ibid., 2, 11.

26. Rowe, 39–53.

27. Wells, 13.

28. Ibid., 15–16. Quoting W. S. Lindsay, *History of Merchant Shipping* (London, 1876), n.p.

29. Wells, 11–12.

5

The Crew

To put a marlinspike in a man's hand and set him to work upon a piece of rigging, is considered a fair trial of his qualities as an able seamen.

—Richard Henry Dana, Jr., 1841[1]

THE MERCHANT CREW

There were great differences among shipowners with regard to how they went about manning a vessel for a voyage. In many cases, the owner simply provided the vessel and supplies through his agents and gave the master particular instructions as to the manner in which he was to proceed in getting a crew. In other cases, the master was given wide discretion in hiring seamen based on more liberal and board suggestions. More rarely for short voyages, the owner allowed his agents to provide the crew without consulting the master, paying so much a head for each and ensuring their appearance on board at the time of sailing. However, on a long voyage, the comfort and safety of all aboard and the success or failure of the entire enterprise might rely on the character of the crew. It was in the interest of both the master and owner in these circumstances to select able-bodied and respectable men. By interesting themselves directly in the process of selecting a crew "a great deal of misunderstanding, complaint, and ill-will [might] be avoided and the beginning, at least, of the voyage be made under good auspices."[2]

The Shipmaster

The person with overall responsibility and power on board an vessel was the shipmaster, or simply the master. He was sometimes called the captain, a term of rank in the naval service not correctly applied to the master in the merchant service. Any officer in command of a vessel is considered its "captain." The master had a good deal of power and influence by which both good or evil could be done during a voyage. With regard to his personality, Richard Henry Dana noted, "If he is profane, passionate, tyrannical, indecent, or intemperate, more or less the same qualities will spread themselves or break out among the officers and men . . . which would have been checked, if not in some degree removed, had the head of the ship been a man of high personal character."[3]

As he prepared for a voyage, the master's duties were mostly confined to outfitting, supplying, and manning the vessel. Everything needed to be in readiness before leaving port, including compliance with all the paperwork, ordinances, and regulations demanded by the port authorities. These could include the preparation of bills of lading, manifests of many kinds, ship registrations, lists of crew members, the payment of port and pilotage fees, and the completion of customs inspections.

The master's responsibility was to get the vessel away from the dock and underway. If a pilot was taken aboard to steer through the intricacies of the harbor mouth or take the vessel "over the bar," the master deferred to his judgment until the ship was clear of danger. A master would rarely contradict the pilot's counsel in these circumstances. Once the pilot left the vessel, the entire control and responsibility for the ship and crew were thrown on to the master's shoulders for the remainder of the voyage.

It was usual for the master to call all hands aft for a talk about the nature of the voyage and his personal expectations with regard to their duties. He was sure to stress his authority and that of his officers and make the rules of conduct perfectly clear to the crew. Thereafter, with the notable exception of Sunday service at which he officiated, the master rarely dealt directly with the crew, choosing rather to act through the influence of his officers. In any case, his own duties were numerous and time consuming.

The master was the navigator for the vessel and was the sole source of course and direction. His first duty was to take a bearing and distance of the last point of departure from the land and have it recorded in the ship's log-book. It was from this point that the reckoning of course and distance was kept. Although the first mate actually kept the log-book, the master examined and corrected it every day. The master also attended the chronometer, made all the navigational observations, took the noon fix of position and any lunar or stellar sightings. He was assisted by the first mate who made simultaneous readings so that the two could be reconciled.

The master had absolute power aboard ship and could make the atmosphere of the vessel almost anything he chose. He was always addressed as "captain" and answered as "sir." He stood no watch and had an entire cabin to himself. If passengers were aboard, he was expected to make an attempt to pay them the attention thought proper for their rank or social station. The master handled all transactions with merchants and port officials ashore. All decisions were made by him with regard to repairs, the dispensation of supplies, and the allowance of food and water. Arguments, discipline, and punishment were left to his discretion and justice. The entire working of the ship lay under his responsibility, yet he never went aloft or did any work with his hands. When on deck, the windward side of the quarterdeck was his. While the officer of the watch was at liberty to trim the yards and make minor alterations to the sails, no major decision could be made by anyone other than the master except in the most pressing circumstances of immediate danger to the vessel.

The master relied heavily on his supervising officers who were called *mates*. The mates were always addressed as **The Mates** "mister" and answered as "sir." Neither the master nor his mates ever took the wheel or tiller. Steering the vessel was left to the men. Every seaman aboard was expected to stand as helmsman at some point in the voyage. The mates divided the crew into two watches—the larboard (port or left side) watch commanded by the first mate, and the starboard (right side) watch directed by the second mate. The master usually allowed the mates to divide the crew into watches based upon their own observations of the qualities of the men. The men were divided as equally as possible, both as to number and ability, as either watch needed to be fully capable of dealing with the necessities of a voyage at sea.

The first mate was an active superintending officer. However, he never pulled, hauled, or did work with his hands. He received his orders directly from the master and transmitted them to the crew. On deck, the first mate often appeared to be the only officer in command of the vessel. Nothing was done unless detailed orders came from him. He needed to be an energetic and vigilant man who was well acquainted with all aspects of a seaman's work. He needed to be a particularly excellent judge of rigging and might go aloft to make an inspection. The setting or lowering of sails and all aspects of the rigging or the repairs on board were done under his superintendence. In the absence of the captain, as in port, the first mate's powers were extended proportionately for cases of necessity, but he would not attempt to exercise any unusual powers, such as punishing a man.

An American naval officer caught in a
mid-nineteenth-century pose. This rare
photo is from the early Civil War period.

The first mate was hired by the owners the shippers, or the insurers
rather than the master. He was essentially the owner's man, given his
position as a check on the master. For this reason, the log-book was
placed in his care as a depository of the evidence of everything that
occurred during the voyage. As a representative of the owners, he could
not be removed from his office by the master except under very peculiar
circumstances closely described in the law. Nonetheless, the master, from
the power of his office, could make the situation of the first mate quite
disagreeable if he was displeased. Maritime law commonly made the
first mate the immediate successor of the master should the latter die or
become unable to perform his duties.

The second mate was the commander of the starboard watch, and
when on deck alone, he had charge of the vessel. He was usually chosen
by the master and did not automatically replace the first mate should
the latter become incapable of performing his duties. His duties included
the maintenance and care of all the spare rigging, blocks, and sails as
well as the tools used to work upon the rigging such as marlinspikes,

heavers, and servers. In the absence of a sailmaker aboard, the care of
the sails was given over to the second mate. Unlike the first mate, the
second mate was expected to do jobs like a common seamen about the
decks and aloft. "He ought to be the best workman on board, or take
upon himself the nicest and most difficult jobs, or to show the men how
to do them." When the whole crew was required for heavy work, such
as taking in or setting studding sails or in bad weather, he placed himself
on the leeward (away from the wind), and he pulled and hauled with
the rest of the men on deck.[4]

Third mates were found only on very large vessels, and they were
usually chosen from among the most senior able seamen by the master.
In some cases they were designated as bosuns (alternate spellings: boatswains, bowswains). This was actually a term applied specifically to a
warrant officer in the navy, and it was a corruption of its meaning when
applied to any seaman in the merchant service.

Almost every merchant vessel of a large size carried a number
of specialized workmen aboard. They were known as idlers be- **Idlers**
cause they stood no watch, did no work common to the seamen,
and held no authority over them. They slept each night and pursued
their trade during the day. Idlers commonly included the carpenter, the
sailmaker, and the cook. On smaller vessels, however, an idler could sign
on as both an able seamen and a carpenter or a sailmaker. Cooks were
never considered seamen, and no seamanship was required of them. It
was not uncommon for the cook to be an older seaman infirmed by age
or the loss of a limb. Very large vessels might also have a cooper, steward, armorer, and persons who followed other trades.

Idlers had no authority aboard ship, not even over the youngest boy.
They were sometimes hired directly under contract by the shipowner,
but they received their orders from the master. Idlers were usually addressed properly as "mister" by the crew, but they were never answered
as "sir." Any order from the mates to the idlers would "come somewhat
in the form of a request."[5]

Although he probably was not a shipwright, the carpenter was perfectly able to tapper a yard, repair a railing or a coaming, and shape an
upper mast. When necessary, the carpenter could repair broken beams,
join and caulk planking, and make emergency repairs of all kinds to the
wooden parts of the rigging and hull. He lived in steerage with the other
idlers and had charge of the ship's tool chest and all things connected
to his trade. Some carpenters also served as coopers, repairing buckets,
barrels, and casks. On whalers, the carpenter/cooper could often be
found assembling barrels. These were fashioned ashore in a cooperage,
the staves numbered, and disassembled to save space for the provisions
needed for the voyage. As the provisions were used up, space in the

hold was made available for the reassembled barrels filled with whale oil or stacks of bone.

Most vessels had one set of extra sails that had been made ashore in a sail loft. At sea, the sailmaker was usually an older seamen with sufficient skill in the trade to mend sails worn over the normal course of their use or make them up in an emergency. Like the carpenter, had he been more skilled, the sailmaker would have made a better and more comfortable living ashore. His tools were generally limited to a pair of shears for cutting canvas, seam formers and pressers made of wood or bone, thick linen thread, a set of large needles, and a palm. This device strapped to his wrist and firmly secured to the hand a small metal and horn button that could be pressed against the end of the needle to drive it through the thick layers of canvas.

The cook spent most of his time tending the fires in the galley where he cooked for both the officers in the cabin and the men in the forecastle. If passengers were on board, he also cooked for them and may have been assigned a helper in the galley in the form of a boy. The need to maintain the galley, boilers, pans, and utensils occupied most of his day. He was able to sleep at night and on some vessels had a bunk in the galley. There was often a good deal of friendly familiarity between the cook and the men. A bad cook was a misery on a good voyage, while a good cook made a bad voyage all the more bearable.

Watches   A *watch* was the term both for the division of the crew and the division of time. The crew was divided into starboard and larboard watches, and the entire twenty-four hour day was divided into watches of either four or two hours. A contemporary seaman described the common practices followed in serving watches.

If, for instance, the chief mate with the larboard watch have the first night watch, from eight to twelve, at the end of four hours the starboard watch is called, and the second mate takes the deck, while the larboard watch and the chief mate go below until four in the morning. At four they come on deck again, and remain until eight; having what is called the morning watch. . . . Where this alternation of watches is kept up throughout the twenty-four hours, four hours up and four below it is called having watch and watch . . . but in most merchant vessels, it is the custom to keep all hands from one P.M. to sundown, or until four o'clock. In extreme cases, also, all hands are kept throughout the day; but the watch which has eight hours on deck at night should be allowed a forenoon watch below.

The watch from four to eight P.M. is divided into two half-watches of two hours each, called dog-watches. The object of this is to make an uneven number of watches, seven instead of six; otherwise the same watch would stand during the same hours for the whole voyage, and those who had two watches on deck the first night would have the same throughout the trip. But the uneven number shifts the watches.[6]

The watches were divided by bells that were struck every half hour. The bells were sounded by two strokes following one another quickly, and then a short interval after which two more were struck. If an odd number, the one was struck alone. This made counting much easier and emphasized both the hour and the half hour.

At noon, eight bells were struck. From that time the bell was struck once each thirty minutes, adding one strike each time, but never going higher than eight. Two bells would be 1 P.M. Three bells 1:30 P.M. However, the eight bells that signified noon also rang at 4 P.M. Two bells struck thereafter meant 5 P.M. and three 5:30 P.M. The system is simplified if one remembers that eight bells were twelve, four, or eight o'clock day or night.

Mariners were generally divided into three classes: able seamen, ordinary seamen, and boys or green hands. All green **Seamen** hands were classified as boys regardless of their age or size. Both in the merchant service and in the navy, each man rated himself when he signed aboard. There were few abuses of this system as every man knew that if found incompetent to perform the duties he signed for his wages would be reduced. More importantly, his shipmates might consider such a deception a fraud against themselves. The officers felt at liberty to punish such a delinquent with unpleasant and inferior work such as sweeping decks, slushing, scrubbing, or tarring.

A "competent knowledge of steering, reefing, furling, and the like" was taken for granted even of an ordinary seaman. It was a common saying that "to hand, reef, and steer makes a sailor," but an able seamen also had to be a good workman upon the rigging. On board, there was always a great deal of work to be done on the rigging. Worn, chaffed, and split rigging needed to be replaced both in port and throughout the voyage. The cutting and fitting of new rigging required a knowledge of neat knots, splices, seizings, coverings, and turnings. It was a man's skill at rigging that tested his seamanship. No man could "pass as an able seaman in a square-rigged vessel who [could] not make a long and short splice in a large rope, fit a block strap, pass seizings to lower rigging, and make the ordinary knots, in a fair, workmanlike manner." Richard Henry Dana claimed that "to put a marlinspike in a man's hand and set him to work upon a piece of rigging, is considered a fair trial of his qualities as an able seamen."[7]

An ordinary seaman was one who from lack of experience or strength could not quite perform the duties of the able seamen. He was expected to hand, reef, and steer under normal weather conditions. He did not need be a complete helmsman, but he could maintain a course under ordinary circumstances. Ordinary seamen were well acquainted with all the running and standing rigging of the ship. They were said to know the ropes. They could usually do the simpler parts of rigging such as

Life on the Ocean: A Midshipmen's Berth in a British Frigate at Sea (HMS "Hyperion"), by Augustus Earle (c. 1830). © NATIONAL MARITIME MUSEUM.

Furling and handling the sails when aloft was difficult and hazardous work. This pencil sketch by the author is based on a bank note engraving.

splicing small ropes, passing a common seizing, and making common knots, but they generally were not skillful with a marlinspike or serving board.

In bad weather an able seaman usually replaced an ordinary seaman at the wheel. Ordinary seamen were not asked to go to the end of the yards or above the tops when furling sails. These stations were left to able seamen, known as topmen—smart young seamen who worked aloft handling the sails. Upper yardmen, the youngest of the topmen and often no more than older boys, worked on the topgallant and royal yards, which were the highest of all. They considered the tops their own, literally and figuratively looking down on other seamen.[8]

Some ordinary seamen had great difficulty working in the rigging but were hired for their strength in pulling and hauling or working at the capstan bar or windlass. These "sheet-anchor men" worked on the forecastle handling the anchors, jibs, and fore yards. Handling the anchors was particularly dangerous work that called for collective strength and coordination rather than individual skill. On the aft deck were the "after-gang" who dealt primarily with the mainsail and spanker and worked on the lines and haliyards in that part of the vessel. In the center of the ship, one deck down was the waist, or well-deck. Here the "waisters" had their duties, and a deck below this were the "holders" who worked among the casks and provisions.[9]

Merchant vessels were generally undermanned when compared to naval vessels. A coasting schooner sometimes carried as few as one seaman for each twenty tons of burden. Ocean traders, Indiamen, and slavers usually carried more, perhaps one seaman for every ten tons. There was no hard and fast rule, and owners hired as few men as could manage the vessel safely. This left merchant vessels easy prey for the generally overmanned pirates and privateers who could overwhelm the crew if they got aboard. Warships often carried hundreds of men.[10]

The ordinary seaman's duties depended a good deal upon the availability of green hands or boys among the crew. If there were sufficient green hands, the ordinary seamen would be given preference over them in the light work and occasionally in working on the rigging. By this means, green hands could extend their knowledge and progress toward the position of able seamen. However, in many merchant vessels, "the distinction between ordinary seamen and boys [was] not very carefully observed," and ordinary seamen were called on to do the duties of green hands even when boys were available. This was generally considered an irritating situation disrespectful of the seaman's skills. If the problem continued it, sometimes caused dissension between the crew and the officers.[11]

If an officer wished for some one to loose a light sail, take a broom and sweep the decks, hold a log-reel, coil a rope, slush or scrub a mast, touch up a bit of tar, or help in the galley, he would call upon one of the boys or green hands. Sometimes when there were plenty of men, boys were never asked to do any but the most simple tasks. Nonetheless, in an ordinary day's work, they were taught a number of skills—somewhat like apprentices, although no formal system existed. These skills included work with knots on ropes and yarns, simple ropework, and the loosing and furling of light sails. They stood a watch like every other seaman and went aloft when working sails. When first aboard, they were immediately sent aloft to accustom them to the motion of the vessel and to moving about the rigging, but in work they were rarely above the tops or to the ends of the yards. They were allowed to take the wheel in light winds and gradually become competent helmsmen.[12]

Richard Henry Dana made the following observations with regard to boys as members of the crew at sea:

Whatever knowledge a boy may have acquired, or whatever may be his age or strength, so long as he is rated a boy, (and the rates are not changed during a voyage unless a person changes his ship), he must do the inferior duties of a boy. If decks are to be cleared up or swept, rigging to be coiled, a man is to be helped in his job, or any duty to be done aloft or about the decks which does not require the strength or skill of a seaman, a boy is always expected to start first and do it, though not called upon by name.[13]

Throughout the nineteenth century, it was common to assign unpleasant and inferior work to the nonwhites among American crews. Chinese were commonly employed in this manner on China trade ships. On the Atlantic runs and in the clipper ships from the east coast to California, the minority members of the crew were more likely to be Africans recruited in the West Indies or the Cape Verde Islands. Many were free men recruited in American port cities.[14]

THE NAVY

A seaman's life in the merchant service was significantly different from that endured while serving in a warship. There is little doubt among historians that the experience, professionalism, training, and morale of the British Royal Navy produced a service superior to that of any other maritime nation during the age of sail. As such, it was the ideal to which all other European navies aspired. The Royal Navy of the eighteenth century formed England's first and most important line of defense. Although many books concentrate on great naval battles and fearsome ships, it was the personnel and officers that made the Royal Navy great. For these reasons, the men of the Royal Navy have come to represent the naval personnel in this period.

The Royal Navy's administration was entirely controlled by the Board of Admiralty. This board was com-   **The Admiralty** posed of seven commissioners headed by the First Lord of the Admiralty, who was usually a political appointee rather than a senior naval officer.[15] There were among the commissioners experienced and distinguished sailors. The commissioners of the Admiralty met every day including holidays and took decisions collectively. At least three of the seven were needed to sign important orders. The Admiralty's responsibilities were divided among several areas, which included the building and repair of ships, the commissioning of officers, the supervision of the Royal Marines, the ordering of the Sea Fencibles (a form of maritime militia), the operation of the Impress Service, and the management of the Navy Board.

The Admiralty had a staff of sixty bureaucrats and clerks overseen by the Board Secretary who wielded a great deal of authority, although he was a mere civil servant. In the 1670s, Samuel Pepys as secretary to the Lord High Admiral had used this power to establish many of the rules and disciplines that ruled the navy in the centuries to come. Pay and working conditions for the staff were very good, and many clerks and administrative officers served for long periods. Experience, talent, and diligence were rewarded. As a consequence, by the standards of the period, the Admiralty as a whole was a very efficient bureaucracy.

The Navy Board, a subsidiary of the Admiralty, designed, built, and supplied the ships, ran the dockyards, appointed the warrant officers, and purchased or manufactured all the navy's stores and equipment except cannon. Cannon were tested, developed, and supplied to both the army and the navy by the Ordnance Board, an independent entity with offices in the Tower of London and test facilities at Woolrich. The Navy Board was further divided into appropriately named boards dealing with the transport of troops and military supplies, the provision of food and drink for the crews, and the care of the hurt and sick. The Transport Board maintained between forty and fifty naval storeships for the use of both the army and the navy. In wartime, it sometimes hired additional merchant vessels, and after 1796, it secured the prisoners of war. The Victualing Board appointed pursers and supplied the navy with food and drink. It had its own breweries for making beer, bakeries for ship's bread, and slaughterhouses for salt pork and beef. The Hurt and Sick Board examined surgeons for certification, provided most medical supplies, and administered the hospitals.[16]

Officers   For centuries, both military and naval officers were part timers. Chosen largely because of their wealth, status, or family connections, officers quickly returned to civilian pursuits once the war they were involved in was over. In 1670, Samuel Pepys tried to professionalize the naval establishment by creating a new approach to the selection and training of young men for the naval service. Interested youths of good birth and breeding were carefully selected and sent to sea under royal patronage "to learn the ropes."[17] These posts, having the title of midshipman, were often made available due to family influence or outright purchase. The rank of midshipman was an intermediate one between that of warrant officer and commissioned officer.

The popular concept of midshipmen as young boys is not always accurate. Certainly some lads of twelve to fourteen years were aboard ships as midshipmen, but the majority were young men in their late teens and twenties. For four years, midshipmen learned the skills of ordinary and able seamen and served as petty officers (or master's mate) at sea for two years more. It was also possible to attend the Royal Naval Academy for three years, join a ship, and serve for three more years of sea duty. In either case, six years of preparation made even the youngest midshipman a more mature individual. Thereafter, they stood for an examination of their skills and knowledge in an attempt to receive a commission. "Although this system had obvious potential for abuse, it worked surprisingly well, and the influence of [family or money] was admitted openly." Nonetheless, regardless of birth or fortune, only by passing a difficult and comprehensive examination could a midshipman receive his lieutenancy.[18]

Officers progressed, thereafter, by seniority. They were given command of vessels by rank. A lieutenant was allowed to command only "unrated" vessels—generally sloops of war with less than 20 guns. A commander (a worthy lieutenant who had not yet been posted) might be given a 6th rater, and a post-captain a frigate or any ship of the line. As with the merchant service, any officer in command of a naval vessel was its "captain." Naval officers that held the rank of captain were said to be post-captains, although they were never addressed using the term. The phrase *post-captain* may have come from the idea that the officer's name was thereafter posted on the advancement list toward the rank of admiral. A senior captain, granted the temporary title of commodore, might be placed in charge of more than one vessel in a squadron. Admirals were flag officers—they had the right to fly their own flag and were given command of whole fleets or parts of fleets.

Advancement to admiral by seniority was not a certainty, and a good reputation as a successful captain and leader of men was essential. Many post-captains, shown to be incompetent, inept, or unfortunate were passed over, serving ashore on half-pay for their entire career, and were moved up to admiral only so the more fortunate or capable captains below them could receive active commands as admirals at sea. There were three grades of admiral (rear admiral, vice-admiral, and admiral) described by the color of their flags: blue, white, and red in ascending order with red being the most senior. Admirals traveled with the fleet on one of its ships, the flag ship, which was commanded by a post-captain. While the admiral commanded the fleet, the "flag-captain" was fully in charge of his own vessel. The ship was usually chosen from among the larger warships of the fleet, or because of the admiral's admiration or trust in its captain. If the admiral "transferred his flag" (moved to another vessel), it became the flagship and its captain became the new flag-captain.

In the late seventeenth century, officers first began to seek a lifelong career in the navy. As there were generally fewer vessels than those needed to staff them, officers quickly found that they could not maintain a berth in peacetime. There were just not enough ships in commission. Yet in a frigate of the period, there were more than a dozen officers: captain, first lieutenant, up to six junior lieutenants, at least two marine officers, and a couple of "passed midshipman" (later called ensigns) who retained their midshipmen's berths until assigned to another vessel. These men ate together in the wardroom. Also of "wardroom quality" were the warrant officers: surgeon, chaplain, sailing-master, and purser. After the wardroom officers came the lesser warrant officers such as the boatswain, chief gunner, and carpenter. Ranking below the midshipmen who had not yet passed their examinations were the petty officers. These were the last to be separated from the seamen by rank.[19]

The navy employed a higher proportion of idlers than that found in the merchant service, including coopers, sailmakers, and ropemakers. Having no naval rank, they formed a more distinctive class among the structured formality of the ship's officers than their civilian counterparts.[20] Each grade among the officers jealously guarded its own rights and prerogatives and "would have jumped overboard before they would have sanctioned the slightest change in the organization of ship-board life."[21]

Many naval officers were placed on half-pay as a fee from the government for remaining available until such time as they were needed. As many as a quarter of all the available officers were on half-pay even during wartime. As there was no seniority list below the rank of captain, many junior officers remained retired. Conversely, many men who were actually too old or too infirm to serve at sea continued to draw half-pay for decades. Nonetheless, an extended period of peace could be disastrous for a career man both financially and professionally if he did not turn to some other means of employment. It was in this area that patronage best served the individual. "The patronage system caused its beneficiaries to be doubly zealous in their conduct to justify their appointments, but it also caused worthy officers without influence to remain unemployed or unpromoted."[22]

Warrant Officers   The Navy Board examined and appointed men as warrant officers on naval vessels. These men were not commissioned but held positions somewhat like that of idlers in merchant vessels. Some of them ate in the wardroom with the lieutenants, marine officers, and the chaplain. These were the purser, the surgeon, and the master. The other warrant officers, such as the boatswain, gunner, and carpenter, lived and messed in the fore cockpit or, on smaller vessels, in the fore part of the gunroom. These were sometimes called standing officers as they tended to stay with the ship in and out of commission.

The purser was a warrant officer in charge of the ship's nonmilitary stores, and he was financially responsible for food and drink if the wastage at the end of a voyage was greater than one-eighth. Many pursers gave short weight and measure when dealing out rations in order to avoid this penalty. Other supplies were purchased by the purser from his own funds and repaid to him at a fixed rate per man per day.

One surgeon was appointed to each warship. They were not necessarily doctors but were examined as to their medical knowledge by a panel of three fleet surgeons before receiving their warrants. Usually they had previously served for some time as surgeons mates (one to three per vessel). Seamen who helped the surgeon and his mates were called lob-lolly boys. Surgeons were paid a stipend per month and a fee per men in the vessels in which they served. Yet there was always a shortage of surgeons, and a substantial bounty, proportioned for service in First to Sixth Rate warships, was paid to attract them. Naval surgeons ranked as equals with army surgeons and could carry a plain officer's sword. In battle, they generally worked in the orlop deck below the waterline.

In the navy, the master was a warrant officer charged with the navigation of the warship. The master thereby freed the naval captain to deal with tactics and strategies. Aspiring masters usually served as master's mates or quartermasters, or they came as masters from the merchant services. They were examined by a senior naval captain and a panel of three masters for their appointments. The master was at the pinnacle of his profession, and there was usually no higher rank that he desired. Nonetheless, some masters sought commissions as lieutenants, hoping thereafter to move up the ladder of naval promotion. Masters supplied their own charts, maps, and instruments, and they kept the official log-book.

The boatswain was a standing officer. Each had served at least a year as a petty officer. Their main duty was to supervise all the deck activity sometimes using a whistle to communicate prearranged signals above the noise of wind and wave. Boatswains were to encourage the men in their work. If friendly persuasion or the force of their personality did not work, they, or the boatswain's mates, might use a rope's end or a rattan cane as a starter. The boatswain's mates did the flogging. The boatswain also oversaw the work of the sailmaker and his crew.

The aspiring gunner served at least four years, one of which was as a petty officer. He was examined by a group of three naval gunners and a mathematical master as to his ability. While the commissioned officers actually directed the action of the guns in battle, the gunner saw to their care, prepared the cartridges for them, and ensured the proper flow of powder and projectile to the gundecks during battle. The gunner needed "quite a few exceptional qualifications, including being expert in higher mathematics, an excellent chemist, and a past master at logistical calculations." He also needed "an almost total disregard for personal safety." He was responsible for testing the quality of the gunpowder brought aboard. His domain was the magazine in which the powder was stored. Herein, with his feet clad in felt slippers and with copper tools to prevent static discharge, he and his assistants made up the ammunition for the guns.[23]

The carpenters on naval vessels were almost indistinguishable from those on merchant vessels except in relation to battle. In an engagement, the carpenter sounded the well to see if the ship was taking water, stopped shot holes in the hull, with prepared plugs, and supervised the repair of damage aloft. To gain access to the hull, the carpenter and his assistants used a narrow passage called the "carpenters' walk" located next to the hull and separated from the gundecks. Only large naval vessels had such a structure.

Petty Officers Able seamen might be promoted to the rate of petty officer if they possessed or developed particular skills. There were three classes of petty officers. The most junior were the quarter gunners, cooper, and trumpeter. The next group included the captain of the tops, the cook, and the mates of the ship's craftsmen. The senior petty officers were the sailmaker, caulker, quartermaster, coxswain, boatswain's mates, and master-at-arms. The rate of chief petty officer was not created until the nineteenth century.

Marines Marines were not seamen and were not used to labor aboard ship except to help with unskilled work. Marines had their own officers who messed in the wardroom. Their training was as infantry, and their purpose aboard was twofold. They made up the bulk of any boarding or landing parties should the situation avail itself, and they were a ready force, separate from the seamen, which the sea officers might use to enforce discipline and prevent mutiny among the crew. They provided the sentries at the captain's door, the magazines, the spirits-room, and the stores. In battle, they took station in the tops where they served as sharpshooters, using standard sea service muskets to fire at the enemy decks below.

Ratings While the commissioned and warrant officers had some permanent connection with the navy, seamen, sometimes called *ratings*, were not considered members of the naval service as a whole. Rather they were part of a ship's company. Mariners did not join the navy in the modern sense. They joined, or were pressed, into the employment of a particular vessel and remained a part of its crew until killed, wounded beyond service, or paid off when the vessel ended its voyage or was put out of commission. Thereafter, sailors moved with relative ease from one vessel to another as their own preferences dictated. Everyone who joined a ship was given a rate by the first lieutenant, which was recorded in the muster book. From this came the man's pay and duties. A seamen could be promoted or demoted from this initial rate at any time by the captain.

The ability of an officer to attract good men to his service was a mark of a successful career and a means by which a reliable ship's crew might be cemented into a successful ship's company. A settled and efficient ship's company was "a precious possession, which both deserved and required careful nurture."[24] A British captain noted, "Nor will I ever [knowingly] keep a dissatisfied man in any ship with me, if he were the best seaman in the world; I would rather have a willing and contented landsman . . . I could make a seaman of." The naval service recognized this importance and shaped the navy so that the men could serve, as far as possible, under officers that they admired.[25]

The men understood that able officers would reward deserving men with advancement possibly to a petty officer's rating—no mean ambition for a seaman. On American vessels, it was generally accepted that ship-masters and officers "from the southern states, who during their formative years had become accustomed to handling slaves, were the most popular with the crew: the northerners, given authority, were apt to become tyrannical." Similar beliefs were held in this regard to those European officers of noble birth—as compared with men who came from an unremarkable or middle class heritage. Neither belief proved infallible in practice.[26]

Any suggestion of drafting men away from a happy ship and well-respected officers aroused instant protest from the crew. When captains changed ships, they hoped to take with them as many reliable men from their former crew as possible. One officer of the period wrote, "I have taken great pains to discipline and make them a tolerable ship's company, which was very bad when I had them first. . . . It would be a little hard . . . losing my people."[27]

Seamen came from a particular class of society with a distinctive life-style. They generally resided along the coasts in sections of town peculiar to themselves. Like other laborers, seamen shared attitudes, language, and a common store of knowledge characteristic of their trade The available evidence from the eighteenth and nineteenth centuries suggests that crews of warships were overwhelmingly composed of young men, typically in their mid-twenties, who were able seamen. By comparison the typical seamen found in the merchant service were in their early thirties and were divided between able and ordinary seamen. Service in a warship was physically taxing in the extreme, and as the experienced man-of-war's men grew older, they became proportionately less attractive to the naval recruiters and press gangs. Unfortunately, in peace time there was no market for a maritime labor force composed of men trained to the rigors of the man-of-war. When paid off, sailors generally drifted from the navy into the merchant service where wages and working conditions varied from port to port and master to master.

Most naval ratings were volunteers. They joined the navy for many reasons. Initially they could expect a bounty when signing on in addition to a couple of months advance in wages. Thereafter, they earned their monthly wage, which, although irregularly paid, accumulated as long as the ship was in commission. Their wages included food, and no deductions were made apart from the costs of slop clothing or tobacco. By way of contrast, the gravest weakness of the merchant service was the risk of being cheated of wages by unscrupulous masters through arbitrary deductions for food, clothing, or claims of damage to the cargo.

The crew of a naval vessel was paid in good English coin while merchant seamen might be offered debased foreign or colonial currency. A seamen from the period wrote, "Naval commanders make it their duty to hoard up poor Jack's money for him—keeping it carefully out of his hands during an entire three years' cruise . . . in order that he may have a chance to spend his pile in drunken orgies at the end of the cruise. However unjust and impolitic such a course seems, it is one almost universally adopted in the navy."[28]

Notwithstanding this testimony, the usual practice aboard a man-of-war was to pay the crew just before they sailed. The Navy Act of 1728 provided a means by which men might remit the money to their families through government agents for a fee either when the ship was paid or at six-month intervals abroad. In 1758, this act was amended to include a new mechanism for remitting money without a fee through government channels. It was required only for a man to sign a simple legal instrument naming the beneficiary of his remittances. These acts had the advantage of making naval service more attractive to married men.

While navy wages were less than competitive with those offered by the merchant service, the major attraction for seamen to the naval life remained the hope of earning prize money. Unlike the privateer where half of the value of a captured ship and its cargo went to the shipowners, in warships of the eighteenth century, the entire value of the prize was distributed to the captors. One-eighth was reserved for the commander-in-chief, one-quarter to the commander, one-eighth to the master and lieutenants, another to the warrant officers, another to the petty officers, and the remaining quarter to the seamen. Inasmuch as each man's share fell with the increasing size of the captor, service in generally smaller and quicker frigates was held at a premium. In a frigate with about 140 seamen, each man could expect approximately 0.02 percent of the value of the prize. While this seems small, it was a larger share than privateersmen serving on similarly sized vessels could expect. Moreover, naval personnel received their wages, food, and medical treatment in addition to their prize money, a situation uncommon among privateers where men served entirely at their own expense. It is no wonder that British privateers were extremely short of seaman.[29]

A considerable number of foreigners served in the Royal Navy as they did in most of the navies of the world. Records indicate that over 10 percent of the crew of *Victory* at the battle of Trafalgar was composed of foreign sailors. At least fifteen different nationalities have been identified among the crew. These included Americans, Frenchmen, West Indians, and Russians. The number of Americans was remarkable as one of the complaints made by the United States, which led to the War of 1812, was with regard to the impressment of American nationals at sea. Many of the men serving in the navy were nonwhite. This was especially

Manning the Navy, by Samuel Collings (J. Barlow, engraver). This period print from June 1, 1870, portrays the ruthless efficiency of the press gang. © NATIONAL MARITIME MUSEUM.

true of the Royal Navy, which, with its far-flung possessions, recruited around the world.

Historians are divided over actually what proportion of seamen were volunteers and what proportion were **Impressment** pressed or conscripted into the navy. Naval historian N.A.M. Rodger noted, "There are few aspects of 18th century history which have aroused more passion and less accuracy than the press gang."[30] The "press" seems to have originated in the thirteenth century, but its most infamous incarnation—the one that figures prominently in novels and movies—dates to the Quota Act of 1795. This legislation compelled every county in Britain to provide a number of recruits according to its population to fill the need for men brought on by the French Revolution. Civic authorities offered bounties and remitted the sentences of criminals and debtors to fill the quota, but forcible impressment still proved necessary.

The Impress Service was naturally unpopular, and the press gang was both feared and physically resisted in performing its duties. The Impress Service was regulated by a captain or commander from a headquarters centered in a seaport district. The press gang was composed of a group of seamen armed with cudgels and commanded by a naval lieutenant. These gangs forcibly abducted men between the ages of eighteen and fifty-five who were "not apprentices or gentlemen." Merchant seamen were their preferred targets; very few landsmen were pressed. Some pressed men were taken directly from incoming merchant vessels before they could come to anchor. Many of the seamen abducted in this manner chose to "volunteer" at a moment's notice and receive the associated bounty.[31]

Clearly the navy in wartime was filled with men of all ages and abilities. However, the idea that men-of-war were filled with pressed civilians from the city streets who had no knowledge of seamanship is not supported by the available evidence. Impressment officers would have been foolhardy to deliberately press men unaccustomed to the sea on whom their own lives might later depend. The related concept that the navy was "a sort of floating concentration camp," as portrayed in novels and movies, is equally ridiculous.[32] Although the government gave the press gangs wide leeway to do as they might—provided they got more men—impressed seamen did not disappear into the holds of warships to be whipped into submission. "Receiving ships"—hulks moored off shore in England and in some colonial ports—legally processed the men into the naval service and sent word to their families as to their disposition.[33]

For all practical purposes, it is impossible to determine if all impressed men were unhappy with their fate, or for that matter, if all the volunteers were content with their lot. It is certain that the impressment system was largely arbitrary, harsh, and unsympathetic to the men that it conscripted, but it also satisfied the manning needs of the navy. Seamen in the Royal Navy had no right to shore leave, making desertion difficult. Entire crews could be "turned over" or distributed to other ships, although this was supposed to happen only in the case of an emergency. In any case, at some point the entire crew, both volunteers and pressed men, were paid off and discharged at the end of a ship's commission so that the naval service was for only a limited period.[34]

CLOTHING

Seaman's Clothing Neither the merchant marine nor the navy issued clothing to sailors prior to the nineteenth century. Most merchant seamen brought a small bag of serviceable clothing with them when they signed on. "A sailor, in the usual striped trousers and short jacket, often carried all his worldly goods wrapped in a kerchief." Replacement items came from the slops chest. This was a supply

Authentically costumed re-enactors tie off a line aboard a replica of a sixteenth-century trading vessel. James Volo Photo.

of personal goods purchased by the master or his agent, kept for sale to the seamen and charged against their wages.[35]

The navies of the world eschewed uniforms for ratings prior to the middle of the nineteenth century. The American and French revolutionaries had no uniform dress for seamen, and these used their own clothes, which sported many regional variations and personal preferences. The mid-nineteenth-century sailor was expected to maintain a uniform that was charged against his wages. This usually took the form of work clothes and dress clothes. In the American navy, sailors wore dark blue at sea. In port they wore white, sometimes even while working.[36]

Yet mariners tended toward certain characteristic items that identified them as seamen. Sailors favored long loose trousers, either white or striped. A coatee with short tails was replaced with time by a short practical jacket without tails, usually dark blue. These were worn with a waistcoat and a white, checked, or striped shirt. Black leather shoes were worn ashore and when going aloft. Round hats were popular. They could be made of felt, straw, or canvass, and they were often tarred or painted to make them waterproof and give them body. A low crowned hat with a narrow brim (much like a civilian top hat) was common in Admiral Nelson's navy. It probably was first created from a tricorn hat with the brim trimmed. The pirate-like bandanna topped with a tricorn hat was less common than Hollywood movies would lead one to suppose and would not have been tolerated in either the merchant or naval service.[37]

When working, sailors often resorted to woolen caps or stocking caps. Petticoat-breeches of white or natural linen, with skirtlike wide legs to midcalf, were worn without stockings or shoes for dirty work. This garment, an ancient one sometimes called a pair of slops, continued to be worn until 1820 and was used over better clothes with a canvass apron for protection.

Woolen pea-jackets and frocks were worn in cold weather, and jackets and pullover frocks of cotton or linen duck were worn in the heat. In tropical climates, sailors might be found barefoot in shirts and slops. Linen canvass coats impregnated with boiled linseed oil were used as slickers (raincoats) in foul weather, but these were used more to keep out the wind than the cold as a sailor's clothing was almost always wet. There were few places in a ship where clothing would dry once wetted.

Officer's Clothing   The connotation of rank through clothing was based on the cut and style as well as the number and arrangement of buttons and braiding in the American and most European services. In the merchant service, officers rated a better set of clothing than seamen, but this varied with the personal preferences and pocketbooks of the individual. The clothing of many merchant officers was chosen to imitate that of naval officers. There was no standard, but it can be assumed that masters and mates dressed better than seamen. Idlers probably had one set of shore clothing and another set of work clothes characteristic of their fellow tradesmen. Petty officers dressed as ordinary seamen.

Naval clothing for officers was dictated by the regulations of the Admiralty, and they changed slowly with time. As they were made by tailors rather than issued by the navy, even uniforms sometimes lacked uniformity. At the beginning of the nineteenth century, the British Admiralty had the most comprehensive clothing regulations of any European service. These included dress and undress uniforms. The small-clothes—waistcoat (vest), shirt, stockings, and breeches—for all officers were white, as was the lining of all officers' coats. Three buttons appeared on the cuffs and pockets of uniforms that had them.[38]

Epaulets were introduced in the regulations of 1795 on the dress uniforms only, to be worn on both shoulders for senior captains and on the right shoulder only for junior captains. No epaulets were worn by officers below the rank of captain. There is evidence that epaulets were worn unofficially as early as 1783. The adoption of the epaulet may have been forced on the Royal Navy as other nations generally acknowledged them as a symbol of authority. They were not universally popular with British officers, who regarded them as a "French Ornament."[39]

The uniforms of French officers resembled those of the army. Blue was the predominant color for coats and coatees. Blues breeches and boots were worn at almost all levels of command in undress. White small-clothes, white breeches, stockings, and buckled shoes were worn in dress. French uniform coats were lined in red. The American navy of the period followed the British in most areas with minor changes in the details of color or devices on buttons. The American Continental Congress initially ordered that the small-clothes and linings be red, but these were changed to white mostly through the badgering of the Naval Committee by John Paul Jones.[40]

Warrant officers in the Royal Navy wore a plain blue single-breasted coat with a falling collar and nine buttons. Pursers, surgeons, and masters wore the same uniform with minor modifications to the devices depicted on the buttons. The surgeon was allowed an officer's plain sword.

The Midshipman's undress uniforms were not regulated but were typically modeled on an officer's plain blue coat worn with gray breeches and white small-clothes. The dress uniform was a single-breasted blue coat with a stand-up collar, blue cuffs, and no lapels. The collar had a white patch with one button at its back edge. The coat had nine evenly spaced buttons. Midshipmen were allowed a dirk rather than a full-length sword. Master's mates had coats similar to these except the coat had pocket flaps. The pocket and front edge of the coat had white piping applied.

The Post-captain's undress uniform was a double-breasted blue coat. The coat had nine buttons a side, arranged evenly for captains of three year's post and in three's for junior captains. The lapels had no lace. The collar was folded over. The pocket flaps and cuffs were blue. The dress uniform was similar but had minor differences, including a blue standing collar, white lapels with gold lace and nine buttons per side evenly spaced, white cuffs, two lines of lace around the cuffs, and pocket flaps for senior captains—one for juniors.

The lieutenant's undress uniform was a double-breasted blue coat, lined in blue and worn buttoned across. It had a standing collar and nine buttons. The pocket, cuffs, lapels, and collar were blue piped in white. The dress uniform was as the captain's but without the lace trim.

The Admiral's undress uniform was a blue double-breasted coat. The cuffs and pocket flaps were blue and had three buttons and loops. The coat had no lace, but nine buttons were arranged evenly for admirals, in threes for vice-admirals, and ten in pairs for rear admirals. No epaulets were worn in undress. Full dress uniforms were based on a single-breasted blue coat closed with hooks and eyes. The stand-up collar was blue with gold trim. The lapels showed a good deal of gold trim with nine buttons and loops evenly spaced on each side of the breast. The cuffs were white with lace bands: one for rear admirals, two for vice-admirals, and three for admirals. Epaulets with pips denoting admiralty were worn on both shoulders.

Tricorn hats for officers were replaced with bicorns hats worn "fore and aft" about 1800. Hats usually sported a large cockade. Buckled shoes were worn with all uniforms. Lieutenants favored Hessian boots when on duty. All officers above midshipman were allowed swords. Light "small swords" were carried on formal occasions, while fighting swords were used at sea. A regulation sword was not established before 1805. Thereafter, its use does not seem to have been strictly enforced. The quality of the buckles and swords was largely a matter of the officer's purse. It was important for officers of lower grades to take care not to offend their superiors by appearing overly ostentatious.[41]

NOTES

1. Richard Henry Dana, Jr. *The Seaman's Friend: A Treatise on Practical Seamanship* (1879; reprint, Mineola, NY: Dover, 1997), 160.

2. Ibid., 131–132.

3. Ibid., 137–138.

4. Ibid., 146–153.

5. Ibid., 154–158.

6. Ibid., 169.

7. Ibid., 158–163.

8. N.A.M. Rodger, *The Wooden World: An Anatomy of the Georgian Navy* (New York: W. W. Norton, 1996) 27.

9. Samuel W. Bryant, *The Sea and the Stars: A Maritime History of the American People* (New York: Thomas Y. Crawell, 1967), 242.

10. Rodger, 40.

11. Dana, 164.

12. Ibid., 166.

13. Ibid., 166–167.

14. Joan Druett, *Hen Frigates: Wives of Merchant Captains under Sail* (New York: Simon and Schuster, 1998), 138.

15. The last Lord High Admiral was Prince George of Denmark (1709).

16. Nicholas Blake and Richard Lawrence, *The Illustrated Companion to Nelson's Navy* (Mechanicsburg, PA: Stackpole, 2000), 8–14.

17. John Laffin, *Jack Tars: The Story of the British Sailor* (London: Cassel, 1969), 131.

18. Philip Haythornthwaite, *Nelson's Navy* (London: Osprey Books, 1993), 7.

19. Bryant, 242–243.

20. Rodger, 113.

21. Bryant, 242–243.

22. Haythornthwaite, 7.

23. *The Practical Sea-Gunner's Companion: An Introduction to the Art of Gunnery; by William Mountaine, Teacher of the Mathematics*, London, 1747. Quoted in Bertram Lippincott, *Indians, Privateers, and High Society* (New York: J. B. Lippincott Co., 1961), 200.

24. Rodger, 122.

25. Quoted in Ibid., 163.

26. Bryant, 242–243.

27. Rodger, 121–122.

28. Charles Nordhoff, *Sailor Life on Man-of-War and Merchant Vessels* (New York: Dodd, Mead, & Co., 1884), 202.

29. Rodger, 129.

30. Ibid., 164

31. Haythornthwaite, 9–10. Rodger notes that "the Admiralty had to reprove officers for accepting 'volunteers' and paying them bounty after they had been pressed." (See Rodger, 163).

32. Rodger, 137.

33. Receiving ships were located in Gravesend, Great Yarmouth, Leith, Greenock, Liverpool, and Bristol. They were also found in Ireland, Malta, Bombay, and Jamaica. For a wider discussion of impressment, see Rodger, 163–182; Bryant, 148–151; and Laffin, 34–46.

34. Rodger, 137.

35. Alan Villiers, *Men, Ships, and the Sea* (Washington, DC: National Geographic, 1973), 184.

36. Nordhoff, 35–37.

37. For those interested in the minutiae of naval clothing, the authors suggest the series of military books published by Osprey Books of London, England. See Philip Haythornthwaite, *Nelson's Navy*, and Rene Chartrand and Francis Back, *Napoleon's Sea Soldiers* (London: Osprey Books, 1990).

38. Breeches had been dark blue prior to 1774. Thereafter, they were white.

39. Haythornthwaite, 18–19.

40. Nathan Miller, *Sea of Glory: A Naval History of the American Revolution* (Annapolis, MD: Naval Institute Press, 1974), 373–374.

41. Haythornwaite, 22–23.

6

Shipboard Environment

The man-of-war's man, on going below, finds a wet and sloppy deck,
up and down which he must puddle, the weary hours of his watch
below.

—Charles Nordhoff, 1884

The living environment aboard any ship alternated
between cold and damp or hot and humid. Merchant   **Accommodations**
seamen's quarters were generally confined to the fore-
castle, since the rest of the vessel carried valuable cargo. Ratings slept
and ate on the gundecks where the gunports could be opened to ventilate
the area. The orlop and hold had no direct ventilation. All ships were
regularly fumigated by burning sulfur, and the below decks were periodically washed down with vinegar. This added to the smell of wet
canvass, tar, stagnant sea water, and rotting wood. Life was made even
less tolerable by the constant motion of a vessel either wallowing in
ocean swells or plunging through rough seas.[1]

The conditions under which naval personnel lived varied both with
rank and type of ship. Admirals and captains always fared best, and
small vessels obviously offered far fewer places in which cabins and
berths could be provided than large ones. In the case of a 74-gun ship,
the captain had a day cabin under the poop deck that opened onto the
stern gallery and had two quarter galleries, one of which was fitted as
a lavatory. Forward of this was the captain's sleeping cabin and a dining

Often the only light in the captain's sleeping quarters was provided by a small porthole. James Volo Photo.

cabin known as the coach. Moving forward along the quarter deck were cabins for the captain's clerk and for the master. The commissioned officers slept in cabins off the wardroom, which was in the space on the main-deck under the day cabin. These cabins were very small with room for only a sea chest and a cot or a hammock. The surgeon and the purser usually berthed on the orlop deck. The other inferior officers berthed on the main-deck in cabins under the forecastle.

In merchantmen, the crew were usually crowded into the forecastle or found space on the open well-deck on which to curl up in a blanket. In warships, even small ones, the crew had the dubious luxury of berthing in the between decks encumbered only by the guns. "[T]he man-of-war's man, on going below, finds a wet and sloppy deck, up and down which he must puddle, the weary hours of his watch below."[2]

Ratings commonly hung their hammocks among the guns while sleeping. Each man was given a hammock number, which he found "among the tinned numbers nailed above the hooks, in the beams and ceiling of the two lower decks." No more than 14 inches of space was allotted to each man. Few ordinary seamen had individual sea chests, but the men of a mess might share one. Each mess of six to eight men ate from a common pot at a table suspended from the rafters in the space between the guns, if they were below deck, or on a square of oil cloth if they were allowed on deck. They usually sat on their sea chests or paid the

The forecastle of a merchant vessel was cramped, wet, and cold, but it was more comfortable than the accommodations on a man-of-war. James Volo Photo.

carpenter to build a pair of benches on which to sit at the table. When cleared for action the table, benches, and chests were displaced, and the meager belongings of the men, held in ditty bags on the bulwark, were wrapped in their hammocks and stowed in the orlop or the hold. On frigates, with less space in the hold, the hammocks were often rolled and placed in the hammock nettings along the railing of the ship. These were some of the activities required when clearing for action.[3]

The wardroom was fitted with two lavatories for the officers in the quarter galleries. Forward of the forecastle on a platform over the bowsprit were the crew's lavatories called the head. There were also two semicircular roundhouses that served as lavatories for the warrant officers and, sometimes, the petty officers. All the lavatories aboard were simple holes cut in plank seats that discharged directly into the sea. Those facilities in the quarter galleries, being like a small closet, offered some privacy, but the lavatories in the fore of the ship were largely open to the wind, weather, and sea spray.

When fitting a ship for sea the captain, or master, was continually engaged in one business matter or another. A good officer **Food** was familiar with all these tasks, and he tried to remain on good terms with the dockyard officials. One of the most important tasks was the purchase and storage of provisions for his crew for an extended voyage. The basic requirement was for food and beverage that would not spoil or otherwise lose its nutritive value, yet provide sufficient calories and a balance of vitamins.

A mess consisted of six to eight men. Charles Nordhoff lends a seaman's view to the details of dining at sea. "[A]t eight bells the crew were piped to breakfast. I speedily hunted up my mess, and found them already assembled about the mess cloth, spread down on the main-deck. The mess cook had gotten us our allowance of coffee, which, with biscuit and salt pork, constituted our breakfast." The mess cook actually did no cooking, but he did receive the uncooked provisions, delivered them to the ship's cook, and retrieved them for his mess-mates.[4]

The staple food for seamen throughout the western hemisphere was sea biscuit, or ship's bread, which was notorious for being virtually indestructible and resembled neither biscuit nor bread. Made with flour, a little salt, and just enough water to make a stiff dough, sea biscuit was baked into a 4 × 4-inch rock-solid square about a half-inch thick. Sailors had to soak it to make it edible or nibble it about the edges. When the biscuit was poor, it was either too hard or moldy and wet. It was noted for being filled with weevils and maggots. These creatures could be evicted by toasting the cracker or breaking it up into a mug of liquid and skimming off the pests. Sea biscuit provided a good quality ration when combined with other foods, and a man could exist on as few as three crackers a day.

When exiting a port, a ship might carry out "a supply of fresh beef and vegetables, sufficient to last the crew for two days, after which sea rations were again served out. The common sea ration of the period consisted of one and a half pounds of biscuit per day (eight to ten crackers), one pint of beans three times a week, three-fourths of a pound of rice twice a week, one-fourth of a pound each of butter and cheese (if available), a gill each of molasses and vinegar twice a week, a daily allowance of either coffee, tea, or cocoa, one and a half pounds of beef four times a week, one and one-fourth pounds of pork three times a week, and a half gill of grog twice a day at breakfast and dinner." With few exceptions, European navies maintained a dietary regimen similar to this throughout the period.[5]

The provisions required for an extended voyage can be exemplified by those needed to prepare the *Bounty* for a solo eighteen-month voyage to the Pacific. *Bounty* was a ship-rigged, lightly armed transport of 230 tons. The captain, Lieutenant William Bligh, thought the ship was over sparred and too small for its crew of forty-six men. The foodstuffs consisted largely of sea biscuit. Also brought aboard were casks of salt pork and salt beef, dried peas, malt, barley, wheat, oatmeal, sauerkraut, rum, beer, wine, and water. Finally, some fancy foodstuffs were taken aboard for the officers. The carpenters built several small cages for livestock such as a dozen chickens, a few pigs, and a half dozen sheep. Hard cheeses

The ship's cook tends the galley fire on board a replica of a sixteenth-century trading vessel. The fuel used aboard such vessels was usually charcoal. James Volo Photo.

were brought aboard. Provisions were replaced at stops made during the voyage.

A contemporary American seaman noted, "Each individual on board ship, from the commodore to the messenger boy, is allowed one ration per day, valued at six dollars per month. In this matter no difference is made by rank, the only distinction being that the officers are allowed to stop their rations, and take the value in money instead, with which, and funds contributed from their private purses, they supply their larder." The seamen could buy fruits, vegetables, and other foodstuffs from the bumboats in port. However, they were "obliged to take the provision furnished by the government" and were expected to keep themselves alive on a daily diet of salt meat, biscuit, grog (rum and water), beer, and wine.[6]

Water
Fresh water was essential aboard ship, but it was all but un-
drinkable under normal circumstances. Beer and grog were considered more healthful, and wine was thought the best drink for
maintaining the health of the crew in the tropics. The daily allowance of
water was left to the discretion of the captain, but the custom was to
allow a gallon per man per day. Every officer received a gallon for his
own use, and an additional pint for washing was drawn by the steward
for each officer. The men received three pints directly (minus that used
in the grog), and a pint for cooking was drawn by the cook for each man
in a mess. The sick were allotted a small additional amount during their
illnesses, and the livestock were given enough to keep them alive. An
account of the use of water was carefully kept in the log even to the
point that the amount boiled off in heating was recorded.[7]

Bounty took on 42 tons of drinking water in its tanks for the first leg
of its journey from England to the Canary Islands. Although there was
no shortage of water, like any good captain Bligh ordered awnings to be
spread to catch the rain, and he filled many hogsheads with fresh water
rather than mixing it with the stagnant water in the ship's tanks. A 42-
gun frigate with a crew of almost 200 was recorded to have taken aboard
102 tons of water that with careful and disciplined husbanding lasted
almost twelve weeks.

Mariner Charles Nordhoff described the task of taking on water in a
foreign port. "For several successive days, the larger boats were now
employed in bringing off water and some few provisions. The water was
brought in large casks, which were towed ashore empty, but tightly
bunged [closed], then rolled up to the watering place, filled, rolled down
to the water's edge, and fastened together in the form of a raft, for the
convenience of towing. The watering parties, which consisted of the
crews of the launch and the first cutter, were the only ones of the ship's
company who got their feet on dry land."[8]

Scurvy
The need to provide foodstuffs that would keep for long periods of time in an age without refrigeration caused a great deal
of the food given to seamen to be dried or salted. An undiffer-
entiated diet of such foodstuffs ultimately led to serious physical difficulties. The most prevalent of the diseases found among seamen was
scurvy. So common was the outbreak of scurvy on long voyages that
many thought the disease to be confined to ships at sea. "The sea was
regarded as an alien, hostile, unnatural and unhealthy element for man,
and those who took to it for gain must perforce risk paying the price."
The disease was thought to originate from the exposure to highly salted
provisions and bad water. In fact, the main cause of scurvy was a defi-
ciency of vitamin C, which could be made up by adding fresh vegetables
and fruits to the diet.[9]

Scurvy was a terribly disabling affliction. If unremediated it could, and did, cause death. William Hutchinson experienced the ravages of the disease in 1739 and lived to write about it in great detail only because his ship reached a port where fresh provisions could be bought in time. Hutchinson's account reflects many of the common misconceptions surrounding the cause of the disease, but his description of the symptoms of scurvy are some of the most graphic recorded in the eighteenth century.

[A]fter being about four months in our passage from the Downs, after eating a hearty breakfast of salt beef, I found myself taken with a pain under my left breast, where I had formerly received a dangerous blow. From this time the sea scurvy increased upon me, as it had done upon many others, a good while before me; and I observed that they soon took to their hammocks below, and became black in their armpits and hams, their limbs being stiff and swelled, with red specks, and soon died. . . . I thus struggled with the disease 'till it increased so that my armpits and hams grew black but did not swell, and I pined away to a weak, helpless condition, with my teeth all loose, and my upper and lower gums swelled and clotted together like a jelly, and they bled to that degree, that I was obliged to lie with my mouth hanging over the side of my hammock, to let the blood run out, and to keep it from clotting so as to [choke] me. . . . [W]ith fresh provisions and fomentations of herbs I got well, and returned on board in eighteen days.[10]

A dried portable soup, regarded at the time as an acceptable substitute for fresh vegetables and fruit, was carried in an attempt to prevent scurvy. In May 1744, Commodore Curtis Barnet led a squadron of four ships from England to the East Indies. In August, as the ships neared the Cape of Good Hope, he wrote a letter describing this mash used to balance the diet of the crew. "I took upon me to order [a pint of] pease to be boiled on Mondays for dinner, and the quart of wheat allowed for Wednesday, to make three dressings, so the men have it for breakfast on Mondays, as well as Wednesday and Fridays, and that issued, each man has a full quart each day, which they eat all up with their sugar."[11]

James Lind experimented with a dozen scurvy victims by giving pairs of men different remedies in an attempt to discover a cure in 1747. He reported his findings to the Admiralty in 1753.

The most sudden and good effects were perceived from the use of the oranges and lemons; one of those who had taken them being at the end of six days fit for duty. The spots were not indeed quite off his body, nor his gums sound; but without any other medicine than a gargarism or elixir of vitriol he became quite healthy. . . . The other [man given oranges and lemons] was the best recovered of any in his condition. . . . Oranges and lemons were the most effectual remedies for this distemper at sea.[12]

Based in part on these discoveries, the Admiralty began to issue bushels of malt in hogsheads, portable soup, and some lemons to vessels proceeding on long voyages. In 1768, Captain James Cook made a report of the efficacy of these remedies.

The ship's company had in general been very healthy owing in great measure to sour krout [*sic*], portable soup and malt. . . . By this means, and the care and vigilance of . . . the surgeon, this disease was prevented from getting a footing in the ship. . . . Portable soup and sour krout were at first condemned by them [the crew] as stuff not fit for human beings to eat.[13]

Dr. William Stone noted in the mid-nineteenth century, "The owners and masters of vessels employed in the United States whale fishery say that, as scurvy never occurs when they have a supply of sound potatoes, they therefore take great pains to obtain and keep a quantity when it is practicable. They pack them in seasoned new oil-casks, also put some in casks in cider vinegar."[14]

In 1775, Admiral Samuel Graves noted that "the seamen always continue healthy and active when drinking spruce beer; but in a few days after New England Rum is served . . . the hospital is crowded with sick."[15] Dr. Stone noted, "In the French and Russian mercantile navies scurvy seldom occurs, owing probably to the general use of the common acidulated wine of France as a drink for seamen."[16]

The efforts made by mariners to solve the problem of scurvy should not be minimized. The true cause of the disease was unknown at the time, and the sciences of nutrition and medicine, as we know them, were in their most formative stages. Using a method of trial and error, seamen found a series of remedies with a wide spectrum of efficacy that prevented scurvy. Only those high in vitamin C—a nutrient that was unknown at the time—could produce a cure. Fresh vegetables, potatoes, oranges, lemons, vinegar (in the sauerkraut), mashes made from grains, fruit wines, and small beers made from the young buds of spruce trees provided this essential vitamin. With time, lemon juice, and the more palatable lime juice, became the focus of those whose responsibility was maintaining the health of crews at sea.

Naval Pay   There was always a good deal of discontent on the lower decks in connection with pay. In the navy, pay was given at a rate determined by the qualities and duties of the individual and by the conditions under which the service was rendered. With regard to the navies of Europe, the pay of the English navy—for which the evidence is probably the best documented—can serve as an example.

In 1545, the rates of pay for the sailors manning the ships of Henry VIII were 1 s. (shilling) a week in harbor and 1 s. 3 d. (pence) when on active service. By the time of the Armada (1588), Elizabeth I had raised the pay to 10 s. a month and had provided for prize money to be distributed among the crew of victorious vessels. Nonetheless, Admiral Sir John Hawkins was honest enough to admit that the men still suffered at the hands of rapacious captains and agents who withheld their wages and their prize money to the point of driving then to mutiny. By 1620, under James Stuart, the basic wage was 14 s. a month, and in 1631, Charles I raised the rate by 1 s.

Notwithstanding the increase in wages, the men remained diseased, hungry, and apathetic under the Stuart kings. "Without better order his Majesty will lose the honor of his seas, the love and loyalty of his sailors, and his Royal Navy will drop," wrote Sir Henry Mervin, a contemporary observer. "Foul weather, naked bodies and empty bellies make men voice the King's service worse than galley slaves." Another officer wrote, "The men stink as they go, and the poor rags they have are rotten and ready to fall off." In the Civil War of 1642 many seamen, unpaid for years, jumped to the side of Parliament when it offered 19 s. a month and paid it punctually. Able seamen—as distinct from ordinary seamen—were given a premium wage of 22 s. 6 d. However, after the Restoration, both pay and the general conditions of service at sea returned to the shameful status they had once had.[17]

At the end of the seventeenth century, an English merchant seamen could expect an average wage of 50 s. a month, whereas the naval wage had risen to as little as 24 s. In 1697, Daniel Defoe described this dichotomy. "[O]ur seamen lurk and hide and hang back in time of war . . . for who would serve king and country and fight and be knocked on the head at 24 s. a month, that can have 50 s. without that hazard?" Nonetheless, the variance in wages continued for centuries. Although the practice of paying enlistment bounties was established in 1660 during the reign of Charles II, in the next hundred years, to the accession of George III in 1760, the naval pay schedule remained totally unaltered.[18]

The government continued to rely on legal prerogative and physical force in the form of the impressment to underpay the naval seamen. Not only did they receive much less than they would have as merchant sailors (by 1790, merchant seamen could earn 85 s. while the naval seamen still got only 24 s. monthly), but all other forms of compensation including working conditions, clothing, and food were dealt with in a haphazard manner. The conditions under which they served were largely based on the good will of the ship's officers. Some naval personnel were treated as little more than slaves.[19] One able seaman, who served with Admiral Nelson at the battle of Trafalgar, and suffered at the hands of a diabolical thirteen-year-old midshipman, wrote in his memoirs that there was a "danger of giving too much power into the hands of a young officer. . . . His conduct made every man's life miserable that chanced to be under his orders. . . . His death was hailed [by the crew] as the triumph over an enemy."[20]

In 1758, Lord George Grenville introduced, and had passed, legislation with a rather wordy, but remarkably cutting title: *An Act for the Encouragement of Seamen employed in the Royal Navy and for establishing a regular method for the punctual, frequent and certain payment of their wages; and for enabling them more easily to remit the same for the support of their wives and families and preventing frauds and abuses attending such payment.* The title alone stands as evidence of the obstacles faced by naval seamen in the arena of just compensation. Unfortunately, although many discrepancies were addressed, it can be shown that the Spithead and Noire mutinies of 1797 were caused largely because of a bitterness due to continuing irregularities in pay. With no change in pay rate for a century and a half, the seamen asked for a raise of 30 s. per month. They received 4 s. 6 d. instead. In 1806, a further 4 s. 6 d. was allowed. Finally in 1853, the annual rate for an able seamen was fixed at £28 (pounds) 17 s. 1 d. (about 48 s. per month). Seamen gunners, divers, and carpenters were all encouraged by special allowances, and the ordinary sailor could receive an extra pence a day for good conduct.[21]

Prize, not pay, was the great incentive for the naval life, but prize money was a matter of chance. An unlucky captain, an old and worn warship, or a determined foe could all deny a sailor prize money for his entire term of service. Nonetheless, it was a powerful inducement, and naval recruiters made a great deal of it. A man could be made richer in an hour of battle than he could ever hope to be after a lifetime of labor ashore. One officer was said to have earned the equivalent of 300 years pay from his share of a single prize. The largest amount paid to a seaman was £850 in 1745 from the capture of two vessels from which more than forty-five wagons of treasure were taken. Moreover, for a long period "head money" was paid the victors with a discrete sum being applied for every member of the crew of an enemy vessel that was sunk. Hunting pirates and slavers could also bring cash rewards. After 1808, when the slave trade was banned by both England and the United States, each slave rescued brought £10 of additional prize to the crew of the patrolling vessel to be shared by the crew. However, much of this was siphoned off to agents, informers, colonial officials, and, of course, the officers and station commanders who received the lion's share in any case.[22]

A routine was established, which remained virtually unaltered thereafter, by which actual money was handed over to the sailor. A white chalk line was marked on the deck and each man "toed the line," gave his full name and a list of his duties to the paying officer, and placed his cap on the pay table. The money was laid on the cap. William Robinson of Admiral Nelson's command noted, "There is not perhaps one in twenty who actually knows what he is going to receive, nor does the particular amount seem to be a matter of much concern; for, when paid, they hurry down to their respective berths [and] redeem their honour with their several ladies and bum-boat men."[23] In 1854, Parliament, under pressure from the war in the Crimea, formalized the entire system with passage of the Naval Pay and Prize Act. No further changes were made in the pay of English seamen until after the first World War.[24]

American merchant shipping ruled the seas in the golden age of the early nineteenth century. Although the early colonials looked to the sea as a tether ensuring succor from their homelands in Europe, later generations thought of the ocean as a great wet moat whose chief virtue was to separate the United States from the rest of the world. Once fear of the wilderness was overcome by a growing familiarity with it, most young men found that frontierism quickly displaced any adventurous or romantic obsession with the sea. For most Americans, life ashore was measurably better than anywhere else in the world even on the edge of the wilderness. When gold was discovered in California in 1848, it was almost impossible to keep a majority of the crew from deserting any vessel that landed on the west coast of America. It was, therefore, generally difficult to find American crews for American vessels anywhere except along the eastern margins of the continent. Although American seamen remained well disposed to the domestic coasting trade, many ocean-going American ships sailed with crews among whom the majority were foreigners.

Paying the Merchant Marine

In the U.S. Navy, able seamen were paid $12 per month, ordinary seamen $10, and green hands between $4 and $8 depending on their age and size. In the merchant service, the wages were about the same on long voyages, but on voyages to Europe, the West Indies, or the American South, they were considerably higher. Still, added to bad food, long wet hours, incivility from the officers, corporal punishments, and the innate dangers of life at sea, the pay offered merchant sailors was incredibly low. Even the British pay scale as higher. Able seamen signing aboard American vessels on the better runs could expect about $18 per month, ordinary seamen $12, and boys as little as $8 in the mid nineteenth century. This was considerably less than the wages earned by a simple store clerk ashore.[25]

Inevitably a few lads, attracted by the adventure and romance, went to sea, but such thoughts were quickly dispelled by the discomforts and perils. Few attempts were made to train apprentice sailors on board, and the available American sailors moved from ship to ship with little remorse if a better offer was presented. Captain Samuel Samuels was one of these. With regard to pay, he has left an interesting record in his journal. As a boy Samuels' first berth was on a coasting vessel, which paid fifty cents for three days work. He later signed for $80 on a run to Liverpool, England, on an American vessel and for 30 s. per month serving as a cook on an English ship going from Liverpool to Galveston, Texas. Ultimately, he signed on a Texas slaver for a two-year voyage at $10 a month. Over and over again, Samuels switched ships, sometimes deserting after only half a voyage. "The sailor's roving disposition costs him dear," wrote Samuels. "I have known men to quit first-rate ships, leaving behind money due them and a good chest of clothes, for the sake of having a short spree . . . [knowing] they would be picked up and shipped off without a cent in their pockets."[26]

Many sailors preferred to ship out on shares rather than work for wages. This was most common aboard fishing and whaling vessels where the profits from the catch would be divided among the officers and men according to an agreement made before the voyage. The lion's share of the profit was usually reserved for the ship owners and investors as they were risking the loss of the entire venture should some evil fate overcome the vessel. The division of the remainder generally followed a scale that depended on both a man's responsibilities and special abilities, or lack thereof. The whole system gave the crew a feeling of ownership in the voyage and ensured their greatest efforts and good behavior. In any case, American law required "an agreement in writing, or in print, with every seaman on board the ship declaring the voyage, and term or terms of time, for which such seaman in hired."[27]

There was no standard scale, and each man could argue for as big a share as he thought he could get before signing on. The process led to a good deal of both bragging and self-appraisal as work at sea quickly unmasked the braggart from the capable seamen. In haggling over these agreements, a knowledge of fractions was essential. The captain might get 1/18th, the first mate 1/27th, the second mate 1/36th, an able seamen 1/50th, and an ordinary seamen 1/75th. Green hands, uneducated or under-educated and new to the process, were known to argue for 1/200th when offered 1/100th. Of course the fractions always needed to add up to a whole of the profits, and some unscrupulous captains signed on men promising generous shares that represented more than the whole hoping that the crew would not know the difference. Cooks and other "idlers" might be on shares or wages, which would be deducted from the profits before the shares were made. If there were no profits, no one got anything, but it was rare that a skipper returned to port with nothing to show for his voyage except in the most dire emergencies.[28]

Punishment   The master of a merchant vessel, or the captain in the naval service, could inflict punishment on a seaman for "sufficient cause," but the correction could not be disproportionate to the offense. "There must not be any cruelty or unnecessary severity exercised." The master's judgment in these cases was commonly accepted, but it needed to be "exercised with due regard to the rights and interests of all parties."[29]

Officers could not be punished because their position protected them. They could only be removed from duty or confined to their cabins until a court of inquiry or court martial could be convened. Of course, an indignant but imaginative captain could find a number of ways for an unrepentant officer to be chastised without violating the regulations. These included service in the masthead for junior officers, standing watch and watch for more senior men, or assignment to other disagreeable duties.

In the merchant service, there was no law or regulation that defined the mode or instruments of punishment, but the master was enjoined to behave in a temperate and decent manner in all cases. The mode of correction might be "by personal chastisement, or by confinement on board ship, in irons, or otherwise." The master could not withhold food and drink, beat, or wound a seamen. In cases of mutiny, "weapons must be used which would be unlawful at other times; but even in these cases, they must be used with the caution which the law requires in other cases of self-defense and vindication of rightful authority . . . and never to gratify personal feelings." Flogging and other criminal punishments in the merchant service, once common, became almost nonexistent in the nineteenth century due to legislation in many countries making the master answerable for what he did and what he permitted to be done aboard his ship.[30]

Most navies had regulations regarding punishment that were commonly referred to as the Articles of War. The Articles of War actually placed the naval captain on a more firm footing with regard to discipline and punishment than the merchant master. The British articles were first embodied in 1731 in the Regulations and Instructions Relating to His Majesty's Service at Sea and later in the Navy Discipline Act of 1749. These were revised in 1780 into thirty-six Articles of War. They applied in war or peace, and the breech of them brought specific punishments or discipline. Nineteen of the articles carried the death penalty. "All other crimes not capital, committed by any person or persons in the fleet . . . shall be punished according to the laws and customs in such cases used at sea."[31]

Charles Nordhoff admitted that the definition of capital crimes could be quite broad. A seamen's complaints, even if justified, needed to be couched in the most careful of terms because crimes such as "mutinous assembly" and "sedition" were largely open to the determination of the ship's officers. "A man-of-war is not the place for too free an expression of opinion. The regulations of the service do not admit of freedom of speech. They contain such a word as *mutiny*, for which they provide 'Death, or such other punishment as a court martial shall provide.' "[32]

A naval captain had wide discretion in inflicting punishment. He could admonish the offender, stop his grog, water his grog, disrate him, put him to work at the pumps (a physically challenging labor), cause him to run the gauntlet, keel-haul him, or flog him. By 1790, running the gauntlet and keel-hauling—dragging the bound man underwater along the length or width of the vessel—had fallen into disuse, but flogging remained a favorite corporal punishment into the nineteenth century.

Until 1806, the British Admiralty allowed any number of lashes to be administered. Thereafter, only twelve lashes for an offense were permitted, but a particularly cruel officer could side-step this regulation by making multiple charges against the offender. Flogging around the fleet—a flogging at each ship in the fleet at the time of punishment—could bring up to 1,000 lashes. Several men were known to have survived this punishment as it was not meant to be a death sentence.

So that the embarrassment to the offender and the deterrent effect on his shipmates were not lost by a lack of showmanship, all hands not needed to operate the vessel were summoned to "witness punishment." Under the supervision of the surgeon, who could stop the ceremony on medical grounds, the offender was stripped to the waist, tied to a grating or the capstan, and administered the lashes by the boatswain or his mates. The instrument used was known as the "cat-o'-nine-tails," a lash with nine thin pieces of line, each with a knot in its length. The "cat" not only raised welts but cut and permanently scarred the skin. It was said that the "cat" was kept in a red baize bag to hide the blood that it drew.[33]

In America, flogging was allowed in the navy until 1850 and in the army until 1864. Charles Nordhoff wrote in 1884,

I fancy that those editors and legislators who sit in their cozy arm-chairs, in office or congressional hall, and talk wisely about the necessity of flogging for sailors, need only once to witness the infliction of the punishment they think so needful . . . to alter their convictions as to the expediency of flogging. . . . Thank God, the counsels of mercy have prevailed and the American Navy is no longer disgraced by the lash.[34]

Courts of inquiry or courts martial were compulsory when a vessel was lost and were required for capital offenses, or when imprisonment or heavy flogging were imposed. Offenders were allowed to mount a defense and call witnesses, but, since the court was composed of officers, and seamen were reticent to be labeled as troublemakers, this was generally ineffective. Officers found guilty of an offense could be dismissed from service, broken in rank or seniority, or shot. Seamen found guilty of capital offenses were usually hanged from the fore yardarm of their ship, having been hauled up by their mess-mates from the cathead. This usually failed to break a man's neck causing him to languish for a long period kicking and struggling as he slowly strangled—"a terrible example to the surrounding spectators."[35]

NOTES

1. Richard Hough, *Captain Bligh and Mr. Christian: The Men and the Mutiny* (New York: E. P. Dutton, 1973), 87.

2. Charles Nordhoff, *Sailor Life on Man-of-War and Merchant Vessel* (New York: Dodd, Mead, & Co., 1884), 179.

3. Ibid., 57.

4. Ibid., 95–96, 164.

5. Ibid., 163–164.

6. Ibid., 163; Hough, 68–72.

7. Alexander D. Fordyce, *An Outline of Naval Routine* (London: Smith, Elder & Co., 1837), 106–107.

8. Nordhoff, 158.

9. Hough, 86.

10. William Hutchinson, *A Treatise on Naval Architecture* (Liverpool: T. Billinge, 1794), 286–289.

11. Extract of a letter by Curtis Barnet, May 1, 1744, *The Health of Commodore Barnet's Squadron*. Online: http://www.cronab.demon.co.uk/barn.htm.

12. James Lind, *A Treatise of the Scurvy in Three Parts* (London: A. Millar, 1753). Online: http://pc-78-120.udac.se:8001/WWW/Nautical/Medicine/Cook.html.

13. David MacBride, *Historical Account of a New Method of Treating the Scurvy at Sea, 1764*. Online: http://pc-78-120.udac.se:8001/WWW/Nautical/Medicine/Cook.html.

14. Robert W. Stevens, *On the Stowage of Ships and Their Cargoes* (London: Longmans, Green, Reader, and Dyer, 1869), vol. VII, 712.

15. Letter of Admiral Samuel Graves to Philip Stephens, Boston, September 22, 1775. Online: http://pc-78-120.udac.se:8001/WWW/Nautical/Medicine/Spruce_beer.html.

16. Stevens, 712.

17. John Laffin, *Jack Tars: The Storm of the British Sailor* (London: Cassell, 1969), 4–8.

18. Ibid., 66.

19. Ibid., 35–41.

20. William Robinson, *Nautical Economy: The Memoirs of William Robinson, An Able Seaman Who Served with Nelson at Trafalgar* (Warwick, UK: Cromwell, 1993), 27.

21. Laffin, 67–73.

22. Ibid., 70–73.

23. Robinson, 53.

24. Laffin, 68.

25. Samuel Samuels, *From the Forecastle to the Cabin* (New York: Harper and Brothers, 1887), 2.

26. Ibid., 23, 32, 72.

27. Richard Henry Dana, Jr. *The Seaman's Friend: Containing a Treatise on Practical Seamanship* (1879; reprint, Mineola, NY: Dover, 1997), 203.

28. Samuel W. Bryant, *The Sea and the States: A Maritime History of the American People* (New York: Thomas Y. Crowell, Co., 1967), 225.

29. Dana, 192.

30. Ibid., 192–193.

31. Nicholas Blake and Richard Lawrence, *The Illustrated Companion to Nelson's Navy* (Mechanicsburg, PA: Stackpole, 2000), 114.

32. Nordhoff, 170.

33. Blake and Lawrence, 114–115.

34. Nordhoff, 169.

35. Blake and Lawrence, 114–115.

7

Pastimes

The sails were all furled and
The work was all done
                    —Sea chanty, "Leave Her, Johnny, Leave Her"

WORK

The work required of seamen was physically demanding. Hauling, pulling, furling, and setting were part of the daily routine of shipboard life.
Bad weather and rough seas kept the watch moving up and down the
rigging adjusting the sails and making repairs. Yet much of the sailor's
life was boring. "Day after day, [the] view continues the same. The ocean,
the clouds, the breeze, the very fish even that gambol about the bows,
seem to be the same, and one could easily fancy the vessel to be set here
in mid-ocean, like one of those little miniature ships which we see on old-
fashioned clocks, rolling and pitching all day, but making no headway."[1]
    A reading of the requirements demanded of ordinary and able seamen
attests to the labor required of them. Besides the obvious tasks involved
in sailing a vessel at sea, there was a good deal of work to be done on
a daily basis, especially in port. Mariner Charles Nordhoff offered an
insight into this aspect of the seamen's life aboard a ship in port during
a single morning.

As soon as the hammocks were stowed, the crew commenced holystoning the
decks. . . . Two parties were sent over the side on catamarans, with slush, sand,

and canvas, to scour the line of copper which appears just above the water's edge. . . . Others were seen suspended on the large copper funnel or smoke-pipe, which served to carry off clear all the smoke of the galley fires. . . . Others blacked stanchions, and cleaned guns and gun carriages.

Holystoning continued until . . . the sand was scrubbed and washed off, the decks swabbed dry, and carefully swept down, and then all the bright-work cleaned. . . . [W]e sideboys were busied scraping and scouring the side-ladder, reaching from a large grating at the water's edge to the upper deck. . . . The boats were [then] sent ashore in charge of officers, and on various errands. . . .

The holders were set to work preparing the water tanks, emptied on the passage out, for refilling. The fore and maintop men were busied clearing away the large boats which are carried amidships at sea, preparatory to their being hoisted out [to get water]. . . . The afternoon was set apart for getting up tackles with which to hoist [the casks of water] out [of] the launch and cutters. This being done, and the decks swept, we were at liberty to amuse ourselves in whatsoever way best suited each one's peculiar idiosyncrasy until supper-time. Then there was a shifting into blue clothing for the night and the morrow's washing decks, after which came quarters, sundown, and tattoo, as detailed of the preceding day.[2]

PASTIMES

The sailor needed diversion from the utter and seemingly interminable boredom which he faced at sea known as "idle time." The uncertainty of surviving severe weather, the adventure of the chase, and danger of the capture were high drama, indeed, but such excitement could be counted in hours on voyages that lasted three and four years. Monotony, homesickness, and tension were natural outgrowths of a situation where crews were forced into limited space for extended periods of time. Men welcomed activities that allowed them to focus on the work at hand, relieving the ennui and furnishing them with a detachment that acted as a surrogate for the privacy denied them in incredibly cramped quarters. With mental escape of more importance than the time that an activity consumed, substantial care and meticulous attention to detail were lavished upon the creation of many seemingly trivial craft items. Additionally, when the work was intended as a gift for a loved one, meticulous effort seemingly rekindled a connection and recreated an intimacy with those loved ones at home.

Scrimshaw Scrimshaw was practiced by many sailors both on merchant ships and naval vessels if the materials came to hand. But it proved a characteristic activity for all members of a whaling crew, including the ship's officers. In fact, captains and masters were among the creators of some of the most exquisite examples of scrimshaw, owing to the latitudes of time and space that their positions afforded. Because of its therapeutic value, the crew was often encouraged to engage in scrimshaw, and on some vessels, instruction was provided to novices. In his 1844 journal from the whaler *Charles Phelps*, Gurdon Hall made the following entries:

The Captain, officers, Boatsteerers and foremast hands Busily employed Sawing up Bone. . . . Almost all hands employed in getting our Busks, swifts fids, gimlet handles, canes and such like Scrimshonting [*sic*] to present to their friends with when we get home.[3]

Most New England households had numerous examples of both decorative and functional forms of scrimshaw. It has been said that every whaler's family had a whale tooth, or two, on the mantel. Surviving examples of whale teeth done in this manner have some of the most elaborate designs of any scrimshaw work. Only the sperm whale has teeth. Highly prized for its superior whale oil and ambergris, the sperm whale had a double row of thirty to forty teeth in its lower jaw. Each tapering tooth ranged from five to eight inches tall. Jawbones were often towed behind the ship for approximately one month before they were hauled on deck to lay in the sun until the teeth fell out. Once free, the teeth were stored in brine. If the crew was anxious to get the teeth, they extracted them with tackles or dug them out with saws and spades. Eliza Williams, who accompanied her husband, Captain Thomas Williams, on a whaling voyage, described the activity aboard ship following the capture of a whale. "The Men saved the jawbones—I suppose they intend to make something fancy from them when there is leisure. They save only the bone out of the head. It is white out of the sperm whale and black out of the other kind."[4]

Once whalemen began to probe the Bering Straits in the 1840s, walrus tusks were also ornamented. Most tusks were obtained in trade with the natives, although some were obtained through routine slaughter for meat by the whalers. In 1848, Mary Brewster, wife of the captain of the *Tiger*, wrote the following entry in her journal regarding trade with the natives in Alaskan waters. "They brought presents of their garments and walrus tusks for scrimshawing for which we paid them in tobacco."[5] The large size of the walrus tusk provided a superior surface upon which the scrimshander could lay out detailed designs. Some of the finest examples of scrimshaw were incised upon walrus tusks, including scenes of naval engagements, classical images of Greek mythology, and engravings of military heroes. American whalemen of the 1860s were particularly keen to depict Civil War battles and generals that they had not even seen.

Many scrimshaw practitioners developed their own tools. Men had little boxes filled with what Herman Melville called "dentistical-looking implements," fine-pointed tools that were self-fashioned from old chisels, filed down nails, or any pointed bit of steel. Files, awls, and gimlets were also employed to bore holes and to prepare the bone.[6] Sometimes the ship's cooper was sought out to make customized tools. The sailor's needles used for mending canvas proved most effective for pricking and inscribing the design. The most basic instrument by far was the jack-knife, for "in general, they toil with their jack-knives alone; and, with that almost omnipotent tool of the sailor, they will turn you out anything you please, in the way of a mariner's fancy."[7]

The creation of a scrimshaw object was often a painstaking process and well suited to the idle time at sea. In preparation for the design, the tooth or whalebone was scraped with a broad-bladed knife and smoothed with a file. Sharkskin sandpaper was then taken to it, and the material was buffed with ashes from the try-pots. It was then softened by soaking it in brine or warm, soapy water. Thus prepared, the design was outlined or scratched upon the relatively smooth surface. Some designs were born of the fertile imaginations of the artist. Others were copied from periodicals or books. The fashion plates of *Godey's Lady's Book* supplied many sailors with an inspiration. Anyone familiar with the celebrated prints from the period can recognize their adaptation from print to bone. *The Pirates Own Book* enjoyed numerous printings throughout the nineteenth century and seems to have been quite popular with the whaling crowd. An illustration from the book entitled *Alwilda, The Female Pirate* provided a popular motif for adorning many whales' teeth. When a paper illustration was to be reproduced, it would be pasted on the tooth or bone and transferred by pricking in the outlines. The scrimshaw piece was finished by inking in the incised lines with the thumb and palm. When India ink was not available, paint, lamp-black, tobacco juice, berries and even tar were employed.

The two most common scrimshaw products were busks and pastry crimping wheels. Busks were wide, center bodice stays used in women's foundation garments. Busks were especially popular with the young men who made them for their sweethearts or wives. The busk was often a sailor's second attempt at the craft, having first tried a tooth. Approximately two inches wide, eight to twelve inches long, and from one-eighth to a quarter of an inch thick, busks were made from panbone or baleen. The long flat bone provided an ample surface upon which the scrimshander could inscribe a multitude of images and even words. The simplistic verses found on many of these may not have risen to a high literary level but a certain sentiment was there. For example:

> Accept Dear Girl this busk from me
> Carved by my Humble Hand
> I took it from a Sperm Whale's Jaw
> One Thousand Miles from Land

or

> In many a gale
> Has been the whale
> In which this bone did rest
> His time is past
> His bone at last
> Must now support thy brest [*sic*].[8]

It was said that a girl who wore the busk of a sailor would always be true to him. While there was a tremendous diversity of design, the nature of such an intimate gift lent itself to more romantic and sentimental images such as stars, circles, hearts, birds, flowers, and for the more accomplished artist, stalwart sailors, forlorn ladies, and embracing couples. The standard ships, whales, eagles, and tropical scenes also appeared. Occasionally, melodramatic scenes were done—such as a long boat being overturned by a breeching whale—perhaps by a sailor hoping to garner increased admiration for his valor, but depictions of fatal and hazardous adventures were more likely inscribed on teeth.

While the extraordinary popularity of crimping wheels has never truly been explained, it has been attributed to the New Englander's passion for pies. Perhaps it was the knowledge that the recipient would use the crimper in her weekly baking and would be reminded of the giver at sea. Perhaps the rekindled memory of a busy kitchen filled with the mouth-watering aromas of baking pies brought comfort to the creator. Whatever the driving force, the design of this small, utilitarian device soared to new heights of imagination and complexity in the hands of the scrimshander. A crimping wheel or jag wheel is a small wheel that turns on a handle and is used to cut pastry and to flute or to crimp together the tops of pie crusts. The five- to ten-inch implements had handles made in the shape of birds, fish, whales, or people, but many were fashioned in intricate cutwork designs. Some crimpers had multiple wheels, and others had small forks that could be used to prick the tops of the pie-crusts.

The myriad of items created by these true folk artists is a tribute to their craft and ingenuity. Some of the more customary domestic items made of bone include swifts, work boxes, bodkins, knitting needles, thread winders, thimbles, clothes pins, candlesticks, butter molds, nut choppers, mortar and pestles, napkin rings, toys, and picture frames. While many scrimshaw elements appear to have been made with female recipients in mind, other loved ones were not forgotten. Masculine items such as canes, cane handles, and watch cases were also devised. Some pieces were work related, such as fids for rope work, seam rubbers used when mending sails, and serving mallets for winding cordage. Blocks,

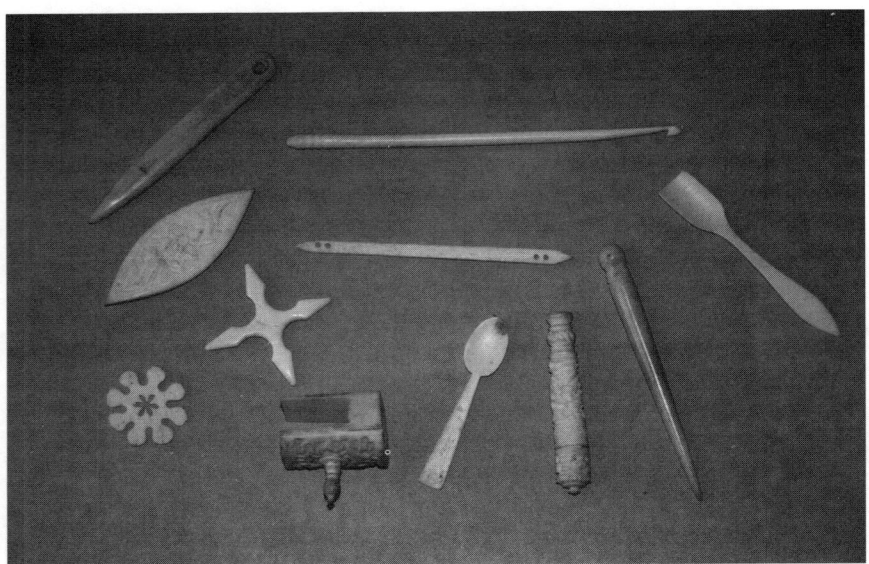

Sailors fashioned many useful household items from whalebone. Items seen here include a tatting shuttle, a crochet hook, bodkins, salt spoons, a needle case, a sewing clamp, and thread winders. James Volo Photo.

dead eyes, and handles for virtually any period tool could be found. Other items were made, not for loved ones or practicality, but for sale or barter when in port.

Scrimshanders also made implements to enhance their shipboard leisure activities. Dice, dominoes, cribbage boards, even cards were made from whalebone. Ink sanders, sealing devices, lead pencil holders, and straight-edges were designed by both officers and the more literate among the crew. Musical instruments were known to have sported scrimshaw keys, bridges, and tail pieces. Whalebone was also used as inlay in wooden boxes or as handles for wooden rolling pins or coconut-bowled dippers.

Decorative Ropework   Shipboard needs required sailors to be skilled with ropes. Eliza Williams wrote, "The Men have been . . . making rope which they do as well as at home in the rope walks. If they want any small ropes for any purpose, they take new large rope and part the strands and lay them up by hand and the reel. . . . They made me a nice, long clothesline."[9] Experienced sailors were also proficient at the practical knots of their calling. Decorative ropework was an outgrowth of everyday seamanship. It was somewhat natural for the knots to be adapted and embellished to produce artistic effects. A simple stopper knot, used to prevent a rope from pulling through an eye, might be fashioned into an ornamental button. Yoke lines could be intricately plaited. A pineapple knot, worked on the end of a fid and varnished, was decorative as well as functional, providing a more secure grip for the large wooden spike.

Fancy ropework had the advantage of requiring few tools. A knife with a spike was all that was essential. A fid, used to separate the strands, became necessary only when larger ropes were employed. A few nails would be driven into a board or spar for more complicated woven mats and rings. Books on seamanship from the eighteenth century discuss decorative ropework. The names given to certain knots, however, were sometimes confusing since crafters were developing knots at different times without the knowledge of the work of others.

Knot makers fashioned billyclub handles, needle cases, rope ladders, decorative chains, lanyards, bracelets, table mats, sashes, bottle covers, shoes, buttons, and toggles. The ropecrafter tended to be most elaborate when the project was personal or purely decorative. Chest handles were a matter of particular pride, as a sailor's chest was his sole personal property on a voyage. To keep knotwork white, pipe clay was applied. A vessel's bell rope was the pride of the ship. Fancy ropework could also be used to create gifts for loved ones. Complex knots were adapted to fashion domestic fancies such as picture frames.

Cards, dice, dominoes, backgammon and checkers were popular games among the crew. Watching the play was likely to **Games** sustain as much interest as partaking in it. Sailor Robert Ferguson wrote about a checker game on the *Kathleen*.

All hands except the man at the wheel and those on lookout, stood around watching every move, even the captain. You could have heard a pin drop. The game lasted two hours and Otto won. All the Portuguese stood around with their mouths open. The captain said he would like to try a game with Otto some day. The cooper told me that our Captain, on the last voyage, beat all the other whaling captains in St. Helena and won fifty dollars.[10]

Checkerboards were likely to be laid out on a piece of painted canvas or on the lid of a sea chest, and the pieces might be made of anything handy even buttons from old garments. More elaborate checkerboards, perhaps inlaid with fine woods and ivory, were handmade by amateur craftsmen on board ship, but these were meant to be sold or given as gifts. Ferguson noted, "For the past few days I have been working on my checkerboard, using pieces of rosewood, ebony satinwood and sandalwood."[11]

Dominoes were especially popular with sailors from continental Europe, but the worldliness of sailors exposed them to many cultures. "An innovative genius from New Jersey, becoming as he said, oppressed with

Fig.39   d   Fig.38.

Fig.40.   b   d

Fig.41.

Fig.42   b   c   a

Fig.43.   b   c   d   a

Fig. 44.   a   b

Fig.45.

Fig.46.

Fig. 47.   b   a   c   c

Fig.49.   d   c   b

Fig.50.

Fig.51.   b   a

Fig.52.

Fig.48.

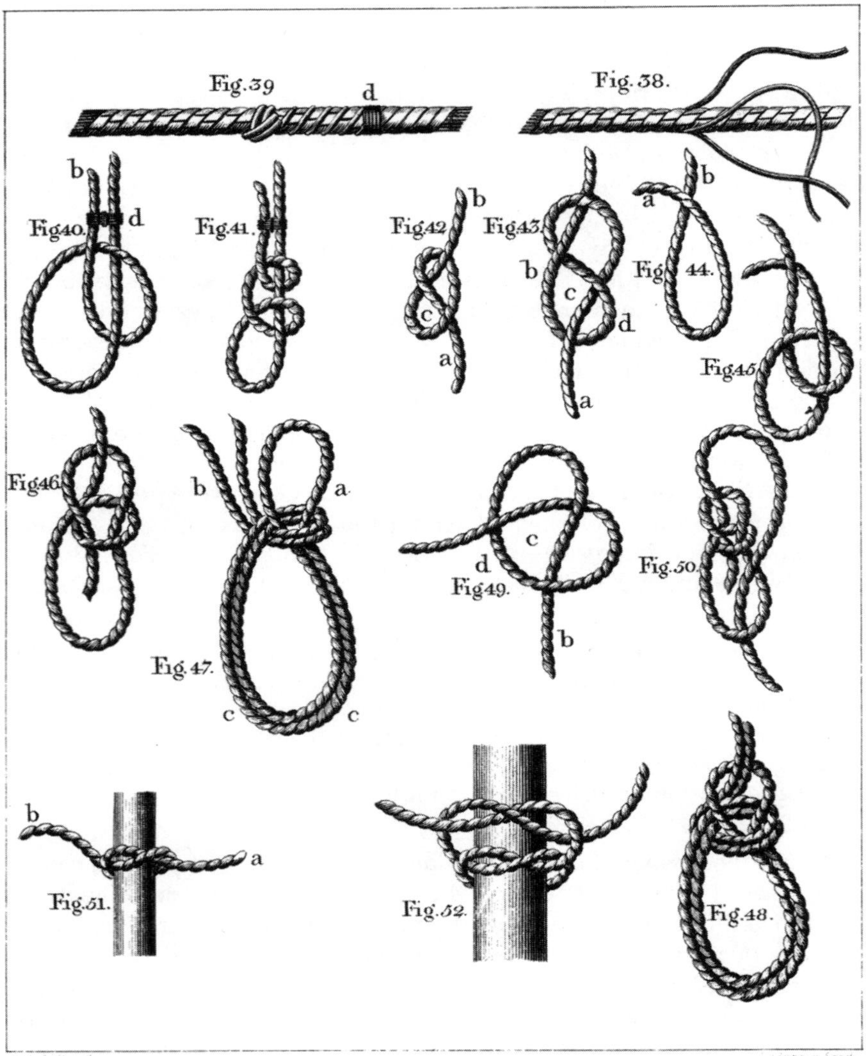

Rope work and knots from nineteenth-century sailor's manual.

ennui, manufactured a set of dominoes from a sperm whale's jaw; another contrived dice; whilst a third made a checkerboard."[12]

The austere Protestant background of some New England captains caused them to frown upon card playing even though the stakes were more likely to be in tobacco than shillings or dollars. "I have seen a half dozen seated around a chest a pile of tobacco in the center, greasy cards, playing bluff or all-fours and watching the game as if their very existence depended upon the winning or losing a few pounds of tobacco." Diarist William Whitecar further related a growing alarm among some members of the crew who saw the green hands repeatedly suffering losses at the hands of a certain group of cronies. High words and quarreling naturally followed. Finally, complaints were made to the captain who offered a bounty of a pound of tobacco for every deck of cards turned in to the officers. This strategy was successful, and several decks of contraband cards were thrown overboard.[13]

Sailors were especially partial to all kinds of music, and the descriptions of sailors' musical activities abound in journals and logs. Music lifted the spirits and furnished an outlet for pent-up   **Music**
emotions. The lyrics were often inconsequential to the solace and camaraderie that the activity provided. During the dog watches, the sailors not on duty would gather and sing or dance to whatever musical accompaniment was available. Although there was little room in such tight quarters for extraneous items, seamen were known to have commonly brought aboard both fiddles and concertinas. Harmonicas, pipes, and penny whistles took up little space in a sailor's ditty bag. In the absence of any instrument, barrels would be impressed into service as drums. Wiser and more compassionate captains appreciated the psychological value of music and used it to maintain good morale. Such a captain might order the boatswain to pipe all hands to dance with the call "Hands to dance and skylark."

Sir Francis Drake was known to have taken highly skilled musicians with him on his voyage to circumnavigate the globe in the sixteenth century. Aboard the *Gazelle* in 1862, the fourth mate noted in his journal that on Washington's birthday "we amused ourselves with the violins, flutina, and tambore. Played some very stirring airs."[14] William Whitecar described a nineteenth-century German whaler that was supplied with "an assorted cargo of German fancy-goods—accordeons [sic], fluitinas, drums, violins, flutes &c . . . which she disposed of . . . to ships she met in want of such articles."[15]

Music provided much more than pure entertainment for the crew. Working songs were an integral part of shipboard labor in the merchant service, although they were seldom used aboard naval vessels. Prior to the widespread adoption of small "donkey" engines in the late nineteenth century, all of the force exerted aboard ship was provided by human muscle. The rhythm needed for an efficient team effort among the crew when setting sails, hauling cargo in or out of the hold, or pushing on the capstan bar to raise the anchor or careen the hull was provided by songs or chanties. "As sailors say a song is as good as ten men."[16] Every ship had a kind of unofficial song leader or "chantyman." In addition to a fine voice and a good set of lungs, the chantyman needed a singular sense of timing and an instinctive feeling for the mood of the men. A well-chosen song that fit the task at hand and suited the spirit of the crew could inspire the hands to peak efficiency.

The chantyman would sing out a line of the song, and the sailors would follow with the chorus. The songs, sung without instrumental accompaniment, were chosen for the specific work goal. Pulling chanties were designed to have all hands pull at the same time. Short drag chanties called for a great exertion followed by a breath before the next pull as when sweating up a halyard the last few inches. The solo line and the chorus were repeated for as long as the effort was needed.

Solo: Oh, Nancy Dawson, hi oh!
Chorus: Cheer'ly man!
Solo: She's got a notion, hi oh!
Chorus: Cheer'ly man!
Solo: For our old bo'sun, hi oh!
Chorus: Cheer'ly man![17]

Double pull chanties were for long hauls such as hoisting heavy yards. For example, hands pulled twice in each chorus of a tune such as "Blood-red Roses," with each pull timed on the word down.

Solo: Our boots and clothes are all in pawn
Chorus: Go down, you blood-red roses, go down!
Solo: And it's mighty drafty round Cape Horn
Chorus: Go down, you blood-red roses, go down![18]

Hand over hand chanties were sung while hoisting light sails. Two or three men on the haliyard all sang together as they hoisted hand over hand. A well-known version of this type of work song is "The Drunken Sailor," also known as "Up She Rises":

What shall we do with a drunken sailor?
What shall we do with a drunken sailor?
What shall we do with a drunken sailor?
Early in the morning.

Haul away, and up she rises.
Haul away, and up she rises.
Haul away, and up she rises.
Early in the morning[19]

Windlass or capstan chanties were for prolonged endeavors such as weighing the anchor, warping, loading or unloading cargo, or working the pumps. These chanties were more harmonious than the others and had two choruses. "Paddy Get Back," which told the tale of a crew that had deliberately been deceived about the ship's destination, was such a song:

Solo: I was broke and out of a job in the city of London;
       I went down the Shadwell docks to get a ship.
Chorus: Paddy get back, take in the slack!
       Heave away your capstan, heave a pawl![20]

A well-known capstan or windlass chanty was "Shenandoah." Although a rivermen's song, its drawling character and rolling rhythm made it popular in more nautical settings.

The solo lines of the song were often old favorites, but sometimes the chantyman would make up his own lines. Chanties might poke fun at the cook or recall a sailor's misadventures in port. The well-known "Drunken Sailor" served as a warning to the crew member who let his workload fall to his shipmates when he was unfit for duty after a celebratory night in port. Chanties could also give voice to displeasure for the captain or officers, which if outspoken, would likely bring stinging punishment. This obviously required the chantyman to be particularly attuned to the officers' tolerance of the subject of a song. The capstan chanty "Leave Her, Johnny, Leave Her" might be sung while entering a port and warping the ship alongside the dock. While there are numerous verses, these lines illustrate how hard feelings, which had accumulated during the voyage, could be given voice.

Solo: It was rotten meat and weevily bread
Chorus: Leave her Johnny, leave her!
Solo: Eat her or starve, the Old Man said,
Chorus: Leave her Johnny, leave her![21]

The chantyman seldom, if ever, selected a minor key chanty in brisk weather. On very hot days, however, when every job required a maximum effort, capstan chanties in the minor key, such as the mournful "Santa Ana," were sung.

> Oh Mexico, sweet Mexico,
>   Hurrah! Santa Ana!
> To Mexico we are bound to go-o
>   On the plains of Mexico.[22]

In the days of early exploration, ships from mainly Catholic countries, such as Spain and Portugal, incorporated songs of prayer into their daily routine. These were often in Latin, the language of the Roman Catholic Church. The sailors were often extremely devout and took this activity quite seriously. The youngest boys would lead the ship's company in religious song. Known as the *pajes de escober* ("pages of the broom") the duty fell to these lads in the same manner that the youngest child of a family might be asked to say grace. At daybreak and sunset, the signal for morning and evening prayers would be the angelic chords of the chants sung by these young boys. Every half hour a boy would sing out at the turning of the glass. At five bells he would sing,

> Five is past and six floweth,
> More shall flow if God willeth,
> Count and pass make the voyage fast.[23]

Protestant sailors were equally resolved in their devotion, but their songs were generally sung in the vernacular of their own country. The Puritan sailors of Admiral George Monck's English navy eschewed music with their Psalms just as they did during services on shore unlike the men of the Restoration navy who sang out lustily to any available accompaniment.

A far different kind of singing took place in the forecastle where the sailors sang for themselves. Fo'c'sle songs were often bawdy and recreational in nature. They were sung during the watch below, on deck during dogwatches, and during any leisure time a sailor might have. These songs were traditionally accompanied by whatever instruments were available. Some songs were popular tunes of the day written by professional songwriters with references to the sea and sailors, but generally, the drawing room sea songs, such as "Nancy Lee" or "The Death of Nelson," found no home in the forecastle.

Other pieces were composed by the sailors themselves. These usually had a narrative quality. They tended toward the sentimental or romantic and were infused with a sense of the vastness and the power of the sea. They provided an outlet for feelings of deep inner sadness, longing for loved ones, or awareness of the proximity of death. Often the subject of the song was dramatic, relating tales of shipwreck, storms, mutinies, or violent death. Tunes were regularly borrowed from other popular ditties or sea songs, and sometimes, the song's original title was incorporated into the lyrics. It was not uncommon for the song-inspired mariner to commence with a call for listeners to gather around. The name of the ship was customarily featured early on in the song and her attributes saluted. The 1746 capture of the French ship *Mars* by the British vessel *Nottingham* inspired the following example:

> Come all ye jolly seamen, a tough old Tar I am.
> I'll sing ye of a fight, my boys, fought in the Nottingham.
> 'Twas by a brisk young Captain, Phil Saumarez was his name.
> And he was bent, with bold intent, old England's foes to tame.[24]

Many others began by fixing the tale in a certain time and place:

> It was in the year eighteen hundred and one,
> March the twentieth day,
> We hoisted up all our topsails
> And for Greenland bore away, brave boys,
> And for Greenland bore away.[25]

Crew members were routinely identified, by position if not by name, and the supposed original composer was sometimes given prominence. American sailors were known to have a propensity to conclude with a moral, extolling the virtue of shunning liquor, loose women, and bad company, as in "Off to Sea Once More."

> Come all ye bold seafaring men, and listen to my song;
> When you come off from your long trips, I'd have you not go
>   wrong,
> Take my advice, drink no strong drink, don't go running on the
>   shore,
> But get married lads, and have all night in, and go to sea no
>   more![26]

DIVERSIONS

The isolation of the sea demanded that sailors be creative in furnishing their own entertainment. Some crews produced their own theatricals. Finding costumes and scenery had its challenges, although the audience was likely not to be too demanding in this respect. There are accounts, however, of plays complete with drop curtains, footlights and props that included even a door with knockers. Slapstick and melodrama were particularly popular. Stellar acting and stimulating scripts were unnecessary, but some performances were given kudos simply for organization and presentation. Admiral Nelson appreciated the therapeutic value of

the theatrical. He not only encouraged such productions but also promoted men who demonstrated a facility and interest in entertaining the
crew.

Arts
In an age before photography, art was both an amusement and a
professional accomplishment. Close quarters and wind tossed
ships did not lend themselves to painting and drawing in a traditional sense, however, seamen did produce a fair amount of artwork
in their log-books, journals, and charts. Officers illustrated their log-
books with unique landmarks, vessels sighted or unusual scenes encountered during a voyage. Charts were embellished with sketches of
dolphins, birds, and islands. Nicholas Pocock, a sea officer in the Royal
Navy, proved so accomplished as an artist that he had a fabulous second
career as a painter and illustrator in the years of his retirement. Pocock
was commissioned by several admirals to depict specific engagements
for their memoirs.

The journals kept by crew members were less common. Some extant
examples contain excellent illustrations portraying shipboard life and
documenting the villages and people of exotic ports. Virtually all of these
works were done in simple pen and black ink, although some used different colors of ink.

The log-books of whalers had their own unique art form. Neat and
very accurate silhouettes of whales were stamped throughout. The silhouettes, which depicted the various whale species—right, sperm, or
humpback—were made by small carved stamps that the captain kept for
this specific purpose. Some of these stamps had beautifully carved,
scrimshaw handles. The center of each whale stamp left a blank space
in the journal into which the captain might enter the number of barrels
of oil that the whale rendered. If a whale eluded capture, the captain
would simply enter a whale's tale in a vertical position indicating that
it had sounded and gotten away. Water spouts, harpoons, and damaged
boats were sometimes also added to the illustrations.

Reading
Some sailors took advantage of the long shipboard hours to
improve their minds. Robert Ferguson recorded that he gave
lessons to two shipmates. Of one, Frank Gomez, he wrote, "He
is very anxious to learn to read and write. To offset the lessons, he does
little odd jobs for me."[27] Some men had gone to sea so early in life that
their formal education was quite limited. It is reported that John Scott
DuBois, captain of the *Ann Alexander*, was such a man and that he paid
shipmates to instruct him in spelling, writing, and reading. Others saw
the opportunity to expand their knowledge into other fields. Ferguson
reported that he had borrowed a book on navigation from the captain
and was "studying navigation the best I could without a teacher."[28]

Charles Nordhoff reported that he had "read all the books in the
ship—many of them treatises on mathematics, political economy, and

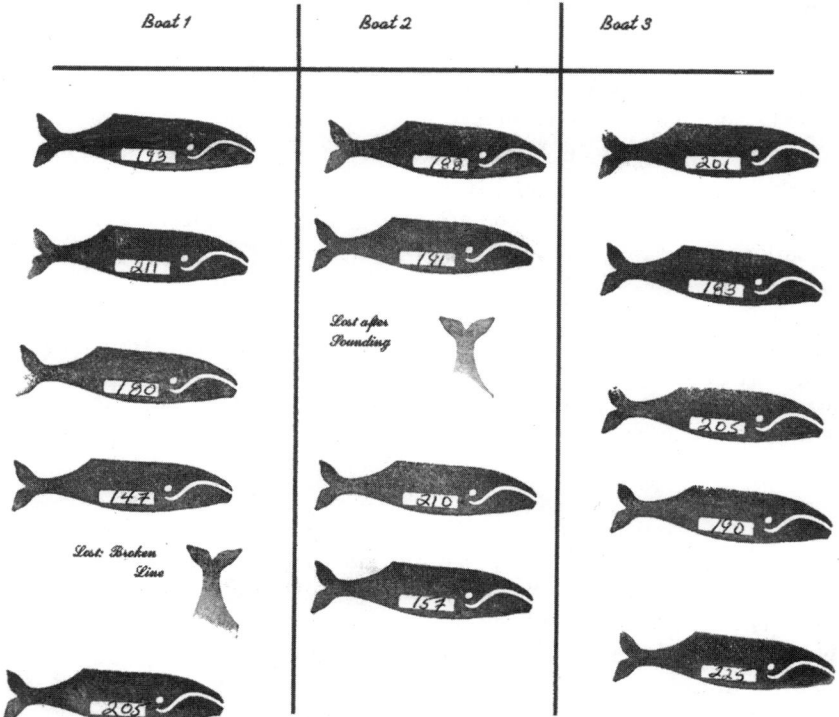

Some captains used stamps in their logs to mark the capture of whales. The yield in barrels of oil was noted in a blank space on the side of the imprint. The flukes of a diving whale signified a whale that got away.

other dry and un-entertaining subjects."[29] Susan Hathorn, who accompanied her husband, Jode, to sea as a bride in 1855, wrote in her journal, "Jode has been reading *Ivanhoe*—he is very much interested in it. I think it is one of Scott's very best stories."[30] Her reading choices were quite typical for the period. "We should die of the dumps if it were not for books—we are reading Byron's Poems."[31]

After visiting the home of a missionary on Strong's Island in the South Pacific, Eliza Williams, wife of Captain Thomas Williams, noted, "They gave us books and papers—some quite late ones—which we were pleased to have."[32] Gifting books was not unique to missionaries. Charles Nordhoff described an incident on a visit to another ship:

I was shown some new books. I looked over them with great interest and chanced to say that I would like to read a certain one. No more was said at the time. When I was about to return on board, in the evening, a package was put in my hand by a stranger, who vanished before I could ask what it was. On opening it when I got on board ship, I found it to be the identical book I had desired to read. To refuse a gift of this kind or even to express any sense of obligation in accepting it would cause pain to the donor, . . . and to offer to pay would be an unpardonable offense.[33]

A ship's doctor, Nathaniel Taylor, also addressed the sharing of books and gave some insight into the amount of reading material available to the sailor:

I had carried from home a large supply of books, and these I freely circulated in both fleets in exchange for others. I was very surprised to find that the sailor was a very good general reader, in fact he rarely leaves port without adding to his stock of books. Upon one occasion we counted the number of volumes which we know to be in circulation at the island, and found that it amounted to over three hundred.[34]

Writing   Whalemen, in particular, were prolific letter writers. Letter writing provided a place for them to air there deepest feelings and most private thoughts. "Here we are 8 days from home. It seems to me more like 8 months. . . . I am more homesick than ever before," wrote Captain DuBois to his wife. In a separate letter he confided, "I think that I will take a barth [sic] this evening [but] I have no towels, that is something I have foregotten [sic]."[35]

Mail delivery from sea was neither swift nor easy yet the desire to maintain ties with loved ones drove seamen to devise numerous methods of overcoming the vast gulf of oceanic distances and the separation of unremitting time. Wives sent letters addressed as simply as "Capt. Nathan Jernegan, Ship *Splendid*, Pacific Ocean."[36] Letters were mailed at embassies, at missions, and even in barrels nailed to trees on lonely islands. Outward-bound ships would drop off letters while ships that were concluding their voyage would pick up letters to be carried back home. Charles Island in the Galapagos became known as Post Office Bay. Its large box, covered with a giant tortoise shell and nailed to a post, was a popular drop-off and pick-up point for whalers. Ships that "gammed" (met at sea or at anchorage) would exchange mail as well as newspapers and news.

Most officers, as educated men, kept personal journals or diaries. Naval commanders were also under some obligation to send out detailed dispatches to their superiors. These were sometimes simple compilations of day-to-day activities, but they often took the form of long, graphic narratives, especially after a particularly successful engagement. These dispatches were a chance for commanders to praise their subordinates and revel in their own success. In this regard, the last paragraph of Brit-

A Snug Cabin by Thomas Rowlandson (1756–1827). Dinner at the captain's table in the eighteenth century was probably not as boisterous as shown in this illustration. © NATIONAL MARITIME MUSEUM.

ish Admiral Cuthbert Collingwood's dispatch written the day after the Battle of Trafalgar (1805) serves as an example:

After such a victory, it may appear unnecessary to enter into encomiums on the particular parts taken by the several commanders; the conclusion says more on the subject than I have the language to express; the spirit which animated all was the same: when all exert themselves zealously in their country's service, all deserve that their high merits should stand recorded; and never was high merit more conspicuous than in the battle I have described.[37]

One of the more common diversions among sea officers was entertaining. Dinner at the captain's table offered an **Entertaining** opportunity for the officers to share with their colleagues an appreciation for good taste brought to each in the sharing of food, wine, and friendly conversation. Dining was deeply rooted in the formalities surrounding the concept of hospitality, but the need to maintain the prestige of each man's rank could make dinners stiff and awkward. By custom, only the captain could start a conversation—even in the presence of passengers—and he was under some obligation to set the tone and pick the topics of discussion for the dinner.

The captain could use an invitation to eat at his table as a sign of approbation for his junior officers, but he needed to avoid inadvertently offending or unconsciously ostracizing any of them. Nor could he show too much zeal for his subordinates, which would be bad for the overall discipline and ordering of the ship.

On a famous occasion before the Battle of Copenhagen, Admiral Nelson entertained all of his fleet captains at dinner at sea. He wrote of these men as "brother officers," and they seem to have returned the compliment by demonstrating a high level of devotion to him.[38] It could be said, and it was certainly true, that men of similar rank and status naturally gravitated toward each other. But Charles Nordhoff, writing of a visit between two men-of-war, showed that such feelings were not limited to the officers alone.

I always found that our crew would consort principally with those of the other vessels who were stationed in the same part of the ship, forecastlemen took their stand in the bows, while the maintopmen were seen congregating in the waist. And not infrequently, when one found an old shipmate, on learning that he was stationed in a different part of the ship there would be an expression of disappointment, and often a positive estrangement. . . . So much are we creatures of habit, that a friend in altered circumstances seems a friend no longer.[39]

Different messes on the same ship might invite others from outside their normal group to dine with them, and visitors to dinner from outside the ship, if available, were commonly made guests. Charles Nordhoff noted,"Visitors are always entertained with the best on board. The stranger has the place of honor at the mess; he is served first, and with the choicest portions . . . [N]o possible mark of attention is omitted. And if there is anything he particularly fancies, yea, even to the half of Jack's possessions, it is his."[40]

Gamming   The term *gam* was used originally to describe a school of whales, but it was later applied to the occasion of whaling vessels meeting at sea and visiting. Gamming was an activity unique to whaling. Merchant ships had schedules to meet, and naval vessels had their stations to keep and their duties to attend. Herman Melville wrote that "Men-of-War, when they chance to meet at sea, they first go through such a string of silly bowings and scrapings, such as ducking ensigns, that there does not seem to be much right-down hearty good-will and brotherly love about it all."[41]

It was the extreme length of whaling voyages that made the gam so popular. The intense isolation of these voyages were pleasantly broken when two ships would meet at sea. If both captains desired to visit, they would signal one another. The weather ship would run across the stern of the ship to leeward. The captain and some of the crew of the first vessel would set out in a boat to the other ship while the mate and some crew members of the second vessel would visit the first. The visitors would gravitate to their counterparts on the other ship, officers to officers, crew to crew. All would be besieged with questions about their birthplace, travels, and experiences. Gams lasted from a day to a week. It was customary for tasty foods to be abundant. Before separating, books, mail, and newspapers were exchanged. Gifts of tobacco, pipes, and needed clothing were also freely given.

The gams served as highlights during the interminable years of a whaling voyage, and they were especially welcomed by the wives of captains who went to sea with their husbands. In early 1853, the unique meeting of four whalers, *Dove, Driver, Candace,* and *Mary,* in a single gam in the Pacific was specially commemorated with an engraving of the event on a whale's tooth. While in port, parties of men often went on visits from ship to ship. It is interesting to note that the customs and protocols reported by whalers were found on other vessels as well.

The variety of interests, skills, and hobbies that seamen drew upon in order to pass their off-duty time and to express themselves was limited only by the number of men who went to sea. Reports survive of a captain who ardently knitted a pair of slippers, one who cross-stitched a pin cushion, and another who was so proficient at net lace that he completed a bedspread on every voyage.[42]

NOTES

1. Charles Nordhoff, *Sailor Life on Man-of-War and Merchant Vessels* (New York: Dodd, Mead & Co., 1884), 174–175.

2. Ibid., 151–157. Blue was the working dress of the American navy. Yet from breakfast until supper white was worn as the ship was open to the view of the public.

3. Edouard Stackpole, *Scrimshaw at Mystic Seaport* (Mystic, CT: The Marine Historical Association, no. 33, March 1958), 11–12.

4. Harold Williams, ed., *One Whaling Family* (Boston: Houghton Mifflin, 1964), 26.

5. Stackpole, 39.

6. Herman Melville, *Moby Dick* (New York: The Library of America, 1984), 1082.

7. Ibid.

8. Eleanor Early, "Mementos of Love from a Sperm Whale's Jaw," in Richard Heckman, ed., Yankees Under Sail (Dublin, NH: Yankees, Inc. 1968), 186.

9. Williams, 112–113.

10. Robert Ferguson, *Harpooner: A Four-Year Voyage on the Barque* Kathleen, *1880–84* (Philadelphia: University of Pennsylvania Press, 1936), 27.

11. Ibid., 75.

12. William B. Whitecar, Jr., *Four Years Aboard the Whaleship in the Years 1855– 59* (Philadelphia, PA: J. B. Lippencott, 1860), 33.

13. Ibid., 32.

14. Emma Mayhew Whiting and Henry Beetle Hough, *Whaling Wives* (Boston: Houghton Mifflin, 1953), 105.

15. Whitecar, 182.

16. Richard Henry Dana, Jr., *Two Years Before the Mast* (Boston: Estes and Lauriat, 1840), 102.

17. Bill Bonyun and Gene Bonyun, *Full Hold and Splendid Passage* (New York: Alfred A. Knopf, 1969), 74–75.

18. John Anthony Scott, *The Ballard of America* (New York: Grosset & Dunlap, 1967), 132–134.

19. Frederick Pease Harlow, *Chantying Aboard American Ships* (Barre, MA: Barre Gazette, 1962), 107–108.

20. Bonyun and Bonyun, 79–80.

21. Scott, 135–137.

22. Harlow, 41–42.

23. Samuel Elliot Morrison, *Christopher Columbus, Mariner* (New York: Meridian, 1983), 41–42.

24. John Laffin, *Jack Tars: The Story of the British Sailor* (London: Cassel, 1969), 184–185.

25. Horace Beck, *Folklore and the Sea* (Middletown, CT: Wesleyan University Press, 1973), 174.

26. Scott, 140–141.

27. Ferguson, 52.

28. Ibid., 163.

29. Charles Nordhoff, *Whaling and Fishing* (New York: Dodd, Mead & Co., 1877), 157.

30. Catherine Petroski, *A Bride's Passage: Susan Hathorn's Year under Sail* (Boston: Northeastern University Press, 1997), 108.

31. Ibid., 56.

32. Williams, 114.

33. Nordhoff, *Sailor Life*, 347.

34. Howard Palmer, ed. *Nathaniel Taylor: Life on a Whaler* (New London, CT: New London County Historical Society, 1929), 132.

35. Clement C. Sawtell, *The Ship* Ann Alexander *of New Bedford 1805–1851* (Mystic, CT: Marine Historical Association, no. 40, 1962), 63–64.

36. Whiting and Hough, 2.

37. Nicholas Blake and Richard Lawrence, *The Illustrated Companion to Nelson's Navy* (Mechanicsburg, PA: Stackpole, 2000), 161.

38. N.A.M. Rodger, *The Wooden World: An Anatomy of the Georgian Navy* (New York: W. W. Norton, 1996), 292.

39. Charles Nordhoff, *Sailor Life*, 345.

40. Ibid., 347.

41. Melville, 1049.

42. Joan Druett, *Hen Frigates: Wives of Merchant Captains under Sail* (New York, Simon & Schuster, 1998), 153.

8

Women and the Sea

A long, long life to my sweet wife, and mates at sea
And keep our bones from Davey Jones, where-e're we be!
                                        —Sea chanty, "Nancy Lee"

From earliest times, sailors were known to be extremely superstitious. Phenomena of the sea such as waterspouts, phosphorescence, and St Elmo's fire spawned a multitude of legends, customs, and charms. Superstitions arose in an attempt to predict and to explain the capricious tendencies of wind and water in concrete terms. "I have never seen an accident occur on shipboard but what someone would step up with prophetic countenance, and engross the attention of every bystander with a relation of some little circumstance that he had taken notice of prior to the occurrence, which he considered as a forewarning."[1]

One widely documented superstition resulted in a strong opposition to having women aboard ships at sea. This particular obsession was an outgrowth of the belief that witches had power over the winds and could, therefore, bring forth deadly storms. This adverse attitude toward women was not confined to simple, uneducated sailors. British Admiral Cuthbert Collingwood wrote in 1808, "I never knew a woman brought to sea in a ship that some mischief did not befall the vessel."[2]

By fact, however, the tradition of taking women to sea was well established in the British Royal Navy by the eighteenth century and persisted through the mid-nineteenth century, despite **Wives** written regulations to the contrary.[3] Captains had considerable latitude in the running of their vessels. While many may have complained about the presence of women on board, female presence was considered virtually an unavoidable nuisance. In the late seventeenth century, it became customary for wives of warrant officers to accompany their husbands to sea. This group included the boatswain, gunner, and carpenter, as well as the purser and master. Idlers such as the cooper, sailmaker, and cook were sometimes also accompanied by spouses. Prior to 1815, some seamen were allowed to bring their wives, but these women were forced to endure the least comfortable situations possible aboard ship.

While the virtue of a woman living amid the crew may arouse suspicion, few, if any, prostitutes remained aboard a ship that went to sea. This was more a function of economics than morality. By the time a ship left port, virtually all of a sailor's money was spent, so that a prostitute's prospect of deriving any financial benefit from a voyage were effectively nil. Additionally, a woman on the lower decks had to depend on a man for her very survival. If she had no husband, she had to find a man who would share both his hammock and his food and serve as her protector.

Although women were present on board, they were essentially ignored. Women were not listed on muster rolls nor were their deaths recorded in ships' records. This disregard persisted despite the fact that, in time of battle, the women joined the ship's company in doing what they could. Recalling the 1798 Battle of the Nile, a seaman wrote, "The women behaved as well as the men. . . . There are some of the women wounded, and one woman belonging to Leith died of her wounds."[4] Women assisted the surgeon and his mates in attending and comforting the wounded. Some women assisted the gun crews serving as "powder monkeys," a physically demanding task they shared with young boys. Seaman Charles M'Pherson recorded his observations after a battle: "Nine of the petty officers had wives aboard who were occupied with the doctor and his mates in the cockpit, assisting in dressing the wounds of the men as they were brought down, or in serving such as were thirsty with a drink of clean water. . . . Two of the number, I think it but justice to mention, acted with the greatest calmness and self possession"[5] Other reports of female courage and dedication were noted in private journals.

Despite their help, women were not even provided rations of food. Husbands had to share their apportionments with their wives and any children they had. This treatment was unique to the navy, as the wife who traveled with her soldier husband in the army received a two-thirds ration and their children a half-ration each in their own right. This allotment was continued even when families of soldiers were being transported by ship, creating the gross inequity of soldiers' families being granted sustenance on the very vessel where the families of the seamen were formally denied any additional rations.

Living conditions for women at sea were harsh as well. Seamen's wives had virtually no privacy. Whatever few possessions the women brought with them had to be stored in their spouse's sea chest. They were forced to share their husband's hammocks in the cramped quarters common to the entire crew. When the boatswain's mate or master-at-arms went about to turn out the sleeping men he would call for anyone still in the hammock to "show a leg." This was used as a means of establishing the gender of the late riser, as the women were not required to turn out for first call. Once the hammocks were stowed away at 8 A.M., the women often congregated on the orlop deck. Below the water line and without gunports, this was a dark and oppressive place, albeit quiet, neighboring the storerooms and the surgeon's quarters. In colder weather, the women may have sought refuge near the galley where there would be some heat provided by the ship's stove. Generally an illiterate population, seamen's wives spent their day in conversation and possibly some sewing. Surely the time passed slowly for them when their main task was to keep out of the way. If they could acquire a tub in which to wash, the women did laundry. Of their laundering one admiral complained, "The hold is continually damp and vapor arising from it highly pernicious."[6] Some women earned a few pence by doing laundry for other men on the ship. Naturally, with drinking water at a premium, they were limited to using salt water. Many captains were constantly suspicious that these laundresses were misappropriating the water stores, which in many cases was probably a well-grounded mistrust. Admiral John Jervis' contempt was quite evident for the women who "infest His Majesty's ships in great numbers, and who will have water to wash, that they and their reputed husbands may get drunk on the earnings."[7]

Wives joined their husbands and their messmates for meals. A mess consisted of six to eight men who ate from a common pot, but the addition of wives brought the number to twelve or sixteen. Food was ordinarily plentiful though monotonous, consisting of boiled salt meat, hard biscuits, and dried peas. Breakfast was at 8 A.M. Dinner was at noon, at which time half the grog ration was distributed. Supper was at 5 P.M. and included the second half of the grog ration.[8]

Late in the day, the men generally had time to relax. Wives would be permitted at this time to join their husbands on deck for dancing and entertainment. The women joined in other recreational activities such as shipboard plays and skits, which often took place at this time.

Childbearing was not uncommon. The storerooms on the orlop deck provided the greatest amount of privacy, but sometimes a paltry piece of canvas was all the privacy that could be found. Following an engagement a seaman reported, "One woman bore a son in the heat of the action; she belonged to Edinburgh." The excitement and chaos of battle often brought on labor and these particularly unfortunate women were left without the benefit of assistance or privacy.[9]

Warrant officers' wives were in a somewhat improved situation in that they shared their husbands' small canvas-sided cabins located on the sides of the lower deck. This enabled them to have some meager amount of privacy and even permitted the possession of some furniture. These women would have employed their time in sewing garments for themselves and their husbands and in attending to any mending that was needed. Having a somewhat larger disposable income, they may also have engaged in decorative needlework such as embroidery or crewelwork. Since warrant officers' wives were much more likely to know how to read than seamen's wives, many of them passed part of the day reading and writing. Prior to the nineteenth century, books would have been few, as they were costly, and there was little space for storage aboard ship, but surely what was had was circulated among the wives of men of similar rank. Wives of warrant officers had the additional benefit of having the service of cabin boys. Commonly aged eleven to twelve years old, these lads acted as servants to the wives, polishing shoes, running errands, preparing special dishes, and such. Often close relationships were formed between the boys and the women, providing the youngsters with maternal nurturing they still required and the women with a motherly fulfillment they most enjoyed.

The wives of officers of wardroom rank ate with the commissioned officers and enjoyed the benefits of a varied diet of fresh meats, delicacies, and wine. Wives of the boatswain, carpenter, and gunner ate separately from both the commissioned officers and the seamen but also had the benefit of being able to supplement their victuals with fresh meat, wine, coffee, and tea. As much as commissioned officers may have loathed the women of the lower deck, they enjoyed the company of ladies of quality who sometimes traveled on naval ships. These women were sheltered in the officers' quarters and entertained at dinners that sometimes rivaled those given ashore.

Sea Widows In either the merchant or naval service, when a seaman was killed by accident or in action at sea his clothing and effects were auctioned off and the proceeds were given to his widow. The wife of a man who died of disease was less fortunate in that his personal clothing was usually disposed of as being disease ridden. Widows were also eligible to receive their husbands' back pay when his ship was finally paid off. Unfortunately, the bureaucracy of the system prevented many widows from ever obtaining this. Richard Dana's 1847 treatise contains a section on "Laws Relating to the Practical Duties of Master and Mariners," which details certain exceptions: "If a seaman dies during the voyage, wages are to be paid up to the time of his death. [However] where the death of a seaman was caused by his own unjustifiable and wrongful acts, his wages are forfeited."[10] If the death was proceeded by a period of sickness or disability, the seaman was "entitled to all his wages . . . during any time he was disabled from preforming duty. But if his sickness or disability is brought on by his own fault, as by vice or willful misconduct, a deduction may be made for the loss of his services." Loose interpretations of the seaman's "own fault" left loopholes for less scrupulous parties to avoid payment. This happened despite the fact that the legal remedies for recovering a seaman's wages were threefold: first, against the master; second, against the owners; and last, against the ship and the freight earned.[11]

The widows of men killed in major actions were sometimes the beneficiaries of private benefactors or public funds that were raised by subscription in honor of these brave men. Beginning in 1733, every commissioned vessel in the Royal Navy kept muster rolls containing two "widow's men" for every 100 men in the crew. Rated as able seamen, the pay for these phantoms was collected in a pension fund for widows. Known as "dead shares," this policy began during the reign of Henry VIII to relieve the widows of commissioned and warrant officers. It was expanded in 1695 to include seamen killed in action and finally extended to any seamen serving in the Royal Navy.

A seaman's wife had to endure a life of loneliness and uncertainty. Naval wives tolerated months of prolonged **Hen Frigates** absence from their men, but merchant seaman's wives often had to resign themselves to marital separation for a year or more. The wife of a whaling captain, however, was one of exceptional trial. As the economics of whaling demanded larger and larger ships, which drew men farther away from their homes, the voyages became extremely lengthy, lasting four and five years. It was not unusual for whaling families to have three or four children each the interval of a whaling voyage apart. Many a man set sail an expectant father only to return years later to learn that his child had died at age two or three, never knowing the comfort of his father's strong embrace nor ever basking in the warmth of his loving smile. Couples married ten years could count their time together in months. An eighteenth-century gravestone on Martha's Vineyard stoically paints the picture of a couple both dead after less than a year of marriage, she in childbirth and he at sea.

> John and Lydia
> That Lovely pair
> A whale killed him
> Her body lies here

In some coastal New England towns, widowhood and separation while on voyage created populations that were largely female. At one point in time on Nantucket, women outnumbered men four to one. Women ran the shops, kept their husband's books, and marketed the exotic goods in which their absent spouses dealt. So ubiquitous was the presence of women in business, that the main street of commerce was nicknamed "Petticoat Row."

Yet some women wanted a more normal life. They wanted to live in a home with their husbands, no matter how abnormal that home might be. Recalling the time her husband was away on a cruise, one wife wrote, "At home though it appeared to some I knew no sorrow then, alas they could not see my feelings nor will they ever know of the many bitter hours I have experienced."[12] By the middle of the nineteenth century, approximately 100 women accompanied their husbands aboard ship. Ships bearing such female residents came to be known as "hen frigates." Merchant captains' wives sailed with their husbands less frequently than whaling captains' wives, but some merchant wives did leave all they knew behind to be with their men. Mary Brewster, a whaling wife, may have spoken for all wives, who, having rejected a life of solitude and trepidation, chose to follow their captain husbands. After twenty-two days at sea, she wrote, "I am with My Husband and by him will remain. No seas can now Divide us. He can have no trouble, no sorrow, but what I can know and share. When perplexed with the duties of the ship and those with whom he is connected, I can soothe all ruffled feelings, take up as much of his attention and mind. If sick, no hand like mine can soothe the sad heart and administer to his wishes."[13]

Accommodations

While accommodations varied from ship to ship, universally they were extremely cramped. Typically, the captain's quarters consisted of two small rooms, a cabin that served the dual purpose of office and parlor and a stateroom for sleeping. The one luxury afforded the captain was a tiny privy, which was little more than a narrow box. The parlor, which would also serve as the family dining room, was illuminated by a skylight shielded by a grill of bars, which could be opened for ventilation in good weather. In addition to such basic cabin furniture as a horsehair sofa, small stove, and captain's table cluttered with navigational aids, the room was commonly filled with sea chests, trunks and, in at least one case, the ship's spare sails. Nonetheless, each seafaring family brought along whatever else meant most for them. For some, it was a rocking chair or parlor organ, for others it was potted plants. "My plants that I brought from home, I think, are all dead. I am watching a geranium very narrowly, hoping it may spring up from the root, but I think it very doubtful. I have planted some orange seeds so that I may have something growing."[14]

The stateroom was almost entirely consumed by a three-quarter bed, which was commonly mounted in gimbals in order to counter a heavy roll of the ship. Unfortunately, the gimbals did little for the pitching and wallowing. Some staterooms also contained a small washstand and a few drawers. The door of the stateroom was usually slotted to allow for modest air circulation. Additional ventilation and light in both rooms came from portholes or small windows high up on the walls. As the century progressed and ships became larger, the captain's quarters were expanded proportionately. Some were lavishly decorated with mahogany, rosewood, or satin-wood paneling; gilt trimmings; and carpeted floors reflecting the captains' social and economic successes.

Life aboard ship could be very lonely for captains' wives. Most men enjoyed their wife's company for a stroll on deck, and many men showed their wives how to take readings and other elements of navigation. There were, however, long periods of time when their attention was entirely consumed by the running of the ship. Victorian convention of the day prohibited the captain's wife from any fraternization with the crew. Propriety and social standing enjoined even casual contact alone with men other than her husband or relatives in all but the most extreme circumstances. However, she could have regular dealings with the steward and occasionally with the cook. Because of the location of the ship's galley, she was often unable to visit the the cook in person. She would sometimes use the steward or cabin boy as an intermediary to carry instructions and premixed ingredients she had prepared for the cook to execute.

The wives of stewards and cooks would sometimes ship with their husbands, serving as assistants to them. Their duty was directly to their spouse, and they functioned under his authority. While the steward reported directly to the captain as his personal attendant, if the steward's wife were aboard she would not be responsible for attending the captain's wife. Although they were the only women aboard ship, class awareness and the maintenance of social position precluded any bonding from occurring. A captain's wife was part of an elite social circle. She could not be expected to befriend the wife of anyone of a lower rank than her husband.

The cabin boy, however, often assisted the captain's wife and became her responsibility. Of her new cabin boy one wife wrote, "Calls himself 16 years old. Should think he is about 12. I am inclined to think that he was a bad boy and his Father was glad to ship him off. He does very well for me and is obedient and naturally pleasant. I think keep a steady hand [sic] and he will do."[15] The women showed their affection for these boys in a variety of ways. Journals report that sometimes the captain's wife altered and repaired their clothes, taught them, and even made sure that the boy's stockings were full for Christmas. After a gamming visit, one whaling wife wrote of another with a nine-month-old baby, "She has an excellent Cabin Boy. He does everything for the Child, washes, irons, and even sews for it. He washes and dresses it, feeds it, and puts it to sleep. I don't see what she would do without him."[16] This was a particularly fortunate occurrence, since the woman in question was so seasick that she was unable to care for her child. Seasickness was a common malady for the women aboard ship, one which never completely abandoned some women. "Pleasant weather but rough which has kept me sick all day. I have been thinking most of the day, when shall I get accustomed to all the changes of wind and weather and have come to the conclusion, by the time this voyage is up I shall, if ever be complete."[17]

Diversions   Knowing full well that the voyage held many lonely hours and days for them, captains' wives brought along much to keep them busy. "Find employment the best amusement to drive away dull care," wrote Mary Brewster.[18] Fortunately, many wives kept journals of their lives at sea leaving us with insight into their unique lifestyle. After two years at sea, a captain inquired of his wife how many yards of cloth she had consumed in her sewing. Not knowing the answer but having the bills for all she had purchased, she discovered (so to her own surprise that she underlined the number) that she "had made up over 600 yards of different kinds of material, some for sheets and pillow cases for the ship, and some for ourselves, tablecloths, towels, curtains, underwear, dresses, linen, jackets, pants, vests, and shirts for the captain." This highlights just how much time was spent in sewing.[19]

In 1855, Susan Hathorn joined her husband, Jode, as a new bride aboard ship and sailed with him for nine months before returning home to await the birth of their first child. She kept a most detailed journal of her work during that time. A tally of these industries shows that Susan spent seventy-five days sewing; thirty-five days embroidering, twenty-three days laundering, nineteen days mending, eighteen days crocheting, fifteen days knitting, thirteen days leather-working, ten days housekeeping, nine days quilting, four days scrap-booking, three days copying "receipts" for cooking, and two days rug-braiding. These activities were typical of those pursued by Victorian women of her social class.[20]

Ladies' magazines such *Godey's Ladies Book* and *Peterson's Magazine* carried a profusion of patterns for fashion accessories and small household items that could be made using embroidery, crochet, and knitting. Ladies made pen wipers, needle cases, toiletry holders, and a myriad of other domestic articles. They made and embellished cravats, suspenders and lounging caps for their husbands. Most of the first two months of Susan Hathorn's journey were consumed by embroidering a pair of slippers for her beloved Jode. In later weeks, most of her time was expended sewing the baby's layette.

Keeping a scrapbook was another popular Victorian pastime. Ladies

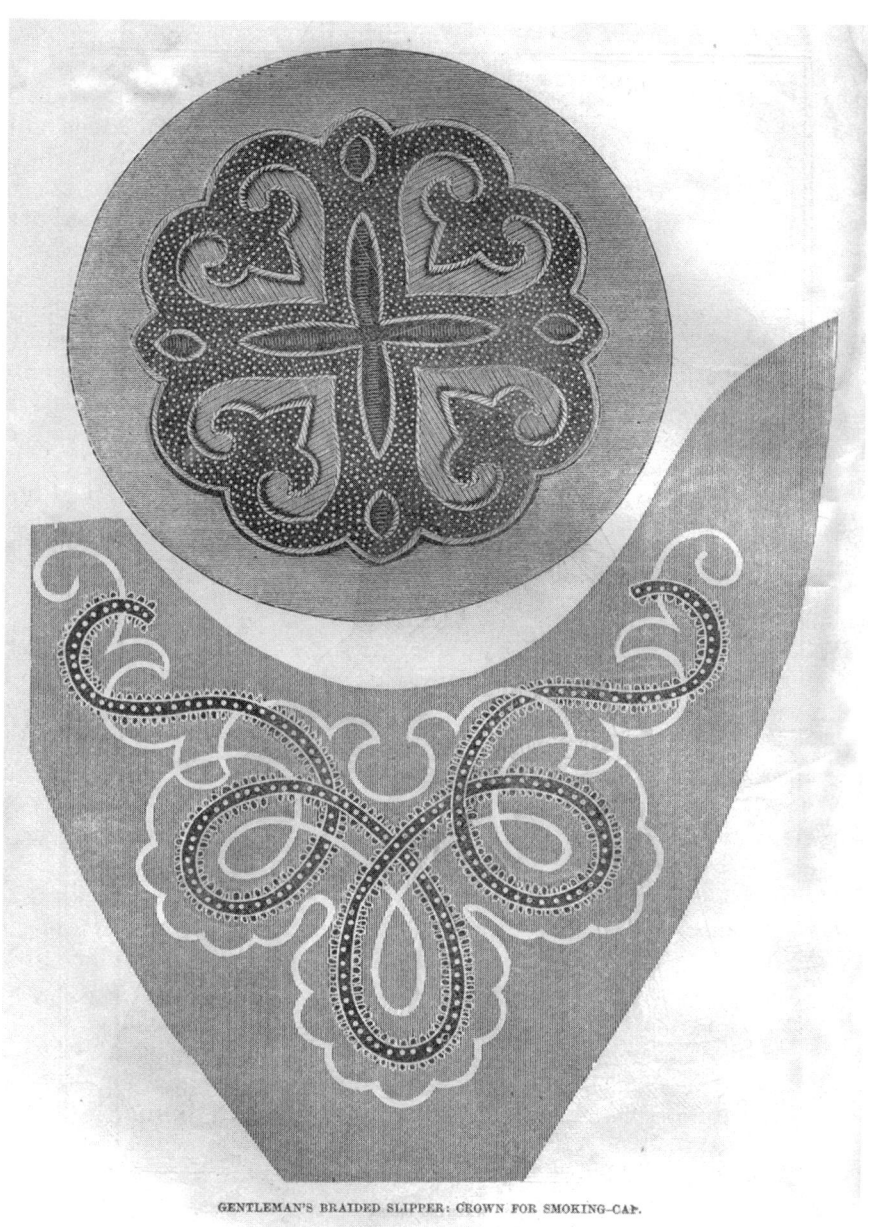

GENTLEMAN'S BRAIDED SLIPPER: CROWN FOR SMOKING-CAP.

To pass the time on their long journeys, captain's wives often brought along a supply of crafts and sewing projects such as this slipper pattern from *Peterson's Magazine*, June 1863.

would clip out inspirational stories of moral fortitude, transcriptions of speeches by prominent personages, and lengthy poems from magazines and newspapers of the day and paste them in scrapbooks, wasting no inch of space. Victorians had a great affinity for nature and enjoyed collecting specimens for both study and decoration. Fireplace mantels and what-not shelves were adorned with interesting pine cones, branches, and mosses. Visiting foreign ports provided the opportunity to gather many unique samples. Like many seafaring women, Susan recorded her finds: "Found about a quart and a half of shells and a beautiful little conch."[21] Susan enjoyed a broad variety of practical and recreational crafts and needlework but even women of narrower interests regularly recorded formidable sewing accomplishments in their journals. Among the personal and domestic sewing accomplishments listed by Lucy Smith were the following nautical accessories: a ship signal flag, a jib for George's boat, a large sail for the starboard boat, a tablecloth for the forward-cabin, and a canvas cover for the chronometer box.[22]

Evenings were often the favorite time for the wives. They walked the now quiet decks with their husbands talking and making plans. Back in their cabin they played cards, dominoes, and backgammon or passed the time reading, something which Victorian families did together. It was common for one family member to read aloud while others listened. Mary Brewster expressed an attitude toward reading that was typical for the period: "I have much time for reading and I desire to fill my mind with such knowledge which will be useful and constructive. Time spent with such books is not lost but profitable and advantageous to all who will read and be benefited by such reading."[23]

Captains' wives generally brought along a supply of reading material sufficient to sustain them on the voyage. Susan Hathorn kept an explicit journal of books she read. Aside from the pragmatic *Mrs. Hale's Cook Book*, from which she copied the "receipts" mentioned in her work list, most of Susan's selections were romantic in nature, dealing with foreign travel, poetry, or historical romance. Six works were by Sir Walter Scott, two by Lord Byron, two by Thomas Moore, and one each by Percy Bysshe Shelly, Harriet Beecher Stowe, George Hilliard, G.P.R. James, Maria McIntosh, and Ann Stevens. These authors would have been popular with Susan's social class and even reflected the newly emerging interest in women authors characteristic of the mid-nineteenth century.

Chores   Not all of a wife's time at sea was spent in what might be considered idle labor. Even a captain's wife had to deal with the realities of life at sea. "Had a regular 'bed bug slaughter' this morning. Found the things in the sofa—under the buttons—a nest under each one. What I shall do with the cock roaches now, is a question of great moment with me. They are fairly taking possession of my quarters."[24]

Laundry was another adventure. One wife described it as "pretty hard work . . . the gale washed faster than I did."[25] The lack of fresh water made a difficult job all the worse. The women hoped for rainwater but depending on the ship's supply of fresh water even that might not be available for washing. Hanging clothes to dry in ocean breezes could be hazardous and many a garment took flight. A green sailor described the manner in which clothes could be successfully hung to dry. "I found that every piece was tied up by the corners with two little strings, or stops as they are called. One of the quartermasters, seeing me without any stops, gave me some rope yarns, and showed me the particular hitch by which they are stopped or fastened to the clothes, and then to the lines, so as to be easily untied."[26] Ironing was not much easier, since the irons had to be heated on the stove, which was in the galley, and then conveyed to the captain's quarters. "The irons do not hold the heat and by the time I got one towel ironed, had to trudge to the galley for a new flat."[27] The required attitude toward life aboard ship was captured in the following diary entry: "Well, I have chosen my own destiny so it does not become me to complain as it was faithfully portrayed beforehand."[28]

Captains' wives provided what assistance they could in many venues. One wrote, "I have often had reason, since I left Nantucket to bless the little knowledge I had of medicine, as it has contributed to take a great care off the mind of my husband. He examines the cases and reports them to me; this his part and I am happy to say that the medicines I have administer'd have never failed their desired affect."[29] Caroline Mayhew, the daughter of a doctor, remained aboard ship in order to tend those of the ship's company stricken with smallpox. When her husband fell ill as well, she took over navigation of the ship in addition to her nursing duties. Nineteen-year-old Mary Ann Patten was on a honeymoon voyage when her captain husband fell ill with "brain fever" and was rendered both blind and deaf. With the first mate incarcerated for insubordination and the second mate lacking skill in navigation, Mary, now pregnant with their first child, accepted her husband's charge to take command of the ship. Mary had carefully studied her husband's calculations during the early months of their journey and was able not only to navigate the ship home, but she safely guided it through a harrowing rounding of Cape Horn.

The demands of the sea become all the more rigorous for women when clothing was factored into the equation. **Clothing** Nineteenth-century fashion did not conform to living aboard ship. Although captains' wives may well have been the most fashionably dressed at home, ship's planking and salt spray would have played havoc with the long skirts of taffeta and silk common to the day. Most women found it more practical to adopt a version of what would have been heavy work dress for chores ashore such as laundry. The fabric of such clothing would have been sturdy, inexpensive, and of a color which would not show dirt. Skirts would be kept at or altered to ankle length. Pregnant Emma Cawse wrote that she found a "nice short wrapper" best to wear on deck. The wrapper was a loose robe that buttoned down the front and was generally used as a dressing gown. Once shortened it would have made for very comfortable attire for a woman in Emma's circumstance. Women also put their "Yankee ingenuity" to work when it came to footwear. Wave-swept decks certainly proved to be a challenge. Some women wore pattens, which were metal or wooden platforms that slipped over the shoe in order to raise the wearer above mud or water. Others wore gaiters to protect their ankles or made protective wear of their own design.[30]

Childbirth Naturally, with wives traveling on such extended voyages, whaling captains were sometimes called upon to deliver their own children. Some women managed to return home to await the event, yet others went to sea so that they would be with their husband for the birth. Skeptical of that decision, Lizzie Edwards wrote in a letter, "Capt. Henry Green's wife is going to have a baby and she has gone north with him to have it on board the ship, for she says she isn't a bit afraid to trust herself to her husband's care."[31] Confident as they must have been, surely these women missed the buttress of the circle of female relatives and neighbors who normally gathered to assist the doctor or midwife at such a time. Whenever possible, the attempt to provide such support was made. If a ship was in the company of another vessel with a woman aboard, arrangements were made for her to be present. If the time of a woman's "confinement," as it was called, could be synchronized with a visit to a port, the mother-to-be might be left to the care of a missionary or other responsible person until the ship could return. Such was the situation of Martha Brown in Honolulu. While it might have been the best decision, her journal entry embodies the distress of this exile as her labor commenced, "Must I be confined without my husband, or one that I can call my friend?"[32]

Caring for a baby shipboard could not have been easy. "It has been a very unpleasant day, blowing a gale all day and the ship rolling very badly. I can't keep the Baby in one place, and he gets a good many bumps."[33] One solution to this problem was to sew the infant into the crib. This is not as extreme a measure as it may seem. Victorian mothers often sewed their babies into their clothing, heeding advice from ladies' magazines, which warned, "A pin should never be used about a child's clothing."[34] Infants wore long gowns that frequently were twice the length of the child. Such clothing was used in place of loose blankets, which could more easily be cast off by a squirming babe. Diapers, or napkins as they were then known, were made of flannel as was much of small children's clothing. Laundering baby's voluminous wraps was a problem, since fresh water was carefully monitored and not always available. Napkins washed in saltwater or dried in salt spray created a surface unsympathetic to the baby's delicate skin. Resourceful mothers used rags, soft paper or any other gentle material available to line the napkins.

Some parents did leave one or more of their children in the care of family when they departed for a voyage, although **Children** hundreds of children were raised aboard their fathers' ships. It is said that young children who learned to walk while shipboard actually had difficulty walking on land once they got to port and reverted to crawling in order to get around. Being a child on board ship must have been quite a lark. In a time when it was likely that a child would not even travel fifty miles from his or her birthplace, children at sea could have the unparalleled adventures of traveling to exotic ports such as Honolulu or being called to play by Eskimo children. Shipboard children generally enjoyed good health, although once they returned home their isolation from other children while on the voyage made them vulnerable to all the childhood diseases from which they had been sheltered.

Despite the bother that the children must have caused aboard ship for the crew, they were often the objects of great affection. "The Men have been mending sails on deck, and I have had the Baby up there. He has been down on the sail, playing with a ball of twine and getting in the Men's way all he could."[35] Crew members made a variety of handcrafted items for shipboard youngsters and tolerated their being underfoot. "The cooper has been making me a bathing tub to bathe the baby in; it is a very nice one. He has taken a great deal of pains with it."[36] One captain wrote that his small son had acquired a veritable fleet of toy vessels. "[H]e has got a sloop yacht that the Carpenter made for him, a full-rigged four-master ship that the second mate made him. I made him a ship about 30 inches long that he can tow on the stern when we are not going too fast, and now the Carpenter has given him a full-rigged model of a ship about 3 feet long."[37]

Perhaps having the sound of children about helped the men deal with separation from their loved ones. Seeing the captain's offspring let them imagine what their youngsters might well be doing ashore, and perhaps in a way, they felt they were not so far apart. A nineteenth-century mariner recalled the painful moment of departure for a voyage: "They that go down to the sea in ships get used to bitter things. It aint [*sic*] so much taking your life in your hands, as other matters that are wuth [*sic*] more than life to you to think on and remember of. If you've married a good woman and set anything by her and she set anything by you, a man takes her eyes along with him as they looked with tears in 'em; and her hands along as they felt when they got around his neck; and her voice, the sound it had, when it choked in trying to say good-by that morning; and the look of the baby in her arms as she stood agin [*sic*] the door."[38]

Living on ship proved one big adventure for most boys, and many became obsessed with it. The rigging made an appealing playground and a perfect place to escape mother or an annoying sibling."Prescott was happy all day in playing with ropes, and he also had a swing, and the small cabin boy used to amuse him."[39] The cook seems to have been a particular favorite of children. The cook was able to slip the youngsters extra snacks, and he would have a more regular schedule, which could accommodate a small person's questions and desire for companionship. Being such a minority amid so many adults, the captain's children were often spoiled and at times would get out of hand. It was not unusual for the vocabulary of these youngsters to include a striking number of colorful sailors' expressions and swear words.

Little girls tended to be kept closer to mother and indoctrinated in the needlework arts and other acceptable feminine pastimes. Six-year-old Laura Jernegan was already keeping a journal almost daily in which she proudly declared her academic accomplishments. "I have had my lessons perfect. I am doing sums in divisson [*sic*]." She also noted her sewing projects, "I am making a toilet cushion," and itemized her readings, "I have just finished a story book called Little Prudy."[40]

Parents set time aside to instruct their children. It was not unusual for this to be a responsibility shared by both parents. Once girls reached adolescence, however, it was highly likely that they were left at home for formal schooling. It was very important for young women of this time to have proper and polished social skills. With no other model than her mother, these were less likely to be complete. Additionally, there was concern for the reputation and virtue of such a young and innocent creature aboard a ship full of men.

Growing up aboard ship brought times of great trial as well. Five-year-old Minnie Lawrence met with what her mother described as "about as severe an affliction as she ever experienced."[41] On their first day out of port, "she lost her Frankie doll overboard, a doll that she dearly loved for its own sake and the more because it was Grandma Annie's. She cried for a long time and wrung her hands in the greatest agony. She insisted so much upon having black clothes made to wear that I was obliged to get her a piece of black ribbon to tie on her arm to pacify her."[42]

Animals aboard ship offered children other opportunities for hardship. "As I went on deck, the first sight that greeted my eyes was the pigs and chickens running about at large on deck."[43] Carrying live poultry, pigs and goats was the best way to ensure fresh eggs, meat, and milk. It was not unusual for the children to become attached to the animals, which, in many cases, became their pets. "There were tears in Minnie's eyes this morning, when we went to the breakfast table, to see her Juba on the dish. . . . She thinks Wiggie must be very lonely."[44]

The most special times for wives and children at sea were when they could "gam" or visit with other ships. Gamming **Gamming** was a time to share stories, to hear news from home, and to enjoy the company of "fresh faces." It was a time for best clothes and special culinary treats. In order to facilitate the transportation of a woman to another ship, the cooper would fashion a barrel-like chair with a rope harness, which would deliver the captain's wife safely, if not comfortably.

For children, visiting usually also meant candy and gifts. "Mr. Morgan brought back a little black dog for Willie. The mate of the Cambria gave her to Mr. Morgan. Willie is much pleased."[45] Some gifts were more exotic. "Captain Howland brought a small pet terrapin for Minnie. . . . He also gave Minnie a little basket of feather flowers."[46] If one of the ships were returning home, it would carry back mail. "I have been writing letters today to have on hand in case we should see an opportunity to send home."[47]

Families also had the opportunity to socialize in port. Honolulu became a major whaling port in the **In Foreign Ports** middle of the nineteenth century with an average of 400 ships per year anchoring there. While ships were refitted, or while they cruised in the cold Arctic waters, many captains' families moved ashore to take up residence in boarding houses under the palm trees. Some women, who did not sail with their husbands, did make the long, arduous journey from home to join them in Hawaii. While in port, these seafaring families established their own little New England community. Days were filled with rides along the beach, picnics, and croquet. Evenings featured dances, suppers, and concerts.

The decision to join her husband brought many extremes to the whaling wife. There was the intimacy of **To Be at Home** being together and the separation from home and fam- **or Aboard** ily. There were tedious days of boredom and exciting visits to exotic places. There were peaceful moonlight walks on deck and terrifying battles between monster whales and courageous men in tiny boats. During her first cruise, Mary Chapman Lawrence wrote, "This is one of the delightful moments of my life. I do not wonder that so many choose a sailor's life. It is a life of hardship, but a life full of romance and interest."[48] For some women, one voyage was enough, yet others repeatedly made the journeys. Having been to sea and seen firsthand the trials and jeopardy of life at sea, Mary Russell wrote to her daughter back home, "This is the way these sons of the ocean earn their money— that is so thoughtlessly spent at home. . . . Could some of these ladies whose husbands are occupied in this dangerous business have been here these few hours past, I think it would be a lesson they would not forget. It would teach them prudence and economy more powerfully than all the books ever written on the subject since the invention of printing."[49] For most women who repeatedly went to sea with their men, the reason is best summed up by Mary Brewster: "I am satisfied with my condition and perfectly contented and of the two, my husband or friends, I must be separated from, leave me him and all the rest I gladly joyfully resign, preferring his society far more than to them who can be found at home or abroad."[50]

Passing as Men There are verified accounts from the late seventeenth through the early nineteenth centuries of over twenty women who joined the British Royal Navy or Marines and successfully passed themselves as men. A number of these women served honorably for years before they were discovered. It can be speculated that there may have been others who were even more successful and never discovered. An 1802 London journal contained an interesting report of a marriage between two sailors. The couple "had been old shipmates . . . during most part of the war, where the lady bore a most conspicuous part in the different actions in which the frigate was engaged. She was always an attendant in the surgeon's department and waited upon Jones (the bridegroom) in his wounded state. An attachment took place which ended in their union."[51] Ships were not the only place where such a phenomena occurred. There are numerous reported cases of women serving as men during the American Revolution and hundreds of documented cases for the American Civil War.

The natural question that comes to mind upon hearing of these occurrences is how could the women possibly have remained unidentified aboard such crowded vessels with virtually no privacy? The first thing to keep in mind is the probability that these women had certain physical traits that made their detection less likely. If they were small in stature, yet strong and athletic enough to perform the assigned work, these women could easily be taken for young men. In 1815, a London newspaper reported, "Among the crew . . . it is now discovered was a female African who served as a seaman in the Royal Navy for upwards of eleven years, several of which she had been rated able on the books . . . by the name of William Brown. [She] has served for some time as the captain of the foretop, highly to the satisfaction of the officers."[52] Captain of the foretop was a prestigious position garnered only by the most agile, steadfast, and experienced topmen. Biases about the physical, emotional, and intellectual abilities of women, as well as limitations regarding acceptable female roles, forestalled the concept of a female sailor and minimized the likelihood that the men would ever consider another sailor's gender. Maleness was simply taken for granted. The disguise would be even more complete if the women were able to sustain rough language and were willing to chew tobacco.

It is also important to understand that clothing did much in this period to establish the trade, wealth, and gender of the wearer. If you dressed as a merchant, it was assumed that you were a merchant. People did not presume to dress out of their station, and proper women simply did not don male attire. While legends and works of literature contain many stories wherein the young maiden disguises herself as a man in order to learn someone's true feelings or to join her beloved, the likelihood of such daring at this point in time was slim The thought might have been titillating, however. Nineteenth-century diarist Sarah Morgan, regretting the limitations of her gender, wrote, "How do breeches and coats feel, I wonder? I am actually afraid of them."[53] One day she boldly decided to unshroud the mystery herself, "I advanced so far as to lay it (the suit) on the bed, and then I carried my bird out—I was ashamed to let even my canary see me—but when I took a second look, my courage deserted me, and there ended my first attempt at disguise. I have heard so many girls boast of wearing men's clothes; I wonder where they get the courage."[54]

The next logical question might well be why would a woman seek a way of life that was so repressed and harsh as that of a seaman? While a sailor's life was generally more restrictive than that of a civilian man, it offered incredible freedom to a woman. In her disguise at sea, the woman received pay equal with that of men, and she was free to dispose of it as she saw fit. An unmarried woman's money was controlled by her father or brother. A single woman in domestic service, an area where most woman were able to find employment, might even have her finances controlled by her employer.

Sarah Rosetta Wakemam disguised herself as a man and worked as a canal boatman in 1862 before enlisting in the Union Army during the American Civil War. She was unique because her situation was known to her parents and her correspondence with them has survived. Naturally, a woman in such a disguise would neither risk keeping a diary nor would she be likely to disclose much in letters. Sarah regularly sent money back to her family with admonitions such as, "Don't save it for me for I can get all the money I want."[55] Few women of her time could make that claim.

Mary Lacy, who served as William Chandler from 1759 to 1771 in the Royal Navy, rose from a carpenter's servant to a fully qualified shipwright. Such an opportunity would never have been offered to her as a woman. Women were commonly prohibited from many trades. When they were permitted in a field, they were routinely given the lowliest work, and if it was a job also given to men, women were paid less for the same work.

Many women, alone and destitute, ended up as prostitutes. William Robinson, who served in the Royal Navy, described the prostitutes he saw in Portsmouth, England. From his description, it is easy to understand why Elizabeth Bowen, in similar straits at age fourteen, willingly disguised herself as a boy and signed on board ship.

Of all the human race, these poor creatures are the most pitiable; the ill-usage and the degradation they are driven to submit to are indescribable; but from habit they become callous, indifferent as to delicacy of speech and behavior, and so totally lost to all sense of shame that they seem to retain no quality which properly belongs to women but the shape and the name . . . whilst this system is observed, it cannot be said that the slave trade is abolished in England.[56]

Of course, some women probably identified emotionally with men. They were not only successful in their disguises, they were comfortable living as a male. During this time in history, it was impossible for a woman to alter her gender role in her own community. Any attempt to do so would not only be met with hostility toward the woman, it would bring shame, humiliation, and social ostracization to her entire family. Mere relocation was not a simple solution, since finding employment in an area where she had no contacts or references was extremely difficult under any circumstances. The sea provided a way to escape the past and begin anew with no questions asked.

Rebecca Johnson served at sea for seven years before her gender was discovered in 1808. It was then disclosed that her mother had also served at sea and fell in battle as a member of the gun's crew. Hannah Witney served five years as a marine and revealed herself only after being picked up by a press gang years later. Women in male disguise always had one advantage over their shipmates. They could disclose their secret and gain immediate release from service. Nonetheless, some women continued to live as men even after their secret was disclosed.

A popularized explanation for women who chose this means of adventure can be seen in the "lost lover" theme of ballads from the period. In the "Marchants Daughter of Bristow," first printed in the 1590s. Maudlin, a merchant's daughter, falls in love with a young man who is thought to be her social inferior. Forced to break off the relationship by her father, Maudlin disguises herself as a ship's boy and goes to sea searching for her sailor love. After numerous adventures, Maudlin meets up with him and the joyous couple return home to inherit the family fortune.

This theme was so often repeated in ballads that it was conceivably included in otherwise factual accounts of women in male disguise for its romantic qualities. In reality, it is highly unlikely that a woman would adopt a male disguise to follow her love when she could have joined him as his wife. A less romantic situation such as that faced by Hanna

Snell, who disguised herself and went to sea to find her sailor husband who had abandoned her and their unborn child, was more likely.

There are examples of women passing as men on American ships as well. In 1848, Ann Johnson served under the name George Johnson on a whaler for seven months. Georgianna Leonard signed on a whaler as a man out of New Bedford in November 1862. She was discovered in January of the following year only after she was ordered to be flogged for having attacked the second mate with a knife.

A few women gained notoriety and infamy as female pirates. Although they dressed as men, the gender of **Female Pirates** these women was no secret. Alwilda, the daughter of a fifth-century Scandinavian king who took to piracy rather than marry her father's selection, gained fame in popular literature and her scandalous tale enjoyed tremendous popularity through the nineteenth century. It is difficult, however, to separate fact from fiction in the details of her adventures and much that was recorded is suspect.

Two very real female pirates, however, were Grace O'Malley of Ireland and Mrs. Cheng of China. Few details are known of their activities beyond their names. In the social climate of the time, however, any woman who successfully commanded men and ships under a variety of hostile circumstances must have been both highly skilled and especially charismatic no matter what nefarious venture she pursued.

The best-known female pirates were probably Ann Bonny and Mary Read. These women fully engaged in pirate attacks and robberies when sailing with the pirate Calico Jack. They were captured, tried, and found guilty of piracy. Upon being sentenced to death by hanging, the women revealed the scandalous fact that each of them was pregnant. Granted a reprieve due to their circumstances, Mary died of fever shortly after being imprisoned. Ann Bonny's fate was not recorded and remains a mystery.

NOTES

1. William P. Mack and Royal W. Connell, *Naval Ceremonies, Customs, and Traditions* (Annapolis, MD: Naval Institute Press, 1980), 285.

2. Edward Hughes, ed., *The Private Correspondence of Admiral Lord Collingwood* (London: Navy Records Society, 1957), 251.

3. Suzanne J. Stark, *Female Tars: Women Aboard Ship in the Age of Sail* (Annapolis, MD: Naval Institute Press, 1996), 50–52.

4. John Nicol, *The Life and Adventures of John Nicole, Mariner* (1822; reprint, New York: Farrar and Rhinehart, 1936), 170–171.

5. Charles M'Pherson, *Life on Board a Man-of-War* (Glasgow: Blackie, 1829), quoted in Henry Baynham, *From the Lower Deck: The Royal Navy, 1700–1840* (Barre, MA: Barre Gazette 1970), 160.

6. Alan Villers, *Men, Ships and the Sea* (Washington, DC: National Geographic Society, 1973), 184.

7. G. J. Marcus, *Heart of Oak: A Survey of British Sea Power in the Georgian Era* (London: Oxford University Press, 1975), 224.

8. Charles Nordhoff, *Sailor Life on Man-of-War and Merchant Vessel* (New York: Dodd, Mead & Co., 1884), 95–96.

9. Nicol, 171.

10. Richard Henry Dana, Jr., *The Seaman's Friend: Containing a Treatise on Practical Seamanship* (1879; reprint, Mineola, NY: Dover, 1997), 222.

11. Ibid.

12. Joan Druett, ed., *She Was a Sister Sailor: The Whaling Journals of Mary Brewster* (Mystic, CT: Mystic Seaport Museum, 1992), 82.

13. Druett, 22.

14. Stanton Garner, ed., *The Captain's Best Mate: The Journal of Mary Chapman Lawrence on the Whaler* Addison, *1856–1860* (Hanover, NH: University Press of New England, 1966), 9.

15. Druett, 23.

16. Harold Williams, ed., *One Whaling Family* (Boston: Houghton Mifflin, 1964), 130.

17. Druett, 79.

18. Ibid., 15.

19. Joan Druett, *Hen Frigates: Wives of Merchant Captains under Sail* (New York: Simon & Schuster, 1998), 62.

20. Catherine Petroski, *A Bride's Passage: Susan Hathorn's Year under Sail* (Boston: Northeastern University Press, 1997), 209–218.

21. Ibid., 37.

22. Emma Mayhew Whiting and Henry Beetle Bough, *Whaling Wives* (Boston: Houghton Mifflin, 1953), 163.

23. Druett, *She Was a Sister Sailor*, 90.

24. Petroski, 23.

25. Druett, *She Was a Sister Sailor*, 188.

26. Nordhoff, 114.

27. Petroski, 12.

28. Druett, *She Was a Sister Sailor*, 82.

29. A.B.C. Whipple, *The Whalers* (Alexandria, VA: Time-Life Books, 1979), 112.

30. Druett, *Hen Frigates*, 46.

31. Ibid., 91.

32. Ibid., 92.

33. Williams, 126.

34. "Editor's Table," *Peterson's Magazine* (September 1864), found in R. L. Shep, ed., *Civil War Ladies: Fashions and Needle Arts of the Early 1860's* (Mendocino, CA: R. L. Shep, 1987), 326.

35. Williams, 98.

36. Ibid., 183.

37. Druett, *Hen Frigates*, 103.

38. Elizabeth Stuart Phelps, "The Voyage of the *America*," *Scribner's Monthly* vol. 12, no. 5 (September 1876): 682.

39. Whiting and Hough, 117–118.

40. Ibid., 127–129.

41. Garner, 85.

42. Ibid.

43. Ibid., 5.

44. Ibid., 12.

45. Williams, 153.

46. Garner, 18.

47. Ibid., 8.

48. Ibid., 5.

49. Whipple, 113.

50. Joan Druett, *She Was a Sister Sailor*, 87–88.

51. Mack and Connell, 293.

52. Stark, 86.

53. Charles East, ed., *Sarah Morgan: The Civil War Diary of a Southern Woman* (New York: Touchstone, 1991), 167.

54. Ibid.

55. Lauren Cook Burgess, ed., *An Uncommon Soldier* (Pasadena, MD: The Minerva Center, 1994), 18.

56. Reprint of *Nautical Economy* (London: 1836), found in William Robinson, *Jack Nastyface: Memoirs of a Seaman* (Annapolis, MD: Naval Institute Press, 1973), 87–92.

9

The Great Trading Fleets of Europe

Play with your fancies; and in them behold upon hempen tackle ship-
boys climbing; hear the shrill whistle which doth order give to
sounds confused; behold the threaden sails, borne with invisible and
creeping wind, draw the huge bottoms through the furrowed sea,
breasting the lofty surge . . . for so appears this fleet majestical.
—William Shakespeare, *Henry V*, act II, scene iv

THE CHARTER TRADING COMPANIES

The age of sail is particularly noted for the giant monopolies granted to
the trading companies of Europe. With the discovery of the New World,
many of the crown heads of Europe found themselves frustrated by their
inability to take immediate advantage of the opportunity to expand their
influence outside their own realms. For centuries, foreign trade was less
spurred by individual initiative than by powerful companies composed
of groups of merchants who received special privileges from their rulers.
Thus, small groups of men, who were willing to risk their wealth by
subscribing to the stock of a chartered trading company, were given an
attentive royal ear when they begged the privilege of exploiting these
potentially profitable new fields of commerce in the name of their country. England, France, Spain, Portugal, and Holland all had great trading
monopolies chiefly in the East and West Indies, while Denmark, Sweden,
and Russia chartered smaller or less extensive enterprises.

A number of kingdoms chartered companies to trade with the East

Indies during the seventeenth century. Chief among these were England, France, and Holland. In the East Indies, direct trading agreements were formed for the first time with local potentates for goods that had been imported into Europe for centuries through the services of Arab and Persian merchants. These middlemen had transferred trade goods from the Indian Ocean to Europe by an overland route, adding a premium to the price of everything they handled and raising the value of these commodities in all of Europe. The new trading companies were cutting out the middlemen and pocketing the profits for their investors.

The profits from American trading posts, on the other hand, could be precarious. Initially the New World trade relied almost entirely on unprecedented agreements with generally unsophisticated native populations who might, or might not, honor their agreements. Moreover, many of the unfamiliar trade goods available from these novel trading partners, such as tobacco, potatoes, or corn, had no established European market. The English Crown chartered the London Company to trade at Plymouth and in Virginia, charging their employees to look for more readily accepted items such as gold, silver, and furs. Holland set up the Dutch West India Company to trade in American sugar and furs; the Swedes established the South Company to develop American trade in furs in the Delaware Valley; and Spain granted monopoly rights in much of North and South America to the Chartered Company of Seville to look for precious metals. In many of these quests, the trading companies were disappointed, but the European rulers who granted the charters were, nonetheless, able to establish colonies and property rights in undeveloped and unexplored places without risking their personal or royal wealth.

Although the various charters differed on specifics, each contained certain essential similarities. In return for sovereignty over the territory in which the company's trading posts and settlements were established, the government gave the company a monopoly over the trade in those areas and over the trade routes established therein. Each company was further given permission to make alliances and contracts with the princes or natives of the region; to appoint and to remove civil, military, and judicial officers; to promote the settlement of fertile and uninhabited districts; to defend themselves if trade should be jeopardized; to build, maintain, and man fortresses; to establish and man their own fleet of warships; and to retain all prizes of war.

The primary obligations of the trading company under such a charter were "somewhat nominal and formal."[1] The company was required to transmit to the home government for approval all alliances and treaties; to report the location of fortresses and settlements; to render an accounting of all profits and losses; to pay for any government troops sent to defend its outposts; and to conduct its activities with wisdom and justice.

It was in vessels like this caravel that many of the voyages of exploration of the fifteenth and sixteenth centuries were carried out. Illustration from an early-twentieth-century text in the authors' collection.

A secondary consideration was that of Christianizing the natives, a responsibility taken quite seriously by most Europeans, especially the Portuguese, Spanish, and French Catholics.

Under the charters, most rulers reserved the right to confirm a number of colonial appointments such as that of governor-general, or viceroy, and they demanded an oath of allegiance from the directors, employees, and any armed forces established by the trading company. The major obligation of the ruler to the charter company was to maintain and defend the company's monopoly with both men and ships against the claims of other companies and other rulers. The assertion of trading privileges by others in the company's territory, the use of its protected trade routes by the vessels of other nations, or any outright attack upon the company's trading establishments or colonies required the intervention of the state. In the age of sail, the governments of Europe increased the size of their own navies largely to ensure their ability to successfully intervene in cases such as these.[2]

Unaware of the potential wealth of the Americas, Spain was initially disappointed by the discovery of a continental land mass, populated by "heathen savages," which blocked the ocean passage to the fabulous spices and riches of the East Indies. Nonetheless, Spain was the recipient of far greater wealth than any other European nation because it was the first to sack the largest, richest portions of the Americas. Yet the Spanish saw these eagerly sought emblems of wealth quickly pass from their hands. Their wealth "being in small bulk on a few ships, following more or less regular routes, was easily seized upon by an enemy, and [the Spanish] sinews of war paralyzed." Therefore, the great fleets of armed naval vessels that plied the oceans from the sixteenth to eighteenth centuries generally owed their very existence to trade.[3]

THE GREAT FLEETS

The giant fleets of the sixteenth century often numbered hundreds of vessels and were generally mere assemblies of armed merchantmen. Indeed, the most permanent characteristic of these older navies was their impermanence.[4] Merchant types were built for stability and hold capacity, not for speed and warfare. When not actively part of a military campaign, they were used solely for trade. In a sixteenth-century sea battle, speed was of little consequence among ships so tightly wedged together in a small area of ocean that any form of maneuver, even had the protagonists wished it, was physically impossible. The vessels served merely as fighting platforms for the troops who battled from deck to deck or fired down from huge improvised wooden "castles" built on the fore and aft decks.

Ordinary weapons such as swords, cutlasses, daggers, axes, polearms, pistols, and muskets—identical to those used on land—were used in these sea battles. Hot pitch, boiling oil, molten lead, clubs, and grapples were also employed. A few "awe-inspiring" cannon were included in each vessel's arsenal of weaponry, but the earliest versions proved "cumbersome" and "singularly ineffective" at sea. The use of superior, long-range naval armament was not a factor in naval warfare until it was introduced by the English late in the sixteenth century.[5]

Unlike the specially trained crews of the war fleets of the eighteenth century, whose duties were more task-specific, the crews of sixteenth-century war fleets evidenced a clear division between the fighting forces on board and those men who were expected to sail the ship, maneuver during engagements, and deal with emergencies or repairs. The fighting forces were often composed of ordinary land infantry with no specific training in fighting at sea, while the vessels were manned by seamen

Weapons common to the eighteenth-century sailor (top to bottom): a blunderbuss .69 caliber, a sea service musket .75 caliber, a sea service pistol .69 caliber, a cutlass. James Volo Photo.

unaccustomed to military tactics. Often they were led by generally competent military men, who had little knowledge of seamanship. A Spanish commander who survived the destruction of his fleet in 1574 exclaimed after the battle, "I told you I was a land fighter and no sailor; give me a hundred fleets and I would fare no better."[6]

The inefficiency of such a naval system was magnified by the common practice of choosing "gentlemen" of high social rank as commanders of individual vessels rather than seamen. Although not lacking in courage or dedication, these men were often unable to subordinate their egos to the exigencies of cooperative fleet tactics.[7] Nonetheless, it was also quite certain that all antagonists in a sixteenth-century sea battle had mobilized their naval forces in much the same way. Moreover, fleets were not asked to do a great deal beyond the transportation of land troops and were assigned far fewer functions to perform than their eighteenth- or nineteenth-century counterparts.[8]

THE PORTUGUESE AND THE SPANISH

During the critical early years of Europe's exploration of the world's seas (in the fifteenth century), it was Portuguese mariners who made the most meaningful advances in maritime technology and achievement. Under the direction of Prince Henry, the Navigator (1394–1460), Portuguese vessels regularly left their long Atlantic-facing seaboard to travel to the Azores, the Canaries, and the west coast of Africa. In 1488, Bartholomew Dias rounded Africa's Cape of Good Hope and entered the approaches to the Indian Ocean. It was Portugal, therefore, that established many of the early skills characteristic of European seamanship.

Until the 1490s, Portugal's more powerful neighbor, Spain, was occupied with the internal problems of consolidating the kingdom and of driving the Moors from the Iberian Peninsula. The expulsion of the Moors from Granada in the last decade of the fifteenth century by Ferdinand and Isabella removed a major obstacle to the voyages of discovery that opened the New World to European exploration.

Spain's ports and possessions surrounding the Caribbean soon became known as the Spanish Main. Although this originally designated only those portions of the continental mainland bordering the Caribbean and Gulf of Mexico, in practical terms, the Spanish Main also included all the islands from Trinidad off the coast of Venezuela to the Straits of Florida. Spain declared the entire Caribbean basin a *mare clausum*, or closed sea. The government refused to recognize the right of any foreign vessel to enter the area and seized those that were found there. Defending this self-proclaimed prerogative assumed that the Spanish navy could control all the shipping in the Caribbean, but of course, it could not. Both French and English privateers and pirates regularly attacked Spanish shipping and burned Spanish towns in the Caribbean. French, Dutch, English, and even Danish traders increasingly refused to acknowledge Spain's American monopoly.[9]

In 1537 in a response to increasing attacks upon their rich New World shipping, the Spanish established the Armada de la Guardia, a convoy system for their treasure galleons. The system included two fleets of merchant vessels sailing under the protection of armed warships. The *flota* left Spain for the West Indian islands in the spring, carrying trade goods, supplies, and personnel. The *galeones* departed in midsummer for Panama and the northeast coast of Columbia. Both fleets met at Havana the following spring to sail back to Spain loaded with treasure.

Spain's absorption of the kingdom of Portugal and its navy in 1580 immediately made it a major naval power. Spanish galleons plied the oceans of the world, and the treasure fleets brought fabulous wealth to her shores. Spain's "black ships" and "Manila galleons" brought the wealth of the East Indies and the Philippines across the Pacific to be trans-shipped across the Isthmus of Panama and the Atlantic to Spain. By the third quarter of the sixteenth century, Spain was the unequivocal ruler of the seas. Yet, with its strength dangerously overextended, Spain found it increasingly difficult to stop intrusions into its vast American trading empire.

Spain's chief rival at sea was England, which had ex- **Anglo-Hispanic** perienced an unprecedented growth in maritime activ- **Tensions** ity since the reign of Henry Tudor (Henry VII). The enmity that flourished between the two kingdoms in the middle of the sixteenth century was fueled by more than a quest for gold and riches. In 1533, Henry's son, Henry VIII, set the English kingdom in opposition to Spain when he divorced his wife, a former Spanish princess. He thereafter set up a Protestant church in England separate from the authority of the pope. Henry's direct heir, Edward VI, drove the English even further into Protestantism. When the youthful Edward died in 1553, the throne passed to Henry's Catholic daughter, Mary Tudor, who had married Philip II of Spain. This circumstance briefly united the two kingdoms, but it was a short-lived alliance.

As queen, Mary's unbridled and severe repression of all English Protestants earned her the title "Bloody Mary" as well as the enmity of a large portion of the English people. Queen Mary's death in 1558 put her sister, Elizabeth Tudor, on the throne. Elizabeth I absolutely rejected Catholicism and earned the hatred of her former brother-in-law, Philip II, who was pledged to defend the Roman Church. The two realms drifted into a state of undeclared naval warfare over commercial, political, and demographic differences. Elizabeth was particularly active in sending out raiders to plunder Spanish colonies and treasure fleets. Philip countered by attacking English ships and seizing English seamen for use as slaves in his row galleys.[10]

In 1587, Philip II attempted to establish maritime dominance in Europe. To that end he gathered a great war **The Armada** fleet, the Armada. Philip prepared the Armada, under the command of the Marquis of Santa Cruz, specifically to chastise Elizabeth and to invade England with a force under the Duke of Parma in the north of Europe. Most of the details surrounding the Armada were formulated by Philip himself. In a single year, he was able to concentrate 130 vessels at Lisbon. Upon the untimely death of Santa Cruz in 1588, the Duke of Medina Sidonia was placed in charge of the operation. This was an unfortunate turn of events as Medina Sidonia was a nobleman with little seamanship.

As the largest Spanish war fleet ever assembled, the Armada was a product of Philip's own naval philosophy and political goals, and it was typical of the giant fleets of the sixteenth century, drawing its 130 ships from all parts of the Spanish empire. The majority of the vessels were designated to convoy a Spanish army, already in the Netherlands, across the Channel to England. These were transports, victualers, and provision ships rather than warships.

The English defense against the Armada consisted of some 90 ships under Sir Francis Drake and about 100 smaller vessels under Lord Henry

Seymour and Sir William Winter. Some 32 of these were race-built galleons especially armed for war and among the first true warships ever
built. The English fleets stood away from the Spanish warships in the
engagements that followed. In unprecedented fashion, they followed the
enemy up the Channel and reached out with their long-range guns to
inflict destruction on the Spanish rear. Contrary winds, adverse tides,
and poor communications kept the Spanish from mounting an effective
response.

An English fireship attack on the Spanish anchored off Calais to await
the Duke of Parma's invasion forces dispersed the survivors of the initial
battle as they cut their cables to escape. Medina Sidonia turned with a
half dozen warships to fight and be defeated a second time. Finally, a
storm in the Channel, combined with English doggedness, scattered the
remnants of the Armada across the North Sea beyond any chance of
reclamation.

Notwithstanding the intrusion of the weather, many historians lay the
failure of the Armada at the door of Philip. His plan to link a fleet with
an invasion force hundreds of miles away, in the face of a determined
enemy, and in an age of unreliable communications was overly optimistic. As a consequence of the English victory over the Armada, Spain
never again rose to the position of a great naval power. But England did
not immediately rise to maritime prominence. It was the Dutch that were
the immediate beneficiaries of the English victory.[11]

THE DUTCH

More than any other country in Europe, the Dutch Republic drew its
prosperity and much of its national character from the sea. Composed
of seven Protestant provinces separated from the Catholic states of the
south by the Low Countries surrounding the rivers Scheldt and Maas,
the Dutch government was actually an association of small sovereign
states governed by the Lords of the States General. Each province had
its own fleet, its own admiralty, and its own policies toward maritime
trade and naval affairs. However, the province of Holland held a disproportionate influence over the other members of the republic, supplying five-sixths of its fleet and 60 percent of its tax revenues. The Dutch
were alternately referred to as the United Provinces or simply Holland
throughout this period.

Much of the territory that made up the provinces had been part of the
vast Spanish empire first of Charles V and later of Philip II. The religious
wars of the Protestant Reformation and Catholic Counter-Reformation
in Europe displaced many people, and the provinces became an asylum
for anti-Catholic religious dissenters. Intensely patriotic and willing to
make sacrifices to protect their freedom, the Dutch formed a "commercial

aristocracy" in the Baltic Sea and North Atlantic. They specialized in building "light and inexpensive ships," which they could sail more efficiently than other nations and charge less freight. Thereby they "were able to compete successfully with all other countries." Commodities from Russia, the Levant, and the Far East entered Europe through these provinces.[12]

Philip II, seeking to punish religious nonconformity among the Dutch, ultimately drove the provinces to armed rebellion. They declared independence from Spain under the Union of Utrecht in 1579. With growing towns and seaports, the Dutch consolidated their commerce and trade in the face of Spanish repression. Although generally adverse to war, they were forced to fight for their continued existence throughout the sixteenth and seventeenth centuries and were willing to make the naval expenditures needed to protect their commerce. The defeat of the Armada by the English gave the Dutch a brief respite from Spanish aggression at sea.

With amazing foresight, the Dutch built upon the navigational skills of the Portuguese. In 1602, they formed the Dutch East India Company. It was remarkably successful. By driving the competition to the ground in the spice market, the Dutch tripled the value of pepper in Europe.[13] The first twenty years of the Dutch company's existence returned the investors initial capital fourfold. The financial success of the company was extraordinary, and it raised the importance of its home city of Amsterdam as a commercial center. In the prolonged contest with Spain, Amsterdam had not suffered as severely as some of the other Dutch cities, leaving it the richest mercantile city in all of Europe. "[T]he treasures of the Indies were unloaded on its docks, its warehouses held the choicest products of the world, [and] the business of Europe was transacted on the Amsterdam Exchange."[14]

The early voyages of Dutch trading ships established posts in the Spice Islands of the East Indies and helped to create a Dutch trading empire in Asia. The company's charter allowed for the establishment of forts and garrisons at strategic locations, and the Dutch government authorized the building of warships to protect her sea-borne commerce. Notwithstanding the fact that the original purpose of the broad powers given to the company was to safeguard its commerce from attacks by the Spanish and Portuguese, at its height the Company had 150 merchantmen, 40 warships, and more than 10,000 soldiers in the field. Moreover, the Dutch navy of this period was, in point of numbers of vessels and the quality of their equipment, the rival of the combined fleets of France and England.

The Dutch had supported England in its struggles with Spain in 1588 through self-interest and religious conviction, but free of a Spanish threat, Dutch shipping in the Baltic quickly outstripped English trading

The galleon was the premier treasure ship of the seventeenth and eighteenth centuries. Note the high stern castle and spreading rake of the masts. Illustration from an early-twentieth-century text in the authors' collection.

vessels by almost seven to one. Fully 80 percent of all European trading vessels called Dutch ports their home by the seventeenth century. The company's warships outnumbered the English in Asian waters by more than three to one and effectively drove the English traders from the East Indies.

However, in 1612, Dutch confidence had been severely shaken when a vastly superior Portuguese fleet was soundly defeated by two small English warships lying in the mouth of the Surat River north of Bombay. Dutch dealings with the English quickly became more strained.[15]

The formation of the powerful Dutch West India Company in 1621 gave Dutch traders a virtual monopoly in North America and Africa that they were able to maintain for more than two decades. Although much of this area was claimed and occupied by Spain, commercial interests in Holland advocated an aggressive trading policy that directly challenged Spanish claims, especially in the West Indies. The directors of the company took immense pleasure "above all in humbling the pride and might of Spain."[16]

Dutch traders sold slaves, knives, mirrors, cloth, and flour to the Spanish colonies, and they brought back to Amsterdam tobacco, sugar, dye stuffs, and hides. Ten ships a month brought salt from the coast of Venezuela. All persons trading without the Dutch company's' permission did so under the threat of confiscation of their ships and goods. The increasing pace of Dutch competition with Spain for sea-borne trade ultimately led to renewed open conflict.[17]

In 1623 the Dutch executed several employees of the English East India Company, forcing the remaining English to retreat to their posts in India. Buoyed by the failure of the English to respond, the Dutch became aggressive. In 1624, they seized Bahia, the Spanish capital of Brazil but could not hold the city. In 1625, a fleet of 17 warships, under Boudewijn Hendricksz, attempted an offensive on Puerto Rico. Hendricksz exhibited a good deal of personal courage as the first attacker to leap ashore under fire. Unable to take the main fortress of El Moro after almost a month of fighting, he looted and burned San Juan before retreating.[18] In 1628, a Dutch squadron of privateers under Pieter Heyn, who had twice been a galley slave on Spanish vessels and had twice escaped, drove several Spanish treasure ships aground, and took riches worth fifteen million gilders out of them. On receipt of the news, the Dutch West India Company declared a 50 percent dividend.[19]

Jan De Witt, a Dutch statesman, came to power in Holland in mid-century. De Witt generally favored the autonomy of Holland within the Dutch Republic, but he also opposed the dynastic claims of the House of Orange. Although his policies often conflicted with the good of the republic as a whole, the importance of Holland as a sovereign member of the United Provinces made him the de facto prime minister of the entire union. De Witt's leadership helped to maintain the Dutch as a major European commercial and colonial power through the third quarter of the century. He viewed every element of Dutch trading as semi-military in character, and his commercial policies quickly evolved from simple competition to ruthless economic aggression.

Although erstwhile allies in the religious wars of the first half of the century, Holland and England came to loggerheads over trade. In 1642, the Dutch had forced the Portuguese out of Malacca. When the Dutch East India Company also drove the Portuguese from Ceylon, the English were left "full of suspicions and accusations," mostly concerned for the security of their own foothold in India. Recognizing that there was little room for two trading nations on the western seaboard of Europe, the English began a shipbuilding program that resulted in a large and powerful fleet.[20]

The First Anglo-Dutch War (1652–1654) was unlike England's war with Spain in which there had been a single giant fleet action. In less than two years, there were six major sea battles, most of which involved large numbers of both warships and trading vessels. During the war, the English were led by admirals Robert Blake and George Monck, and the Dutch were commanded by Admiral Martin Tromp. The second major sea battle of the war saw 66 English warships pitted against 70 Dutch warships and 250 merchantmen. The battle lasted for three days. Even though the battle proved indecisive, for the first time in the age of sail, there was a determined contest "on the sea for command of the sea."[21]

Although a seemingly equal struggle, the Dutch were quickly beaten in the First Anglo-Dutch War because they lost command of their vital sea approaches in the North Sea and the Channel. Nonetheless, the English fleet was badly mauled in the final sea battle of the series, and De Witt was thereby able to negotiate a favorable treaty. Dutch naval prowess had been humbled, but they had not been pushed off the world stage of trade. During the next decade, De Witt greatly enlarged his navy, and he placed it under command of the brilliant naval strategist Admiral Michael De Ruyter.

The First Anglo-Dutch War was fought under the Parliamentary government that had come into power during the English Civil Wars (1640–1649). The Protectorate was displaced in 1660 by the return of the Stuart monarchy in the person of King Charles II and his brother James, the Duke of York, who served as Lord High Admiral. Charles did his best to precipitate a war with the Dutch, sending a fleet to raid their trading stations on the coast of New Guinea and expanding English trade in the East Indies through his holdings in Bombay. The English attitude was summarized by a naval officer who bluntly remarked, "The trade of the world is too little for two of us: therefore one must go down."[22]

The Second Anglo-Dutch War began in 1665. The Dutch declared war but were not anxious to completely alienate their sometime ally. Their war aims simply required a modification of the British Navigation Acts (first enacted in 1660), a recognition of Dutch trading hegemony in the East Indies, and a reaffirmation of Dutch possession of several sugar islands in the Caribbean.

The initial sea battles were large affairs with nearly 100 ships to a side. Admiral Monck sent part of his fleet under Sir Robert Holmes into the Dutch port of Texel, where about 150 Dutch ships were destroyed. Admiral De Ruyter retaliated by capturing the English colony at St. John's, Newfoundland, and by defeating a large English fleet in 1666. In 1667, finding no English opposition in the Thames River, De Ruyter passed the unfinished shore fortifications on the riverbanks and destroyed the English fleet at anchor. To add insult to injury, he appropriated the English flagship *Royal Charles* for his own use and had several first-raters towed from their moorings and burnt as they lay in shallow water within sight of London. The blow to English morale could not be overestimated.

In the subsequent peace treaty of 1667, the Dutch won all of their war aims and gained special trading privileges in Sumatra. They mollified the English by giving them the New World colony of New Netherlands. This concession, taken together with existing claims and colonies, gave the English an uninterrupted Atlantic seaboard in North America from the Bay of Fundy to Florida. This momentous transfer of sovereignty was noted by almost no one at the time except the residents of the small Dutch town of New Amsterdam at the mouth of Hudson's river (then called the North River). The immediate impact of the exchange was simply to rename the place New York in honor of the Duke of York, the king's brother.

In 1668, Louis XIV of France threatened the Low Countries of Europe, which bordered Holland. This caused De Witt to formulate a triple alliance with Sweden and England against the French. However, De Witt resigned his office as soon as the French invaded the Lowlands, and he was subsequently killed by an unforgiving mob. In 1672, the republic passed away to be replaced by the rule of William of Orange. Nonetheless, during De Witt's tenure in office, Holland had changed from a simple merchant nation into a major sea power. The Dutch remained a major player in worldwide sea-borne commerce. In 1678, the English stripped her of much of her European trade. But for almost a century thereafter, the Dutch remained supreme in the Far East and retained much of their Asian trading empire into the twentieth century.

THE FRENCH

The French tendency to treat their maritime interests as secondary in importance to their dream of dominating the European continent should not be minimized when studying their naval history. The standard policy of using sea power solely to ensure positions ashore inevitably made the French navy a mere extension of the army for the duration of a particular campaign. The subordination of sea power to this role must be considered when analyzing French conduct on the world stage, since it seems to be a permanent facet of French strategy, transcending the many monarchs, republican directories, and emperors. According to a French naval historian, "The French navy has always preferred the glory of assuring or preserving a conquest to that more brilliant perhaps, but less real, glory of taking some ships."[23]

Before the establishment of the Royal Marine, France had regularly relied upon the impressment of private vessels to attain her war aims. These objectives rarely included prolonged control of the sea lanes and were usually limited to the pursuit of French interests on the continent.

A national interest in the development of a French navy was briefly kindled in 1627 by an unexpected and overwhelming victory over an English fleet sent to relieve the Protestant Huguenots besieged in the city of La Rochelle. But the development of a world-class fleet, requiring vast sums of money for its support and maintenance, was not immediately possible in a nation disrupted by civil unrest and a weak administration.[24]

In 1643, a child-king, Louis XIV, ascended to the French throne, and the early decades of his reign kept France embroiled in internal affairs. During this period, there was also a great deal of corruption initiated by Nicolas Fouquet, the finance minister. Not until 1661, when Fouquet was finally brought to trial, were the funds needed to build a navy available. Louis' new finance minister, Jean-Baptiste Colbert, played a significant role in producing a vast revenue surplus, which he used in part to establish the foundations of the French navy for the eighteenth century.

Colbert was was a mercantilist. He believed that prosperity could be brought to France by commercial regulation, closely supervised colonization and trade, and a determined enforcement of French navigation laws. In a letter to Cardinal Mazarin, Colbert outlined part of the program that he was to use so successfully: "We must reestablish transport of commodities by sea and land, [and] the navy must be strengthened in order to afford protection to merchant ships." To this end, Colbert helped to establish both the French East and West India companies, and he set about creating a navy and merchant marine to support and protect them.[25]

In spite of the drastic measures that he took to protect French colonial interests from attack in America and India, Colbert was unable to attract sufficient support for the efforts of the French trading companies at home. Nonetheless, once appointed Minister of the Marine in 1669, he provided his assistance to the shipbuilding industry, organized a merchant service, and built a number of warships adequate to protect at least the domestic commerce from enemy raiders. Colbert established formal training for naval architects and port facilities and dry docks for shipbuilders. During his administration, the port of Rochefort was improved and expanded, and several naval training schools for officers were opened.[26]

In just a few years, Colbert's administration had incorporated the whole theory of sea power that was to characterize the eighteenth century. At several points during the reign of Louis XIV, the French fleet nearly equaled the combined naval strength of England and Holland. But even Colbert's unsparing exertions could not make France a world maritime power overnight. A costly and protracted war against Holland undid the greater part of his reforms, and all this growth withered away when he lost the king's favor in the 1680s.

THE ENGLISH

Immediately after 1588, England's fleet was outnumbered by those of other European powers. Even so, English warships were demonstrating that they were to be feared at sea. In 1612, a Portuguese fleet of four galleons and several frigates came in sight of two English vessels, commanded by Captain Thomas Best, lying at anchor at Surat, India. One of these was the warship *Red Dragoon* and the other the *Ozeander*, an armed pinnace. Nicholas Withington, an employee of the Honourable East India Company, left an account of the engagement:

Then our general in the *Dragon* presently weighed anchor and worthily encouraged our men not to fear them nor the greatness of their ships or fleet but to show themselves true Englishmen; and so met their admiral and vice-admiral and shot not one shot till he came between them and then gave each of them a broadside and a brave volley of shot which made them give way and no more come near her that day. [On the next day] the fiery *Dragon* bestirring herself, in some three hours hot fight drove three of the galleons on the sands and then *Ozeander*, drawing little water, danced the hay about them and so paid them that they durst not show a man on their decks, killing and spoiling their men, and battered their ships exceedingly.[27]

Captain Best's brilliant defensive action was the first blow to Portuguese dominance in India. The factors of the company quickly established a base for four warships at Swally near Surat and formed an alliance with the local Mogul ruler. In 1615, Captain Nicholas Downton, attacked by a Portuguese armada and again greatly outnumbered, beat them off no less decisively than Best. The actions of Best and Downton served notice on the maritime powers of Europe that the English sailor was to be taken seriously.

However, these "fierce little battles" with the Portuguese alone could not establish the English traders with the Indian powers. The Mogul emperor of India exhibited a profound lack of interest in commerce with England. The servants of the Honourable East India Company soon learned to be diplomats as well as traders. As a result of careful posturing, the English representative of the company, Sir Thomas Roe, was able to devise an advantageous agreement with the emperor, giving the company "free leave to trade at any port in the Mogul empire, on the east coast as well as the west [and] also the privilege of paying customs once but thereafter no further dues . . . on the same goods." In this regard, the emperor refused to be bound by a treaty, but he deigned to issue a set of imperial orders that produced the same effect.[28]

Notwithstanding these successes for the Honourable East India Company, the accession of the Stuarts to the combined English and Scottish thrones in 1603 introduced a severe reversal of fortunes for the English navy. The general attitude of peaceful coexistence exhibited by the Stuarts for the Catholic thrones of France and Spain led to the Royal Navy's immediate decline. Although several of the largest warships in Europe were built by the English during the period, all four kings of the Stuart line showed an ambivalence toward the development of English sea power to some extent over the next eight decades.[29]

Although ships were used to transport troops around the British Isles, King James I minimized the need for a navy and thought it very expensive to maintain. James' successor, Charles I, came into conflict more than once with Parliament over "ship money" even though he had a royal prerogative to use all the money from the Cinque ports for this purpose. It is difficult to say how much influence such conflicts had in causing Charles to lose his throne to the Parliamentary forces in the 1640s. Nonetheless, the practical concerns generated by the English civil wars overshadowed any development of a truly professional navy for almost a decade. Only during the Republican Period (1649–1658), ruled by the Lord Protector, Oliver Cromwell, was England able to build its sea power. In 1655, an English fleet of 38 ships and 2,500 men wrested the strategic post of Jamaica from the Spanish. Under Cromwell, the fleet rose from 49 vessels to more than 200. By 1660, the English navy had more, better, and larger ships of war than at any time to that date.

Following the restoration of the Stuart line to the throne in 1660, King Charles II exhibited a fondness for ships, and a number of large vessels were built during his reign, including the *Royal Charles*, the largest warship built to that time. Nonetheless, he was particularly indifferent to the decay of English sea power in part because he did not wish to resurrect the disputes with Parliament over ship money. In India, the island of Bombay came as part of the dowry of Charles' Portuguese queen, but it was not until 1665 that the Portuguese, still protesting, handed it over to the English crown. However, Charles did not press for money for its maintenance.[30] Instead he made over the island to the Honourable East India Company in 1668 for a nominal annual rent. Almost immediately, trade came to Bombay as merchants, at the mercy of the mainland Indian powers, came to settle on an island where their goods and persons were secured by the growing reputation of the English fleet.[31]

Historians are greatly divided with regard to the place Charles II should hold in the development of the greatness of the Royal Navy. Any claim to pre-eminent maritime power by the English under Charles II has to be tempered by the facts. While the English were able to destroy an entire Dutch merchant fleet in 1665, the Dutch had little trouble burning much of the English fleet within sight of London only two years later.

Finally Charles II made a dangerous move, contracting an alliance with France against Holland. The Third Anglo-Dutch War was an "unnecessary war" with four major actions. In 1673, James, Duke of York, engaged De Ruyter in the Texel in a bloody and stubborn conflict. The French fleet abandoned the English and sailed clear of the battle. It proved to be the final action of the war, resulting in the French and English being driven from the Dutch coast.[32]

Notwithstanding this controversy, during the reign of Charles II, a number of positive steps were taken that laid the foundations for England's ultimate rise to maritime prominence in the age of sail. One of these was the acquisition of New York. The other came in the person of a bureaucrat, Samuel Pepys.

In the 1670s, while Colbert was establishing the Royal Marine in France, Samuel Pepys—controller of the com- **Samuel Pepys** mission in charge of providing victuals and maintenance for the British fleet under Charles II—was promoted as secretary to the

Lord High Admiral, who was the nominal head of the Admiralty. Pepys was a reformer who brought order and discipline to the workings of the Navy Board, which built and supplied ships, ran the dockyards, and examined the warrant officers under the authority of the Admiralty. He took a number of much needed measures against waste and corruption in government. Nonetheless, he was disappointed to see almost all the reforms he had established quickly forgotten when his policies came into conflict with those of his political enemies. Beginning in 1679, the naval administration quickly reverted to the practices of former times.

Returned to office in 1683, Pepys set to rebuilding the Royal Navy in earnest, and his efforts were met with considerable success.[33] In 1688, he was able to prepare for sea, with little previous warning, a total of seventy-six warships. He devised rules and procedures that provided for almost every contingency of naval operations, and he created the first genuine strategic doctrine for the British navy. Pepys—like DeWitt in Holland and Colbert in France—made the English navy a respected maritime power. It was under Pepys' framework that the Board of Admiralty would operate for more than two centuries.

As the seventeenth century turned, French aspirations of placing a Bourbon on the Spanish throne brought a decade of indecisive conflict known as the War of Spanish Succession. The English, of all the maritime powers involved, was the only nation to exit this war well enough placed to assume a position of maritime supremacy in Europe—building their navy, strengthening and extending their sea-borne commerce, and seizing strategic positions astride some of the most frequented sea lanes, particularly Gibraltar.

Ironically, the Dutch were forced to neglect both their navy and their maritime trade during the war due to "the inherent weakness of a State narrow in territory and small in the number of its people." Holland thereby gave English shipping a virtual monopoly in sea-borne commerce. Dating from the Peace of Utrecht, which ended the war in 1713, Holland ceased to be numbered among the great maritime powers of Europe.[34]

Spanish maritime interests suffered little during the war because their naval presence had not been significant for many decades. The dawn of the eighteenth century found Spain with a motley collection of mostly foreign-built naval vessels. Although Intendant of the Navy, Jose Patino, tried to establish a more potent Spanish sea presence, in 1717 his fleet was all but annihilated in a running series of single combats with the English off Corsica. Not until 1771 would Spain again have more than 100 warships.[35]

France was severely damaged in terms of the immense drain placed on French resources by an extended period of land warfare. Although the French had backed the successful claimant to the Spanish throne, they came out of the conflict strife-torn and exhausted. In the Peace of Utrecht (1713), the French ceded considerable territory on their northern and eastern borders to their enemies, and gave Nova Scotia and Newfoundland in America to England.

The English navy that exited the War of Spanish Succession knew no equal. In the words of Alfred Thayer Mahan, England built "her sea power upon the ruins of her rivals, friend and foe alike." Not only was England now first among the naval powers of Europe, "she controlled the great commerce of the open sea with a military shipping that had no rival."[36]

NOTES

1. Lucy M. Salmon, *The Dutch West India Company on the Hudson* (Poughkeepsie, NY: Published privately, 1915), 19.

2. Ibid., 15–20.

3. Alfred Thayer Mahan, *The Influence of Sea Power upon History, 1660–1783* (New York: Dover, 1987), 42.

4. Michael Lewis, *The History of the British Navy* (Fair Lawn, NJ: Essential Books, 1959), 13.

5. Ibid., 14. Only recently had specialized "warships" made their appearance.

6. William O. Stevens and Allan Westcott, *The History of Sea Power* (New York: Doubleday, Doran, 1943), 98.

7. Mahan, 127–129.

8. Lewis, 15.

9. Alexander Winston, *No Man Knows My Grave: Privateers and Pirates, 1665–1715* (Boston: Houghton Mifflin, 1969), 16.

10. The role played by religion in these relations should not be minimized.

11. The *Mayflower*, which brought the Pilgrims to Massachusetts in 1620, was a member of the English fleet that sailed out against the Armada. It was originally constructed as a wine transport.

12. George Masselman, *The Cradle of Colonialism* (New Haven, CT: Yale University Press, 1963), 49.

13. Winston, 15.

14. Salmon, 22.

15. Philip Woodruff, *The Men Who Ruled India: The Founders* (New York: Schocken Books, 1964), 31.

16. Winston, 16.

17. Stevens and Westcott, 100.

18. National Park Service, *The Forts of Old San Juan: San Juan National Historic Site, Puerto Rico* (Washington, DC: U.S. Department of the Interior, 1996), 38–48.

19. Winston, 16.

20. Brian Gardner, *The East India Company: A History* (New York: Dorrset Press, 1971), 41.

21. Fred T. Jane, *The British Battle Fleet: Its Inception and Growth Throughout the Centuries* (1912; reprint, London: Conway Maritime Press, 1997), 48–49.

22. Lewis, 88.

23. Mahan, 287. Mahan quotes the author Ramatuelle, *Tactique Navale* about which he gives no further information.

24. From 1662 to 1684 France increased its net revenues by 30 million livres.

25. Maurice Ashley, *Louis XIV and the Greatness of France* (New York: Collier, 1962), 37.

26. Ibid., 37–38.

27. Woodruff, 31.

28. Ibid., 33–34.

29. Kevin Phillips, *The Cousins' War: Religion, Politics, and the Triumph of Anglo-America* (New York: Basic Books, 1999), 14.

30. Charles married Catherine of Braganza in 1662, receiving both Bombay and Tangiers. The English abandoned Tangiers to the Moroccans in 1684.

31. Woodruff, 57–58.

32. Lewis, 92–93.

33. John Laffin, *Jack Tars: The Story of the British Sailor* (London: Cassel, 1969), 9–10.

34. Mahan, 209.

35. G. J. Marcus, 246–247. G. Douglas Inglis, "The Spanish Naval Shipyard at Havana in the Eighteenth Century," in *New Aspects of Naval History: Selected Papers from the Fifth Naval History Symposium* (Baltimore, MD: Nautical and Aviation Publishing, 1985), 48–49.

36. Mahan, 209, 224.

10

The Art of War at Sea

What the country needs is the annihilation of the enemy.
                                        —Admiral Lord Horatio Nelson

In clear weather, two ships could see each other over a considerable distance. A man at the masthead with good **The Meeting** eyes and a good telescope could see as far as ten miles.[1] **Encounter** Nonetheless, it was nearly impossible to tell if the sails that appeared over the horizon were those of a friend or an enemy. A ship-of-the-line and a merchantman can have almost identical sail plans. Differences in the size, the number of decks, or the number of guns on a vessel were not obvious at this distance. Many merchant captains painted black squares along the bulwarks of their vessels hoping that they would be mistaken for the gunports of a warship.

A meeting at sea usually brought increased exertions on the part of each commander to ascertain the actual characteristics of an approaching vessel before irrevocably committing himself to an encounter. A lightly armed merchantman or a slaver would immediately run from the appearance of any unexpected sail, even if it proved to be friendly. Privateers or pirates, relying on the speed of their vessels, might try to run along a parallel course before abandoning a possible prize. The warship, however, was under some obligation to stand and make a fight with any enemy vessel near its own size. Nonetheless, during wartime it was almost inevitable that any but the most aggressive commander of a single warship would overestimate the strength, speed, or agility of an enemy and take to his heels. Even aggressive commanders approached an unknown sail with apprehension.[2]

Warships were designed to fight, but in practice, they did so infrequently. When all of the conditions for a sea battle were established—including bringing an enemy to action—the officers and seaman of each vessel faced the supreme test of their readiness and organization. Sea battles were bloody and desperate encounters that stressed the courage and resolve of even the best crews, and officers were under a disproportionate strain to keep themselves and their men steady and under command. While the majority served the guns on the lower decks, part of the crew was always needed to effect repairs quickly and to effectively maintain control of the vessel while under fire.

The Strategic Use of Sea Power

Strategy and tactics are related, but they are not equivalent. Strategy is done in a planning room by heads of state or commanders of military forces (usually on maps), while tactics are applied by the on-site commanders at the point of contact with the enemy. Both English and French naval strategies can serve as classic examples of different attitudes toward sea power in the age of fighting sail.

The primary strategy of the British Royal Navy of the eighteenth century was to bring the enemy fleet to battle and destroy it, thereby preventing a possible armed invasion of Britain, Scotland, or Ireland. Admiral Horatio Nelson identified the ultimate goal of British naval strategy as "the annihilation of the enemy." To attain this objective, the English needed to maintain an overwhelming strength at sea.[3] In the 1740s, for example, the British had 90 ships-of-the-line and 84 frigates, a number that increased during the next decade. By comparison, the French had 45 ships of the line and 76 frigates, and the numbers of French vessels fell as those of British increased during the Seven Years War.[4]

The disparity in fleet size is best explained in terms of French naval strategy. The French objective in maintaining a fleet was to protect their trading establishments, island outposts, and colonies. The Royal Marine was also used to facilitate ulterior objectives on the Continent such as the movement of troops or the distribution of supplies. The French needed, therefore, to have only enough ships to resist scattered incursions of their empire or to similarly threaten British interests. The policy of the French admirals was "to neutralize the power of their adversaries, if possible, by grand maneuvers rather than to destroy it by grand attack."[5] This strategy, known in maritime circles as that of a "fleet in being," required a stronger enemy to take extraordinary measures to maintain its preponderance of strength while allowing the weaker the economy of maintaining a smaller naval establishment and applying its national resources elsewhere.

Alfred Thayer Mahan noted that the reliance on the defensive use of sea power alone harbored an intrinsic inadequacy for a nation with many posts and scattered colonies, compelling the strategist "to distribute his force so as to be strong enough to stop the enemy on any line of attack that he [might] adopt."[6] These differences in naval strategy must not be forgotten as it is only against this backdrop that some of the naval campaigns of the period can be interpreted.

The tactics employed by the British Royal Navy in the age of fighting sail defined the art of war at sea in the period and can be categorized into several groups. Histor-   **Fleet Tactics** ically, the earliest fleet tactic was the melee—characteristic of the great fleets of the sixteenth century in which individual vessels became entangled and sea battles were fought much like land battles. The line abreast and the line ahead, referred to in written records as early as 1653, were undeniably adopted as fleet tactics in 1665 by the Lord High Admiral, the Duke of York (later King James II). The development of gunports along the sides of each vessel allowed guns to be placed below the upper deck in two or more banks. The line abreast, with ships sailing one beside the next using the guns in their bow, therefore, was quickly abandoned, as the firepower of the ship came to reside along its sides. The line ahead, essentially a "follow the leader" approach to the control and ordering of the fleet by its admiral, maximized the number of guns that could be brought to bear upon the enemy fleet at one time for the same reason. The line ahead came to dominate fleet tactics in the age of sail, and it was not to be displaced until the widespread deployment of the gun turret after the American Civil War.

Other tactics followed no set chronological order moving in and out of fashion with the prejudices of the sea lords. These included numerous variations on line maneuvers such as doubling the enemy's line—having one set of ships on both sides of the enemy line at the same time—and breaking the enemy's line by sailing through it in one or more places. Although occurring in the happenstance of battle in earlier engagements, breaking the line was first successfully introduced as a preordained part of a battle plan by British Admiral Lord George Rodney in the War of American Independence. A variation was also used by Admiral Nelson at Trafalgar in 1805.

The chase, commonly used by cruisers in running down merchant shipping at sea, was an ancient tactic that had largely fallen into disuse in the eighteenth century. However, the chase was successfully used in two naval battles in 1747, jointly called the Battles of Finisterre. In the first of these, Admiral Lord George Anson, with fourteen warships, intercepted a French escort of six warships convoying two separate fleets

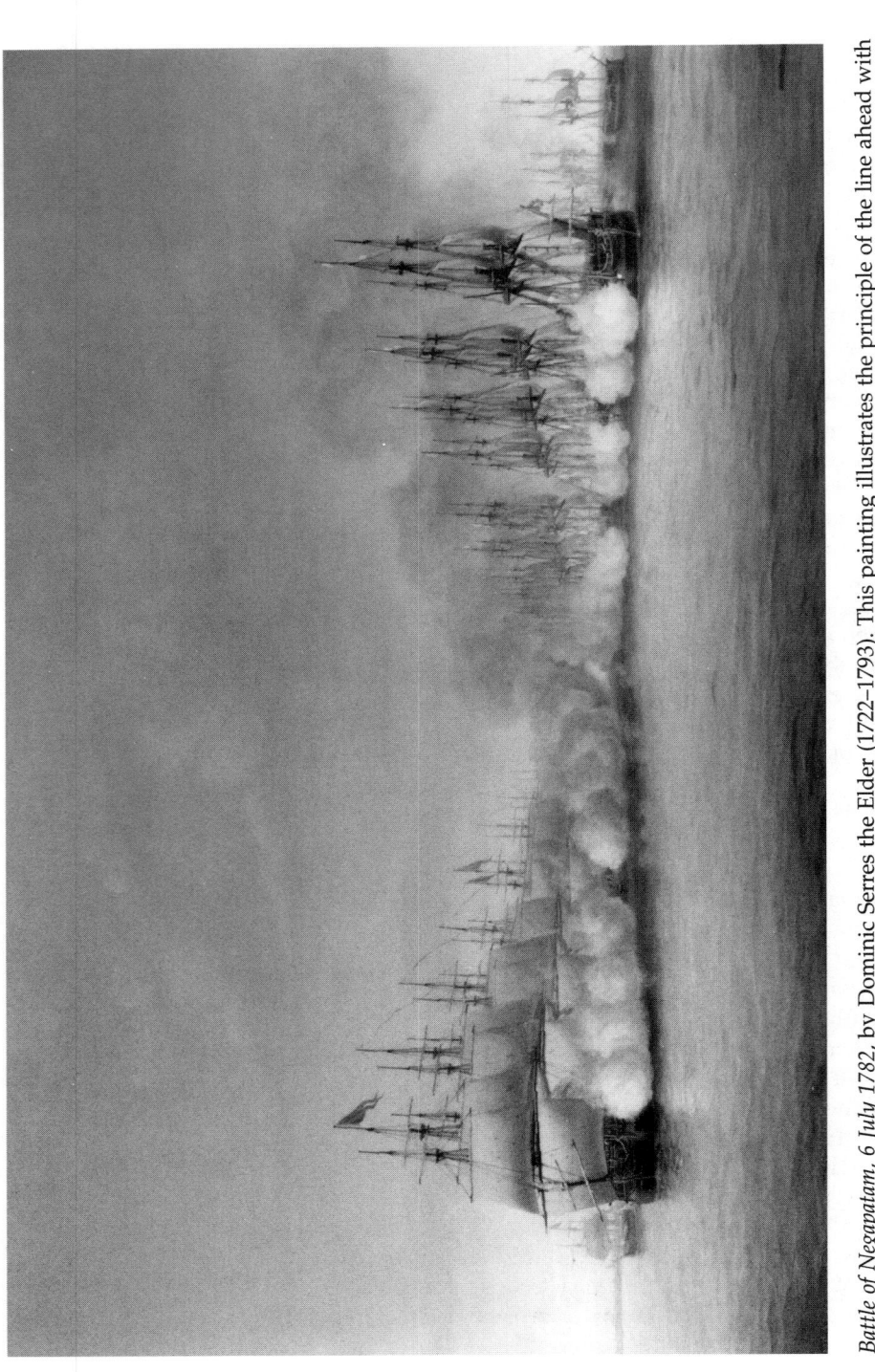

Battle of Negapatam, 6 July 1782, by Dominic Serres the Elder (1722–1793). This painting illustrates the principle of the line ahead with precision but with unrealistic detail. © NATIONAL MARITIME MUSEUM.

of merchantmen—one bound for America, the other for India. It took Anson almost two hours to order his fleet along a proper line of attack, and then he ordered a chase. This set his captains free to "catch as catch can" with staggering results. All six escorts were taken, as well as three lightly armed Indiamen. Later, five additional merchant ships were captured. Admiral Sir Edmund Hawke used chase tactics later in the same year with similar results: six of eight French warships captured.

French naval tactics are much simpler to summarize. The French fleet fought in a line ahead almost without exception throughout the eighteenth century. Moreover, French commanders most often chose to fight from the lee gage (or downwind) of their opponent. They rarely expended their resources in "slugging matches" meant to sink or capture enemy vessels, choosing rather to happily break off an engagement after dismasting, diverting, or otherwise slowing the enemy fleet. Once this design was accomplished, the French generally ran for port.

The greatest failure of the British navy in this period was the adoption of tactics that did not force the French to remain in the conflict until the battle was decided. British tactics called for the attack to be pressed from the weather gage (or upwind) and for the guns to be aimed at the hull of the enemy—between wind and water—killing the crew and damaging the hull. British tactics, therefore, generally complimented the desires of the French, who favored the leeward position and appreciated the fact that their rigging and sails were not being shot to pieces in the initial stages of the battle. Barring mere accident or an initial disabling shot, nothing conclusive can issue from such an arrangement.

Logically, with fleets of equal speed and weatherliness, the fleet to windward cannot be forced to engage, and the fleet to the lee cannot avoid an engagement if the wind holds steady.[7] Nonetheless, the choice of the leeward position benefited the French ships, which were generally better designed than the British vessels of the period and could be sure of winning a downwind race unless severely damaged. "British shipwrights were of a conservative turn of mind and were content to provide ships that were soundly built . . . but they seldom looked beyond that, whereas the French . . . were constantly effecting minor improvements."[8]

So illogical were the fleet tactics of the British navy in this regard that no French ship of the line was sunk during a sea battle for a period of ninety years when only line ahead tactics were followed![9] Losses among French warships in this period, whether by sinking or capture, were limited to situations where the order of an immediate chase, a general melee, or a breaking of the enemy's line was issued by a British admiral. Nearly half of the eighteenth century passed before some steps were taken to deal with a fleeing enemy who did not wish to be engaged.[10]

Notwithstanding the strategic shortcomings of its tactics, the eighteenth century British navy was vastly superior to all of the navies sent against it in terms of the number of warships it maintained at sea. By the end of the Seven Years War (1754–1763), the English had more than 130 ships-of-the-line and more than 100 frigates and smaller war vessels. The British achieved their original objective of becoming the single great maritime power of the period by driving all of their rivals from the sea lanes.[11]

Command and Control

The overall command of the British navy resided solely in the Lord High Admiral until 1660 when two parliamentary committees—the Navy Board and the Admiralty Committee of the Council of State—took responsibility for most of his administrative duties. The latter was the precurser to the Board of the Admiralty. This body, composed of the heads of the other departments of state, was characteristically efficient, level headed, and quite markedly incorrupt. While the Lords of the Admiralty adopted a number of regulations viewed with disbelief by the ordinary seaman, their foresight in some areas showed a genuine underlying excellence.[12]

Nonetheless, the command of a fleet at sea was the sole responsibility of the admiral-in-chief. The organizational control fell to the squadron commanders who acted as rallying points for the vessels under their direct command. The fleet normally was composed of three squadrons flying white, red, and blue pennants respectively. The white squadron commonly led the line as the van; the red took the center; and the blue brought up the rear. The tripartite division of van, center, and rear was common throughout the age of sail among many nations. The center was the normal position of the admiral-in-chief. The second-in-command, also an admiral, was normally offered the van, while the most junior admiral commanded the rear. An "admiral of the red" would thereby be senior to an "admiral of the white" or an "admiral of the blue," better known as a rear admiral. These distinctions were somewhat superfluous, however, as the fleet often reversed direction several times in trying to come to grips with an illusive enemy with the rear and van exchanging responsibilities. The leadership of the admiral-in-chief remained somewhat remote from the other parts of the fleet spread at times over many miles. This sometimes resulted in a lack of direct leadership when it was most needed. Nonetheless, the overall fleet commander was expected to be with the center, and opposing fleet commanders often sought out each other in major engagements, hoping to lay their respective flagships along side like chivalric champions.

In most naval engagements, the commanders of the opposing fleets chose to sail along parallel courses rather than drifting about during the conflict. As warships had no motors, they required a certain momentum in order to maneuver, bring their guns to bear, and maintain their relative positions alongside the enemy. While there were some notable exceptions, such as Drake's attack on the Spanish squadron at Cadiz in 1587 or Nelson's attack on enemy fleets at anchor at the Nile and at Copenhagen, most battles took place over many miles of ocean. Such fine control of the speed of the vessels was needed that, with time and experience, it was found to be mutually advantageous for the opposing fleets to sail along a line "close hauled" to the wind.

By sailing as much into the wind as possible without being blown backwards, individual captains were able to fill their sails to gain speed or, by backing their sails slightly, to use the wind as a brake. Judicious use of the wind allowed the captain to keep his vessel on station in the line and allowed the admiral to keep his fleet in contact with the enemy. The position between filling and backing was called lufting, with the sails taking on a flapping mode. Should the vessel lose momentum while lufting, it might be taken in irons—unable to maneuver or gain speed without resorting to extraordinary measures such as falling away before the wind or sending out her boats to tow her into a proper position to make use of the wind. It could be disastrous for a warship to be taken in irons during a close engagement, as she would either be left behind by her own fleet or become a ripe target for boarding by the enemy.

A ship in the mist of battle might turn away quite easily if in the downwind position. Turning with the wind was called waring the ship. Turning into the set of the wind was tacking. Even with damaged rigging, the force of the wind would tend to take a damaged ship away from the battle line, and unless engaged by a determined opponent, the vessel might make an escape or take time to make repairs. The French may have been more comfortable with the leeward position for this reason. However, for a ship to turn away from the battle line from the weather or windward position was much more difficult and required a good deal of preparation. The force of the wind naturally drove the ship in the windward position into the enemy "to fight or surrender; there was little chance of her running away."[13] It was generally accepted that a ship could strike its colors with honor if too badly damaged to escape or with too many of the crew wounded or killed to fight effectively.[14]

The period between first sighting an unfriendly sail and closing with the enemy in battle was always one of con- **Clearing for** siderable activity. A thing of beauty when under sail, a **Action** large warship was also clumsy and ponderous to maneuver, requiring perfect timing and seamanship of its captain. It was very difficult, therefore, to fight under full sail and maintain the fine control needed to prosecute a battle with some finesse. Any ship going into battle needed to "clear for action." Therefore, during the closing minutes of the approach, the commander would give orders to place the vessel

A large naval cannon with its training tackle and heavy breeching rope. Note the sponge, powder ladle, and worming iron. Also note the tub holding the slow match. Illustration from an early-twentieth-century text in the author's collection.

under "fighting sails"—topsails and jib set, the mainsails clewed up, and the royal and topgallant yards sent down if there was time. Nonetheless, there were times when ships went into battle with all sails set. Duplicate sheets and braces were put in place to ensure control of the ship, and the rope slings that supported the great yards were reinforced with chains to eliminate much of the potential injury from falling debris.

On deck, hammocks, bedding, and spare canvas were bundled into the nettings along the sides of the railings to serve as some protection from small arms fire and flying wood splinters, as well as to deter boarders. The decks were wetted to resist fire, and sand was scattered about to improve footing. The ship's boats were cast overboard to be towed or retrieved later.

Below decks, the partitions that formed the officers' cabins were removed, and the furniture, mess tables, and any other loose objects were stowed away. The carpenter and his crew would prepare their shot-plugs (cone shaped pieces of wood that could be hammered into any hole near the water line), and the surgeon and his mates would establish a medical station on the orlop deck or in the cockpit. The powder monkeys would bring a limited number of charges up from the magazine for each gun. This was to prevent accidental explosions. The charges would be replenished throughout the battle. Tubs filled with water and sand held the burning slow match with which to fire the charge.[15]

In an engagement between two vessels of roughly
equal firepower, the opposing commanders would use   **Naval Gunnery**
their judgment of speed and distance to close to within
the range of their guns. This could be a considerable distance, as the
maximum range of naval guns could be well over a mile. However, the
practical range of cannon in the seventeenth and eighteenth centuries
was usually no more than a "cable length" (about 200 yards), and fighting ranges may have been as close as a "pistol shot" (under 50 yards).
Carronades, very short cannon of large caliber developed at the Carron
gun foundry in 1779, were designed to be fired at point blank range.[16]

As the distance between the contestants closed, each commander
would attempt to maneuver his vessel so as to bring the largest number
of guns to bear as possible upon his opponent while simultaneously
avoiding those of the enemy. Modern vessels equipped with gun turrets
can sweep through most of a 360-degree circle, taking aim at almost any
target without changing the orientation of the vessel. However, the
smooth bore cannon of the seventeenth- and eighteenth-century sailing
ship were mounted on wooden trucks, and the great weight of the guns
allowed little lateral sweep, which was accomplished only by the brute
power of men with handpikes. As the guns could be aimed only a few
degrees forward or aft through the gun ports, one of the skills needed
in a fight was the ability to place the ship in positions that allowed the
gun crews a shot at the enemy.

Most warships had a pair of long-range bow and stern "chasers" for
use in running down merchant vessels or warding off pursuit. The
greatest concentration of guns, however, resided along the sides of the
vessel and combined to produce the broadside—a nearly simultaneous
firing of the main battery of guns perpendicular to the long axis of the
ship. The effectiveness of the broadside was first proven in 1567 when a
single English privateer fought a two-day action against seven Portuguese ships near Terceira in the Azores. The *Castle of Comfort* beat off
every attack by using a number of overwhelming broadsides at long
range. "The news of this victory was received in England with enthusiasm."[17]

Ten years later, the English were using broadsides aimed at the hulls
of Spanish galleons with equal success. Military historian John Keegan
has noted that "few ships were sunk in these encounters, for the wooden
ship was virtually unsinkable by solid shot unless it caught fire."[18] Yet
broadsides could be devastating even if they did not damage the hull of
the ship below the waterline, blowing out great holes in the masts, over-
turning cannon, producing flesh-piercing splinters and killing the gun
crews directly. This new and formidable tactic did not immediately
change the way sea battles were fought in the English navy, and it also
seems to have been lost on the commanders of other navies.

The need to reload cannon from the muzzle, a time-consuming process, exposed the gun crews of the sixteenth century to the small arms fire of the enemy as they climbed outside the bulwarks to ram home the charge. A major advance in this regard was the method of running in the guns to reload them behind the bulwarks of the ship. Working in cooperation with the laws of physics—for every action there is an equal and opposite reaction—the guns recoiled from the ship's side automatically when fired. Previously the gun had been fixed to the side of the ship to keep it from flying across the deck with every shot. This placed tremendous strain on the ship's timber and required that the ship's guns be small and of low velocity to prevent damage. The concept of containing the recoil and expending the energy by dragging long lengths of rope through a block and tackle allowed the muzzle to come to rest just inside the railing of the ship where reloading could be done behind the safety of the ship's side. The block and tackle were then used to run out the gun, pulling the muzzle forward before firing. This innovation led directly to the adoption of gun ports and the positioning of additional guns on the lower decks of many large warships.

British gunners of the period generally aimed for the area between the water and the railing of the ship in an attempt to strike it where the damage to the guns and crew would be maximized. Expert gunners could "skip" a cannon ball along the water's surface like a stone to hit their target at great distances. A good gun crew could fire one broadside every five minutes, and an excellently trained crew might fire one every three minutes. To the modern mind—familiar with rapid fire weapons—this is a very slow rate of fire, but it must be remembered that an entire engagement might unfold over many hours, or days, as the antagonists drifted along under shortened sail at 2 or 3 knots.

French gunners—less expert in their trade than the British, especially after the French Revolution—generally aimed for the masts and rigging of their enemy. Since naval cannon could not be elevated much above seven degrees, they tended to fire on the uproll of the ship to send their shot high in the air. A well-aimed solid shot could take down a mast while chain shot and bar shot were designed so that they tore away the sheets and stays like rotating sickles as they flew through the air. Grape and canister (clusters and cans of smaller projectiles) were more commonly used for the purpose of killing the crew rather than for damaging the ship. All of the navies of the eighteenth century used similar ordnance.

Experience showed that any shot smaller than 12 pounds did very little damage to the timbers of a man-of-war, and 12, 18, 24, and 32 pound projectiles were commonly used in various warships. The lightest guns (4, 6, and 9 pounders) were placed on the highest decks above the waterline to work upon the rigging and decks. The 32 pounders, which were the most effective in terms of penetration and speed of loading, were almost always restricted to the lowest deck in a ship-of-the-line to improve the vessel's stability and sailing qualities. The 32 pound carronade was adopted in 1779, and most men-of-war had at least some of these as part of their armament thereafter. Frigates rarely carried any guns larger than 18 pounders in their main battery.[19]

In the last two decades of the eighteenth century, Sir Charles Douglas, Flag Captain to Admiral Rodney, suggested several improvements in naval gunnery practices. He changed the cartridge-casings holding the gun charges from silk to flannel to prevent static discharge, utilized steel springs to absorb some of the recoil of the cannon, and introduced the flint and steel gun lock to replace the slow match. Douglas' improvements were officially approved by the Admiralty in 1781. They were first used by the West Indian Squadron in the Battle of the Saints in 1782 (the first great carronade battle) where more men were killed in the French flag-ship alone than in the entire British fleet.[20]

Although a majority of actions, both between individual ships and squadrons of the fleet, were essentially artillery duels, in an engagement the individual commander had several tactics available to him besides participating in a simple slugging match. It was in this area that captains could demonstrate their skill and initiative. One tactic was that of "raking" the opponent. Raking was accomplished by crossing the enemy's stern, where few guns were mounted, and firing through the stern counter and down the length of the enemy vessel as the guns came to bear. Shot fired in this manner often traveled the length of the ship, splitting timbers, upsetting guns, and killing the crew. Raking could also be accomplished by passing before the enemy and firing through the bow section.[21]

Single Ship Tactics

If a skipper had a handier and more agile vessel than his opponent, he could rake with one broadside, tack, and fire the other broadside in a similar manner without taking opposing fire. The process could also be accomplished in light winds by backing across an opponent's wake. Enemy commanders were well aware of what their opponents would try if given the opportunity, and they were quick to react to the potential danger by attempting counter measures. Being raked was almost the worst thing that could happen to a vessel in an engagement short of an explosion in the powder magazine.

All the tactics used by a commander were aimed at one objective—to adversely affect the ability of his opponent to make further resistance. Either he had to hold his enemy in play sufficiently long for his own firepower to take effect, or he had to sufficiently weaken his opponent so that he might carry the enemy vessel by boarding. Centuries of actions at sea in which hand-to-hand fighting decided the issue were not easily forgotten, and tactics that culminated in slashing, close-quarters fisticuffs

HMS *Victory Raking the Spanish at the Battle of Cape St. Vincent, 14 February 1797*, by Robert Cleveley (1798). © NATIONAL MARITIME MUSEUM.

Captain William Rogers Capturing the "Jeune Richard," 1 October 1807, by Samuel Drummond (1765–1844). This painting illustrates the chaos and violence of the hand-to-hand fighting that followed a boarding. © NATIONAL MARITIME MUSEUM.

on the enemy's deck were still regarded with great favor. Attempts to grapple the enemy vessel, entangle the rigging, or ram the opposing vessels into a conglomerate mass were all based on the hope that a boarding party might successfully decide the issue. Boarding parties were often led by the first lieutenant who hoped to establish himself as a man worthy of advancement to captain's rank.

When not formed as part of the boarding party, marines were generally sent with their muskets to the fighting tops from where they could fire down on the deck below or drop hand grenades into the open hatches of the enemy. British Admiral Nelson lost his life to a French marksmen in the tops at the Battle of Trafalgar, and the American Captain, John Paul Jones, forced the warship *Serapis* to surrender during the War of Independence when a grenade, dropped from the main yard of *Bonnehomme Richard*, caused the powder charges stacked among the British guns to explode.[22]

The conditions under which engagements were fought placed the utmost strain not only on the structural integrity of the ship but also on the physical resources of the crew. The participants might be engaged for hours in "grindingly hard physical labor . . . much of it within a few yards of the mouths of thirty or forty cannon." Physical exhaustion, the apprehension of immediate and unremitting danger, and the intense mental strain that accompanied the control and maneuver of a vessel in battle left many believing that they had done all that they could do. Naval authority David Davies noted that during a prolonged encounter "one did not think too clearly about what to do next, one collapsed." Although fate sometimes decided the issue, often it was the skipper and crew that rose above these trials that were favored with victory.[23]

Sailing and Fighting Instructions Historians and maritime scholars know much about the nature of British naval tactics because, from an early date, they were formalized into a written body of signals and maneuvers called the *Sailing and Fighting Instructions*. Although these documents do not provide exciting reading for the armchair admiral, they are the tinder that naval scholars use to build great controversies from what are otherwise commonplace naval operations.

In fleet engagements comprising many ships on each side, the admiral needed to command the actions of his subordinates and of individual vessels as he saw the needs of the overall conflict develop. As there were only rudimentary means of communication by sight, speaking trumpet, or messenger boat, a series of prearranged visual signals were instituted, each with its own meaning. These signals were the basis for the *Instructions*.

The admiral's pennant, a long narrow flag colored to suit his rank, was flown from the masthead of his flagship, locating him in the center squadron. Signals were made by raising colored flags and pennants in different positions on the admiral's flagship. These were repeated on all the ships throughout the fleet. Smaller warships, usually frigates, were stationed to windward of the battle, outside the pale of the smoke, as signal repeaters to ensure good visual contact with the entire line of battleships. The signals were severely limited in scope, most being sailing instructions that pertained to the movements of the fleet at sea. However, some signals were deemed fighting instructions in that they were used in combat.

The evolution of the *Sailing and Fighting Instructions* is fairly well documented. Sir Walter Raleigh included fighting instructions in the orders that he issued in 1617 on his voyage to Guiana, and Sir Edward Cecil reissued the same set in 1625. These were rather simple signals calling for an "attack in succession." Each ship was expected to come down to the enemy from windward; close and fire its broadside; change tack; fire the other broadside; and then haul away as close to the wind as possible to allow the next ship in line to repeat the process. On its surface, this instruction seems to be rooted in a somewhat naive assumption that the enemy vessels would calmly allow successive ships to bombard them without taking counter measures. But it was thought in the seventeenth century to be more efficient to reload out of the enemy's range. Certainly Raleigh and Cecil could not have seriously envisioned such a scenario without leaving unspoken and unwritten latitude to their individual captains with which they might react to the tactics of the enemy.

As the technology of gun loading improved, the thought of hauling out of action to reload disappeared from the instructions. A first indication of changes in the written instructions appears in 1653 when *The Instructions for the Better Handling of the Fleet in Fighting* were issued by the parliamentary Admirals Robert Blake, Richard Deane, and George Monck. These called for vessels to come at the enemy in line ahead, "tak[ing] best advantage they can to engage the enemy next unto them . . . all the ships endeavor[ing] to keep in line with the Admiral." The signals now included for the first time directions to "close with the enemy." The line ahead remained the most widely used British tactical formation into the nineteenth century.[24]

The *Instructions* evolved as they were used by various fleet admirals of the Royal Navy after 1688. At the Battle of Cape Barfleur in 1692, the English fleet went into battle with the *Instructions Made by the Right Honorable Edward Russell, Admiral*. These articles were modified from the 1672 instructions laid down by the Lord High Admiral, the Duke of York, because of the disastrous experiences of the English navy in the Second Anglo-Dutch Wars. There were fewer articles in Russell's instructions, and less reliance was placed on orders transmitted by speaking trumpet or by boat. Moreover, the use of signals sent by flags was now firmly established.

In 1704 at the Battle of Malaga, Admiral Sir George Rooke issued fighting instructions that included thirty-two articles amended to a set of twenty-six sailing instructions. Although called "fighting instructions," twenty-two of the signals were sailing maneuvers; five regarded disabled ships; and only five dealt with tactics. The entire document was made into a thirty-four-page folio titled *Sailing and Fighting Instructions for His Majesty's Fleet*. Thereafter copies of this folio were available from the Admiralty printing office for promulgation to the fleet by successive admirals. While this avoided the need to compose new sets, Rooke's instructions took on an unwarranted aura of permanence, especially as his successful campaign was the last for almost forty years.

The *Signals and Instructions for 1784–1796* were so little changed from Rooke's that they also gave the impression of permanent orders. However, the term *permanent* was not attached to the title of Rooke's instructions until an otherwise noteworthy student of naval tactics did so in 1905. His work gave the mistaken impression that Rooke's instructions were considered immutable, entrenched rules issued to all future commanders by the Lords of the Admiralty. It is unfortunate that this error has carried over through so many years of study and research to contaminate our understanding of this period in naval history.[25]

It is quite incomprehensible why any authority on the Royal Navy (historians, authors, and documentary filmmakers) would continue to claim that the *Fighting Instructions* of this period were the immutable directives of the Lords of the Admiralty to be followed to the letter. Throughout the eighteenth century, each admiral-in-chief was free to dictate his own instructions, and many did. Even the "permanent" fighting instructions, which were run off at the Admiralty press were constantly and continuously amended by the addition of instructions unique to the character of the admiral in command. An addendum to the standard folio was printed by the Admiralty in 1757 and issued as *Additional Signals and Further Additional Signals*. The title of this publication urges the student away from the position that the *Fighting Instructions* were immutable. The Admiralty, itself, was freely participating in opening them to numerous amendments and alterations.

Just when these unique movements, called *Additional Instructions*, were first amended to the standard *Fighting Instructions* is difficult to pin down. Admiral Lord George Anson and Admiral Sir Edward Hawke showed no reluctance in issuing additional instructions when they were needed, and extant copies of their instructions show that they have been modified in manuscript. In a copy issued by Hawke in 1747, there were fifteen handwritten entries unnumbered and interspersed among the *Sailing Instructions*. Some of these may have been inherited by him from previous commanders of the Western Station. Many of the instructions initially laid down for the convenience of a particular station were later incorporated into the printed Admiralty folio.

Anson, "one of the greatest administrators and strategists in [British] history" went on to be First Lord of the Admiralty in 1755. Anson's instructions are the first to mention a signal for a general chase as well as a signal to allow a single squadron to chase. These two additional instructions would seem to fly in the face of Article 26 of the "permanent" Admiralty copy, which allowed a chase only if the entire enemy fleet were on the run. Moreover. Anson included printed signals for particular ships to chase to windward or to leeward, and further signals allowed him to send his ships to any of the four points of the compass. The existence of such printed and manuscript signals deals a severe blow to any theory that held that individual commanders could not deviate from the "permanent" instructions without tempting the wrath of the Admiralty.[26]

No single seaman's experience did more to enhance the myths surrounding the *Fighting Instructions* of the Admiralty than that of Admiral John Byng. When he was executed on the deck of a ship-of-the-line in 1757, it was generally understood by Byng's contemporaries **The Tragedy of Admiral John Byng** that his death was due to his own stupidity in abandoning the British base at Minorca when he could have come to its aid and not for a breech of Admiralty directives.

Since there was no article of war under which a commander might be adjudged guilty of poor judgment, and since a scapegoat was needed to explain the loss of Minorca, Byng was charged with failing to "do his utmost to take and destroy every ship which it shall be his duty to engage, and assist and relieve all and every of his Majesty's ships which shall be his duty to assist and relieve." While none of his majesty's ships were in need of assistance, it seems that the Lords of the Admiralty chose to extend the duty to aid and relieve to the island garrison at Minorca so that they could try Byng.[27]

There should be no sympathy for Byng. He handled his fleet very poorly. With about equal force, Byng approached an oncoming French fleet from at an angle with head-on of about seven points—equivalent to about 70 degrees. Byng proceeded to sail by the French, bringing his van beyond the French rear before ordering his fleet to tack in succession (rather than at the same time) thereby bringing his rearmost ships onto a course of attack with the French van one at a time. All of the maneuvers used by Byng were well established in the *Sailing and Fighting Instructions*.

However, Byng failed utterly to realign the angular bearing of his fleet with respect to the French line. The *Sailing Instructions* encompassed signals for the remediation of this problem, but Byng chose to disregard their use and attacked as he was. Moreover, his order to tack in succession was simply "incomprehensible" under the circumstances. This failure placed his leading ships at a severe and needless disadvantage as they came to the attack bow on and one at a time. Since few guns can be brought to bear on the enemy from the bows of a warship, the leading vessels took an unanswered pounding from the broadsides of the French as they approached to make their attack. Moreover, each succeeding British vessel was forced to sail further and further under this relentless fire in an attempt to reach the French line and bring its own broadsides to bear. As the line of the French fleet bore away from the British attack, greater and greater distances needed to be covered by the hindmost warships. Byng's own squadron, the van in this case, never made contact with the enemy at all, and his hindmost ships were well to windward throughout the engagement.

There was no hesitation to attack among the ships of the leading British squadron under the command of Rear Admiral Temple West, who signaled for "close action." Nonetheless, no vessel on either side was lost, and Byng ultimately lost contact with the French when the wind shifted unfavorably. Byng, fearing that his force was not strong enough to relieve the besieged garrison in Minorca, chose to abandon the effort and to retreat to Gibraltar.

Byng's court martial acquitted him of charges of cowardice and disaffection, but found him guilty under Article 12 of the Articles of War, as stated above, which called for a sentence of death. Testimony at the trial showed that Byng had consulted the *Sailing Instructions* (specifically Article 17) before ordering his fleet to tack. A late-nineteenth-century researcher focused on this circumstance, drawing an unwarranted conclusion that the article was the crux of the prosecution and, thereby, contributing to the myth of a vengeful Admiralty. The court unanimously requested mercy of the King, but it was refused. It was clearly understood by all in attendance, including Byng, that he was going to die for abandoning Minorca and not for disobeying the Admiralty's *Instructions*.

Byng was subsequently shot by a file of marines on the quarterdeck of the flagship *Monarque*. Ironically, he had been a member of the court martial that had found Admiral Thomas Matthews guilty of mishandling his fleet at the Battle of Toulon in 1744. In that case Byng, a junior rear admiral at the time, had voted with the majority of the court to simply cashier Matthews and four of his captains because of their disgraceful handling of the engagement.[28]

The Vocabulary Signal Book In 1778, Admiral Richard Howe devised a numerary code based on the ideas devised during the American War of Independence by British Admiral Richard Kempenfelt, "an officer [of] high professional abilities" whose "tragic death" prevented him from implementing them.[29] Kempenfelt had drafted his original ideas as a captain in the Channel fleet under a series of admirals, and he refined them under his own blue pennant as a squadron commander. Specific words and phrases were given numbers that could be combined into orders. Although the signal flag set remained the means of communication, with a signal book based on Kempenfelt's numerary code, Howe was able to say most of the things he wished to his captains directly.

Naval authority J. S. Corbett found Howe's numerary code "was no mere substitution of a new set of *Instructions* but a complete revolution of method. The basis for the new tactical code was no longer included in the *Instructions* which thereafter took the place of being explanatory to the signals." Such a system placed much less emphasis on the prearranged instructions of former years and allowed orders to be issued to individual ships as the battle developed.[30]

By 1790, Howe, considered the "Grand Old Man of the Navy," was able to have his signal book and code adopted by the entire British naval establishment. Howe's signal book was used at the battles of the Glorious First of June, St. Vincents, and the Nile. Better communications had come just in time for Britain's entry into a long naval war with France—first with the republic and later with Napoleon—"a truly maritime war . . . [in which] the magnificence of sea power and its value had perhaps [never before] been more clearly shown."[31]

In 1800, Sir Home Popham improved the signal book with the *Telegraphic Signals or Marine Vocabulary*. For the first time, the commander could spell out specific words and phrases. At the most decisive naval battle in history—Trafalgar—armed with an adequate system of intercommunication, Admiral Nelson was able to communicate his wishes directly to his captains.[32] Nelson's immortal "England expects that every man will do his duty" was spelled out using Popham's numerary code.[33]

253—England
269—Expects
238—Every
471—Man
958—Will
220—Do
370—His
4—D
21—U
19—T
24—Y[34]

NOTES

1. David Davies, *Nelson's Navy: English Fighting Ships, 1793–1815* (Mechanicsburg, PA: Stackpole, 1996), 60.

2. C. S. Forester, *The Age of Fighting Sail: The Story of the Naval War of 1812* (Sandwich, MA: Chapman Billies, 1956), 60.

3. Allan Westcott, ed., *Mahan on Naval Warfare: Selected from the Writings of Rear Admiral Alfred Thayer Mahan* (Boston: Little, Brown & Co., 1919), 80.

4. Alfred Thayer Mahan, *The Influence of Sea Power upon History, 1660–1783* (1890; reprint, New York: Dover, 1987), 259.

5. John Creswell, *British Admirals of the Eighteenth Century: Tactics in Battle* (London: Allen and Unwin, 1972), 48.

6. Westcott, 89.

7. Creswell, 46.

8. Ibid., 15–16.

9. Michael Lewis, *The History of the British Navy* (Fairlawn, NJ: Essential Books, 1959), 118.

10. Creswell, 40.

11. Mahan, 209, 224.

12. Lewis, 77–80.

13. Davies, 67.

14. N.A.M. Rodger, *The Wooden World: An Anatomy of the Georgian Navy* (New York: W. W. Norton, 1996), 55.

15. Forester, 64; John Laffin, *Jack Tars: The Story of the British Sailor* (London: Cassell, 1969), 153–154.

16. Creswell, 93.

17. G. J. Marcus, *The Formative Centuries: A Naval History of England* (Boston: Little, Brown & Co., 1961), 52–53.

18. John Keegan, *The Price of Admiralty: The Evolution of Naval Warfare* (New York: Viking Press, 1988), 6.

19. Creswell, 23; Nicholas Blake and Richard Lawrence, *The Illustrated Companion to Nelson's Navy* (Mechanicsburg, PA: Stackpole, 2000), 30; James M. Volo, "The War at Sea," *Living History Journal* (January 1987): 3.

20. Marcus, 348.

21. Rodger, 54–60.

22. Keegan, 6.

23. Davies, 70.

24. Creswell, 17–18.

25. Ibid., 28.

26. Marcus, 286. The authors are indebted to John Creswell's research into the controversial area of the *Instructions*. While there remains some romance associated with the heroic captain forging ahead into battle although restrained in his tactics by an authoritarian and dogmatic Admiralty, the authors believe that such notions are better left in armchair fiction rather than being incorporated into serious historical research.

27. Creswell, 94.

28. Ibid., 94–103.

29. Mahan, 408.

30. J. S. Cobert, *Signals and Instructions* (London: Navy Records Society, 1908), 233.

31. Mahan, 338.

32. Ibid., 338.

33. Marcus, 350–351.

34. William Robinson, *Nautical Economy: The Memoirs of William Robinson, An Able Seaman Who Served with Nelson at Trafalgar* (Warwick, UK: Cromwell, 1993), 19.

11

Pirates and Privateers

Privateering became a craze the like of which had never been seen in Britain.
     —Francis R. Stark, nineteenth-century naval historian[1]

Only a fine line existed between piracy and privateering, with the distinction essentially a legal one—an attack by either pirates or privateers made little difference to the victimized vessel. Of course, pirates were less likely to provide the crew and passengers of a seized vessel with polite handling than privateers. Pirates were outlaws attacking and plundering shipping upon the high seas or at anchor in bays and inlets. Privateers were commissioned to raid enemy vessels during wartime. Many pirates attacked the shipping of all nations indiscriminately, while others evaded the wrath of particularly powerful maritime nations by carefully avoiding certain vessels and preying solely on the shipping of less powerful countries. In many cases, pirates killed every person aboard a victimized vessel in order to conceal their deeds. They were known to wantonly destroy property "just for fun, since they gained nothing by it."[2]

PIRATES

Much of what historians think they know of pirates is based on legend, myth, and anecdotal accounts. Pirates kept few records, since their continued success depended largely on anonymity. Since piracy was a capital crime, pirates went to extraordinary lengths to cover their tracks. They changed the names of their vessels, adopted aliases repeatedly, and shifted their operations from their original vessels to prizes better suited to their trade. The only dependable records about pirates seem to come from the government agencies and naval squadrons assigned to suppress them.

The New York colony seems to have earned the questionable distinction of becoming a major haven for pirates in the 1690s largely through the connivance of the royal governor, Benjamin Fletcher. Several of the most prominent merchants in New York quietly garnered large profits from slave trading, smuggling, and piracy—euphemistically calling this the "Red Sea Trade." New England, Pennsylvania, and Maryland also offered a welcome to buccaneers. With liberal governors, weak administrators, and no Admiralty courts in the colonies to try them for their crimes, the temptation to turn to piracy was almost irresistible. In 1696, the crown tried to suppress piracy in the colonies. "In the case of the encouragement of privateers by Governors. We conceive that the King can order all his Governors, and the Proprietors also, to give no privileges to privateers. . . . But we understand . . . that what are here called privateers are in reality freebooters (pirates), who ought to be wholly suppressed."[3]

The suppression of piracy and the restraint of privateers became a major problem for the British Crown in the last years of the seventeenth century. However, the Red Sea Traders worked their dealings principally in the Indian Ocean, and they maintained bases on the island of Madagascar away from British rule. St. Mary's Bay was one of their favorite haunts on the island. Founded through the efforts of Frederick Philipse, a New York merchant and property owner, this pirate den offered security, entertainment, and proximity to the shipping lanes from the East Indies to Europe. Piracy was also common in the Mediterranean, and it flourished in the Caribbean. However, piratical activities made the stockholders of the East India Company indignant, and the outraged directors of the Honourable Company forced reforms in the law that brought some order to the sea lanes between 1692 and 1712.

Some of the men charged with the responsibility of capturing pirates were pirates themselves. Two of these were outstanding: Henry Morgan and William Kidd. Sacking and pillaging along the Spanish Main, Henry Morgan frequented the pirate dens at Tortuga and Old Port Royal. As long as England tried to open a door into the trade of the West Indies, Morgan and his contemporaries raided Spanish treasure galleons under the spurious cover of privateering commissions. But Morgan ruined his buccanneering reputation when he accepted the position of deputy-governor of Jamaica in 1672 from Charles II. He was also made a knight,

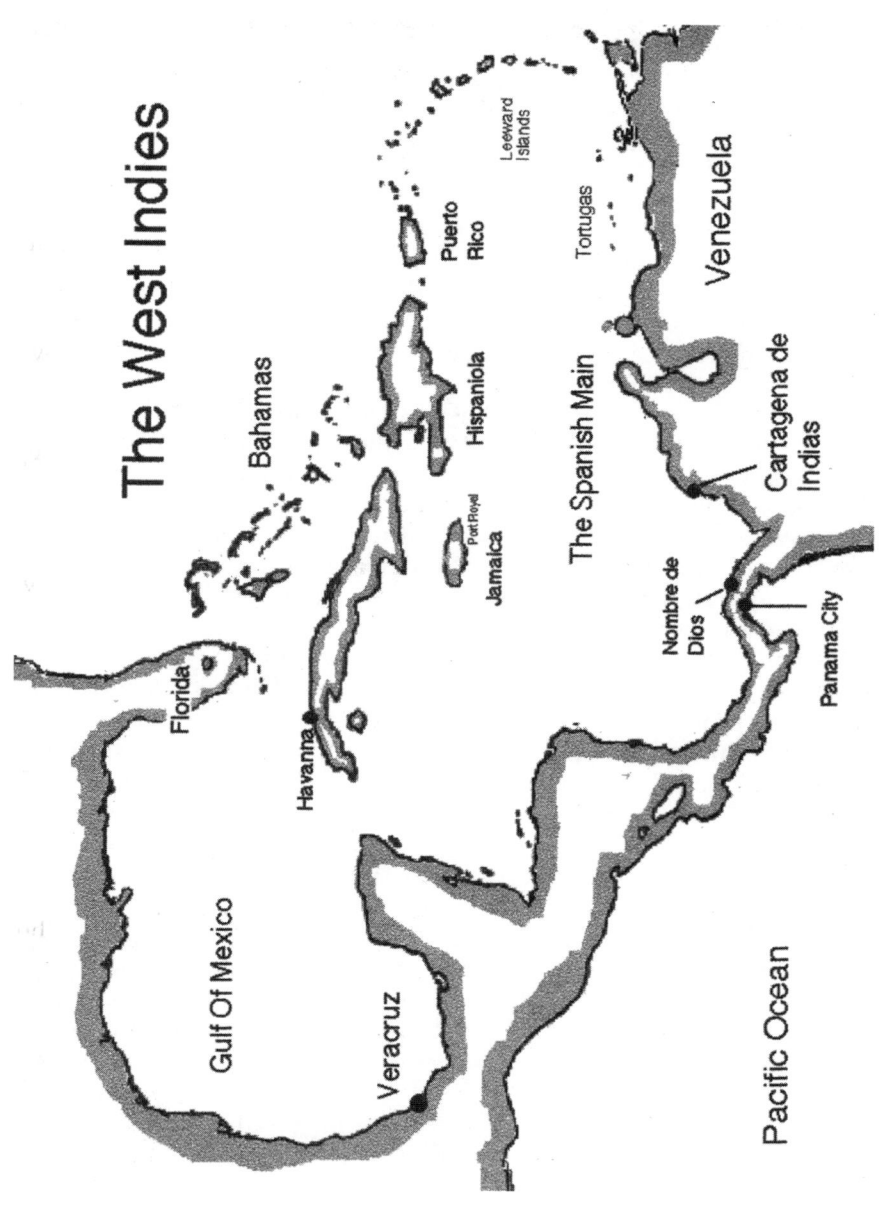

The West Indies

Bahamas

Florida

Gulf Of Mexico

Havanna

Veracruz

Port Royal
Jamaica

Hispaniola

Puerto Rico

Leeward Islands

The Spanish Main

Tortugas

Venezuela

Cartagena de Indias

Nombre de Dios

Panama City

Pacific Ocean

senior member of the Council, lieutenant general of all the forces on the island, and judge-admiral of the Admiralty court. This was the pinnacle of his power. Thereafter, he was plagued by political enemies in London. Nonetheless, by 1680, Sir Henry was able to state with complete confidence, "I have put to death, imprisoned, and transported to the Spaniards for execution all English and Spanish pirates that I could get within this government . . . [and] I use the utmost severity of the law against them . . . God forgive 'em. I do."[4]

Captain William Kidd was a legitimate privateer working out of New York colony. In 1691, Kidd became an acquaintance of Richard Coote, Lord Bellomont, who had replaced Benjamin Fletcher as governor. Bellomont quickly and effectively attacked piracy and ruined the profits of the Red Sea Traders. Kidd accepted a commission to capture several well-known New York pirates known to use Madagascar as a base. He recruited a crew and gave chase.

Historians are divided as to what happened thereafter. Kidd seems to have made several captures in and near the Indian Ocean. Two of these were seized as legitimate prizes, but three of them were plundered, several people killed, and the spoils divided out among Kidd's crew. This was patently illegal. Whether Kidd turned pirate voluntarily or was forced into piracy by his crew is debatable. Nonetheless, with the hue and cry against pirates so universal, when Kidd returned to New York, Bellomont shipped him off to London for trial as a pirate and murderer.

Captain Kidd's trial was a political one. The Tories hoped to use it to embarrass Lord Bellomont's friends in London. Evidence favorable to Kidd disappeared, and the parts of the law that he had violated were filled with ambiguities. Kidd was found guilty, hanged, and his body left in chains on the gibbet in London. Before his death William Kidd was supposed to have said, "For my part, I am the innocentest person of them all."[5]

PRIVATEERS

Privateers were legitimate commerce raiders who attacked mostly unarmed or lightly armed merchant vessels during wartime. These depredations were considered "acts of war" endorsed by the government that had issued the commissions, or letters of marque, under which the privateers operated. As with mercenary armies hired to fight on land, privateering was a form of private enterprise in which vessels fought on the high seas in the hope of being rewarded with prize money for the capture of the enemy's shipping. While not condoning indiscriminate activities such as rape, unrestrained cruelty, or murder, the privateer's commission allowed the seizure, capture, or destruction of the vessels and cargo of only a specified enemy (or enemies). Privateers were allowed to kill any person resisting the seizure of the vessel, and they could deprive the crew and passengers of their liberty until they could be brought to port. More importantly from the point of view of the privateers, they were allowed to pocket the proceeds of the sale of the captured ship and cargo—without being exposed to a charge of piracy.

Privateers was tolerated because governments wished to maximize their ability to attack the commerce of an enemy with the greatest economy of force. By applying the principles of capitalism, self-interest, and entrepreneurship to war at sea, hundreds of vessels and thousands of sailors were **The Origins of Privateering** motivated to take up privateering. The royal charters granted to the European trading companies that colonized the New World recognized the right of the directors to seize and to sell prizes taken from the enemy for their own profit as an inducement to prospective investors.[6] Officials sent to govern the colonies and trading posts were often given the right to issue commissions to privateers and to condemn prizes. The principles behind privateering are sometimes baffling to the modern student, but they were codified and well understood by most seamen at the time.

In medieval times, many nobles waged war on land to redress personal grievances. Ultimately some of these disputes spilled over on to the seas, especially in the Mediterranean. A growing number of merchant shippers, distressed at the prospect of having their vessels stopped or seized indiscriminately, found that their business affairs were being hampered by vessels involved in these private wars. A loud cry of resentment went out from the business community, and a system of licenses was instituted to put calm to the resulting chaos and provide some governmental control. The earliest known permit granted by a sovereign to wage private war at sea was that issued by Holy Roman Emperor Frederic II to Rudolph de Caprarja of Tuscany in the twelfth century.[7] Once such licenses became popular, any seizure of shipping resulting from a private war waged upon the seas without such a permit was widely viewed as piracy, and the crew of the offending vessel, if caught, were quickly executed. Pirates were generally hanged, and their bodies were left to rot on the gibbet in rusted chains either at the dockside or on islands in the harbor.[8]

From such scattered and foggy beginnings, privateering developed into a recognized instrument of war with rules of engagement, a system of courts to decide ambiguities, and a growing body of legal precedent. Privateering continued for five centuries until it was finally outlawed by the Declaration of Paris in 1856. Almost all of the great European maritime powers used privateers as commerce raiders at one time or another, and almost all agreed to its prohibition in the nineteenth century. After 1856, the privateers of all signatory nations were treated as pirates and were subject to prosecution, imprisonment, or death if captured.

In the United States, privateering was a popular form of business and investment. Largely because of internal resistance from influential New Englanders, the United States failed to sign the prohibitory agreement prior to the outbreak of the Civil War. The last privateers to legally sail the seas, therefore, were the sailors of the Confederate States who, ironically, preyed upon these same New England shippers, who complained bitterly as they became the victims from 1861 to 1865. Only in the late stages of its development did privateering take on the romantic image of a maritime militia.[9]

Business as Usual   The financing of a privateer was usually accomplished only by the selling of "shares." After the customary eight shares had been set aside for the vessel's captain, additional shares were assigned to the ship's officers and crew. The remainder was divided out among the land-bound investors whose money supported the acquisition and operation of the cruiser. Mates, bosuns, surgeons, and those with special skills often received a fraction more than the single share allotted to common seamen. Boys who shipped as part of the crew generally drew one-half share. Even with a fractional interest in a single bounteous prize, several boys were known to have become quite wealthy by serving on privateers.

The owners of the vessel commonly shared as much as 50 percent of the value of any prize. They received the lion's share of the profits because they risked their entire investment if the privateering vessel was lost at sea or captured. It was virtually impossible to get insurance for privateers. Nonetheless, the profits from a single capture and the condemnation of its cargo often paid back the entire privateering investment with additional captures bringing almost pure profit.

Equipping a private warship was often more difficult than financing one. If there were no cannon available, which was often the case in time of war, some commanders would ship out with nothing more on board than pistols, muskets, knives, and swords in the hope of making an easy capture by boarding a lightly armed merchantman. The cannon or swivels from the victim would then be transferred to the captor. Several small victories of this sort could quickly equip a privateer with a good number of small cannon, making her the match or superior of most merchantmen.

Some audacious fellows actually began their privateering careers without a ship, putting to sea in whaleboats, skiffs, and fishing smacks. Many privateers initially operated without a proper license, a fact often overlooked by a friendly prize court in wartime. These catch-as-catch-can privateers were most successful at the beginning of a conflict, often seizing vessels unaware of the state of war. In American coastal waters, with their numerous coves and inlets, small boats would dash out after almost any enemy flag vessel. The waters of the Chesapeake Bay and the areas around Cape Cod and the Long Island Sound near New York abounded in these miniature vessels of war. During the American Revolution, Britain sent more than eighteen warships and 2,000 soldiers to burn the town of Norwalk, Connecticut, on the Long Island Sound.[10] Described in British records as a "nest of privateers," Norwalk housed more than sixty whaleboats used to attack vessels bringing provisions to British-held New York City.[11]

The capture, libeling, condemnation, and sale of a prize was more involved legally than it would at first seem. To **Prize Courts** be a proper prize, a vessel captured at sea or in an enemy port had to belong to the enemy, or citizens of a country then at war with the captor. Neutral shipping was immune from capture unless it was carrying contraband. The captured vessel was brought into a friendly port where both ship and cargo went through a condemnation process in a prize court. If there was no prize court in a particular port, a captured vessel might be held for months until the case was adjudicated. Some harbors served as reception points for captured vessels for long periods. From 1656 to 1783, for example, Dunkirk served as a point of condemnation for 4,000 vessels. Boston and Baltimore served a similar function during the American Revolution and the War of 1812.[12]

In a prize court, documents were studied, testimony was taken, and a defense by the owners was made. Each vessel was libeled (a claim was filed), and each case was judged separately. Additionally, more than one privateer might lay claim to a single prize or conflicting titles of ownership were offered—all of which muddied the legal waters. Prize courts kept careful records of their proceedings. These included written records, interrogatories, bills of lading, and logs. If the ship and/or cargo were deemed to be legitimate prizes, they would be condemned and sold at auction. The proceeds were then distributed by the court among the owners, officers, and crew of the captor.[13]

Most European maritime powers used privateers in one form or another; nonetheless, it was the English **Private Warships** that established the rules that were to prevail into the **Instead of Navies** nineteenth century. In Britain prior to the thirteenth century, it was the habit of the English kings to require that the owners of merchant vessels make themselves and their ships available to the needs of the army upon command. Once dragooned into service, these merchantmen were used to transport troops and provisions to the Continent. In 1242, the Crown expanded this role to include offensive warfare. English vessels from the Cinque Ports (Hastings, Romney, Hythe, Sandwich, and Dover) were ordered by Henry III to commit every possible injury upon French shipping. The king, thereby, converted every English merchant vessel into a privateer with no ceremony at all.

The formal and systematic use of private war vessels by the English began one year later in the form of "licenses" granted to Geoffney Piper, Adam Robernolt, and William Sauvage to prey upon the French as private warships in partnership with the king. The text of the surviving commission reads in part:

Relative to annoying the King's enemies. The King to all, etc., greetings. Know ye that we have granted and given license to Adam Robernolt and William Sauvage, and their companions whom they take with them, to annoy our enemies by sea or by land, wheresoever they are able, so that they share with us the half of all their gains; and therefore we command you neither to do nor suffer to be done, any let, damage or injury to them or their barge, or other ship or galley that they may have; and they are to render to the King, in his wardrobe, the half of all their gains.[14]

Henry III gave his thirteenth-century privateers "a license," or permission, to act as a private navy in the service of the Crown. By so doing, he covered with a cloak of legality many actions that would otherwise have been construed as piracy. In issuing the commission, the king made himself a partner in the venture by requiring half of all the plunder. Private vessels were generally used as privateers only in wartime as an essential auxiliary to the operation of land forces, thereby filling the need for a large navy.

English privateers often operated under an "Order Of Council for General Reprisals" issued against a specified enemy. This allowed them to take an unlimited amount of booty from the enemy as long as a state of war existed between the contesting countries. The names *Revenge, Vengeance*, and *Reprisal* appear regularly among the favorites given to privateering vessels.

Although licensed private warships were in use for almost five centuries, there is no known record of the use of the term *privateer* before the seventeenth century. The term appears for the first time in a letter written by Sir Leoline Jenkins in 1665. There seems to have been no specific term used to describe them prior to this date. Nonetheless, there is evidence that private warships were commonly said to be upon a "cruise" (first used in 1651) and may have been called "cruisers" as early as 1679.

Letters of Marque Merchant vessels, whose primary purpose was commerce, were sometimes provided with a "letter of marque" (or mark), which allowed them to make seizures if the opportunity availed. These went out on "voyages" rather than "cruises," and the difference seems to have been recognized at the time.

As early as the thirteenth century, there was a distinction between the private warship and a letter of marque. The letter of marque was issued as a legal instrument that allowed the holder to redress purely private grievances by granting a property right to the unspecified goods of another person or monarch. In 1295, for example, a letter of marque was issued to Bernard D'Ongressil. His cargo of fruit from Spain was robbed by some Portuguese.[15] The letter of marque gave him the "license of *marking* [or picking out] the men and subjects of the Kingdom of Portugal, and especially those of Lisbon, and their goods by land and sea," until such time as he regained just compensation for his loss.[16]

The letter of marque was widely considered a "measure short of war," and it was limited to a specific period of time with the stipulation that an accounting would be made of any surplus to the Crown. Both Humphrey Gilbert and Martin Frobisher armed themselves with letters of marque on their voyages of discovery to the New World. The full legal title of the license was a "letter of marque and reprisal," and the idea that it originated as a "reprisal" against a particular person or country for their own attack or plunder is only one of many competing scenarios for the origin of the term. An alternate theory suggests that the term originated simply from the seal or stamp with which the document containing the license was officially marked.[17]

In the fifteenth and sixteenth centuries, the depredations of pirates and privateers became almost indistinguishable. While the privateers had their commissions and the pirates did not, it became common practice for some monarchs to share in the spoils of both rather than establish their own regular navies. The Mediterranean of the fifteenth century was so filled with privateers from the Italian city states, Spain, and Greece that merchants once again demanded protection. As the enforcement of the piracy laws tightened, many privateers found that they were being treated like pirates in any case. The enforcement of the laws against piracy had an unexpected effect. Many privateers found that they could cut their unscrupulous monarchs right out of their share of the booty by simply abandoning any allegiance and keeping the whole of the profit for themselves.

In 1544, King Henry VIII reinvigorated the English privateering system by allowing the privateers to keep "the **The English** whole property in prizes which they took." This change in **Sea Hawks** the established structure of privateering brought many adventurous skippers back to the legal side of the ledger. However, with Henry's death, the gentlemen known as "Sea Hawks" (Francis Drake, Walter Raleigh, and John Hawkins, for example) found Henry's daughter, Elizabeth, less generous by half than her father. Notwithstanding the fact that the Crown once again had its hand in their pot, these gentlemen adventurers found working within the law profitable. Moreover, they received not only the approbation of the English Court, but also its diplomatic defense for their raids against Spanish shipping as long as the Queen got the lion's share of the profits.

Initially, English interest in the New World lagged behind that of Spain and France. The earliest attempts by the English to exploit the New World were intimately tied to the exertions of the English Sea Hawks. Sir Francis Drake, best known of the Sea Hawks, made a habit of attacking Spanish shipping in the Caribbean, and his exploits underscored the vulnerability of the Spanish treasure convoys. Few men knew Caribbean waters better than Drake. To the Spanish he was a "devil," and his name was used to frighten little children. The skillful aggression of men such as Drake brought home the plunder of fat Spanish galleons loaded with gold and silver from the New World. Considering the tremendous bulk of the Spanish New World trade, however, very few ships were actually taken. Nonetheless, the loss of a half dozen treasure galleons in a year more than once paralyzed the Spanish and helped to provide money for the English treasury as well.

In an age of small navies and many private vessels, the Sea Hawks rallied to the Crown when the nucleus of a fleet was needed in 1587 and 1588, and several played major roles in planning and implementing the defeat of the Spanish Armada. In 1587, Drake sailed into Cadiz with an English fleet and destroyed a great part of the ships preparing to join the Armada. The defeat of the Armada in 1588 was one of the most decisive naval actions ever fought. The battle immediately shifted the balance of naval power in Europe toward England.

The stories of fabulous wealth taken by privateers spread the practice into New World waters. Among Sir Walter Raleigh's goals in supporting the settlement of coastal Virginia was the establishment of bases for the interdiction of Spanish treasure fleets in the Straits of Florida. Every royal governor sent to the English colonies concurrently held the rank of vice-admiral with the right to issue commissions to privateers and condemn prizes. Privateering flourished, especially along the sea lanes favored by Spanish treasure galleons, and almost every outward bound English merchantman carried a letter of marque.[18]

Privateering in New World waters soon grew beyond the bounds of reasonable control. In 1595, Queen Elizabeth gave Drake and his cousin, John Hawkins permission to attack Puerto Rico and Panama. The prime target was Panama because a great deal of treasure passed through there from Spanish enterprises in the Pacific, but intelligence reached Drake that a crippled galleon carrying more than two million ducats in treasure was bound for repairs at Puerto Rico. Drake sailed with 27 ships and 2,500 men to attack San Juan, but his plans faltered when he failed to wrest away the treasure in the ensuing attack. Moreover, Hawkins died of fever on the outbound voyage, and Drake died at sea almost immediately thereafter.

Sir George Clifford, another noted Sea Hawk, was probably the most prominent privateer to be found among the English nobility. He commanded the ship *Bonaventure* in the Armada fight. Clifford organized no less than eleven privateering expeditions against the Spanish, and he suggested several others to the Queen. In 1598, he led a fleet of 21 vessels and 1,700 men into the Caribbean to attack San Juan. Although he succeeded in capturing the city, Clifford failed to hold it. For nearly a century, no English force again threatened Spain in the Caribbean.[19]

The privateers sent out by the first and second earls of Warwick attacked Spanish shipping from bases in England, Holland, and the West Indies. When England made peace with Spain, the privateering captains provided themselves with letters of marque from Holland. When the Dutch made peace, they obtained commissions from the Duchy of Savoy. Although the attacks were always directed toward Spain, and can be seen as a form of anti-Spanish patriotism, the actual goal seems to have been the continued flow of a substantial amount of revenue for the Warwick family.[20]

The ascension of the Stuart kings (James I and Charles I) in the first quarter of the seventeenth century and the internecine battles of the English Civil Wars of the 1640s overshadowed any increase in privateering in Britain. From 1649 to 1660, Oliver Cromwell was more interested **A Decline of English Privateering**
in building the English navy than fostering privateering, and Charles II was particularly disruptive to its further development. Louis XIV of France influenced Charles' marriage to the Catholic Infanta of Portugal and helped to focus English naval enmity on Holland. Louis also negotiated the return to France of the port of Dunkirk, which had been seized through the strategic foresight of Cromwell. Naval historian Alfred Thayer Mahan found the return of Dunkirk to French control "inexcusable from the maritime point of view" as the port quickly became "a haven for [French] privateers, [and] the bane of England's commerce in the Channel and North Sea."[21]

In 1688, the English Parliament deposed James II in favor of William of Orange. William had been the focus of an anti-French, antipapist movement in Europe since his childhood. The alliance of Dutch and English interests in the person of William caused an immediate deterioration of England's relations with France. During the War of the League of Augsburg (1688–1697) the activities of the English privateers became irrelevant when compared to the might of the combined English and Dutch navies.

Nonetheless, as King William's War opened, both Dutch and English commerce came under attack by French privateers who were very active in this regard. William did nothing to engender privateering but was careful, nonetheless, to reserve for the Crown one-fifth of any prizes taken. By the beginning of the eighteenth century, all indications were that the practice of privateering among the English was in decline while that of the French was flourishing.[22]

The Prize Act of 1708 In 1701, Queen Anne quietly ascended to the British throne upon the death of her widowed and childless brother-in-law, King William. Although the elderly queen was well loved by her people, Anne's reign was to see no peace. In 1700, the grandson of Louis XIV came to the Spanish throne as Philip V, virtually combining the French and Spanish thrones. In 1702, the War of Spanish Succession began on the Continent and continued until 1713. The period was one of almost constant warlike disputes on the continent of Europe, better characterized by the land conquests of the great English war captain the Duke of Marlborough than by the movements of great fleets.

Although Parliament procrastinated in undertaking badly needed naval reforms for many years, they made a remarkably good job when they finally tackled the problem. The passage of the Prize Act of 1708 proved a crucial point in the history of both the Royal Navy and British privateering. The Prize Act marked a positive change in Crown policy toward the privateers, codified many of the procedures and rules that governed privateering, and established bonds to ensure the "good behavior" of the privateering crews and officers. More importantly, the Prize Act showed that "the days of the government's conniving at piracy were past" by eliminating payment to the Crown of any part of the value of ships or cargo captured in wartime.[23]

In part, the act openly encouraged private persons to take up privateering by establishing a bounty to all sailors and officers who chose to ship out on a privateer, and it further applied the same principles governing prize money for privateers to the Royal Navy, stating:

That from and after the 26th of March, 1708, if any ship of war, privateer, merchant ship or other vessel be taken as [a] prize in any of Her Majesty's Courts of Admiralty, the flag-officer or officers, commander or commanders, and other officers, seamen, and others who shall be actually on board such ship or ships of war or privateers, shall after such condemnation have the *sole interest and property* in such prize or prizes.[24]

The people of Britain became actively involved in privateering in one form or another immediately after the Prize Act went into effect. Adventurers, former smugglers, merchants, and investors recognized the inherent profit to be made in fitting out a vessel as a privateer if no share went to the Crown. Although neutral vessels carrying war material were not added to the list of proper prizes until the middle of the eighteenth century, there were plenty of vessels to prey upon in the sea lanes between Britain and the Continent. It was at this point that the interest in privateering began in earnest among many Anglo-Americans, who were to prove particularly adept at building fast and inexpensive vessels that were well adapted to the privateering role.

The Peace of Utrecht ended the state of war in Europe in 1713. Queen Anne died in 1715 with no living direct heir, and the throne passed to George I of Hanover. After the Treaty of Utrecht, Europe passed through a peaceful period of twenty-five years. With no enemy to prey upon, interest in privateering once again waned. Nonetheless, it is interesting to note that piracy increased during this period of peace and that many privateers turned to smuggling rather than to the less intriguing life of common seamen.

When a minor conflict (called the War of Jenkin's Ear) broke out between England and Spain in 1739, the original Prize Act of 1708 was reissued as the General Prize Act. Englishmen initially seemed unwilling to send out cruisers against the Spaniards. During the first three or four years of the conflict, there were few active British cruisers. Records show that in 1744, there were fewer than sixty English cruisers at sea and that they captured as few as 10 percent of the prizes brought into British Admiralty Courts in that year. However, this minor Anglo-Spanish conflict turned into a major European confrontation (the War of Austrian Succession, 1740–1748) when France entered the fray as Spain's ally. It was not long thereafter that a larger number of British privateers were plying the oceans. In 1745 there were almost 200 British cruisers at sea, and fully half of the prizes seized by the British in that year were made by private warships.

The Prize Act of 1708, along with its many updated versions, provided the basis upon which all privateering was controlled and justified throughout the remainder of the eighteenth and nineteenth centuries. The admiralty court bureaucracies, the formal condemnation procedures and defenses, and the underlying distinctions between proper prizes and neutral shipping that the Prize Act of 1708 established were imitated by European and American governments and applied throughout the world until the practice of privateering was outlawed in 1856.

During the War of Austrian Succession, English privateering became "a craze the like of which had never been seen in Britain."[25] George II, realizing that the English were being disadvantaged by allowing the free passage of neutral Dutch vessels carrying French

The Golden Age of English Privateers

and Spanish supplies, extended the definition of a proper prize to cover Dutch bottoms transporting contraband goods. The royal definition of *contraband* was so expansive that there was almost no limit to the items that now might be condemned by the Admiralty Court. There was little that the outraged Dutch could do short of war, and until the peace was negotiated in 1748, they lost well over £1 million in shipping and cargo to English cruisers.

During each of the wars of the eighteenth century, Anglo-American colonists participated as commerce raiders by building vessels of considerable size and armament specifically for privateering. The colonists also became adept at darting out from the innumerable coves and inlets that characterized the American coastline in whaleboats, launches, and canoes to gobbled up unwary coasting vessels. Many colonials created large fortunes for themselves by investing in privateers.

Advantageous legislation and political influence also urged many Englishmen to take up the privateering trade in response to the Seven Years War (1756–1763). Men and ladies of the court, gentlemen, common laborers, and fishermen—almost everyone with a few shillings—invested in hundreds of ships, barks, cutters, and longboats sent out to prey upon the commerce of the sea. Many adventurous spirits actually served on these vessels as part of the crew, but most participated from the safety of their own homes as mere investors and let the professional seamen take the risks. The privateering craze continued to spread in the American colonies where the availability of good, fast vessels at a reasonable cost, and the geographical separation from Europe, remote from the protecting navies of the world's maritime powers, made privateering even more alluring. For example, Isaac Sears, at the age of twenty, served as the captain of the privateer *Harlequin*, creating a substantial fortune from the seizure of a single prize during the "French" wars. In the 1770s, Sears became an active leader of the American Revolution in New York.

The Seven Years War began in the forests of America, but it soon entangled all of the major nations of Europe and their colonies in India, the East Indies, and the Pacific in a struggle for empire. The cruisers of the major maritime powers had a field day indiscriminately hauling in vessels of every description with little regard to their possible neutrality or the nature of their cargo. The prize courts were swamped with disputes over ownership and insurance, claims for the reparation of unjustifiable losses, and charges of abuse at the hands of the privateering crews. Many of the excesses were traced back to the group of neophyte privateers who stood out from the coast in small vessels and fishing boats to seize whatever shipping availed itself. It was found that the more professional and better financed privateering operations caused less trouble. Subsequently English cruisers smaller than 100 tons burden with fewer than 10 guns firing at least 9 pounds of metal shot were refused licenses. The heavy-handed excesses of the cruisers during the Seven Years War—on all sides—tended to put the business of privateering into ill repute.

While the English freely used their privateers to enhance their superior navy, the French used them largely because they had nothing else. Few French monarchs had ever shown any desire to attain a naval status greater than that **The French Corsairs** of parity with the English. There were a mere 35 French ships-of-the-line in the middle of the eighteenth century. Of course, with both the French and Spanish thrones connected by close family ties after the War of Spanish Succession, a combination of their individual fleets could still be daunting for the English who arguably had the strongest single navy in the world.

The history of French privateering is somewhat less complicated than that of the English and Anglo-Americans. By royal ordinances in the fifteenth and sixteenth centuries, French privateers, generally referred to as corsairs, were held strictly responsible should they do damage to any vessels other than those of a specified enemy, and the distinctions between a privateer and a pirate seem to have been quite as clear for the French as they were for the English. From the beginning, French privateers were required to post a bond with the government of up to 15,000 livres, to receive the permission of the fleet Admiral to proceed on a cruise and to submit themselves to his discipline. The fleet Admiral required one-tenth of all prizes as his fee over and above any share that went to the Crown.

In the second quarter of the sixteenth century, France was almost constantly at odds with Spain. Attracted by Spain's New World treasure galleons, many French corsairs left their more usual haunts off the coast of Spain and positioned themselves in the Caribbean to seize Spain's wealth both afloat and ashore. Prominent among those privateers who used the unfortified islands of the West Indies as bases were Jean Florin, François le Clerc, and Jacques Sores. In 1523, Florin seized two Spanish treasure ships. Five years later, French corsairs burned a town in Puerto Rico; and Jacques Sores, with a single ship, was credited with burning at least five other Spanish towns in the Caribbean. Ultimately, Spain strengthened her convoy system and began to build forts to defend her settlements.

Thereafter, French interest in privateering waned until it was promoted by the Minister of Marine, Jean-Baptiste Colbert. French privateering reached its zenith two decades later during the War of the League of Augsburg (1688–1697). In 1690, nearly 300 corsairs were operating under French commissions. Their number was so large that they began traveling in squadrons, a concept popularly attributed to the creativity of Jean Bart, the best-known French privateer.

During the War of Spanish Succession (1702–1713) a group of French privateers known as Filibusters (*filibusters*), including Jean Bart and

Light 3 pounders like this one were often the only weapon found on small trading vessels and privateers. Weapons like this were almost useless against ships, but they were efficient man-killers. James Volo Photo.

Duguay-Troulin, proceeded to take upwards of 4,000 English vessels worth £30 million. The Filibusters (or Brothers of the Coast) became known for their merciless ravaging and pitiless plundering of both ocean-borne commerce and coastal cities. The English considered the Brothers of the Coast little more than pirates. Nonetheless, the services that they rendered to the French crown, especially in the Caribbean, were of such value to the state that their excesses were often overlooked.

During the War of Spanish Succession, Louis XIV reduced France's finances to the point of exhaustion. Under the rule of Louis XV, who at the age of five assumed the French throne after his father's death in 1715, privateering went into decline. Fortunately for France, the world experienced a period of relative peace while the child-king grew. When the adult king of France, now thirty, determined to enter the War of the Austrian Succession (1740–1748), he encouraged privateering in much the same way as had the English. Yet the French eschewed making neutral bottoms legitimate targets for capture. At the beginning of the Seven Years War (1756–1763), Louis XV abolished the Crown's share of prizes, and in 1758, he removed the traditional admiral's share of all prizes. The corsairs, thereafter, were given the entire value of any vessels and cargoes they captured. Subsequently, many small, active vessels put to sea as commerce raiders.

As British colonials, the Americans had grown wise in
the ways of privateering. During all the colonial wars of   **The American**
the eighteenth century, Anglo-Americans had operated   **Privateers**
cruisers under the watchful and protective eye of the
British Royal Navy. As relations between the mother country and her
colonies along the Atlantic seaboard deteriorated into rebellion and war,
Americans turned once again to privateering. However, this time their
prey was British commerce. The bulk of the American naval force during
the Revolution was made up of privateers. These operated under a "license" or commission issued by the individual American states or the
Continental Congress.

Simple economic self-interest spurred most men to serve in privateers,
and hundreds of Americans served in private warships from 1775 to
1783. Yet there was no guarantee that the licenses issued by the states
or Congress would protect the individual sailor from a charge of piracy.
After all, the "governments" issuing the licenses were in rebellion against
their rightful king. Many privateers dispensed with the time-consuming
formalities of getting a license and simply forged their own papers.[26]
Throughout the rebellion, the British held all captured American sailors
under a bill of attainder, charging them with piracy and treason. Naval
historian Francis R. Stark has pointed out that

it would be idle, of course, to pretend the they [those Americans serving in
privateers] were all inspired by patriotic motives only; but it is certain that the
patriotism of most of them was of a purer character than that of their English
and French predecessors. For the first time in history the privateer system assumed approximately the shape of a marine militia or volunteer navy.[27]

New England sailors took naturally to privateering, and American
shipbuilders and designers provided vessels that were generally superior
to those of the mother country as to their speed and their ability to sail
to windward. Yet even a small British frigate carried more guns and had
a larger, better disciplined crew than a privateer, and a ship-of-the-line
might carry 60 to 80 large guns and 600 men. In a ship-to-ship engagement, a British man-of-war would simply blow most American privateers out of the water. Consequently, American privateers relied upon
their speed to make captures and to make good their escape from patrolling British warships. American privateers paid for this advantage by
carrying fewer guns and sacrificing what little cargo capacity they had
to essential stores. The usual plan was to overtake and to attack unarmed
or lightly armed merchant vessels, detach a few men as a prize crew,
and make for a friendly American or foreign port, where both ship and
cargo would be condemned as a prize.

Privateers attacked not only merchant vessels but also unescorted supply ships sent out by the Royal Navy to support the British forces in America. The London *Chronicle* reported that the store ships *Nancy* and *Concord*, after becoming separated from their escorts, were taken by the privateers "within sight of the fleet in Boston."[28] Vice Admiral Samuel Graves so feared the American efforts in and around Boston that he "ordered the [Royal Navy] ships of war in the harbor to be secured with booms all around to prevent their being boarded and taken by rebel whale-boats."[29] In February 1776, Admiral Molyneaux Shuldham, who replaced Graves as the commander of the Atlantic Squadron, which was charged with suppressing the American privateers, wrote: "However numerous our cruisers may be or however attentive our Officers to their Duty, it has been found impossible to prevent some of our ordnance and other valuable stores, in small vessels, falling into the hands of the Rebels."[30]

Privately armed vessels came to characterize American maritime warfare after 1778, and their success may have served to fuel war weariness in England. A favorite American hunting ground was at the entrance to the Gulf of St. Lawrence where small fishing and trading vessels could be taken with little risk from the Royal Navy base at Halifax because of the fog and storms that ravaged the region. Another favorite spot was the West Indies, but here the Americans had to deal with the West Indian Squadron, based in Jamaica, and well guarded convoys of merchant vessels. The failure of the Royal Navy to stop American privateers from attacking British commerce in American waters was overshadowed only by its equally frustrating inability to drive the Americans from the English Channel. British newspapers were filled with stories of the recurring appearance of American privateers in home waters.

A comparison of the American (Continental) navy and the privateer fleet is interesting and enlightening in this regard. A total of 47 vessels served as a regular naval force during the entire course of the Revolution. These vessels carried 1,242 cannon and swivel guns (man-killing weapons larger than a musket and too heavy to fire unsupported). The Continental Navy captured a total of 196 vessels valued at about $6 million (Spanish). During the rebellion, there were 792 American privateers mounting more than 13,000 guns. Many of these cruisers operated throughout the entire eight years of the war. Admittedly, many of the vessels were small with light weight armament, yet the privateers captured more than 1,000 prizes valued at almost $18 million. After 1778, some American cruisers were formidable warships carrying 150 crewmen and upwards of 20 guns.[31]

During the American Revolution, the successes of the citizen soldier on land and the citizen sailor at sea took on an importance of legendary proportion in future American thinking that blocked out the realities of just how they were accomplished. The ships of the Continental Navy had some obligation to stand their ground and make a fight, while the privateers, built for speed, were free to choose their battles. Yet, the myth of American invincibility, taken together with a characteristic aversion to standing professional forces, caused the new United States to eschew a large army and a line of battleships for reliance on a citizen militia and a minuscule navy supported by a heavy dependence on privateers.

American fondness for privateering continued into the nineteenth century. Within six months of the dec- **Privateers of 1812** laration of war in 1812, more than 1,100 privateers made their way out of Baltimore, Maryland, and the surrounding Chesapeake Bay to attack British commerce. New England shipowners, who were generally against the war, sent out only a few cruisers. The vessels dispatched from Baltimore in 1812 were unlike their revolutionary cousins of 1775. They carried scores of men and larger, if not more numerous, guns. In anticipation of the conflict, ten privately financed warships of more than 300 tons each had fitted out in the shipyards of Baltimore alone.

Certainly vessels like these would have posed an enormous obstacle to the operations of the Royal Navy had they stayed in the Chesapeake, but the promise of enormous profits afloat on the sea lanes of the world quickly lured them away. Consequently when the British attacked Fort McHenry in the Baltimore harbor and burned the American capital at Washington, D.C., they were opposed only by a minuscule fleet of gunboats originally designed by Thomas Jefferson to provide for a coastal defense. Fortunately for the Americans, Fort McHenry was a state-of-the-art fortress that denied the British a firm foothold on American soil.

Nonetheless, with the armistice of 1815, it was found that not a single American war aim had been attained. Two of the six 44-gun frigates— *Chesapeake* and *President*—which were the pride of the American navy had been taken in combat. Yet history has largely dismissed the dismal failure of American arms for the less bitter illusions of success offered by the stirring victories of the frigates *Constitution* and *United States*; the successful defense of Fort McHenry; and the minimal successes of American naval forces on Lake Erie, Lake Champlain, and at Fort Erie. None of these victories, however, had proved decisive. The British, finally successful against Napoleon, had simply wearied of war. Nonetheless, American privateers had helped to wear down the British fighting spirit by capturing more than $40 million (US) worth of shipping in less than two years, sometimes at the rate of more than thirty prizes per month. Private warships, in fact, proved to be the only effective American offensive weapon in the war. A contemporary observer noted that the American privateers of 1812 "sustained the honor of their country almost singlehandedly."[32]

The French also maintained their privateering traditions
Napoleon's against the British. Privateers of the French Revolution cap-
Privateers tured over 5,500 British vessels from 1793 to 1801, and from
1803 to 1814, more than 5,300 were taken. The fall of French
privateering bases such as Ile-de-France and Guadaloupe in the West
Indies posed little problem to the cruisers as they simply found new
bases. In the Caribbean, a number of privateers worked from the coast
of Columbia.

Robert Surcouf was the most outstanding and successful of the privateers in the Napoleonic Era. His daring capture of the East Indiaman
Kent of 38 guns and a crew of 437, including troops, with the 18-gun *La
Confiance*, which had a crew of 120, was possibly his most impressive
action.

The general peace that ensued after the defeat of Napoleon left little
opportunity for privateering. The nations of Europe became increasingly
involved with internal strife and colonial trade matters. Mariners in the
United States generally turned away from privateering to focus on the
foreign carrying trade, worldwide whaling, and a growing trans-Atlantic
immigrant trade.

NOTES

1. Francis R. Stark, *The Abolition of Privateering and the Declaration of Paris*
(New York: Columbia University Press, 1897), 72.

2. George Masselman, *The Cradle of Colonialism* (New Haven, CT: Yale University Press, 1963), 51.

3. James G. Lydon, *Pirates, Privateers, and Profits* (Upper Saddle River, NJ: The
Gregg Press, 1970), 48.

4. Alexander Winston, *No Man Knows My Grave: Pirates and Privateers, 1665–
1715* (Boston: Houghton Mifflin, 1969), 86–95

5. Lydon, 51–54. See also Winston, 112–162.

6. Lucy M. Salmon, *The Dutch West India Company on the Hudson* (Poughkeepsie, NY: Published privately, 1915), 30–32.

7. Jerome R. Garitee, *The Republic's Private Navy: The American Privateering
Business as Practiced by Baltimore during the War of 1812* (Middletown, CT: Wesleyan University Press, 1977), 3.

8. Robert Carse, *Ports of Call* (New York: Scribner's, 1967), 95. Although the
letter of English law required that pirates be sent to Britain for trial, this was
deemed to be impractical in all except the most noteworthy of cases.

9. Contrary to maritime mythology, the navy of the Confederate States of
America (1861–1865) was not solely composed of these privateers but rather of
regular naval vessels that filled the role of commerce raiders much like the sub-
marines of the world wars of the twentieth century.

10. An American prize court, one of only five in New England, was located
at Norwalk, Connecticut. During the attack, many of the town records were

burned, almost completely erasing the existence of Norwalk's prize court from American maritime history.

11. It should be noted that many American Loyalists also operated as British privateers under the royal flag, attacking rebel shipping in much the same manner.

12. Garitee, 6.

13. Such records serve as a useful source of primary materials for historians.

14. H. Nicolas, *History of the Royal Navy* (London, 1847), 200; Stark, 51.

15. Fred T. Jane, *The British Battle-Fleet: Its Inception and Growth Throughout the Centuries* (1912; reprint, London: Conway Maritime Press, 1997), 16.

16. Stark, 52.

17. Garitee, 4.

18. Kenneth R. Andrews, *Elizabethan Privateering: English Privateering during the Spanish War, 1585–1603* (Cambridge: Cambridge University Press, 1964), 16–18. Also see Ivor Noel Hume, *Martin's Hundred* (Charlottesville: University Press of Virginia, 1979).

19. National Park Service, *The Forts of Old San Juan: San Juan National Historic Site, Puerto Rico* (Washington, DC: U.S. Department of the Interior, 1996), 34–37.

20. Kevin Phillips, *The Cousins' War: Religion, Politics, and the Triumph of Anglo-America* (New York: Basic Books, 1999), 30.

21. Alfred Thayer Mahan, *The Influence of Sea Power upon History, 1660–1783* (1894, reprints New York: Dover, 1987), 105.

22. Mahan, 61.

23. Stark, 68–69.

24. Ibid., 69. Emphasis added.

25. Ibid., 72.

26. Samuel W. Bryant, *The Sea and the States: A Maritime History of the American People* (New York: Thomas Y. Crowell, 1967), 86.

27. Stark, 121.

28. The London *Chronicle*, December 30–January 2, 1776, as reported by William Bell Clark, *George Washington's Navy. Being an Account of His Excellency's Fleet in New England Waters* (Baton Rouge; Louisiana State University Press, 1960), 61.

29. Ibid., 63.

30. Gardner W. Allen, *A Naval History of the American Revolution*, vol. I (Williamstown, MA: Corner House, 1970), 83–84.

31. James M. Volo, "The War at Sea," *Living History Journal* (January 1987): 2–18. Also see William Bell Clark, *Ben Franklin's Privateers: A Naval Epic of the American Revolution* (Westport, CT: Greenwood Press, 1969).

32. Garitee, 244.

12

The Age of Fighting Sail

Admiral De Grasse's 1781 offensive was "the most important and
most perfectly executed naval campaign of the age of sail."
—Jonathan R. Dull, naval historian

The Age of Fighting Sail can safely be viewed as a single prolonged
conflict covering a period of about a century and a quarter beginning
with the Glorious Revolution in 1688 and ending with the British victory
at Trafalgar in 1805 during the Napoleonic Wars. It was a period in
which the armed merchantmen of the age of trade were replaced by
genuine warships whose task was to control the sea lanes. As the naval
tactics of the period changed gradually and the shipbuilding technology
and effectiveness of naval gunnery changed very little, consideration of
the naval tactics used by either side can be viewed as a simple evolution
in strategy and implementation.[1]

There were seven distinct wars fought during this period with France
and England allied on opposite sides with the other states of Europe: (1)
the War of the League of Augsburg (1688–1697); (2) the War of Spanish
Succession (1702–1713); (3) the War of Austrian Succession (in two stages
between 1740 to 1748); (4) the Seven Years War (1756–1763); (5) the War
of American Independence (1775–1783); (6) the wars fought with the new
French Republic; and (7) the wars fought with Napoleon's empire.

There were two primary motives for all the Anglo-French wars. The
first is best described as English unwillingness to stand by as France tried

to dominate the European continent. The second involved both British and French ambitions in the area of world trade. At the end of the age, only one European nation would dominate the seas.

THE WAR OF THE LEAGUE OF AUGSBURG

Known in America as King William's War, this conflict began as the Glorious Revolution, which toppled James II from the English throne. The initial stages of the conflict were bloodless. James' army deserted him, and the small part of the navy that did not openly declare for William of Orange sat in the Thames River unable and unwilling to prevent the invader from moving down the Channel from Holland to Devon. William landed unopposed at Torbay, and James fled to the protection of Louis XIV in France. The French king could not abide William, a dedicated Dutch Protestant, on Britain's throne. William had been the center of Dutch Protestant unrest since he was a child. When he became king of England, he quickly became the champion of "global Protestantism," and he used the newly combined Anglo-Dutch fleet to foster that cause.[2]

The England of earlier times had been reluctant to expand in the face of the pope's division of the New World between Spain and Portugal. The cause of Protestantism led England—free of papal restraint—to a more active and sustained quest for maritime power. The desire to secure England and the English colonies from the specter of Roman Catholic popery became an distinctive characteristic of English patriotism and national identity. Militant Protestant sea captains thereafter gave a crusading tenor to the battles waged against the Catholic Bourbon monarchies of Spain and France.

The ascension of William and Mary to the English throne had a positive influence on English sea power mainly because it brought the Dutch and English fleets together as allies. The Dutch fleet, however, remained subservient to the control of English admirals. Nonetheless, Louis of France concluded that he might win a naval war against England if he made judicious use of both his navy and his privateers in support of James without overly exposing his own position on the Continent. Louis' plans began with a resounding success. The exiled James, with the backing of French arms, was transported to Ireland by the French navy. James, backed by the Catholics in Ireland, quickly controlled almost all of the island.

A small British squadron under Admiral Sir George Rooke was detached to relieve Londonderry. Almost immediately thereafter, King William took an army of opposition over to Ireland under the protection of another fleet commanded by Admiral Cloudisley Shovell. A third squadron of the fleet, under Admiral Henry Killigrew, was sent to Gibraltar to prevent a joining of the French fleets stationed at Toulon and Brest. William, either through incompetence or overconfidence, had split his naval forces in a most dramatic and dangerous fashion: Rooke and Shovell in Irish waters, Killigrew off the coast of Spain, and the remainder of he fleet, under Admiral Earl Torrington, in the Channel.

Unfortunately, Killigrew's squadron failed in its mission and missed the outgoing Toulon squadron. For the first time, a united French fleet of some 80 warships, under Admiral Comte Anne de Tourville, was dominant in the Channel. Torrington's Anglo-Dutch fleet of 55 warships was the only naval force available to stop a French invasion of England. Unknown to the English, Tourville had overestimated the difficulty of bringing his fleet into the Channel, and he had not taken sufficient troops for an invasion. Queen Mary, in William's absence, ordered Torrington to immediately attack the French. Torrington initially objected hoping to engage in a defensive maneuver that might save his fleet from annihilation, but Mary and her counselors insisted.

The English waited for Tourville off Beachy Head hoping to attack the French rear from windward but refusing **Beachy Head** action elsewhere to compensate for their numerical inferiority. Somehow the Dutch in Torrington's van, misunderstanding or disobeying his orders, rushed headlong into the French and were badly mauled by their van and center. With some skill, Torrington extricated them at the cost of several Dutch warships and one English vessel, which were scuttled so they would not be captured. He then retreated up the Channel as he had originally planned before the Queen had interfered with his strategy.

Tourville, although victorious and in control of the Channel, failed to follow up his victory. The French were unprepared for their success, and by the time they had an invasion force ready for embarkation, both Shovell and Killigrew had returned to the Channel. In a remarkably short time, the English had once again amassed a major fleet to threaten Tourville's operations. The chance for invasion had passed, and Tourville knew it. Louis XIV was never again to see its like.[3]

Two years after Beachy Head, Admiral Tourville— this time with an inferior fleet—was driven from the **Barfluer/La Hogue** Channel by an Anglo-Dutch fleet under Admiral Lord John Russell at Barfleur. Tourville had tried to imitate Beachy Head in reverse, but the French fleet was too widely dispersed. At Barfleur, Tourville's rear was doubled, and his center was cut to pieces by Russell. Seeing that further action was unprofitable, the French admiral ordered his fleet to run downwind for whatever ports they could make. The main body entered St. Malo intact, and three ships, including Tourville's flagship, made Cherborg. However, twelve of the French warships took refuge in La Hogue closely followed by two English squadrons under admirals Sir Ralph Delavall and Sir George Rooke. The English sent their seamen and marines in the fleet's boats on a "cutting out expedition," which destroyed or damaged beyond repair every one of the twelve refugees in the harbor.

The war ended in 1697 in a tactical stalemate with William unable to defeat the French on the Continent and with Louis unable to effect an invasion of England. Thereafter, Louis gave up his efforts to gain command of the sea, and he never resumed them. In succeeding years, the only French vessels found at sea were the occasional merchant vessel and some French privateers.[4]

THE WAR OF SPANISH SUCCESSION

In 1700, the grandson of France's Louis XIV claimed the vacant Spanish throne as Philip V. The potential for Louis XIV to wield excessive influence over Europe under this circumstance galvanized the Protestant states of Europe into an alliance. The War of Spanish Succession (1702–1713) was the last naval war characterized by great fleets composed of hundreds of vessels. After 1713, national fleets of more specialized warships numbered in the twenties and thirties rather than in the hundreds. Notwithstanding the great size of the opposing fleets, few major actions took place during this war. Only once did the French stage an invasion of England, but the mere presence of the Royal Navy proved more than a match for them. Admiral George Byng tried to bring them to action, but the French refused.

There were no decisive sea battles during the thirteen years of the War of Spanish Succession, but the allied Anglo-Dutch fleet proved to be of great indirect military value in support of the Duke of Marlborough's land war on the Continent. Alfred Thayer Mahan pointed out that to appreciate the effect of the sea power of the allies, it was necessary to take account of the quiet, steady pressure that control of the sea brought to bear against France. "It is thus indeed that sea power usually acts . . . so quiet in its workings."[5]

Gibraltar An important part of the Duke of Marlborough's strategy centered on the ability of the Royal Navy to prevent a juncture of the French fleets based in Toulon and Brest. With no nearby base, autumnal gales from the west forced the British to abandon their Mediterranean posts each year by late October. Campaigning in the Mediterranean, therefore, was reduced to a few months clustered around the summer.

In 1702, Admiral Rooke directed his fleet into an attack on Gibraltar. The French garrison on the island was totally surprised by the successful landing of Rooke's marines, and the French fleet immediately put to sea to gain the island back. The Battle of Malaga, which followed, was bloody, but indecisive with no ships taken by either side. Both antagonists sailed for home almost immediately thereafter. However, Rooke left behind a squadron under Admiral John Leake, a remarkably able officer, who held Gibraltar and also captured another strategic base at Minorca.

In 1713, the Treaty of Utrecht secured both Gibraltar and Minorca for the British as well as several islands in the West Indies, but the Bourbons successfully set one of their own on the Spanish throne. In light of these results, the importance of the capture of Gibraltar, the "Rock," cannot be underestimated. Events and geography had combined to make this island one of the most strategically important spots in the world.[6]

JENKINS' EAR

For almost a quarter century after the Treaty of Utrecht, Europe was at peace. Then in 1739, England became involved in a meaningless conflict with Spain known as the War of Jenkins' Ear. Captain Robert Jenkins reported to the House of Commons that he had been stopped by a Spanish warship. When he refused to allow the Spanish to search his vessel "one of his ears was torn off." The vindication of Jenkins soon became a national cause, and war was declared against Spain. Yet it was commonly rumored that the entire affair of the ear was a simple fiction scripted to gain public support for an aggression against Spain.[7]

In their greed to dispossess the Spanish of some of their most valuable sugar-producing islands in the Caribbean, the British fitted out a fleet of 124 vessels, 29 of which were ships-of-the-line, to attack Cartagena. Aboard were 12,000 soldiers—among them more than 2,000 American volunteers. The entire enterprise was commanded by Admiral Edward Vernon. Although Vernon was an admirable seamen, the expedition was an utter failure. The army commander refused to cooperate with the navy, tropical disease laid the troops low, and the colonials insisted on being brought home when their relatively short enlistments expired in the middle of the contest. Fewer than 3,000 men survived the expedition, and only about 700 Americans returned to the colonies. Besides the obvious failures, the most significant result may have been the scarring of American attitudes toward the British regulars.[8]

THE WAR OF AUSTRIAN SUCCESSION

In 1740, Charles VI of Austria died with no male heir. Charles had taken pains to ensure that Europe would support the accession of Maria Theresa in his place. Nonetheless, France demurred and immediately formed alliances with Maria Theresa's enemies. The British, characteristically opposed to any French position, declared war on France in 1744.

The land war did not go well for the British. They lost battle after battle on the Continent, and the French were able to wrest the important trading center of Madras in India from the armies of the Honourable East India Company. The apparent weakness of English arms led Scottish adherents of the Stuart line, deposed in 1688, to attempt to regain the British throne from its present occupant, George II. The resulting Scottish Rebellion of 1745—although initially successful in winning battles in the north of Britain—was absolutely crushed at the battle of Culloden in 1746.

Louisburg   In America, several New England colonies joined together to strike a blow at the French. Their target was the formidable fortress of Louisburg on Cape Breton Island. "To many of the colonists this Catholic stronghold was a den of Satanic iniquity," and their desire to eliminate the French presence in Canada was sometimes fueled by extreme hatred for the adherents of a rival religion.[9] Notwithstanding their religious prejudice, the proposed campaign was wise strategically. Not only was Louisburg a location from which the French could potentially incite Indian raids into the New England frontier, it also directly threatened the ability of the colonial fishing fleet to utilize the cod fisheries of the Grand Banks and dry and salt their catch on the Canadian shore.

The colonials assembled a fleet of close to 100 vessels, mostly small sloops, shalops, and schooners. The fleet was commander by Captain Edward Tyng of Massachusetts. The land forces, composed of more than 4,000 provincial troops, was commanded by Colonel William Pepperell of Maine. The "All-American" expedition was belatedly joined by four ships-of-the-line of the Royal Navy commanded by Commodore Peter Warren. This was the only part of the force provided by the home government.

Warren immediately blockaded Louisburg and silenced the main defensive guns on an island in the harbor. He then covered the amphibious landing of the colonial troops that was carried out in open boats through a heavy surf. After forty-seven days of siege, the fortress surrendered. In the meantime, several French ships, unaware that the harbor was not in safe hands, had been taken by Warren's ships. The commodore's refusal to share the prize money with the colonial skippers created a good deal of friction.

On a wider scale, the war at sea was somewhat of a draw with each side taking about 3,000 merchant vessels. The fall of Louisburg to the British proved their one shining accomplishment. By the Treaty of Aix-la-Chapelle in 1748, the British gained Acadia (Nova Scotia)—from which they promptly removed the French inhabitants and established a major naval base at Halifax. The American colonials were outraged when the government returned Louisburg to the French in exchange for Madras. It was obvious that a further final contest was approaching between England and France for possession of North America.[10]

THE SEVEN YEARS WAR

The Seven Years War (the French and Indian War in America) actually began in 1754 with a skirmish in the wilderness of western Pennsylvania between French colonial troops and Virginia militia commanded by a young and inexperienced officer named George Washington. The action was something of a diplomatic embarrassment for the British government, and it quickly escalated into a worldwide conflict. Battles on sea and land were fought in North America, the West Indies, Europe, India, the East Indies, and the Pacific between vast alliances on both sides, making it a true "world war."[11]

In 1756, England understood that it could not fight the French on land in Europe, India, and North America and simultaneously maintain a fleet strong enough to beat them at sea. Therefore, the government concluded a treaty of alliance with Frederick the Great of Prussia. England would help in the land war with supplies, funds, and a few regiments of British regulars, but the brunt of the fighting on the Continent would be borne by the Prussians. The British would concentrate on fighting the French in North America and at sea. For their part, the French allied themselves with Catholic Austria. Thus two Catholic empires with their associated satellites were ranged against two eminently Protestant nations. Frederick quickly defeated the Franco-Austrian forces at the battle of Rossback in 1757. With France severely crippled on land, the English were free to pursue them with greater vigor at sea.

The French entered the Seven Years War with almost 80 ships-of-the-line, but the British had more than 120 manned by 70,000 trained seamen. Admiral Edmund Boscawen scored the first naval victory of the war near the entrance to the Gulf of St. Lawrence in Canada. Boscawen intercepted four French warships and gave chase. Captain Richard Howe in the *Dunkirk* (60) engaged the French *Alcide* (64) and opened such a furious cannonade that the French ship struck its colors. This victory helped to make both Boscawen and Howe significant figures in British naval history thereafter.

Several unsuccessful military campaigns were then undertaken by the British. The first of these proved the most notable failure in land warfare of the period. The defeat of General Edward Braddock and of the Coldstream Guards by the French and their Indian allies on the Monongahela River in America shocked the British public in 1755. Also widely remarked upon was the expedition of Admiral John Byng in the Mediterranean in the same year. After abandoning the British base at Minorca to an enemy fleet, Byng was tried and executed for mishandling his command. Less dramatic was the botched attempt to retake Louisburg by Admiral Francis Holbourn in 1757. The English fleet sailed up to the harbor, saw sixteen large French warships ranged about the fortress, and retreated precipitously without engaging. This failure was particularly noted by the Anglo-Americans, who were still smarting over the return of the fortress at the end of the last war.

Undaunted by embarrassment, the British pushed on. An "All-American" expedition sent to secure the lake passage from Canada to New York in 1756 won a stunning victory over the regulars of the French army. In 1758, a new fleet was assembled at Halifax to attack Louisburg once again. Numerous transports, 40 men-of-war, and 8,000 sailors were placed under the command of the capable Boscawen. A land force of 12,000 British regulars was placed under generals Jeffery Amherst and James Wolfe. Boscawen blockaded the Louisburg harbor after Amherst and Wolfe successfully landed their troops. With the fortress besieged and with no hope of a relieving force breaking the blockade, the French surrendered within a few weeks.

The Wonderful Year—1759   Bolstered by the success at Louisburg, General Wolfe returned to Canada in 1759 to attack Quebec with a massive body of regular troops supported by 49 men-of-war, almost 200 transports, and 14,000 sailors and marines. Temporarily delayed by late-season ice, the ships threaded their way up the tricky channel of the St. Lawrence River with the help of excellent navigators under Admiral Charles Saunders and James Cook, then master of the fleet.

By autumn, the great citadel at Quebec had fallen to the ill-fated Wolfe. But the threat of having the fleet frozen in during the coming Canadian winter caused Admiral Saunders to withdraw, leaving a small land force to hold the city until relieved in the spring. The importance of the prompt arrival of the Royal Navy at Quebec of 1760 cannot be under-estimated. It confirmed the victory of 1759 and led directly to the fall of Montreal and all of French Canada with it.

The year 1759 was also wonderful for the British at sea. The Royal Naval virtually annihilated a French fleet slated for the invasion of England and Scotland. Admiral Rodney destroyed the French invasion barges at Le Havre, and in August, Boscawen fell upon a French fleet led by Admiral de la Clue, chased it into Lagos Bay, and destroyed or captured every ship. The West Indies Squadron took the sugar island of Guadaloupe, and the warships of the Honorable East India Company took the initiative from the French squadron in India.

At the Battle of Quiberon Bay on the French Channel coast in November 1759, Admiral Sir Edward Hawke attacked the Atlantic Squadron of Admiral Comte de Conflans under remarkably severe weather conditions and drove Conflans' ships onto a lee shore in a tempest. Although

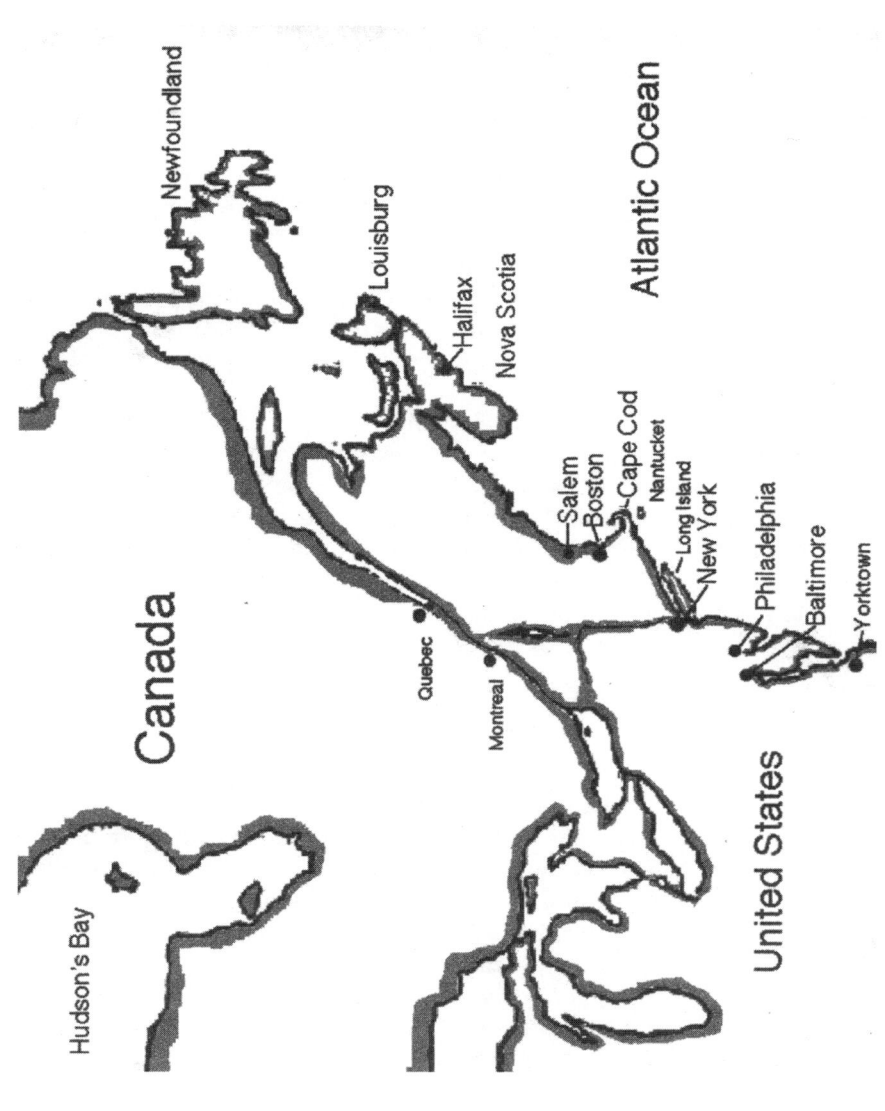

Canada

Hudson's Bay

Newfoundland

Louisburg

Halifax
Nova Scotia

Quebec

Montreal

Salem
Boston

Cape Cod
Nantucket

Long Island
New York

Philadelphia

Baltimore

Yorktown

Atlantic Ocean

United States

not joined in formal battle, France lost 10 warships and the temporary use of 13 more on the shoals, rocks, and sand bars of the bay. More than 2,500 French sailors lost their lives. "Although few contemporaries realized it, the Battle of Quiberon Bay, and not the more celebrated Battle of Quebec, was the decisive military event of 1759."[12]

The French lost a total of 27 ships-of-the-line and 8 smaller vessels in 1759 alone. With half of its major warships gone, besides a large number of damaged frigates, the French navy was ruined for the remainder of the conflict. Nonetheless, even as the end of the war neared, the French minister of marine, the Duc de Choiseul, continued to work to restore the naval power of France. Rather than turning away from sea power, he turned to privateers. Subsequently, French privateers swarmed over the sea lanes. Notwithstanding the vigilance of the blockading English navy (the British had more than 130 active ships-of-the-line and more than 100 frigates and smaller war vessels on stations around the world), French privateers took a total of more than 2,500 merchant vessels during the war.

In the Peace of Paris (1763) that followed, the French lost almost all their possessions in North America except a few islands in the Caribbean. Spain, which had belatedly entered the war on the side of France, quickly lost Minorca, Havana, and Manila to the wide-ranging Royal Navy—a circumstance that served to underscore Spain's continued position as a secondary naval power. By the provisions of the treaty, Havana and Manila were restored to Spain by Britain in exchange for Florida and all the Spanish territory east of the Mississippi River. Britain kept Minorca and the Grenadas, Dominica, Tobago, and St. Vincent in the Caribbean. France gave Spain all of Louisiana as compensation for her losses, especially the loss of the strategically important Mediterranean island of Minorca.

Empire   The British won a great empire in the Seven Years War. The Royal Navy that had helped to accomplish this left the war with almost 300 warships in commission. Naval historian Alfred Thayer Mahan summed up the British position at the end of 1763. "The one nation that gained in this war was that which used the sea in peace to earn its wealth, and ruled it in war by the extent of its navy."[13] Nonetheless, this successful conclusion created many of the political and economic conditions that permitted the Anglo-American colonists to attempt to sever their ties with Britain in the 1770s.

In the years after the war, the British ruling classes became indifferent to the needs of maintaining the navy. Having won an empire and having humiliated their traditional enemies, they seemed to have misunderstood the perils that continued to exist. The failure to maintain the Royal Navy in fighting trim was to have devastating consequences in the next decade.

Many of the vessels that fought in the Seven Years War were to enter the next war as overaged derelicts.

By contrast, the French continued building warships with greater resolve during the interwar years. Briefly, under the leadership of Minister of Marine Choiseul, the French took the lead in marine design. Choiseul restored discipline to the navy, reorganized the artillery of the fleet, and arranged for the training of a body of 10,000 naval gunners. By 1770, the French had 64 of the finest ships-of-the-line and an additional 50 state-of-the-art frigates. These vessels were some of the swiftest warships in the world. Moreover, Choiseul had taken great pains to bolster the alliance of his country with Spain, which had built or refitted another 50 ships-of-the-line. The British viewed this build-up with a certain amount of disquietude, but after the war they were largely distracted by internal affairs, particularly the deteriorating relations with their own colonies in North America.

THE AMERICAN WAR FOR INDEPENDENCE

In the years between the Seven Years War and the American war, the Royal Navy had been systematically sold off. From 1771 to 1775, ninety-seven warships had been struck from the Admiralty lists, and just fifty-seven had been added that were of inferior size and weight of metal. It was a period of "political jobbery and corruption" controlled by King George III's ministers and friends. Although the navy had been allotted funds, the money had been "diverted to [political] party needs and private pockets all the way from Westminster to the dockyards and back." Stores were ordered and never used, ships that might have been repaired were written off and sold to private firms, and appropriations were made for new vessels but the ships were never built. There was also a severe shortage of timber made worse by the loss of the great stands of oak and pine in North America.[14]

It is beyond the scope of the present discussion to delve into the reasons for the American Revolution. Regardless of the causes, the British navy in the American war was unable to keep French and Spanish munitions from being landed in the Anglo-American colonies during the formative months of the Revolution. This failure was largely due to the extreme length and intricate topography of the American coastline. France and Spain, although officially neutral, supplied guns, muskets, flints, saddles, uniforms, and especially gunpowder to the British colonials as early as 1774.

An analysis of the disposition of the Atlantic Squadron of the Royal Navy in the months before the Battle Lexington shows that of the 24 warships on station more than half were guarding the approaches to New England, with seven of the largest in Boston harbor. This left the remaining thousand miles of coast virtually unpatroled except for a half dozen sloops-of-war of approximately 20 guns and a handful of cutters having 6 or 8 small cannon.

It was inconceivable that the Anglo-American colonies could have overcome the overwhelming military superiority of Great Britain in their struggle for independence without the help of some established foreign power. The bulk of the American naval force during the Revolution was made up of privateers. These, like their cousins in the nascent Continental Navy, were no match for British warships. As British naval power closed off outside commerce with the Americans and kept them from renewing their stocks of firearms and munitions, the cause of independence became increasingly unlikely.

French Intervention The victory of the American army at Saratoga, New York, in late 1777 has traditionally been cited as the impetus needed to establish an alliance with France in 1778 that would help to ensure the success of independence. This traditional view may need revision. By 1777, the French Council of State had already faced the necessity of entering the American war under the leadership of Charles Gravier Vergennes, the minister of state.

Through both overt and clandestine schemes, Vergennes pursued an aggressively anti-British policy. His plan was to weaken Britain economically by separating her from her important North American colonies, especially the wealth-producing sugar islands of the West Indies. He hoped thereby to re-establish the balance of power in Europe that had been lost in the Seven Years War.[15] France dared not risk a commitment from which she could not retreat, but Vergennes was a skillful diplomat who used a program of restraint and moderation to dominate the French Council of State. He proved to be one of the great war leaders of his century.[16]

Initially, Vergennes hoped to sustain the American war effort with only military supplies, money, and the support of American privateers.[17] Fearing that a compromise Anglo-American peace was in the offing in 1777 and mistrusting the assertions of the American commissioners to Paris to the contrary, Vergennes sought a reason to actively enter the war and thereby bolster American hopes for full independence without concessions. When the French frigate *Belle-Poule* was fired upon by the British fleet in 1778, the Foreign Minister declared that France considered herself to be at war with England.[18]

France's contribution to the war was largely a naval one. Vergennes policies relied upon the naval reforms and building programs begun by Choiseul, whose efforts had prepared France for a war in terms of ships and men. When war broke out in 1778 France had 80 ships-of-the-line in good condition and almost 67,000 seamen. When the Spanish entered the war in 1779 as a Franco-American ally, they added nearly 60 ships-of-the-line and frigates with sailors in proportion. To answer this combination, the British had, in 1778, about 150 ships-of-the-line—a fairly equivalent number. However, these had been working the Atlantic station for almost three years in an attempt to blockade the American ports, and they were worn and badly in need of repair.[19]

French entrance into the war transformed it from a ground engagement in the colonies into a multi-ocean naval war. The conflict at sea, so neatly focused for the Royal Navy on the New England coastline, quickly blurred to include the need to defend the Channel, the Mediterranean, the Indian Ocean, and the Caribbean. Britain was forced to "severely modify her strategy for suppressing the American rebellion." Initially the British planned to destroy the American army by crushing the rebellion at its urban centers, but this strategy failed. Alternately, they planned to wear down American resistance by detaching mobile forces from the colonial urban bases, particularly New York. This strategy proved to be seriously deficient, especially in view of the need to detach troops to counter the French potential of invading the undermanned British possessions in the West Indies.[20]

Events were to show that the actual center of the naval war would be the West Indies. While little campaigning could be done there during the hurricane season, at other times, the French fleet massed to assault the British sugar islands, taking them piecemeal until almost all had fallen. Moreover, it was from the West Indies that Admiral De Grasse would launch the decisive expedition to support the American army in the Chesapeake in 1781.

Inasmuch as the French took command of the seas from the Royal Navy during the American war, their general strategy can be considered appropriate. This was especially true in that they were able to obtain a

The Battle of the Chesapeake

tactical superiority for Admiral De Grasse's 1781 campaign. Historian Jonathan R. Dull sees this as "the most important and most perfectly executed naval campaign of the age of sail."[21] The pinnacle of this campaign was the Battle of the Chesapeake, which directly led to the surrender of the British army under General Cornwallis in Virginia and the creation of the United States. These results make it one of the most decisive battles in world history.[22]

In 1781, the British Atlantic squadron was based in New York under Admiral Lord Thomas Graves. New York City was, at that time, a British stronghold, and from its great harbor, Graves kept a cautious eye on a small squadron of 8 French warships based in Newport, Rhode Island. The more numerous British warships were more than a match for the French, and the distinguished Admiral Lord Richard Howe had chased them back into Newport in a series of maneuvers in 1778. However, Graves, although an able sea officer, lacked the flexibility and ingenuity of Howe. He tended to follow orders cautiously and deliberately. Nonetheless, in March 1781, Graves led a fleet of warships sufficiently well to drive the small French squadron once again back to Newport.

When Cornwallis' land forces were maneuvered into Yorktown, Virginia, by the combined American and French armies in September 1781, the British general was confident that he had completed the most dangerous part of his campaign. Though besieged to landward, Cornwallis had a reasonable expectation that he would be relieved on the York River side of his position by Graves' fleet of 19 warships. He was seemingly unaware that the French fleet campaigning in the West Indies under Admiral De Grasse had stolen a march on the Royal Navy squadron under Admiral Rodney and had run north into the coastal waters of Virginia. While Rodney frantically tried to locate De Grasse's fleet in the Caribbean, Graves found the 24 French warships quietly sailing for the mouth of the Chesapeake.

The immediate relief of Cornwallis was impossible under the circumstances. Knowing the consequences of abandoning the British army to their fate and noting that the French were "in no sort of battle-order," Graves cautiously edged his well-formed battle line down upon the French. De Grasse moved away from the bay close-hauled to take up the challenge. What followed was little more than a long-range cannonade. Having engaged less than half of Graves' line, De Grasse cleverly maneuvered and sailed back into the mouth of the bay. Finally, joined by the French Rhode Island squadron that had sailed to Virginia in the interim, the French now numbered 36 ships-of-the-line.

Graves was left at sea with a substantially inferior fleet and unable to do anything but return to his base at New York. He had lost no engagement. No ships had been lost on either side. Yet Graves had lost America. Left without relief, Cornwallis could do nothing but surrender. By most standards, one of the most decisive sea battles in history had been a somewhat boring affair. Yet this battle points out one of the great principles of naval warfare—being stronger than the enemy at the right time and place.

Winning the Peace

The momentum generated by the success of the allied war effort on land and sea in 1781 led to an increasing likelihood that the war would come to a speedy conclusion. The Americans were almost assured of independence, but their European allies were under some stress to extricate themselves from the war with their war aims fulfilled. However, before a peace could be concluded, the French suffered a series of misfortunes. In 1782, De Grasse was captured and his fleet scattered by Admiral Sir George Rodney at the Battle of the Saintes. Rodney, either by accident or design—naval historians disagree—attacked from windward, cut through De Grasse's line, and laid his ship to leeward of the _Ville de Paris_, forcing

De Grasse to remain in the fight. A melee ensued in which 5 French ships were taken in the first stand-up naval battle in more than half a century. This serious setback was followed by the capture of virtually an entire convoy of 60 French supply ships and the loss of almost all the islands in the West Indies that had been captured by the French during the war.

The one bright spot was the incredible success of the French Royal Marine in India. In the space of only fourteen months, ending in June 1783, the French, under Admiral de Suffren Saint Tropez, faced off with the Royal Navy under Admiral Sir Edward Hughes no less than five times. Each fleet action proved indecisive except the last. Suffren attacked so fiercely that Hughes' fleet was left incapacitated. All of India lay before Suffren, but just as he was about to claim it, word came that the war was over.

The Treaty of Paris had been signed in January 1783. The French minister, Vergennes, had found the peace talks complicated by the unpredictable consequences of European politics. Although Vergennes had urged better Allied coordination to avoid a bad peace, the peace negotiations had centered more and more on Spanish, rather than Allied, war aims. He had also been hampered by a fear that the Americans would agree to any peace proposition that explicitly or implicitly recognized American independence without regard to their allies. While there was no doubt that the Americans could not have forced their separation from Britain without foreign aid, they were still more closely tied to Britain by cultural, religious, and economic similarities than they were to France. Nonetheless, the American ministers in Paris remained faithful to their allies until the peace had been signed.[23]

In the War of Independence, the American navy was essentially driven from the seas by Britain, yet America gained its freedom. Spain did very little to further the allied cause, yet Spain regained Minorca. The French navy had gained control of the seas and beaten Britain for the first time, yet France failed to gain much in the peace other than bragging rights and a single sugar island (Togabo). French participation in the American Revolution proved ultimately to be tragic, helping as it certainly did to prepare a financial and political crisis that was to lead France into its own revolution in less than a decade.[24]

Although far stronger than it needed to be to overwhelm the Americans, the Royal Navy was simply unprepared to match its European rivals. The entry of the French alone expanded the scope of the conflict from the Atlantic seaboard of North America into the West Indies, India, and Europe. When the Spanish joined the Allies in 1779, they brought an overwhelming advantage in ships-of-the-line, which was increased by the entrance of Holland into the war in 1781. However, the Spanish were

The Failure of the British Navy

interested in little beyond the recovery of Gibraltar and Micorca, and the Dutch had entered too late to make more than a minor contribution.

The British resorted to endless maneuver and countermaneuver, following the "fleet-in-being" theory, but failed to exploit a number of tactical opportunities offered to them by concentrating on countering French strategy rather than taking the naval initiative. The British navy missed over a dozen strategic opportunities by ignoring the realities of naval operations and repeatedly obtaining a meaningless naval superiority in autumn in storm tossed Europe and in summer in the Caribbean, with its annual potential for hurricanes. "For such strategic ineptitude the British could have no excuse."[25]

THE FRENCH REVOLUTION

Throughout the eighteenth century, the French had the second strongest navy in the world, with England's the first by far. The French were able to maintain some semblance of equality with the English until the Seven Years War, when they were exposed to a disastrous series of demoralizing setbacks. During the American War of Independence, they managed several successes that brought them revenge and rejuvenated their officer corps.

The officers of the French navy were almost exclusively the sons of less imposing noble houses. An aspiring midshipman (*Eleve de la Marine*) had to apply to the Ministry of Marine with a certified copy of his family genealogy to ensure that he had the required family background to be an officer. The system had the potential for grievous consequences in terms of ability, but it worked fairly well in producing good officers mainly because the aspirants were highly trained before being put into service.

The American war had placed severe financial strains on the French treasury and had highlighted several fundamental weaknesses in the structure of the Royal Marine. In 1786, the entire French navy was reorganized for its greater efficiency, and many measures were taken for its improvement. Among these was the establishment of a single category of seaman-gunners. Known as the *Corps Royal des Canonniersmatelots*, these men were specialists trained in gunnery, small arms, and seamanship. On warships there were seven *canonniers-matelots* assigned to every gun. The men were volunteers recruited from among merchant seamen by promises of glory and prize money. The French had no "press," but they did resort to a form of conscription in times of war. Every French sailor had to register with the authorities and was obligated to serve on a warship in one of every three cruises. While the system seemed more reasonable than impressment, events were to prove that French sailors were less tolerant of forced service than English seamen.[26]

Before the French Revolution of 1789, all was not well in the officer corps. There were two types of French naval officers. Officers *de plume* ("of the pen") were administrative men who built and maintained ships as naval engineers, technicians, and commissaries. Officers *d'épée* ("of the sword") were sea-faring men who faced the enemy across the muzzles of cannon. The active sea officers held the administrative types in low regard. In 1783, the French crown instituted a number of budget restraints that put the fighting officers at odds with the administrative staff, whose job it was to carry them out effectively. As ships were taken out of commission, the sailors were abandoned to the vagaries of supply and demand for mariners in the merchant service, and large numbers of shipworkers, sailmakers, and other craftsmen were thrown out of work in the seaport towns due to a lack of naval contracts.

When the French Revolution came, the navy was one of its first casualties. Civil disturbances spread to the military ports of Brest and Rochefort, and scuffles ensued between the officers of aristocratic birth and the common-born sailors. The shipworkers, in particular, supported the revolution and formed themselves into National Guard units. The *canonniers-matelots* in Rochefort refused to fire on the National Guards and mutinied. In Toulon, the admiral commanding the port was chased out of town, and in Brest both the sailors and the soldiers mutinied.

The majority of the officer corp, noble by birth, remained loyal to the king or left the service to become emigres. Several who stayed were attacked by a mob in Toulon in 1792 and hanged from lampposts in the town. While several mutinies occurred on warships serving on colonial stations, the entire Windward Island squadron—four ships with officers and men—sailed to Spanish Trinidad and placed themselves at the disposal of the king of Spain, the Bourbon cousin of the French monarch, rather than submit to the revolutionaries.

A new officer corps was raised by the French Republic, mostly by commissioning former petty officers and merchant marine officers. A surprisingly large number of the midshipmen and ensigns also accepted promotion, though their aristocratic backgrounds left them under a cloud of suspicion. The new officer corps was, therefore, fairly well versed in the mechanics of seamanship, but it did not have the training or experience to confront the tactical and logistical problems that accompanied a competent naval strategy at the highest levels.

As an example, at the battle of the Glorious First of June in 1794, the French commander Louis Villaret-Joyeuse, a lieutenant a mere three years earlier, had been directly promoted to admiral without ever serving as a captain. His successful opponent, the venerable Admiral Lord Richard Howe, had been promoted lieutenant fifty years earlier, had served as a post-captain in the Seven Years War, and had commanded the Atlantic squadron of the Royal Navy in the American war for a time.

The French fleet also suffered from administrative mismanagement and a general distrain for discipline among the men. The Committee of Public Safety was now the virtual government, and its greatest fear was of counter-revolution by those who had enjoined privileges under the former government. In response, the elite *canonniers-matelots* were sent to fight as artillerists with the republican infantry, and the National Guard volunteers were placed aboard warships as gunners. The pro-revolution volunteers knew nothing of naval artillery. Many of the line infantry were also assigned to the navy as sea-soldiers. These measures caused a great deal of chaos aboard ship and a good deal of resentment among the men.

The successful structure of the Royal Marine had been deliberately abolished based on the grounds that it constituted a system of privileged classes, but it had been replaced with no rational structure at all. The only aspect of the Royal Marine that was retained by the republican government was the habit of underfunding the navy. The ships were neglected. New building was cut back, and provisions for the maintenance of storehouses, arsenals, and dockyards remained inadequate.[27]

While the revolutionary army won land battles through sheer enthusiasm and weight of numbers, the republican navy was perhaps never worse prepared for war. In 1793, British Admiral Lord Hood sailed into Toulon harbor where he found 30 French warships, one-third of the fleet. He brought out 3 and burned 9 more. In 1794, Admiral Howe won a tactical victory over Villaret-Joyeuse at the battle of the Glorious First of June, but the French fleet of transports, filled with vital grain from America, escaped. Hood then captured Corsica in a series of actions that brought Captain Horatio Nelson to prominence.

Holland fell to the republican armies in 1794, and Spain entered the French alliance two years later. These events forced the Royal Navy to abandon the Mediterranean altogether. However, two major British victories in 1797 caused France to quickly revert to her historical role of naval inferiority. The first was the Battle of Cape St. Vincent and the second was at Camperdown.

At Cape St. Vincent, Admiral Sir John Jervis, with 15 ships-of-the-line, sighted a Spanish fleet almost twice his number making for Cadiz in a poorly formed line. Jervis made for a gap in the Spanish formation, hoping to separate the two halves of the fleet and defeat each in detail. However, it was quickly plain that his timing was off, and the Spaniards would be able to consolidate. Closest to the critical point was Horatio Nelson in *Captain* (74). Nelson saw the difficulty and without orders threw his two-decker into the gap and engaged, single-handed. Having been given additional time, the rest of Jervis's fleet came to Nelson's support. Four prizes were taken by nightfall—two by Nelson—and ten of the enemy were badly crippled. The victory made Nelson's career.

At Camperdown, Admiral Adam Duncan blockaded the Dutch part of Texel with 16 warships. The Dutch fleet was also 16 strong. Sailing at right angles to the enemy line, Ducan fell upon them from windward in two parallel lines, smashed through in two places, and brought on a fierce melee. Duncan came away with the Dutch commander, 9 enemy ships-of-the-line, and 2 of their frigates. With these victories, the Spanish and the Dutch fleets had effectively been removed as meaningful threats to the Royal Navy.

In 1798, Nelson, now a junior rear admiral, was sent with a fleet into the Mediterranean to disrupt French plans for the Toulon fleet under Admiral Francois Paul d'Brueys. Unknown to Nelson, the French fleet was to escort a large expeditionary force under the command of General Napoleon Bonaparte to Egypt. Bad weather caused Nelson to lose contact with the French, who made for Malta, took the island without serious opposition, and just as quickly disappeared. Given the strategic importance of both Italy and Egypt, Nelson made for Egypt (guessing correctly but arriving before the slower sailing French invasion fleet). Assuming that he had guessed incorrectly, Nelson then made for Sicily.

Meanwhile, the French arrived in Egypt. Brueys sailed directly to the Nile, disembarked Napoleon's troops, and sent his 13 warships into nearby Aboukir Bay. Brueys placed his warships in an outward-facing line anchored so near the coastal shallows that he imagined it safe from attack in that quarter. The confidence inspired by Napoleon's nearby coastal batteries caused some French captains to send their crews on shore leave.

Unexpectedly on the evening of August 1, 1798, Nelson's fleet appeared on the horizon. Having wandered the Mediterranean for almost a month he had picked up the French scent in Sicily and sailed again to Egypt. Nelson threw his fleet into action immediately. One British ship, *Culloden*, went aground, but Captain Thomas Foley, in *Goliath*, courageously made for the landward side of the French fleet, followed by four more warships. Nelson, sixth in line, made for the outside thereby doubling part of the French line. With their van and center anchored and attacked from both sides, the French fought desperately into the night. The French flagship of 120 guns, *L'Orient*, hotly pressed, caught fire and blew up with a dreadful roar at 10:30 P.M. Brueys and all but seventy of the crew were killed. This tragedy was the climax of the battle, creating a terrible pause in the fighting. By dawn, all but three of the French had been taken one by one. The remaining French vessels fled under Admiral Pierre de Villeneuve, but only two escaped as the third went aground on the same shoals that had failed to protect the fleet from attack.

For the first time in all the Anglo-French engagements since the French

Revolution, the enemy's fleet had been brought to battle and annihilated.[28] Moreover, Napoleon's campaign in Egypt had been disappointing, and without ships he was forced to abandon his army in Egypt. The Mediterranean thereafter became "almost a British sea." Admiral Jervis regained Minorca in 1798, and Captain Sir Alexander Ball recovered Malta in 1800.[29]

Nonetheless, Napoleon escaped Egypt to reinvade Italy and win a land battle at Marengo in 1800. Fearing French domination in Europe, Russia, Prussia, Denmark, and Sweden formed the League of Armed Neutrality by year's end. As part of their strategy, they excluded Britain from trading in the Baltic. This cut off the Royal Navy from its main source of vital naval stores without which it could not prosecute an effective naval war. In response, Admiral Sir Hyde Park was sent to Denmark with a fleet to require Danish withdrawal from the league. With Park's thinly veiled diplomacy failing, Admiral Nelson, who was second-in-command, offered to attack the Danish fleet anchored in a line under the shore batteries in the harbor at Copenhagen.

The carefully planned attack required that part of the fleet negotiate the dangerous shoal waters of the harbor under the guns and mortars of several well-placed batteries. Nelson avoided these by hugging the Swedish side of the harbor in the night and returning up the channel to anchor outside the Danish fleet. The shore batteries were thereby made less effective as they were required to fire over their own ships. The rest of the fleet, under Park, was to attack directly from the sound.

Nelson's squadron began fighting in mid-morning, but Park was prevented from joining the battle by adverse winds. Park signaled Nelson to discontinue the action, but he persisted. Nelson is said to have put his blind eye to his telescope and commented to his flag-captain that he saw no signal from Park. By afternoon, the Danish fire stopped, but as no ships offered to surrender, Nelson threatened to burn all that did not. The ultimatum ended the battle. He later wrote, "[T]he French could not have withstood for one hour what the Danes suffered for four." A large part of the Danish fleet had been taken. Shortly after Copenhagen, the League of Armed Neutrality dissolved.[30]

In January 1801, the French made a weak attempt to relieve their army in Egypt but were foiled by a Royal Navy squadron stationed in Aboukir Bay. Instead, it was the British army that landed in March and defeated the French two weeks later at the Battle of Alexandria. Ultimately, both nations became exhausted and recognized that a stalemate had been reached. In 1802, the Peace of Amiens gave a brief respite to the warring nations of Europe. Nonetheless, the trading community soon discovered that peace with the French was little better than war. The foreign policy of France remained provocative and disquieting.[31]

THE NAPOLEONIC WARS

In 1802, a plebiscite declared Napoleon Bonaparte Consul for Life, and France quickly returned to a monarchy. But despotic rule by Napoleon was an improvement over the terror, civil strife, and corruption that had characterized the Republic. The French navy was in a desperate state with only 13 of 42 ships-of-the-line in commission. Bonaparte and his foreign minister, Charles Maurice de Talleyrand, began a naval building program that would bring 23 new battleships to the French fleet.

By 1803, Britain found that continued peace was beyond hope. The Royal Navy had 55 ships-of-the-line ready for the coming war. Britain declared war in May and seized all French merchant vessels in British ports. In the next two years, the Royal Navy swept up several French and Dutch islands in the West Indies and blockaded the French-held coasts of Europe. With an unprepared fleet, there was little that the French could do at sea, so they attacked Britain's only continental possession, Hanover, and forced the surrender of its army. Having substantially consolidated his position on the Continent, Napoleon made himself emperor in 1804.

Bonaparte's grand design thereafter was to invade England by way of the Channel. In March 1805, Admiral Villeneuve escaped the blockade at Toulon and joined Spanish Admiral Don Frederico Gravina at Cadiz. The combined fleets concentrated in the West Indies in the hope of dispersing the Royal Navy and making the Channel vulnerable. Villeneuve returned from the islands with a Franco-Spanish fleet of 20 ships-of-the-line making for Ferrol, where he would join with more French and Spanish ships. In July, Villeneuve fought an indecisive engagement with 14 British ships under Admiral Sir Robert Calder, but by August, he had been reinforced with enough vessels to protect Napoleon's cross-Channel invasion.

During Villeneuve's return journey, he was chased by Admiral Nelson with a squadron of 11 battleships. Nelson once again failed to find the French, and he returned to Gibraltar to reprovision. He then sailed northward, joining with Admiral William Cornwallis off Ushant on August 15. Within a month, he also joined with Admiral Lord Cuthbert Collingwood who had been watching Cadiz and now became second-in-command.

Nelson had accumulated a fleet of 27 ships-of-the-line besides frigates by October. Although the French had 33 battleships, Nelson considered it unlikely that Villeneuve would come out without being enticed to do so. He, therefore, moved his fleet fifty miles west, leaving only his frigates—the eyes of the fleet—to keep watch. Several warships were stationed between the frigates and the bulk of the fleet to provide word if Villeneuve went to sea. Meanwhile, Napoleon canceled the invasion of

England and ordered the French fleet to Italy to support an attack on Austria. Although Villeneuve had guessed Nelson's strategy, in response to the emperor's orders, he left Cadiz on October 20. The stage was now set for one of the most famous naval battles in history.

Trafalgar On the next day, the two fleets sighted each other at six miles' distance near Cape Trafalgar, which was about twenty miles away, and formed for the most celebrated battle of the age of sail. No naval battle has had more written about it. Reports of the maneuvers used during the engagement remain varied and sometimes conflicting. Nelson's handling of the fleet has been discussed for almost 100 years. His death during the engagement prevented his own account of the details of the strategy he had in mind. Nonetheless, several facts have been established through the memoirs of his officers, particularly Collingwood and Nelson's flag-captain, Thomas Hardy.

The Franco-Spanish fleet formed in two groups in one long line. One of these groups, a line of 21 ships, was commanded by Villeneuve in *Bucentaure* (80). The other group of 12 ships was formed under Gravina in the *Santisima Trinidad*, the largest warship in the battle, with 136 guns. Nelson came down perpendicular to the Franco-Spanish line in two parallel columns much as Duncan had done at Camperdown. Eleven ships in one column formed on Nelson's flagship, *Victory*, of 100 guns. The remainder formed on the equally powerful *Royal Sovereign*, which was Collingwood's flagship.

Villeneuve, recognizing the unordered condition of his fleet, signaled them to turn back to Cadiz. This further disordered the Franco-Spanish line, which was about five miles long. The wind was barely perceptible, making the British approach long and tedious. Collingwood's flagship, the best sailer in the fleet, was the first to see action. The rearmost warships barely made it at all. *Britannia* (100) took three hours to get into the fight.

Once battle was joined, it became a confused and furious melee. Nelson's flag-captain, Hardy, blasted *Bucentaure* with triple shot as *Victory* passed, putting the French flagship out of action. Hardy then closed on *Redoubtable*. It was from the fighting tops of this French warship that the bullet came that mortally wounded Nelson as he walked the quarterdeck. The Spanish flagship *Santisima Trinidad* was attacked by no less than two 74s and a 98, *Neptune*, to which it finally surrendered. Gravina escaped to *Principe de Asturias* (112), signaled for the remaining allied ships to form on him, and then sailed toward Gibraltar. Villeneuve, who had transferred his flag from *Bucentaure* to *Mars*, was captured.

No naval battle was more decisive than Trafalgar. Eighteen vessels of the combined fleet, equally divided between the French and Spanish, struck to the British. The others scattered. Only 11 made Cadiz. "So overwhelming a defeat of his fleet by a lesser number of British ships . . .

The Fall of Nelson, by Denis Dighton (1792–1827). This early-nineteenth-century painting illustrates the moment in which Lord Nelson fell during the Battle of Trafalgar. © NATIONAL MARITIME MUSEUM.

made it clear to Napoleon that . . . he had no real hope of reviving a feasible plan for the invasion of England, whatever the success of his continental campaigns." Although Napoleon continued to build warships for the remaining ten years of the war, the French remained powerless to compete with the British at sea.[32]

NOTES

1. Alfred Thayer Mahan, *The Influence of Sea Power upon History 1660–1783* (1890; reprint, New York: Dover, 1987), 209.

2. Kevin Phillips, *The Cousins' War: Religion, Politics, and the Triumph of Anglo-America* (New York: Basic Books, 1999), 11.

3. William suspected that Torrington had deliberately sacrificed the Dutch. Torrington was jailed for disobeying orders, but he was cleared by a court martial of naval officers.

4. Michael Lewis, *The History of the British Navy* (Fairlawn, NJ: Essential Books, 1959), 104–108.

5. Mahan, 191.

6. Lewis, 108–110.

7. Samuel W. Bryant, *The Sea and the States: A Maritime History of the American People* (New York: Thomas Y. Crowell, 1967), 53.

8. See Douglas Edward Leach, *Roots of Conflict: British Armed Forces and Colonial America, 1677–1763* (Chapel Hill: University of North Carolina Press, 1986).

9. Bryant, 56.

10. See Leach.

11. John Ferling, *Struggle for a Continent: The Wars of Early America* (Arlington Heights, IL: Harlan Davidson, 1993), 197. Also see Timothy J. Todish, *America's First First World War: The French and Indian War, 1754–1763* (Ogden, UT: Eagle's View, 1988).

12. Fred Anderson, *Crucible of War: The Seven Years' War and the Fate of Empire in British North America, 1754–1766* (New York: Alfred A. Knopf, 2000), 383.

13. Lewis, 137.

14. Ibid., 140–141.

15. Jonathan R. Dull, *The French Navy and American Independence: A Study of Arms and Diplomacy 1774–1787* (Princeton, NJ: Princeton University Press, 1975), 11.

16. Ibid., 108.

17. Ibid., 100, 165.

18. Ibid., 118–120.

19. James M. Volo, "The War at Sea," *Living History Journal* (January 1987): 2–18.

20. Dull, 105.

21. Ibid., 239.

22. Lewis, 145.

23. Dull, 273.

24. Ibid., 294–344.

25. Ibid., 188–225, 263.

26. Rene Chartrand and Francis Back, *Napoleon's Sea Soldiers* (London: Osprey Books, 1990), 5–8.

27. Ibid., 9–12.

28. John Creswell, *British Admirals of the Eighteenth Century* (London: Anchor Books, 1972), 15–16.

29. Lewis, 167.

30. Nicholas Blake and Richard Lawrence, *The Illustrated Companion to Nelson's Navy* (Mechanicsburg, PA: Stackpole Bools, 2000), 170–171.

31. Michael Glover, *The Napoleonic Wars: An Illustrated History, 1792–1815* (New York: Hippocrene Books, 1979), 89.

32. Creswell, 251–252.

13

The American Revolution

These people show a spirit and conduct against us they never showed against the French, and everyone has judged of them from their former appearance and behavior . . . which has led many into great mistakes.

—A British officer, 1775

Soon after the end of the Seven Years War, Americans began to revitalize their maritime activities. Free of the French threat and under the protection of the Royal Navy, American trading vessels, whalers, and slavers inundated the ports of the world. Although Americans shared a common history, culture, and religious tradition with England, they began showing a general dissatisfaction with British rule and the Royal Navy as early as 1764. There were many areas of contention prominent at the time including disagreements over expanding the colonies, relations with Indians, and political control of the colonial governments, but the one point that struck sparks was the colonial passion for avoiding taxes by smuggling.

The foundation of the British economy and the empire was based in regulated trade. The home islands were supposed to be the centers of manufacture, while the colonies were to provide both the raw materials and the market for British manufactured goods. British shippers and merchants made their profits by moving the raw materials to England

Smugglers favored small, quiet coves and inlets to unload their wares, as shown in this 1792 painting by George Morland (1763?–1804). Their use of shallow draft boats and skiffs prevented the revenue cutters from following them to the shore. © NATIONAL MARITIME MUSEUM.

and returning the finished goods to the colonial markets. The government took its part in the form of taxes and duties.

Smuggling was an old and widespread activity practiced throughout the British Empire, but American smugglers proved particularly adept at evading the customs, especially with respect to trade with the West Indies, southern Europe, and the west coast of Africa. Smugglers operated as little more than pirates. Nonetheless, they enjoyed a certain prominence among their fellow colonials largely because they provided manufactured goods and luxuries at much lower prices than could legitimate sources. Many highly born and well-respected men in America dabbled in contraband wines, brandies, and rum; fine fabrics; glassware; finished metal objects; and other goods manufactured outside of Britain. John Hancock, a respected merchant and member of the colonial upper crust, was held to be one of the most notorious smugglers in colonial America.

Illegal colonial manufactures and smuggling disrupted the plan for the British trading empire. The stockholders of legitimate trading companies were apprehensive at the loss of a large proportion of their profits to the colonials and complained bitterly to the government. The loss of tax revenue was also considerable. The Exchequer estimated the losses due to smuggling to be in the tens of thousands of pounds each year. In response, the customs officials fitted out a number of lightly armed sloops and schooners to patrol the American coastal waters and halt the smuggling.[1]

To better maintain their trading strategy, the government passed a whole series of maritime reg-   **The Navigation Acts**
ulations called Navigation Acts. Such regulations
had long been characteristic of the relations between Britain and her American colonies, the first having been passed in the reign of Charles II. Initially the Crown allowed a good deal of trade to take place between the individual colonies and foreign markets under the watchful eye of their royal governors. South Carolina traded rice for wine, fruit, and salt directly with the Mediterranean. Connecticut traded vegetables, Maryland wheat, and Pennsylvania corn.

Massachusetts, and much of New England, traded cod with the Caribbean for molasses to make rum. The average American drank almost four gallons annually, but much of the rum was used to trade for African slaves. This three-way traffic—molasses, rum, and slaves—was actually fueled by the fisheries of the Grand Banks. This trade was called the Triangular Trade, and it was extremely lucrative.

As the colonies grew, so did the volume of trade with foreign nations. Soon the colonies were trading with other countries as much as they were with Britain, and it became obvious to the Crown that its colonies were slowly approaching economic independence. Britain attempted to reassert its authority over trade with the Molasses Act of 1733, which imposed such heavy import duties on molasses from non-British Caribbean islands that it should have eliminated the trade. Instead it made both the colonials and their French suppliers eager to work together in the contraband rum industry.

Immediately after the Seven Years War, with the French threat in North America eliminated, the government began to strictly enforce the navigation laws in the colonies. It was the vigorous enforcement of the principles underlying the acts rather than the actual financial burden of the taxes that was the cause of much of the colonial alienation. The colonials viewed new regulations, such as the Sugar Act and Townsend Revenue Act, as violations of fundamental principles rather than as simple trade regulations.

The Sugar Act put a six-penny tax on each gallon of molasses, but it contained more than forty provisions for changes in the customs and commerce regulations that amounted to a unprecedented change in the status of the colonies with regard to the mother country. Regulatory paperwork was vastly increased, and enforcement was extended to almost all coastwise traders, including the smallest intercolonial shippers

A British sloop rigged cutter of the mid-eighteenth century. Small vessels like these were charged with the enforcement of the revenue laws.

who might move cargoes only a few score miles along the shore. Many seaside towns had no customs facilities, making the regulations so bothersome that they could be strictly followed only in the largest ports where the wharfs and customs facilities were near each other. Gloucester, Massachusetts, for example, was a legally recognized trading port of some size, but it did not have even a single customs official.[2]

Moreover, violation of the acts was no longer considered a mere breech of trade drawing a small fine, but was now considered a crime punishable by seizure of both ship and cargo. Hostility grew toward the representatives of the Crown, especially in the ports where enforcement was most vigorously prosecuted. Spontaneous demonstrations erupted at the sight of a revenue cutter, and Royal Navy press gangs looking to man a short-handed vessel at a colonial port met with unprecedented levels of noncooperation and violence among the people. As relations deteriorated between New England and Britain, the Crown repeatedly responded with the worst possible moves, inexplicably further restricting trade to English ports and barring New England fishermen from the Grand Banks. It is not surprising, therefore, that the centers of the American revolutionary movement should be found in northern port cities such as Newport, Providence, and Boston.[3]

In 1772, lack of cooperation changed into overt violence. The Royal Navy revenue cutter *Gaspee*, commanded by Lieutenant William Dudingston, intercepted the colonial packet *Hannah*, commanded by Benjamin Lindsay. The **The Burning of Gaspee** master of the *Hannah*, inbound to Providence from New York, refused to heave to in Narragansett Bay and have his ship's papers examined. Lindsay had become annoyed by Dudingston's arrogant manner and had taken advantage of a fresh wind, an ebb tide, and a shallow draft to avoid the cutter, which ran aground on a bar. A frustrated Dudingston sat aboard the stranded cutter, waiting for the flood tide to float it off.

The *Hannah* continued on to Providence, where word spread of the revenue cutter's predicament. Eight longboats under the direction of Captain Abraham Whipple were launched, each filled with vengeful colonists armed with staves, stones, and a few firearms. In the dead of night, the colonials overwhelmed the crew of the lightly armed *Gaspee* and burned the vessel to the waterline. It is unclear why so many men should have so quickly taken advantage of this particular opportunity to express their resentment toward the Royal Navy. The British government was outraged; the colonial government of Rhode Island expressed regret and sympathy; but no one could identify the assailants.

The burning of the *Gaspee* was closely followed by a more celebrated incident. The object of colonial anger this time **The Boston Tea Party** was a shipment of tea belonging to the Honorable East India Company sitting aboard ships at the dock in Boston. In response to colonial outrage over the Intolerable Acts, the government had rescinded all the duties except the tax on tea. However, the colonials remained agitated, and the tea quickly became a symbol for deeper grievances. On the night of December 16, 1773, a group of Bostonians dressed as Indians boarded one of three East Indiamen in the harbor and threw 350 bales of tea into the water. The demonstration has come to be known as the Boston Tea Party.

Once again, the government was outraged, but no one would identify the guilty parties. This time, however, the British closed the entire port of Boston as a punishment and as a warning to the colonies. This circumstance led directly to an enhanced support for the Bostonians throughout the colonies. As the situation worsened, the outbreak of serious violence became more likely. Ultimately, the colonials took the stance that open warfare was necessary and conciliation impossible.

The later incidents on Lexington Green, at Concord Bridge, and in Boston immediately led to a real shooting war that spread throughout the colonies. Circumstances led the colonial Continental Congress to provide for an army, but the colonial representatives doubted the practical value of forming a navy. It was inconceivable that the colonies could deploy a fleet with any chance of matching the Royal Navy. Nonetheless, the enterprising Americans were not prone to miss an opportunity to profit from a little privateering. The Americans began their naval war, therefore, as commerce raiders.

American Cruisers
Both George Washington and Benjamin Franklin commissioned a number of vessels to act in the cause of American independence. In the earliest days of the Revolution, during the siege of Boston, Washington authorized Nicholas Boughton to take several soldiers and proceed to the port of Beverly, Massachusetts, where he was to take command of the *Hannah*, a schooner fitted out with a few small cannon as a privateer. This was the first of six vessels that ultimately formed "George Washington's Navy." The remaining vessels were *Hancock, Franklin, Lee, Warren,* and *Harrison.* When *Hannah* was found to be too damaged from a grounding, she was replaced by the *Washington.* Each vessel sailed under a white ensign bearing a green pine tree with the words "An Appeal to Heaven" inscribed below it. In forming this force, Washington acted solely on his own authority as commander-in-chief of the Continental Army.[4]

Franklin acted later but with more authority. As a member of the Naval Committee of the Continental Congress and as a representative of the nascent American government in Paris, Franklin issued commissions to likely officers and provided funds for the arming and fitting of American warships in foreign ports. The *Black Prince*, the *Black Princess*, and *Fearnot* were among the vessels that Franklin commissioned as "Continental Cruisers" in 1779. Many in the crew of *Black Prince* were Irish and English smugglers who had used an American sea captain to obtain a commission from Franklin. Nonetheless, these three vessels were active in the American cause, patrolling European waters for about a year, and capturing 114 enemy merchant vessels.[5]

Colonial consciousness of the military value of prosecuting a war at sea was fueled largely by necessity. The American army was woefully short of gunpowder and arms, and it was hoped that American ships could run to France, Spain, or the islands of the West Indies to procure a supply. No one expected the result of the cruise of Captain John Manly, in *Lee*, in November 1775. Manly, one of Washington's finest captains, intercepted a Royal Navy storeship, *Nancy*, that had become separated from its convoy. The lightly armed *Nancy* was quickly taken. She disgorged a stockpile of military stores desperately needed by the infant Continental Army, including 100,000 flints, 2,000 muskets, and a 13-inch mortar—"the finest piece of ordnance ever landed in America."[6] Vice Admiral Samuel Graves, who commanded five British warships in Boston harbor, wrote: "It is much to be lamented that a cargo of such consequence should be sent from England in a vessel destitute of arms even so to protect her from a rowboat."[7]

In quick succession, supplies and arms were also taken from the store ship *Concord*. Four lightly armed transports (*Anne, George, Lord Howe,* and *Annabella*), carrying almost 400 Scotch Highland troops to fight in America, were also captured. Of 36 store ships and transports dispatched to New England during the brief British occupation of Boston, only eighteen arrived safely. The others were captured, dispersed to the West Indies, or forced to return to England.[8]

The privateer navy was deemed an immediate success by the rebellious colonials. A tavern song was altered to praise the intrepid captains:

> Then rouse up, all our Heroes, give MANLY now a cheer,
> Here's Health to hardy Sons of Mars who go in Privateers . . .
> They talk of Sixty Ships, Lads, to scourge our free-born Land,
> If they send out Six Hundred we'll bravely them withstand . . .
> Then rouse up all my Hearties, give Sailor Lads a Cheer,
> Brave MANLY, HOPKINS, and those Tars who go in Privateers.[9]

The Congress, elated by this chain of successes, quickly appropriated 100,000 dollars to buy four merchantmen to be immediately converted into warships. **The Continental Navy** Further, the members approved the construction of thirteen warships to be built from the keel up in the overly optimistic time of just three months. Five ships of 32 guns, five of 28 guns, and three of 24 guns were authorized. Although the building contracts were spread among seven states with considerable shipbuilding facilities, neither the materials nor the crews were available. Congress' new-found commitment to an American navy can be measured by the fact that almost one million dollars was appropriated to provide for a Continental Navy.

The Naval Committee also drew up an ordered list of officers to serve in the new navy. Unfortunately, the men on the list were given precedence mainly because of political or social patronage rather than ability. None of Washington's captains was listed, except John Manly (1st) who topped the list. Some months later, John Paul Jones (18th) wrote to Robert Morris, the vice chairman of the Marine Committee of Congress, "I cannot but lament that so little delicacy hath been observed in the appointment and promotion of officers in the sea service, many of whom are not only grossly illiterate, but want even the capacity of commanding merchant vessels."[10] In 1781, a congressional committee investigating how the list was generated could not "fully ascertain the rule by which that arrangement was made."[11]

Ezek Hopkins was made commander-in-chief of the navy, a purely political appointment made to please his brother Stephen Hopkins of Rhode Island, who was chairman of the Naval Committee. Ezek Hopkins' name did not even appear on the precedence list possibly because he had been ashore since 1772.[12] He was described by a contemporary as "an antiquated figure, shrewd and sensible . . . only he swore now and then." He had gained prominence in the Revolution by helping to prepare the defenses of the port town of Providence, Rhode Island. The designation of "commander-in-chief" rather than "admiral" seems to have been intended to give Hopkins a status equivalent to that of George Washington on land. Contemporary sources refer to him as "commodore." The Naval Committee gave Hopkins command over only those ships being fitted out in the Delaware River. Several other Continental vessels were at sea, but they were clearly not under his orders.[13]

Also included among of the new American naval officers were other friends and relatives of the Rhode Island representative. John B. Hopkins (13th), Ezek's son, was made captain of *Cabot*. The younger Hopkins had taken part in the burning of the British revenue cutter *Gaspee*. Dudley Saltonstall (4th), a Hopkins cousin, was given command of the flagship, *Alfred*. Saltonstall was from an old maritime family in New London, Connecticut, and he had been a privateer in the French Wars of mid-century. He was something of an enigma, described by some of his contemporaries as morose, ill-natured, or narrow-minded and by others as sensible and indefatigable. John Paul Jones, whose own temperament was cold-blooded and autocratic, disliked Saltonstall intensely, declaring that the man had "a rude unhappy temper."[14]

Abraham Whipple (12th), who led the expedition that burned *Gaspee*, was made captain of *Columbus*. He came to Philadelphia in the sloop *Katy*, which he turned over to the Continental service and renamed *Providence*. This vessel was also fitted as a warship and given to the command of Captain John Hazzard (unlisted), a New Yorker. There is little known of Hazzard except that he was described as "a stout man, very vain and ignorant."[15]

Nicholas Biddle (5th) of Pennsylvania was given command of *Andrea Doria* and proved to be a most capable officer. He was unrelated to the other captains. In fact, Biddle was the only non-New Englander on the precedence list, and he was the only one to have served in the Royal Navy. He had been appointed midshipman in 1771 and had served with another midshipman named Horatio Nelson. Biddle gained his command from the Naval Committee primarily because he had run in a shipment of six and a half tons of badly needed gunpowder from the French island of Santo Domingo. Biddle had also demonstrated his ability to command as captain of the row-galley *Franklin* on the Delaware River in the earliest days of the rebellion.[16]

Shortages of seamen and supplies dogged the Naval Committee throughout the war, yet by January 4, 1776, the needs of the tiny squadron were, at least temporarily, met. Commodore Hopkins ordered all the officers and men to immediately repair on board their respective ships to "avoid being deemed deserters." *Alfred, Columbus, Cabot,* and *Andrea Doria* cast their moorings and moved slowly down the ice-filled Delaware toward the sea. Ten days later, first *Providence* and then a small armed sloop, *Fly,* joined the fleet at its anchorage opposite Philadelphia. Finally, in mid-February, two small vessels fitted out in Baltimore completed the fleet as it anchored near the mouth of Delaware Bay. The sloop *Hornet* was armed with 10 small guns, and the schooner *Wasp* had 8 guns.[17]

On January 6, the Naval Committee wrote to Hopkins with instructions. In part, these directed, "[P]roceed directly for Chesapeake Bay in Virginia . . . enter said bay, search out and attack, take or destroy all the naval forces of our enemies that you may find there. . . . [Then] proceed immediately to the Southward and make yourself master of such forces as the enemy may have both in North and South Carolina." These orders reflected a knowledge of the scant disposition of British warships in the Southern colonies (see table), and they acknowledged Southern support for the creation of the navy in Congress.[18]

On February 14, the commodore called the commanders of each vessel in the fleet to the flagship *Alfred.* Captains Whipple (*Columbus*), J. B. Hopkins (*Cabot*), Biddle (*Andrea Doria*), and Hazzard (*Providence*) met with captains William Stone (unlisted, skipper of *Hornet*) and William Hallock (15th, skipper of *Wasp*) as well as Lieutenant Hoystead Hacker (16th, formerly first officer of *Cabot,* but now skipper of *Fly*). These men would lead the first American naval expedition under the commodore's fine yellow flag emblazoned with a thirteen-segment serpent (representing the colonies) and inscribed with "Don't Tread On Me."

Commodore Hopkins immediately informed these men that he would use the discretion he assumed from his instructions to recast the mission. Hopkins now planned a raid on New Providence (Nassau) in the Bahamas to capture a store of gunpowder and arms said to be stored there. He issued orders to that effect and set both general and specific signals for his captains. The immediate destination of the fleet was to be Grand Abaco Island in the Bahamas. The fleet mounted a total of 114 guns— the largest being 9 pounders. Besides officers, 700 sailors and almost 200 marines made up the personnel of the fleet.[19]

With a fresh wind, the fleet sailed on February 14, 1776. By March 1, six of the eight vessels lay at anchor off Grand Abaco. *Hornet* and *Fly* had disappeared during the voyage. For two days, the fleet waited, using the time to train their men and refill their water casks. Two small British merchantmen were taken, and from the prisoners, Hopkins received intelligence about New Providence. From this information and his own knowledge of the place, Hopkins drew the specifics of his raid. As the harbor was guarded by two forts, a direct assault by the fleet seemed ill-suited to the task. Although he had made "no attempt to hide his

Disposition of Royal Navy Warships on the North American Station, January 1775

Ship	Guns	Men	Station
Boyne	70	520	Boston
Somerset	68	520	Boston
Asia	64	480	Boston
Preston	50	300	Boston
Mercury	20	130	Boston
Glasgow	20	130	Boston
Tartar	28	160	Halifax
Rose	20	130	Rhode Island
Swan	16	100	Rhode Island
Hope	6	30	Rhode Island
Fowey	20	130	Virginia
Lively	20	130	Salem
Scarborough	20	130	New Hampshire
Canceaux	8	45	New Hampshire
Kingfisher	16	100	New York
Tamer	14	100	South Carolina
Cruizer	8	60	North Carolina
Savage	8	60	East Florida
St. John	6	30	East Florida
Magdalen	6	30	Philadelphia
Halifax	6	30	Maine
Diligent	6	30	Maine
Gaspee	6	30	Maine
Diana	6	30	Unassigned

presence or to take advantage of the speed and surprise that was his," Hopkins decided, instead, to employ a subterfuge and send in the marines.[20]

The Marines American marines, like their British counterparts, were carried aboard naval vessels for several reasons. Primarily, they served as a force trained specifically for close combat. Their station in an engagement was in the fighting tops or as boarders. They also served as a force, separate from the seamen who formed the nucleus of the crew, that the officers could count on to help control the men. With this purpose in mind, marines were kept separate from the seamen, sleeping and eating in an area between the ratings and the officers. They had their own officers.

The initial corps of American marines that shipped out with Commodore Hopkins had been raised in Philadelphia. The Tun Tavern seems to have been the main source of volunteers. Robert Mullan, owner of Tun Tavern, and Samuel Nickolas were made captains of marines. The marines adopted a dark green uniform coat with white cuffs and facings. Their small clothes—shirts, waistcoats, and breeches—were white. They wore black leather necks stocks, and their leather accouterments were white.

Packed into the two captured vessels, two and a half companies of marines and fifty sailors—270 men in all—approached the harbor of New Providence. Although Hopkins' plans called for the fleet to remain over the horizon until the marines landed, the commodore misjudged his timing. The fleet came barreling into the port immediately in the wake of the island vessels. Nonetheless, the marines stormed ashore in their first amphibious landing as Americans and swept through the forts that were abandoned after a nominal defense.[21]

The raid was a success limited only by the fact that the governor of New Providence had spirited 150 barrels of gunpowder out of the islands upon word of Hopkins' arrival. Seventeen large cannon (32s, 18s, and 12s) were taken, as well as thousands of round shot and other ordnance supplies. Once the town was taken, the total number of guns removed was eighty-eight of various sizes, as well as a variety of mortars. The marines also found twenty-four barrels of powder that remained in the forts, an amount far less than hoped.

While the fleet was lying in the Bahamas, it was rejoined by *Fly*, which had collided with *Hornet* in a storm. *Hornet*, damaged in the collision, had made for the South Carolina coast and had returned to Delaware Bay. With sickness ravaging his crews, Hopkins ordered his captains to sail north and rendezvous in the Block Island Channel off Rhode Island. Here *Andrea Doria* and *Fly* captured an armed schooner, *Hawke*, and the bomb vessel *Bolton*. Both were taken with little trouble—Hawke was the first Royal Navy warship captured by the Continental Navy. Shortly after the reunion of the fleet, two more sail were sighted, the British frigate *Glasgow* of 22 guns, Captain Tyringham Howe commanding, and its tender, a sloop.

Although all the ships cleared for action, no orders came from Hopkins. In fact, not one order was issued by the commodore during the engagement that followed. *Cabot* and *Glasgow* came within pistol shot of one another when an overzealous marine tossed a grenade on the *Glasgow*'s deck. Both ships immediately opened with broadsides but *Cabot*'s six pounders were no match for the 9 pounders aboard *Glasgow*. *Cabot* sheered away, while being hit with a devastating broadside that killed four and wounded seven including Captain Hopkins. Biddle, in *Andrea Doria*, was forced away from the battle in order to keep from colliding with *Cabot*. The flagship *Alfred* now joined the battle. *Alfred*'s twenty 9 pounders were a match for *Glasgow*, and Lieutenant Jones was below on the gun-deck urging on his crews. Suddenly the American's wheel and tiller were struck, and the ship broached. In this condition, it could be raked at will. However, Biddle had come back into range of the British frigate, and *Columbus* was nearing. *Glasgow's* captain, having acquitted himself brilliantly so far, decided that there was no future in taking on the entire fleet, broke off the action, and fled using the ship's stern chasers to ward off any pursuers. *Columbus* had one last chance to rake the fleeing Britisher, but most of the shot went high. After four hours of fighting and pursuit, Commodore Hopkins signaled for a recall. This was the only direction he gave to his captains in the action.

Five Americans had been killed and nine wounded. The British tender had been taken by the prize *Hawke*. The *Glasgow* was later reported to have sustained a good deal of punishment. The British frigate was "considerably damaged in her hull, had 10 shot through her mainmast, 52 through her mizzen stay sail, 110 through her main sail, 88 through her fore sail, had her spars carried away and her rigging shot to pieces." *Glasgow* lost one man and three wounded. Each of these had been hit by sharpshooters—American naval gunnery had been notably ineffective.[22]

The successes of the first American naval expedition quickly wore off as the details of the *Glasgow* action came to light. Captain Hazzard of *Providence* made no attempt to join the battle, seeming content to sail back and forth out of range. Numerous questions were raised as to how a single ship could do so much damage to an entire fleet and make good her escape. This failure was emphasized when Captain John Barry, in command of the brigantine *Lexington*, captured the Royal Navy sloop *Edward* in a sharp fight. Abraham Whipple demanded and received a court martial in order to validate his actions. The court found him to have been ineffective due only to an error in judgment and not from cowardice. Captain Hazzard of *Providence* was also hauled before a court martial, but, this time, the court found him guilty of neglecting his duty. Hazzard was cashiered, and Lieutenant John Paul Jones was given his command.

Although no ship had been lost and several had been taken, Commodore Hopkins quickly became a target for criticism. Politics and preferment among his officers prevented the fleet from putting to sea again. The details of his demise as commander-in-chief are complicated and unimportant. Hopkins, Saltonstall, and Whipple were called before the Marine Committee of Congress to answer charges of neglect of duty and disobedience of orders. The accusations against Saltonstall and Whipple were disposed of swiftly, but those against Hopkins lingered. Ultimately, he was admonished for taking an initiative without the express orders of Congress in attacking New Providence and was censured by Congress for keeping the fleet inactive thereafter. The remainder of Hopkins' career was marked by antagonism, hostility, and disaffection.

On January 2, 1778, the Continental Congress resolved: "Congress having no further occasion for the service of Ezek Hopkins, Esquire who, on the 22 December, 1775, was appointed commander-in-chief of the fleet fitted out by the Naval Committee, Resolved, That the said Ezek Hopkins, Esquire be dismissed from the service of the United States." Never again was the rank of commander-in-chief given to another American naval officer.[23]

Eighteenth on the list in precedence was John Paul Jones. Born in Scotland in 1747 as John Paul, this American naval officer is the best-known single-ship commander to have served in the Continental Navy. Having brushed with the wrong side of British law when he killed the ringleader of a mutinous crew in the merchant service, John Paul quickly vanished from sight and changed his name. There is some evidence that before the Revolution, John Paul Jones made his living as a smuggler and pirate in North Carolina.

John Paul Jones

Nonetheless, when the war began he was able to use the patronage of several influential colonial shipowners to receive a place in the Continental Navy. Jones was made the first lieutenant of Admiral Hopkins' flagship *Alfred*. After surviving Hopkins' fiasco and receiving command of *Providence*, Jones quickly proceeded on a series of independent cruises, taking sixteen prizes in a short period. Although *Providence* mounted only 12 four pounders, Jones found the ship fast and maneuverable and said the crew was the best he ever commanded.[24]

Jones next traveled to France in the new American sloop-of-war *Ranger*. Armed with 18 four pounders, Jones ravaged the Channel and the Irish Sea. Palpable fear overtook the British public when he attacked the home of Lord Selkirk on the west coast of England, stole his silver plate, and burned several vessels in the nearby port of Whitehaven. The alarm was sounded all along the coast, and several British cruisers were sent in pursuit of the Yankee "pirate." One of these was the *Drake* (20 6-pdrs.), built in Philadelphia before the war and taken into the Royal Navy.

The two ships came into sight of one another an hour before sunset on April 24, 1778, in the Belfast Lough. Jones, with his yards set back and his courses clewed up, waited for the *Drake* to approach. The Britisher sent a lieutenant in a boat to discover if *Ranger* was a peaceful merchant ship or an enemy. The lieutenant was immediately taken as a prisoner of war. *Drake* raised the Union Jack. The Britisher was approaching *Ranger's* stern when Jones broke out the Stars and Stripes, identifying himself as an American Continental ship, and opened a broadside. The British captain was caught unaware and allowed Jones to suddenly cross his bows, raking him from stem to stern. Wanting a prize, Jones stood off blasting *Drake's* rigging with chain shot and her deck with grape and canister. The British captain was killed in the first minutes of the battle. The first lieutenant was mortally wounded, and forty-two of the crew were killed or wounded. Within an hour, *Drake* became unmanageable and the British struck their colors.[25]

Drake was the first Royal Navy warship taken by an American in European waters. *Ranger* lost only three men and had five wounded. Jones sent his first officer, Lieutenant Thomas Simpson, to take the prize. Jones disliked Simpson, a political appointee, and found fault with his handling of the *Drake* on the return cruise to France. In fact, Jones placed Simpson under arrest for insubordination.

This was only the first of many problems that were to plague Jones for the next nine months. Confident that he would be given a better command after his raid and victory, Jones was frustrated by how slowly a new ship was forthcoming. He also found himself at odds with a large segment of his crew over prize money, bad treatment, and his charges against Simpson (who was generally well liked). Seventy-seven sailors and twenty-eight warrant and petty officers complained to the American commissioners in Paris, charging that Jones was arbitrary, bad tempered, and insufferable. Supported only by Benjamin Franklin, who promised him command of *L'Indien*—a new powerful frigate building in Amsterdam, Jones dropped his charges against Simpson, who sailed away as the new commander of *Ranger*.[26]

Once again Jones was frustrated. His chances of obtaining a new warship dimmed when *L'Indien* was sold to the French, and Franklin's counsel to be patient was wearing thin. Finally, in late 1778, a ship was found that could serve the American purpose. The *Duc de Duras* was a tired French East Indiaman of 900 tons built in 1766. Like the type, *Duc de Duras* was sturdy but ponderous and slow.

The upper deck was armed with 6 nine pounders, the gun-deck with 28 twelve pounders, and 6 ancient eighteen pounders. The largest cannon had been secured from French ordinance stores previously condemned as unfit. They were mounted in the midshipman's berth so close to the waterline that they could not be run out in any weather other than a flat calm. Jones handpicked his officers and approved the 380 men that served aboard, many of whom were British deserters or former prisoners of war. Before sailing Jones renamed the ship *Bonhomme Richard*.

Serving as the commodore of a small squadron including *Bonhomme Richard* (40), the corvette *Pallas* (26), the brig *Vengeance* (12), the small cutter *Cerf* (18), and the American frigate *Alliance* (36), Jones sailed in search of the enemy. Each of his companion vessels, except *Alliance*, were outfitted and maintained by France but sailed under American commissions. *Alliance* was commanded by Captain Pierre Landais, an honorary citizen of Massachusetts.

On September 23, 1779, the *Bonhomme Richard* sighted a large number of sails that turned out to be a Baltic convoy of forty-one supply ships under the protection of the frigate *Serapis* and the sloop-of-war *Countess of Scarborough*. The sloop-of-war was armed with only 22 guns, but *Serapis* was a fast, new frigate rated at 44 guns but carrying 50. Captain Richard Pearson had added additional armament (20 nine pounders and 10 six pounders) to the frigate's massive main battery of 20 eighteen pounders.

Since the wind was light, it took more than three hours for Jones' squadron to make its approach. *Pallas* made for the *Countess of Scarborough*, engaged her, and quickly made her a prize. *Vengeance* inexplicably took no part in the action, and *Alliance*, though initially making to engage *Serapis*, sheered off at the last moment. With darkness falling, *Bonhomme Richard* and *Serapis* maneuvered for advantage.

With the first fire, two of the ancient 18 pounders on *Bonhomme Richard* blew up, killing most of their crew and blowing a hole in the deck above. Pearson attempted to obtain a raking position and failed. Finally the two vessels entangled, with *Bonhomme Richard*'s bow hung upon *Serapis'* stern. With his guns unable to bear, Jones attempted to board *Serapis* but was driven back. By this point in the action, Pearson, feeling that he had demonstrated his superior firepower and tactics, called out to Jones, "Has your ship struck?" From the deck of the *Bonhomme Richard* came the reply, "I have not yet begun to fight!"[27]

Bonhomme Richard backed off, and the two antagonists were again broadside to broadside. Now the pounding match began. So close did the ships come that the fluke of *Serapis'* anchor caught *Bonhomme Richard*, and the bowsprit and mizzen riggings became entangled. Grapples were thrown and made fast. Sharpshooters in the American fighting tops began clearing the British deck. Suddenly, *Alliance* came out of the growing darkness, and the Americans gave a cheer, supposing that Captain Landais would put his vessel along *Serapis'* unengaged side. To their horror, Landais swung to the other side and let go a broadside into *Bonhomme Richard*. He then put about and put another into the bow. Jones was astonished at the action of his subordinate, who may have mistaken his consort for the enemy in the dark.

With the *Bonhomme Richard* sinking under him, Jones was once again asked to surrender. "No, sir, I haven't as yet thought of it, but I'm determined to make you strike." At about this time, William Hamilton, who had been fighting in the tops, inched his way out onto a yardarm with a basket of grenades, determined to drop them into the open hatches of *Serapis*. After several tries, one grenade fell through, exploding among a pile of loose cartridges on the British gundeck. A terrible roar followed the exploding ammunition as the flame passed from pile to pile. About twenty men were killed, and many more were terribly burned. When a final British attempt to board failed, Pearson struck his colors. Anxious that *Alliance* might return, Pearson thought further battle "in vain and in short impracticable from the situation . . . to stand out any longer with the least prospect of success."[28]

One of the most bitter ship-to-ship actions in naval history was over. It had lasted for more than three hours. Jones lost 150 killed and wounded; and Pearson had 120 casualties. Although *Countess of Scarborough* was made a prize by *Pallas*, not one of the Baltic supply fleet had been taken. This was remarkable as *Vengeance* and *Cerf* had remained unengaged. The *Bonhomme Richard* was a total loss. No amount of effort could save the ship. When Jones transferred his command to *Serapis*, he found his prize a leaking wreck. Only with the effort of both surviving crews did the ship make harbor in Texel, Holland.

Pearson later faced a court martial for losing two warships, but the safety of the convoy and the number of enemies ranged against *Serapis* saved him. He was later knighted, causing Jones to remark, "Let me fight him again . . . and I'll make him a lord!" Jones was immediately raised to the status of a legend. His victories in American and European waters stood in sharp contrast to the failure of the rest of the Continental Navy and the Allied fleets. Nevertheless, it must be remembered that it was the Franco-Spanish fleet of Admiral De Grasse that saved the war at sea for the Americans in 1781.

NOTES

1. Samuel W. Bryant, *The Sea and the States: A Maritime History of the American People* (New York: Thomas Y. Crowell, 1967), 34.

2. Mark Kurlansky, *Cod: A Biography of the Fish that Changed the World* (New York: Penguin Books, 1997), 94.

3. Oliver M. Dickerson, *The Navigation Acts and the American Revolution* (New York: A. S. Barnes, 1963), 172–183, 295–300; Kurlansky, 96–97.

4. See William Bell Clark, *George Washington's Navy: Being an Account of His Excellency's Fleet in New England Waters* (Baton Rouge: Louisiana State University Press, 1960).

5. See William Bell Clark, *Ben Franklin's Privateers: A Naval Epic of the American Revolution* (Westport, CT: Greenwood Press, 1969).

6. Nathan Miller, *Sea of Glory: A Naval History of the American Revolution* (Annapolis, MD: Naval Institute Press, 1974), 72.

7. Clark, *George Washington's Navy*, 62–63.

8. Arthur Bowler, *Logistics and the Failure of the British Army in America, 1775–1783* (Princeton, NJ: Princeton University Press, 1975), 53. Also see Robert W. Neeser, ed., *The Dispatches of Molyneux Shuldham, Vice Admiral of the Blue and Commander in Chief of His Britannic Majesty's Ships in North America: January–July, 1776* (New York: Naval Society Publications, 1913).

9. Clark, *George Washington's Navy*, 228. Ezek Hopkins was the first commander of the Continental Navy.

10. Miller, 214.

11. William M. Fowler, Jr., *Rebels under Sail: The American Navy during the Revolution* (New York: Charles Scribner's Sons, 1976), 295.

12. In what follows, the place of each officer will be given as an ordinal number, or marked as unlisted, in parentheses.

13. Miller, 56.

14. Ibid., 118–119.

15. Ibid., 93.

16. Bryant, 78–79.

17. See Miller, 84–99.

18. Ibid., 93–94.

19. Ibid., 93. See also Fowler, 92.

20. Fowler, 92.

21. While this is celebrated as the birth of the U.S. Marines, Americans had made amphibious landings during the French wars—in particular the landing at Louisburg under William Pepperel during the War of Austrian Succession.

22. Miller, 115.

23. Ibid., 217.

24. Ibid., 128.

25. Ibid., 365–366.

26. Ibid., 369–370.

27. Author Nathan Miller points out that it was earlier in the battle than is normally thought that this famous phrase was uttered.

28. Miller, 384–385.

14

The Sea and the States

All the coasting trade is being done by screw steamers and a few side wheelers. . . . The few sailing vessels building are small craft of no great burden.

—*New York Times*, 1866

The excellence of American ships in the first half of the nineteenth century is unquestioned. American maritime design and shipbuilding technology were the envy of the world, and American sailing ships were soon the fastest on the seas. Americans were master windship builders, and this same excellence lent itself to the design of naval vessels. Nonetheless, by the third quarter of the century, contemporary observers could rightly speak of the virtual extinction of American commerce and unfavorably compare the ships of the late nineteenth century U.S. navy to ancient Roman galleys.

THE U.S. NAVY

The official Continental Navy was disbanded immediately after the American Revolution, but the insults of the Barbary pirates from Algiers, Tripoli, Tunis, and Morocco spurred the young nation into building a permanent naval force. In 1785, two American merchant ships were captured in the Mediterranean, and a score of American citizens were held for ransom in North Africa. The Congress of the United States authorized the construction of six large frigates to defend the American flag around the world and a flotilla of small gunboats to defend the harbors and coastline.

Congress officially re-established the Department of the Navy in 1798 due to the insults that American shipping was receiving from the French and the British. By 1800, other warships had been added to the navy such as the 18-gun *Hornet* and the 22-gun *Wasp*, which followed a tradition of reusing the names of famous U.S. Navy ships. To these were added the newly built 36-gun frigate *Essex* and the 38-gun frigate *Philadelphia*. Other vessels were taken into the American navy like those captured from the French in the undeclared Quasi War (1798–1803), among them the 14-gun *Croyable* and the 36-gun *Insurgente*.

The undeclared naval war with revolutionary France and the Tripolitan War of 1801–1805 tested the new navy and produced officers such as Stephen Decatur, John Rodgers, and Edward Preble. Several warships were dispatched to the north coast of Africa to express American displeasure with the Barbary states under Commodore Richard Dale in 1801 and again under Preble in 1803. When negotiations failed, Congress gave the squadron permission to be more aggressive. This included authority to blockade the coast and take prizes.

Exactly what caused Captain William Bainbridge to chase a Tripolitan corsair into shoal waters in 1803 is unclear. Nonetheless, his frigate, *Philadelphia*, struck and held fast on the Kaliusa Reef. Bainbridge and his crew worked tirelessly to free the ship until, surrounded by Tripolitan gunboats, he cast his guns into the sea and tried to scuttled the ship—all to no avail. Three hundred American sailors and their officers were captured, imprisoned, and held for ransom. Moreover, the Tripolitans salvaged the guns and began making *Philadelphia* ready for sea.

By February 1804, it was decided that the *Philadelphia* must not be allowed to go to sea. In an action, which British Admiral Horatio Nelson called "the most bold and daring act of this age," young Stephen Decatur and eighty volunteers, disguised as Maltese sailors, slipped aboard the frigate from the ketch *Intrepid*, overpowered the watch, and set the vessel ablaze. Decatur then retreated without the loss of a single man. Preble then set to bombarding the city of Tripoli with little result. When Commodore Samuel Barron arrived with a dozen warships to beef up the Mediterranean squadron, he assumed command. But the sickly Barron died leaving the operation to Captain John Rodgers, who was next in seniority. In a combined operation with a landside army commanded by William Eaton, the former American consul to Tunis, the Bashaw of Tripoli was forced into an agreement in June 1805. Bainbridge and his men were released after nineteen months of imprisonment during which six men died. With the immediate problem of the Barbary pirates put behind them, the American navy moved forward, having accomplished little other than forging a tradition of daring and bravery among its officers and men. A satisfactory agreement to the Barbary Wars was not reached until 1816.[1]

Both Britain and France continued to take advantage of the United States on the high seas. French warships stopped American vessels at sea and demanded to examine their papers. They searched merchantmen for contraband and seized cargoes although they had no right to do so. British vessels acted in much the same way, but they also impressed American seamen into the Royal Navy if there was the least question as to their U.S. citizenship. Some sailors provided themselves with documents attesting to their citizenship. The activities of both France and Britain were generally outside the scope of international law, but the American navy was too weak to do much about them other than to complain to the court of world opinion. **The Embargo**

In an effort to stem this crisis, the U.S. Congress passed the Non-Importation Act of 1806, which made it illegal for American shippers to deal with either the French or the British. By 1807, it was obvious that nonimportation alone was not going to solve the problem, as both Britain and France seemed unaffected by the loss of American business. By executive order, Thomas Jefferson, then president of the United States, declared an embargo in 1807, which closed all U.S. ports to foreign shipping. It is difficult to say just what strategy Jefferson had in mind by doing this other than attempting to keep American vessels out of harm's way. The immediate result was simply to put a large segment of the American merchant service out of business. Ships sat rotting at the docks; sailors wandered the waterfront looking for work on coasters and fishing vessels; and shipowners tried to weather a financial disaster. New England was particularly hard pressed, and Jefferson, a southern planter, was correctly portrayed as the villain in a botched attempt at world diplomacy at the expense of northern manufacturers and shippers.

In 1810, Congress authorized James Madison, Jefferson's successor, to open trade with Britain or France provided that when one changed its behavior, trade would be cut off with the other. On the strength of an assurance by Napoleon that the objectionable French measures would be raised, Madison issued a proclamation of nonintercourse ending all commerce with Britain.

The American entry into the Napoleonic War in Europe in 1812 is somewhat of an enigma, and the study of the decision has filled numerous volumes. The Federalists of New England were vociferously opposed to the war. Yet the political influence of about two dozen outspoken proponents of war with England in Congress convinced President James Madison to declare war in June 1812. These War Hawks expected the war with England to be **The War of 1812** short, and they were convinced that the United States could gain part or all of Canada while the British were expending most of their energy fighting Napoleon in Europe. The British policy of inciting Indian raids on the American frontiers and of impressing American seamen at sea for the Royal Navy were used as a justification for the opening of hostilities.[2]

The Americans entered the war in 1812 with six frigates, five sloops of war, two brigs, and sixty-two gunboats ready for sea. Nine new vessels were building in various harbors including two new 74s, but these would not be ready until 1814. Only one American vessel was patrolling Lake Ontario, and several other war vessels were building or refitting for service on the Great Lakes. It seems obvious, therefore, that the American plan for its naval defense was somewhat optimistic. A navy twenty times the number would have been needed to stand eyeball to eyeball with any of the fleets of Europe. The Royal Navy had more than 100 warships larger than 64 guns, while the six frigates fielded by the Americans had no hope of standing up to even a single 50-gun fourth rate.

The reasoning of both Madison and the War Hawks was quickly shown to be faulty as the British immediately set almost 100 warships on the station solely directed against the American coastline. Although most of these warships were 32- to 40-gun frigates and smaller vessels, some were mighty 74s, having three decks. To counter the British presence the Americans had six large frigates designed to carry 44 guns (although only three had this armament) and several smaller vessels of the *Essex* class. But the double-banked American frigates proved vastly superior to any other warship in their class. Naval authority and author C. S. Forester pointed out that they were not "extra powerful frigates" but rather "not-too-small two-decked ships of the line."[3]

The United States had been fortunate in its choice of a naval designer for these vessels. Joshua Humphreys was gifted with a combination of original thought, professional competence, and technological shrewdness. He had first suggested the fortified frigate design to Congress in 1794. The resulting warships had been built with stout timbers of live oak from the swamplands of Georgia in order to add strength and durability, and they were designed with a flush spar deck with stalwart protective sides, allowing more guns to be mounted on two decks than was common with vessels that had well decks amidships. Like many American merchant vessels of the day, these frigates were particularly fast and could run from any vessel they could not match in size. Nonetheless, their superiority over other warships in their class was largely due to Humphrey's attention to detail and to the talent of their officers and crews.[4]

Of the six vessels—*Constitution, President, United States, Chesapeake, Constellation,* and *Congress*—only the first three were armed with 44 guns.

The others varied between 36 and 38 guns. The best known of the group was *Constitution*, with its many single-ship actions including the defeat of the British frigates *Guerriere* and *Java*. The strength of *Constitution's* sides in these battles was so great that many of the enemy's shot bounced off into the sea. This observation led to the frigate's nickname "Old Ironsides." The *United States* served to bring Captain Stephen Decatur to prominence when he trounced the 38-gun *Macedonian*, which was later brought into the American navy. The 38-gun *Chesapeake* was lost in an ill-considered ship-to-ship duel with *Shannon* (36) in sight of Boston. Late in the war, *President*, the fastest of the six Humphrey frigates, was pounded into submission by a small squadron of British ships including the 44-gun *Endymion*, a British large frigate. *Constellation* (36) spent most of the war blockaded in Norfolk after being chased back into its hole by two ships-of-the-line, three frigates, and two sloops-of-war. Finally, the *Congress* (36) spent much of the war in consort with *President*, before that ship's capture. *Congress* captured a few merchant vessels in the Atlantic but generally failed to distinguish itself otherwise.

With the war at an end in 1815, and with Napoleon removed from the stage of European politics, the world entered an era during which many nations turned their focus inward. For most of the next fifty years, European countries struggled with the civil unrest caused by internal social upheavals that culminated in the widespread revolutions of 1848 to 1860. The Sicilians and Neopolitans revolted in Italy under Garibaldi; the Piedmontese struggled with Austria; and the Sepoys mutinied against the British in India. In 1854, the French and British allied against Turkey and Russia for control of the Crimea.

Meanwhile, the United States passed through a long period of internecine brawling over states rights and slavery, which ultimately led to the Civil War. By this time, the merchant marine and the navy had grown in size and experience. The Confederate States by contrast had no navy, only scanty shipbuilding facilities, and its ports existed largely to service northern shipping. In its struggle with the North, the South turned to commerce raiding, as had so many Americans in former times. The *Southern History of the Civil War* stated the goals of these Southern raiders: "The militia of the seas . . . would penetrate into every sea and find splendid prizes in the silk ships of China and the gold-freighted steamers of California." To what degree the Confederate States Navy was successful is open to question.[5]

THE CONFEDERATE COMMERCE RAIDERS

The damages due to the attacks of Confederate commerce raiders have continued to serve as the keystone of the traditional explanation for the years between 1866 and 1890 being called "The Dark Ages of American Oceanic Enterprise." Several maritime authorities, however, consider the reasoning underlying this explanation faulty. Historian Lawrence Allin claims it to be the "most loudly heralded . . . and erroneously quoted . . . explanation for the decline of the U.S. maritime trades."[6] Robert Albion and Jennie Pope label the traditional arguments "extravagant" in their study of the effects of war on maritime trade;[7] and Clinton Whitehurst describes the reasoning as "a simplistic notion at best" in his study of the shipbuilding industry.[8]

On November 6, 1865, *Shenandoah* ended a journey of destruction in Great Britain, after capturing or destroying 38 vessels. *Shenandoah*, powered by sail with auxiliary steam, was the last of approximately 18 commerce raiders commissioned by the Confederate government. Of these, only eight achieved any substantial results. *Shenandoah, Tallahassee, Florida,* and *Alabama* are generally credited with the lion's share of the damage. The raiders captured or destroyed a total of 239 vessels, or 105 thousand tons, causing a direct loss to northern shipping interests of between $20–25 million. Allegedly, about 800 thousand tons of U.S. flag vessels had been legally sold and registered under another flag in response to the actions of the raiders. Foreign registry was used to avoid both capture and potentially ruinous war risk insurance rates. These predatory cruisers formed the South's only deep-water weapon and have come to represent the high point of Confederate naval history.[9]

The Alabama Claims Since the Confederate raider *Alabama* made the largest share of the Civil War–era seizures, the resulting litigation between the United States and Great Britain came to be know as the Alabama Claims. The United States, in an arbitrated settlement, received over $15 million in reparations from the British for that nation's complicity in building, supplying, manning, and otherwise aiding the raiders. In laying the foundation of its case against the British, Charles Francis Adams, representing the government, also demanded payments for the virtual destruction of the maritime commerce of the United States during the war years. This demand amounted to an assertion that the raiders and, by extension, Great Britain were entirely responsible for the decline of the U.S. merchant marine during the Civil War period. These indirect damages were ultimately disallowed by the Geneva Arbitration Tribunal that oversaw the settlement of the case.[10]

The rationale of the government's argument for indirect damages, which serves as a foundation for the "Flight from the Flag" theory, was rooted in the concept that the existence and reported success of the Confederate raiders had undermined American pre-eminence in the foreign carrying trade to the extent that British carriers were unfairly able to displace the Americans. By driving war risk insurance premiums higher than was warranted by the accomplishments of the raiders, U.S. commerce was forced to suffer. American shippers were forced to seek neutral carriers, often British ones. Moreover, it was charged that Lloyd's of London, which set the underwriter's standards for vessels and held the position as the largest marine insurer of the world's fleet, had given British vessels favorable treatment. Northern shippers, already working on small profit margins, had been forced to sell foreign (legally sell to foreign owners), in the face of the financial ruin brought on as port charges mounted on their unused vessels.

The terminology of *selling foreign* and that of *flying a flag of convenience* are often confused. Vessels that were sold foreign were considered to actually have been sold so that their former owners no longer held a financial stake in their operations. Flying a flag of convenience was a different matter. It amounted to a paper transaction, wherein the former owners still retained financial and practical control the vessels but had legally transferred their ownership to another national registry.[11]

The high rate of war risk insurance served as the driving mechanism of the supposedly disastrous effects on U.S. com- **War Risk** merce during the war years. War risk rates were supplemen- **Insurance** tal premiums set beyond the cost of ordinary marine insurance for which the fees were considerably lower. In the case of loss due to natural disaster or act of war, the insurance covered the financial damage to the owners up to, but not beyond, the value of the vessel and cargo.

War risk rates were set by taking into consideration the route of the vessel, its type and cargo, and the ability of its navy to protect it. In 1775, for instance, the war risk premium for British-owned shipping on a run from Philadelphia to Europe was 2.5 percent, little more than the normal rate, as it was supposed that the Royal Navy could effectively protect British commerce. However, by 1781, insurance rates for a voyage to Havana or Jamaica had risen to almost 50 percent, with the average rates to other destinations lying between 20 percent and 30 percent, mostly because of the success of American privateers in these waters. Rates for U.S. flag vessels during its involvement in the War of 1812 reflected its naval weakness in comparison with the British. Insurance rates ranged from 40 percent to 75 percent on runs to the Far East, and insurance at any cost for an American vessel was unavailable to Europe, the Mediterranean, and the West Indies.[12] At no other time in its history was the United States so completely cut off from the sea as it was by the Royal Navy in 1814.[13]

Used in this manner, war risk rates are a significant indicator of the control of the seas in a conflict. Since the southern naval forces in the American Civil War were never comparable to that of the North, it may be concluded that the higher rates reflected a "panic" in northern ship-

ping circles, which did more damage than the actual ravages of the raiders.[14] As an example, in the winter of 1863–1864, Captain Raphael
Semmes and the *Alabama* were reported to be in the Pacific, and his
presence was confirmed when the raider stopped at Singapore for provisions. For three months, not a single American vessel left the harbor
of Hong Kong because of these reports. Yet in March, when the *Alabama*
was reported to have rounded the Cape of Good Hope for France, these
American vessels flew across the Pacific.[15]

This panic may have been rooted in America's own experience with
commerce raiding. During the American Revolution, the Continental
Navy posed no significant threat to the might of the Royal Navy. However, they were able to capture or destroy 196 vessels valued at more
than $6 million. Moreover, added to the regular naval forces of the col-
onies were almost 5,000 privateers whose sole purpose was to raid British commerce. These captured more than 1,000 British vessels, including
twelve British warships, worth an astonishing $18 million.

During the Civil War period, the Confederacy had no genuine navy.
It relied on its ability to disrupt Federal commerce in much the same
way that privateers in the Revolution and War of 1812 had done. The
premiums for war risks on northern shipping ranged from 1 percent to
3 percent in 1861, to 10 percent in 1863, at the height of Confederate
raiding activity. These insurance premiums were small when compared
with historically high rates for war risk in other periods. Moreover, the
highest war risk rates in the Civil War period reflected insurance only
to the more distant runs in the East Indies and the Pacific. War rates on
northern vessels to Europe, the West Indies, and along the Atlantic coast
remained remarkably low, ranging from as little as 0.5 percent to 3.5
percent throughout the period.[16]

Although the single richest prize of the war, the ship *John Bell*, worth
$1.5 million, was taken by *Florida* off the Windward Islands in the West
Indies, both *Florida* and *Alabama* generally preferred the more distant and
safer waters off the coast of Brazil, the Straits of Sunda, the China Sea,
or the Bay of Bengal. Moreover, *Shenandoah*, although logging more than
50,000 miles, failed to ever approach U.S. coastal waters during its career,
preferring to prey on whalers in the Bering sea and the South Pacific.
Only in 1864 was *Tallahassee* active on the Atlantic coast. As the war
progressed, strategic commercial intersections, such as the English Channel, Gibraltar, Capetown, and Bahia in the South Atlantic, proved to be
patrolled by an ever-increasing number of Federal cruisers purposely
detached from the blockading squadrons to these locations in an attempt
to stop the raiders. This may account for the disparity in war risk rates
for these destinations.[17]

The panic found in northern shipping circles was effectively supple-
mented at the time by the efforts of Confederate agents in Europe, such

as James D. Bullock who was responsible for building and arming a number of Confederate vessels in Britain. Bullock has been characterized as "worth far more to the Confederacy than most of its best-known generals."[18] Other less notable agents were George N. Sanders, who would later play an important role in the secret service activities in Canada, and several regular Confederate naval officers, including Raphael Semmes, skipper of the *Alabama*. These agents proved sufficiently effective in portraying the success of the raiders' activities that as early as 1863 the *New York Times* reported that British opinion was of the mind that "American shipping had almost become valueless in consequence of the seizures made by the Confederate cruisers."[19]

Unchallenged, Bullock claimed that Confederate efforts had caused 715 American vessels to be transferred to the British flag by 1864, together with an assertion that three-quarters of American trade had been transferred to foreign bottoms.[20] In like manner, J. Thomas Scharf, a Confederate naval officer writing in 1887, claimed that the raiders had caused "the approximate extinction of American commerce."[21] Little effort was made to determine the reliability of these assertions at the time, and direct and indirect references to them continue to be made by authors and historians to this day.

The depredations of the Confederate raiders did little to depress the domestic coasting trade, and coasters found the nearby Atlantic waters generally safe throughout the war.[22] Although their loss was to produce the greatest panic, as few as 50 coasting vessels, exclusive of other types of craft, fell prey to the Confederates. There were calls for harbor protection and coastal convoys as fear spread from port to port. Fortunately such coastal forays were relatively rare events, and the raiders had to hit and run as word of their presence spread by telegraph to Union bases. Ironically, the reports of the raiders proceeding along the coasts probably did more damage than the actual captures.[23]

For a brief period in the summer of 1861, the Confederate raider *Sumter* was active along the Atlantic coast and in the West Indies, capturing or burning 17 vessels, but the raider quickly crossed the Atlantic to be bottled up in Gibraltar. Lieutenant Charles Read, commanding a series of converted prize vessels, termed the "tenders" of *Florida* in Scharf's account, destroyed several small vessels in his cruise along the Northeast coast. Read's exploits raised great alarm in June 1863, when he was reported to be in Long Island Sound off the port of New York. Although the navy would not detach a single warship from the blockade to pursue him, Read did merit the attention of about thirty regular and improvised naval vessels sent out from the Philadelphia, New York, and Boston navy yards. Read burned or bonded 21 vessels before his three-week raid was ended in Portland, Maine.[24]

The Depredations

Early in 1864, Lieutenant John Taylor Wood seized and destroyed a Union gunboat in the Chesapeake and, having done some further damage among the Federal vessels, was made a commodore in the Confederate navy. Wood's expedition shocked the North and embarrassed the Potomac Flotilla.[25] In July of the same year, he was given command of *Tallahassee*. He headed for the New Jersey coast and was so successful at evading Federal vessels that he contemplated entering and bombarding New York Harbor. As he could not find a pilot willing to direct him, he settled for a cruise from Montauk Point to Boston Bay and then along the New England coast. He captured 26 vessels, including several pilot boats, in ten days, releasing one of his prizes with the numerous prisoners that he had collected.[26]

In October 1864, *Tallahassee* (renamed *Olustee*) and *Chickamauga*, now commanded by Lieutenant William H. Ward and Lieutenant John Wilkinson, respectively, escaped from the Federal forces blockading Wilmington and burned several coasting vessels, ships, and a pilot boat off the New Jersey coast, Sandy Hook, and Block Island. Although they destroyed 20 vessels, the ships proved to be of little monetary value. Even so, the presence of these raiders did cause considerable local panic, and the psychological impact of the depredations on the northern public was enormous. However, they no longer had the impact of the depredations of Read and Wood in the summer of 1863, which had coincided with the pinnacle of war risk insurance rates.[27]

Moreover, as commerce destruction was considered a secondary objective of the Confederate naval effort when compared to the primary goal of drawing Union blockading vessels away from the Atlantic and Gulf coasts, the 1864 exploits of the Confederate navy were considered by some contemporaries to be counterproductive. No blockading vessels were dispatched north to intercept the raiders. Instead, the success of the raiders resulted in a tightening of the blockade that denied the South badly needed supplies when they were needed the most. Even Lieutenant Wilkinson urged that the raiders be removed from service and returned as blockade runners.[28]

The Whaling Fleet As a single identifiable class, the whalers were the most preyed upon of U.S. flag vessels during the Civil War. Of the 239 vessels captured or burned by the Confederate raiders, *Alabama* had burned fourteen whalers; *Shenandoah* had destroyed 29; and the other raiders brought the total to 50 vessels, a mere 8.4 percent of the U.S. whaling fleet. However, these represent almost 21 percent of the craft destroyed by the raiders. In addition, the whaling industry sold 39 vessels to the federal government in 1861 to be sunk as a "stone fleet" to block the harbor entrances of southern ports. The total loss to the whaling fleet during the war,

The ship's wheel of a New England whaler. The glass skylight brought sunshine to the captain's day cabin below. James Volo Photo.

therefore, amounted to 89 vessels. Less than half of these losses were related to the raiders.[29]

In 1860, the total number of whaling vessels in the U.S. fleet amounted to 596, down from its maximum size in 1846 of 735 vessels in a world fleet of only 900. Since 1858, the fleet had been steadily shrinking. Coupled with the normal rate of retirement and loss from natural causes, there was a significant additional decline in the whaling fleet of 46 percent during the war years. The demise of U.S. whaling was symptomatic of deep weaknesses in the industry that included overharvesting and depressed market prices. The whaling fleet, in fact, saw a 25 percent increase in the whaling tonnage in 1866, which suggests that wartime losses were not insurmountable, but statistics indicate that the whaling fleet underwent a sudden collapse in 1867, which is generally attributed to the introduction of cheap petroleum fuels and lubricants. These products had begun to gain a market share as early as 1859. Whale oil as a lighting fuel was driven from the marketplace by 1873 to be replaced by kerosene, and only less profitable whale by-products retained any market. Consequently, the whaling fleet gradually shrank as vessels became worn out. The process was enhanced by the twin disasters of 1871 and 1876 in which 41 whaling vessels were crushed in encroaching polar ice.[30]

In the face of close scrutiny, therefore, the Confederate commerce raiders fade as a cause for the severe distress documented to have taken hold of the U.S. merchant marine trades, and the importance of the raider's depredations in the patchwork of causes for the decline of the foreign carrying trade seems to be based more on anecdotal evidence provided by former Confederates and the owners of economically distressed shipyards rather than on documented statistics. While the wartime figures evidence a decline, they do not seem to support a general abandonment of the U.S. flag or an extinction of its commerce.[31]

Rather than a general abandonment of U.S. registry, the facts seem to indicate that only a minority of owners, generally of large sailing vessels, deserted the flag. Moreover, the reliance on the psychological apprehension of loss and on the fear of high war risk rates as compelling mechanisms for owners to change registry fails to answer one salient question convincingly. Since the owners of vessels captured or destroyed by the Confederates were paid for their vessels and cargoes by the insurance or by the foreign purchasers in the case of sale, why were these vessels not replaced after the Civil War as the hundreds of captured and destroyed merchant vessels had been after the colonial and revolutionary wars of the eighteenth century? Furthermore, the insurance rates returned to their prewar levels with the end of hostilities, but foreign carrying continued to decline even in the absence of the raiders. Here is a central weakness in the argument of the "continuing effect" of the raiders, especially as it fails to suggest a mechanism by which the immediate effects of the raiders could prove so enduring.[32]

The decline of the U.S. foreign carrying trade, especially the profitable trans-Atlantic trade, seems to be best understood in terms removed from a continued emphasis on the activities of the Confederate raiders and the permanence of their consequences. The continued recourse to the activities of the raiders as an explanation of the decline have even been described as simple attempts to bolster southern morale and armchair efforts to enlarge the annals of sea adventure.[33]

The failure to modernize the foreign carrying fleet, at a point in time when America's standing in world commerce was already under attack, serves as a more rationale mechanism for the enduring nature of the decline. Conversely, the strengths found in domestic waterborne shipping seem to be due to the application of the very techniques of modernization and innovation found lacking in the foreign carrying trade. The Confederate cruisers may have acted as an accelerating factor in causing the foreign trade decline to peak during the war years, but the factors that had begun the decline, in the decades before the war, were to figure prominently among those that caused it to continue into the postwar period. As one historian noted: "The elements contributing to the decline of the merchant marine were already apparent before the Civil War, and the results would have been the same if the conflict had not occurred."[34]

THE CARRYING TRADE

Due to the utilitarian nature of marine architecture, vessels designed for deep water, lacking the adaptability necessary to deal with the exigencies of the shallow-water coasting trade, were sold off rather than redeployed to coasting. The predominantly square rigged clipper ships generally required larger crews than the more maneuverable and innately efficient fore and aft rigged coasting craft. Moreover, the cargo capacities of many ocean-going designs proved too large to make the smaller "harbor jumping" cargoes economical to carry.[35] Even the deepwater clippers ships "were born, flourished, and faded from sight in a single decade" because they failed to make the transitions required by the changing patterns of trade and economic activity.[36]

The discovery of the gold fields in California, and later in Australia, heightened the demand for clipper ships, but they were expensive to build and uneconomical to operate. Only the willingness of passengers, crazed with gold fever, to pay exorbitant rates for a quick passage kept the clipper ships in service. They lasted only a few years—generally from 1849 to 1859. The "down-easters" resembled the clipper ships of the 1850s, but this distinctive, Maine-built vessel had neither their sharp lines nor their hollow contours. To increase their cargo capacity the downeasters had little dead rise; in other words, they had a flatter floor in their cargo hold. Although they could spread a good deal of canvas, they were not as heavily sparred as the clippers mainly because they were intended as cargo carriers. The down-easters were able to fill the need for large ocean-going carriers on the less prestigious sea lanes of the world.

Large ocean-going windships were perfectly designed for bulk cargoes such as southern cotton; West Coast grain; Chilean copper ore; Scandinavian salt; or French timber. Typical outbound cargoes included Pennsylvania coal, kerosene, and case oil; locomotives and wheelbarrows; and ready-made clothing and "Yankee notions." When trade slackened, the down-easters carried ice from the Arctic Circle to the West Indies, Calcutta, and Bombay and Chinese from Singapore or Hong Kong to Hawaii and California. Some down-easters were so busy completing a sequence of these long tedious voyages that they did not put in at an American port more than once or twice in a decade.[37]

Notwithstanding the variety exhibited by these cargoes, it was the guano dug from the Peruvian islands of the Pacific that furnished the paying cargoes for most wooden windships during the decline of the cotton-carrying trade, the failure of the grain crop, or the weakening of the gold fever. *Guano* is a Peruvian word for "manure"—not the brown, steaming heaps found on horse and dairy farms—but rather the dried, powdery droppings of millions of sea birds. The Humboldt or Peruvian

The yards on this ship have been "cock-billed" to make the snow and ice run off more freely. James Volo Photo.

current that flows along the west coast of South America has an amazing abundance of sea life that attracted sea birds for millions of years. These birds nested in the Chinchas Islands a few miles off the coast of Peru, and their droppings accumulated and dried on the arid coasts, rising in places to heights of seventy or eighty feet. In many places, vessels could cozy-up to the deposits lining the shore with their yards cock-billed (set at a slant) and let the cargo pour through chutes directly into their holds. In 1865 alone, more than 20,000 shiploads of nitrate-rich guano, of some 2,000 tons each were taken away to enrich the farm fields of the America, England, and Holland.

Guano proved to be intrinsically more valuable than it would at first appear. Between 1851 and 1872, more than 10 million tons, with a market value up to $30 million, was removed. Although the yellow dust carried into every corner of the ship and smelled strongly of ammonia, guano was a cargo that needed no container other than the vessel itself; it could not shift; and it could not spoil. "It was not uncommon to see two hundred square-riggers lying in the protected anchorage between the north and central islands awaiting cargoes." When the Peruvian deposits were depleted in the 1870s, guano mining moved to other more southern points along the coast of Chile.

THE COASTING TRADE

With regard to economy of operation, moderate-sized sailing coasters were best suited as bulk cargo carriers for short hauls, but these were receiving competition from steamers. Nonetheless, a distinctive type of sailing schooner was developed for the coasting trade that allowed them to hold their position in competition with the steamers until the twentieth century. Inexpensive to build and operate and built with traditional American wooden hull technology, these sailing schooners of between 300 and 700 tons capacity were kept busy carrying lumber, coal, ice, and other cargoes up and down the Atlantic, Pacific, and Gulf coasts. The sailing schooners of the coasting trade "formed a hard core of shipping on which the nation could rely."[38]

Protected by a series of navigation acts from foreign competition, the coasting trade had continually grown as a percentage of the merchant marine fleet from 25 percent in the Federalist era, to 41 percent just before the Civil War, and 57 percent by war's end. It was to retain this level of representation throughout the decades of the 1870s and 1880s.[39] A growing national population, the effects of industrialization, and absolute protection from foreign competition allowed coasting to supplant foreign trade as the major activity of the merchant marine as early as 1857. The coasting trade was very active, with cotton, tobacco, lumber, turpentine, rosin, rice, indigo, and grain making up the bulk cargoes.[40]

Coastal steam lines developed slowly in the first half of the nineteeth century because of monopolies granted by individual states to local investors. In 1824, the Supreme Court overturned the state grants as invasions of the federal power to regulate interstate commerce. A willing public advanced the cash needed to develop the coastal steamship lines, and by 1840, all the major East Coast ports were connected by steam. Steam lines had been established from the northeast directly to New Orleans and Savannah prior to the Civil War, and they met with some success. The technological quality of many steam-powered blockade runners during the Civil War overshadowed that of the U.S. merchant sailing fleet, and a large number of shippers took note of the advantages of steam.[41]

In the aftermath of the war, a few innovative American owners began to use efficient steel-hulled, multiple expansion steamships of significant size to operate in the cotton coasting trade even though the initial costs of the vessels were quite high. Steamers seemed to be losing the traditional grip that sailing vessels had on this important fraction of U.S. maritime commerce. A contemporary observer noted in 1866, "All the coasting trade is being done by screw steamers and a few side wheelers ranging from 800 to 1,500 tons. The few sailing vessels building are small craft of no great burden."[42]

The shift from sail to steam can be seen in this illustration of the docks in Hoboken, New Jersey, found in *Leslie's Illustrated Magazine* in 1865. The military and commercial use of sail began to decline before the Civil War and virtually disappeared as early as 1900.

Closely related to the coasting vessels were the numerous wooden fishing schooners that dominated the nineteenth-century fishing industry. These were generally small vessels in terms of tonnage, and their relatively small representation in the merchant fleet is slightly misleading.

THE ADVENT OF STEAM

The wooden windship design had reached its practical engineering limits with the development of the clipper ships of the 1850s. It can be demonstrated that the U.S. shipbuilding industry was simply not competitive in the years after the Civil War and that a change to steam-driven, metal-hulled vessels was essential to the U.S. shipping industry. The failure to accomplish this may have served as a primary mechanism for much of the decline in the foreign carrying trade while concurrently explaining the sustained the growth of the coasting trade and inland navigation.

At midcentury, the engineering fundamentals of steamship construction for the oceanic trade had several common characteristics. The hulls were made of wood; the vessels were propelled by paddle wheels housed amidships; the engines were physically very large and of a single expansion, low pressure type, also located amidships; and the steam was exhausted into jet condensers so similar to those devised by James Watt in 1769 as to be considered identical. Low pressure water tube boilers had been common since their invention in 1791. Paddle wheels, by design well suited to low pressure, were slow, rotating devices of large area that maximized the impulse imparted to the vessel; increased the reliability of the engines; and minimized the stress on the hull. While economical in terms of fuel consumption, the low pressure steam boilers retarded the introduction of the screw propeller. Moreover, paddle wheels provided greater acceleration than the screw propellers of the period.[43]

Nonetheless, steam was usually considered to be an auxiliary to sail, and many vessels were designed with combinations of motive power. However, these vessels commonly experienced some disadvantages as both screws and paddle wheels produced considerable drag when the vessel was under sail. Paddle wheels were particularly noted for adversely effecting the overall sailing qualities of a vessel. When equipped with the higher pressure fire tube boilers, introduced in the 1850s, and screw propellers, the restrictions of increased fuel consumption served to severely limit the speed that the steamer could maintain for any extended period of time.

Windships, by comparison, could make hundreds of miles in a day. A record 400 nautical miles in twenty-four hours was reached in the

1850s by the American clipper ship *Challenger*. Under these conditions, it seemed unlikely that steam would ever compete economically with sail, particularly on the long distance routes where fuel and fresh water for the engines became major limiting considerations.[44]

These disadvantages left the windships with a decided economic edge, at least on the long-haul routes. Nevertheless, wooden-hulled American clippers saw severe competition in the Oriental trade from British windship designs that utilized composite hulls, wood with cast iron beams and bracing, before the war. Although generally smaller than the American ships, and somewhat slower under the best of conditions, the British vessels proved to be better suited to a variety of weather extremes. Even these British windships—the *Cutty Sark* is a prime example—were driven from the trade by steamers in the decade after the Civil War.[45]

U.S. TECHNOLOGICAL STAGNATION

American technological distress in the postwar years may be attributed, in part, to the very success for which U.S. shippers and shipbuilders were noted at the end of the age of sail. In the first half of the nineteenth century, American shipbuilders had no equal in the world. With modern wood-working and wood-turning apparatus, American shipyards could crank out their best work at as little as 60 percent of the cost of British builders, who generally did not invest in such devices. Although profits from investments in the domestic shipping industry could vary with time, the expected financial return from the foreign carrying trade was "effectively tied . . . [to] how well U.S. shipyards could compete in price with their foreign counterparts." Americans found themselves saddled with expensive shipbuilding apparatus made obsolete by the sudden popularity of metal hulls and steam. British builders, by contrast, had made no large investment in wooden windship technology and were able to update their shipyards directly to metal and steam production without taking a loss.[46]

The vessels remaining in the U.S. merchant fleet after the Civil War were described as "old, obsolete, and nearly worthless craft." This description was quite probably accurate and may suggest an alternative explanation for the decline of the U.S. sailing ship other than the damage done by the Confederacy. The day of the windships had passed.[47]

The demand for a quick passage to California created by the gold rush frenzy of the 1840s and 50s had run its course. In the China trade, the Suez Canal particularly hastened the decline of the windships. Sailing vessels simply could not maneuver in the narrow canal and were placed at a severe disadvantage in comparison to the steamers, which also benefited from the fuel savings inherent in a voyage shortened some 4,000 miles. The fabulous clipper ships built in the glorious 1850s had outlived their useful purpose, which resulted in a condition in the 1860s and 1870s known as "block obsolescence," a repetitive phenomenon in American shipbuilding history in which large numbers of vessels became outdated at the same time.[48]

As early as 1856, the foreign carrying trade, which was the life blood of the windship, "had collapsed in fact, if not in the consciousness of a frustrated people who would find it more comfortable to blame that collapse on the [Civil] war." While metal-hulled, steam-powered marine technology advanced, the traditional technology of the wooden-hulled sailing vessel grew stagnate. Iron-hulled steamers began driving the windships of all nations off the most profitable routes.[49]

NOTES

1. Frances D. Robotti and James Vescovi, *The USS* Essex *and the Birth of the American Navy* (Holbrook, MA: Adams Media, 1999), 96–106.

2. See Harry Fritz, "The War Hawks of 1812," *Capital Studies* 5 (Spring 1977): 3–10.

3. C. S. Forester, *The Age of Fighting Sail: The Story of the Naval War of 1812* (Sandwich, MA: Chapman Billies, 1956), 44–45.

4. Robotti and Vescovi, 32.

5. Edward A. Pollard, *Southern History of the War* (1866; reprint, New York: Fairfax Press, 1990), 218.

6. Lawrence C. Allin, "The Civil War and the Period of Decline, 1861–1913," in *America's Maritime Legacy: A History of the U.S. Merchant Marine and Shipbuilding Industry since Colonial Times*, ed. Robert A. Kolmarx (Boulder, CO: Westview Press, 1979), 65–66.

7. Robert G. Albion and Jennie B. Pope, *Sea Lanes in Wartime* (Portland, ME: Archon Books, 1968), 173.

8. Clinton H. Whitehurst, *The U. S. Shipbuilding Industry: Past, Present, and Future* (Annapolis, MD: Naval Institute Press, 1986), 22.

9. K. Jack Bauer, *A Maritime History of the United States: The Role of America's Seas and Waterways* (Columbia: University of South Carolina Press, 1989), 241. It is of interest to note that not a single merchant sailor was killed during any of the episodes leading to the destruction of these 239 vessels. Further, these figures do not include several vessels taken by southern privateers at the beginning of the conflict. Confederate privateers were all but driven from the seas by the time of the establishment of the Federal blockade. See the Introduction to Wm. M. Robinson, Jr., *The Confederate Privateers* (Columbia: University of South Carolina Press, 1990).

10. James D. Bullock, *The Secret Service of the Confederate States in Europe*, 2 vols. (New York: Putnam's, 1884), 185.

11. Flags of convenience are still sometimes used by American companies to evade strict maritime legislation passed at the beginning of this century, and since, involving safety standards and sailors' rights. See Bauer, 247.

12. Albion and Pope, 63, 70.

13. Ibid., 110.

14. Ibid., 169.

15. William Hutchinson Rowe, *The Maritime History of Maine: Three Centuries of Shipbuilding and Seafaring* (Freeport, ME: Bond Wheelwright, n.d.), 220.

16. G. W. Dalzell, *The Flight from the Flag: The Continuing Effect of the Civil War upon the American Carrying Trade* (Chapel Hill: University of North Carolina Press, 1940), 239–240; see also Albion and Pope, 169–170.

17. Richard S. West, Jr., *Mr. Lincoln's Navy* (New York: Longmans, Green and Co., 1957), 277–282.

18. Philip Van Doren Stern, *The Confederate Navy: A Pictorial History* (Garden City, NY: Doubleday, 1962), 34.

19. *New York Times*, August 4, 1863, 1:1.

20. Bullock, 185.

21. J. Thomas Scharf, *History of the Confederate States Navy* (1887; reprint, New York: Fairfax Press, 1978), 782–784.

22. Albion and Pope, 159.

23. Ibid., 164.

24. Scharf, 817–818.

25. Ibid., 806–807, 806 n.

26. Stern, 200–201.

27. Albion and Pope, 164–171.

28. Stephen R. Wise, *The Lifeline of the Confederacy: Blockade Running during the Civil War* (Columbia: University of South Carolina Press, 1988), 201–202; see also West, 271.

29. Scharf, 436.

30. Clark, vol. II, 125; see also U.S. Bureau of the Census, *Historical Statistics of the United States, Colonial Times to 1970.* Bicentennial edition, 2 vols. (Washington, DC: U.S. Department of Commerce, Bureau of Census, 1975), 751.

31. U.S. Bureau of the Census. The figures are arrived at by taking the sum of Q 485 and 486, which represent the inland navigation portion of the fleet and the total documented tonnage for the fractions that are kept as a separate statistic in Q 417. These figures are then use to determine the total fleet tonnage as percentages.

32. Dalzell, 240–241.

33. Gerald Simmons, ed., *The Blockade: Runners and Raiders* (Alexandria, VA: Time-Life Books, 1983), 161.

34. See Bauer.

35. Samuel W. Bryant, *The Sea and the States: A Maritime History of the American People* (New York: Thomas Y. Crowell, 1967), 334–335.

36. Henry C. Kittredge, *Shipmasters of Cape Cod* (Boston: Houghton Mifflin, 1935), 293.

37. Rowe, 207–220.

38. Bauer, 127.

39. Bryant, 335.

40. Bauer, 106–127. The author's discussion of the coasting trade is very helpful, especially as this aspect of the topic is neglected by many other authorities.

41. See Bauer.

42. Clark, vol. III, 90.

43. Wise, 102.

44. K. T. Rowland, *Steam at Sea: The History of Steam Navigation* (New York: Praeger Publishing, 1970), 81. Much of the technical information about steam vessels of this era has come from this source. Also useful for the development of steam engines is Donald L. Canney, *The Old Steam Navy: Frigates, Sloops, and Gunboats, 1815–1885,* vol. I (Annapolis, MD: Naval Institute Press, 1990).

45. Richard Natkiel and Anthony Preston, *Atlas of Maritime History* (New York: Facts on File, 1986), 110.

46. Clinton H. Whitehurst, *The U.S. Merchant Marine: In Search of an Enduring Maritime Policy* (Annapolis, MD: Naval Institute Press, 1986), 1–2.

47. Dalzell, 247; see also Albion and Pope, 171.

48. Robert Uhl, "Masters of the Merchant Marine," *American Heritage* (April, 1983): 71–72.

49. C. Branford Mitchell, "Pride of the Seas," *American Heritage* (December 1967): 83.

Selected Bibliography

Albion, Robert G., and Jennie B. Pope. *Sea Lanes in Wartime: The American Experience, 1775–1945*. Portland, ME: Archon Books, 1968.

Allin, Lawrence C. "The Civil War and the Period of Decline: 1861–1913." In *America's Maritime Legacy: A History of the U.S. Merchant Marine and Shipbuilding Industry since Colonial Times*, ed. Robert A. Kolmarx. Boulder, CO: Westview Press, 1979.

Balch, Thomas W. *The Alabama Arbitration*. 1900. Reprint. Salem, NH: Books for Libraries Press, 1969.

Bauer, K. Jack. *A Maritime History of the United States: The Role of America's Seas and Waterways*. Columbia: University of South Carolina Press, 1989.

Baynham, Henry. *From the Lower Deck: The Royal Navy, 1700–1840*. Barre, MA: Barre Gazette, 1970.

Beck, Horace. *Folklore and the Sea*. Middletown, CT: Wesleyan University Press, 1973.

Bernath, Stuart L. *Squall across the Atlantic; American Civil War Prizes and Diplomacy*. Berkeley: University of California Press, 1970.

Blake, Nicholas, and Richard Lawrence. *The Illustrated Companion to Nelson's Navy*. Mechanicsburg, PA: Stackpole, 2000.

Bonyun, Bill, and Gene Bonyun. *Full Hold and Splendid Passage*. New York: Alfred A. Knopf, 1969.

Bowler, Arthur. *Logistics and the Failure of the British Army in America, 1775–1783*. Princeton, NJ: Princeton University Press, 1975.

Bryant, Samuel W. *The Sea and the States: A Maritime History of the American People*. New York: T. Y. Crowell, 1967.

Bullock, James D. *The Secret Service of the Confederate States in Europe*. 2 vols. New York: Putnam's, 1884.

Burgess, Lauren Cook, ed. *An Uncommon Soldier*. Pasadena, MD: The Minerva Center, 1994.

Campbell, George F. *The Neophyte Shipmodeller's Jackstay*. Bogota, NJ: Model Shipways, 1969.

Canney, Donald L. *The Old Steam Navy: Frigates, Sloops, and Gunboats, 1815–1885*. Vol. I. Annapolis, MD: Naval Institute Press, 1990.

Chartrand, Rene, and Francis Back, *Napoleon's Sea Soldiers*. London: Osprey Books, 1990.

Clark, Victor S. *History of Manufactures in the United States*. 3 vols. New York: Peter Smith Publishers, 1949.

Clark, William Bell. *Ben Franklin's Privateers: A Naval Epic of the American Revolution*. Wesport, CT: Greenwood Press, 1969.

———. *George Washington's Navy: Being an Account of His Excellency's Fleet in New England Waters*. Baton Rouge: Louisiana State University Press, 1960.

Coppin, Brigitte. *The Compass: Steering Towards the New World*. New York: Penguin, 1995.

Creswell, John. *British Admirals of the Eighteenth Century: Tactics in Battle*. London: Allen and Unwin, 1972.

Dalzell, G. W. *The Flight from the Flag: The Continuing Effect of the Civil War upon the American Carrying Trade*. Chapel Hill: University of North Carolina Press, 1940.

Dana, Richard Henry, Jr. *The Seaman's Friend: Containing a Treatise on Practical Seamanship*. 1879. Reprint. Mineola, NY: Dover, 1997.

Davis, Charles G. *American Sailing Ships: Their Plans and History*. New York: Dover, 1984.

Dickerson, Oliver M. *The Navigation Acts and the American Revolution*. New York: A. S. Barnes, 1963.

Druett, Joan. *Hen Frigates: Wives of Merchant Captains under Sail*. New York: Simon & Schuster, 1998.

———. *She Was a Sister Sailor: The Whaling Journals of Mary Brewster*. Mystic, CT: Mystic Seaport Museum, 1992.

Dull, Jonathan R. *The French Navy and American Independence: A Study of Arms and Diplomacy 1774–1787*. Princeton, NJ: Princeton University Press, 1975.

East, Charles, ed. *Sarah Morgan: The Civil War Diary of a Southern Woman*. New York: Touchstone, 1991.

Engle, Eloise, and Arnold Lott. *America's Maritime Heritage*. Annapolis, MD: Naval Institute Press, 1975.

Ferguson, Robert. *Harpooner: A Four-Year Voyage on the Barque* Kathleen, *1880–84*. Philadelphia: University of Pennsylvania Press, 1936.

Ferling, John. *Struggle for a Continent: The Wars of Early America*. Arlington Heights, IL: Harlan Davidson, 1993.

Forester, C. S. *The Age of Fighting Sail: The Story of the Naval War of 1812*. Sandwich, MA: Chapman Billies, 1956.

Fowler, William M., Jr. *Rebels under Sail: The American Navy during the Revolution*. New York: Charles Scribner's Sons, 1976.

Fritz, Harry. "The War Hawks of 1812." *Capital Studies* 5 (Spring 1977): 3–10.

Gardner, Brian. *The East India Company: A History*. New York: Dorset Press, 1971.

Garner, Stanton, ed. *The Captain's Best Mate: The Journal of Mary Chapman Lawrence on the Whaler* Addison, *1856–1860*. Hanover, NH: University Press of New England, 1966.

George, Henry. *Protection or Free Trade: An Examination of the Tariff Question with Especial Regard to the Interests of Labor*. New York: Henry George and Co., 1886.

Gibbons, Tony. *Warships and Naval Battles of the Civil War*. New York: W. H. Smith, 1989.

Gibson, Marjorie Hubbell. *H.M.S. Somerset, 1746–1778: The Life and Times of an Eighteenth-Century British Man-O-War and Her Impact on North America*. Cotuit, MA: Abbey Gate House, 1992.

Glover, Michael. *The Napoleonic Wars: An Illustrated History, 1792–1815*. New York: Hippocrene Books, 1979.

Hacker, Louis M. *The United States since 1865*. New York: Appleton-Century-Crofts, 1949.

Harlow, Frederick Pease. *Chantying Aboard American Ships*. Barre, MA: Barre Gazette, 1962.

Haythornthwaite, Philip. *Nelson's Navy*. London: Osprey Books, 1993.

Hollett, David. *The Alabama Affair: The British Shipyards Conspiracy in the American Civil War*. Wilmslow, Cheshire, UK.: Sigma Leisure, 1993.

Hough, Richard. *Captain Bligh and Mr. Christian: The Men and the Mutiny*. New York, E. P. Dutton, 1973.

Hughes, Edward, ed. *The Private Correspondence of Admiral Lord Collingwood*. London: Navy Records Society, 1957.

Kitteridge, Henry C. *Shipmasters of Cape Cod*. Boston: Houghton Mifflin, 1935.

Kurlansky, Mark. *Cod: A Biography of the Fish that Changed the World*. New York: Penguin Books, 1997.

LaFeber, Walter. *The Cambridge History of American Foreign Relation*. Vols. I–IV. Cambridge: Cambridge University Press, 1993.

Laffin, John. *Jack Tars, the Story of the British Sailor*. London: Cassel, 1969.

Leach, Douglas Edward. *Roots of Conflict: British Armed Forces and Colonial Americans, 1677–1763*. Chapel Hill: University of North Carolina Press, 1986.

Lewis, Michael. *The History of the British Navy*. Fairlawn, NJ: Essential Books, 1959.

Mack, William P., and Royal W. Connell. *Naval Ceremonies, Customs, and Traditions*. Annapolis, MD: Naval Institute Press, 1980.

Mahan, Alfred Thayer. *The Influence of Sea Power upon History, 1660–1783*. 1890. Reprint. New York: Dover, 1987.

Marcus, G. J. *The Formative Centuries: A Naval History of England*. Boston: Little, Brown & Co., 1961.

———. *Heart of Oak: A Survey of British Sea Power in the Georgian Era*. London: Oxford University Press, 1975.

Masselman, George. *The Cradle of Colonialism*. New Haven, CT: Yale University Press, 1963.

McGregor, Tom. *The Making of C. S. Forester's Horatio Hornblower*. New York: HarperCollins Publishers, 1999.

Miller, Nathan. *Sea of Glory: A Naval History of the American Revolution*. Annapolis, MD: Naval Institute Press, 1974.

Morrison, Samuel Elliot. *Christopher Columbus, Mariner.* New York, Meridian, 1983.

National Park Service. *The Forts of Old San Juan: San Juan National Historic Site, Puerto Rico.* Washington, DC: U.S. Department of the Interior, 1996.

Natkiel, Richard, and Anthony Preston. *Atlas of Maritime History.* New York: Facts on File, 1986.

Neeser, Robert W., ed. *The Dispatches of Molyneux Shuldham, Vice Admiral of the Blue and Commander in Chief of His Britannic Majesty's Ships in North America: January–July, 1776.* New York: Naval Society Publications, 1913.

Nicol, John. *The Life and Adventures of John Nicole, Mariner.* 1822. Reprint. New York: Farrar and Rhinehart, 1936.

Nordhoff, Charles. *Sailor Life on Man-of-War and Merchant Vessels.* New York: Dodd, Mead & Co., 1884.

———. *Whaling and Fishing.* New York: Dodd, Mead & Co., 1877.

Owsley, Frank L. *King Cotton Diplomacy: Foreign Relations of the Confederate States of America.* Rev. ed. Chicago: University of Chicago Press, 1959.

Palmer, Howard, ed. *Nathaniel Taylor: Life on a Whaler.* New London, CT: New London County Historical Society, 1929.

Paullin, Charles Oscar. *Paullin's History of Naval Administration, 1775–1911.* Annapolis, MD: Naval Institute Press, 1968.

Pérez-Mallaína, Pablo E. *Spain's Men of the Sea: Daily Life on the Indies Fleets in the Sixteenth Century.* Trans. Carla Rahn Phillips. Baltimore, MD: Johns Hopkins University Press, 1998.

Petroski, Catherine. *A Bride's Passage: Susan Hathorn's Year under Sail.* Boston: Northeastern University Press, 1997.

Pollard, Edward A. *Southern History of the War.* 1866. Reprint. New York: Fairfax Press, 1990.

Robinson, William. *Jack Nastyface: Memoirs of a Seaman.* Annapolis, MD: Naval Institute Press, 1973.

Robinson, Wm. M., Jr. *The Confederate Privateers.* Columbia: University of South Carolina Press, 1990.

Robotti, Frances D., and James Vescovi. *The USS* Essex *and the Birth of the American Navy.* Holbrook, MA: Adams Media Corporation, 1999.

Rodger, N.A.M. *The Wooden World: An Anatomy of the Georgian Navy.* New York: W. W. Norton, 1996.

Rogers, John G. *Origin of Sea Terms.* Mystic, CT: Mystic Seaport Museum, 1985.

Rowe, William Hutchinson. *The Maritime History of Maine: Three Centuries of Shipbuilding and Seafaring.* Freeport, ME: Bond Wheelwright, n.d.

Rowland, K. T. *Steam at Sea: The History of Steam Navigation.* New York: Praeger Publishing, 1970.

Salmon, Lucy M. *The Dutch West India Company on the Hudson.* Poughkeepsie, NY: Published privately, 1915.

Sawtell, Clement C. *The Ship* Ann Alexander *of New Bedford 1805–1851.* Mystic, CT: Marine Historical Association, no. 40, 1962.

Scharf, J. Thomas. *History of the Confederate States Navy.* 1887. Reprint. New York: Fairfax Press, 1978.

Scott, John Anthony. *The Ballard of America.* New York: Grosset & Dunlap, 1967.

Semmes, Raphael. *Memoirs of Service Afloat.* New York: Carlson, 1869.

Sheer, George F., and Hugh F. Rankin. *Rebels and Redcoats*. Cleveland, OH: World Publishing, 1957.

Shep, R. L., ed. *Civil War Ladies: Fashions and Needle Arts of the Early 1860s*. Mendocino, CA: R. L. Shep, 1987.

Simmons, Gerald, ed. *The Blockade: Runners and Raiders*. Alexandria, VA: Time-Life Books, 1983.

Sinclair, Arthur. *Two Years on the* Alabama, ed Wm. N. Still. 1895. Reprint. Annapolis, MD: Navy Institute Press, 1989.

Spence, Bill. *Harpooned: The Story of Whaling*. New York: Crescent Books, 1980.

Sprout, Harold, and Margaret Sprout. *The Rise of American Naval Power, 1776–1918*. 1939. Reprint. Princeton, NJ: Princeton University Press, 1967.

Stackpole, Edouard. *Scrimshaw at Mystic Seaport*. Mystic, CT: The Marine Historical Association, No. 33, March 1958.

Stark, Suzanne J. *Female Tars: Women Aboard Ship in the Age of Sail*. Annapolis, MD: Naval Institute Press, 1996.

Stern, Philip Van Doren. *The Confederate Navy: A Pictorial History*. Garden City: Doubleday, 1962.

———. *When the Guns Roared: World Aspects of the American Civil War*. New York: Doubleday, 1964.

Stevens, William O., and Allan Westcott. *The History of Sea Power*. New York: Doubleday, Doran, 1943.

Still, William N., Jr. *Confederate Shipbuilding*. Athens: University of Georgia, 1969.

U.S. Bureau of the Census. *Historical Statistics of the United States, Colonial Times to 1970*. Bicentennial edition, 2 vols. Washington, DC: U.S. Department of Commerce, Bureau of Census, 1975.

U.S. Offices of Naval War Records. *Official Records of the Union and Confederate Navies in the War of the Rebellion*. 31 vols. National Historical Society, 1987.

Villiers, Alan. *Men, Ships, and the Sea*. Washington, DC: National Geographic, 1973.

Wells, David. *Our Merchant Marine: How It Rose, Increased, Became Great, Declined and Decayed*. New York: G. P. Putnam's Sons, 1890.

West, Richard S., Jr. *Mr. Lincoln's Navy*. New York: Longmans, Green and Co., 1957.

Westcott, Allan. *Mahan on Naval Warfare: Selected from the Writings of Rear Admiral Alfred Thayer Mahan*. Boston: Little, Brown & Co., 1919.

Whipple, A.B.C. *The Whalers*. Alexandria, VA: Time-Life Books, 1979.

Whitecar, William B., Jr. *Four Years Aboard the Whaleship in the Years 1855–59*. Philadelphia, PA: J. B. Lippencott, 1860.

Whitehurst, Clinton H. *The U.S. Merchant Marine: In Search of an Enduring Maritime Policy*. Annapolis, MD: Navy Institute Press, 1986.

———. *The U.S. Shipbuilding Industry: Past, Present, and Future*. Annapolis, MD: Navy Institute Press, 1986.

Whiting, Emma Mayhew, and Henry Beetle Hough. *Whaling Wives*. Boston: Houghton Mifflin, 1953.

Williams, Harold, ed. *One Whaling Family*. Boston: Houghton Mifflin, 1964.

Wise, Stephen R. *The Lifeline of the Confederacy: Blockade Running during the Civil War*. Columbia: University of South Carolina Press, 1988.

Index

Page numbers in *italics* indicate illustrations.

About the Authors

DOROTHY DENNEEN VOLO is a teacher and historian. She is the co-author of *Daily Life in Civil War America* (Greenwood, 1998) and *Encyclopedia of the Antebellum South* (Greenwood, 2000).

JAMES M. VOLO is a teacher, historian and living history enthusiast. He is the co-author of *Daily Life in Civil War America* (Greenwood, 1998) and *Encyclopedia of the Antebellum South* (Greenwood, 2000).